THE NEW
ASTROLOGY
for women

Jessica Adams

HarperCollinsPublishers

HarperCollins*Publishers*

First published in Australia in 1997 as *Astrology for Women*
Reprinted twice
This edition published in 1998
Reprinted in 1999, 2000 (twice), 2001
by HarperCollins*Publishers* Pty Limited
ABN 36 009 913 517
A member of HarperCollins*Publishers* (Australia) Pty Limited Group
http://www.harpercollins.com.au

HarperCollins*Publishers*
25 Ryde Road, Pymble, Sydney NSW 2073, Australia
31 View Road, Glenfield, Auckland 10, New Zealand
77–85 Fulham Palace Road, London W6 8JB, United Kingdom
Hazelton Lanes, 55 Avenue Road, Suite 2900, Toronto, Ontario M5R 3L2
and 1995 Markham Road, Scarborough, Ontario M1B 5M8, Canada
10 East 53rd Street, New York NY 10022, USA

National Library of Australia Cataloguing-in-Publication data:

Adams, Jessica.
  The new astrology for women.
  New ed.
  ISBN 0 7322 6433 2.
  1. Astrology. 2. Women—Miscellanea. I. Adams, Jessica.
  Astrology for women. II. Title. III. Title: Astrology for women.
133.5082

Cover design by Katie Mitchell, HarperCollins Design Studio
Cover photograph by Karin Catt, Patrick Jones Studios

Printed and bound in Australia by Griffin Press on 79gsm Bulky Paperback White

10 9 8 7 6 5   01 02 03 04

This book is dedicated to Richard Sterling and Gwyn Turner, who got me started.

CONTENTS

YOUR FUTURE

WORKING IT ALL OUT

Acknowledgements

The most bizarre thing happened when the first edition of *Astrology For Women* was toasted with the HarperCollins staff — a bottle of Bollinger slowly uncorked itself and exploded all over the pristine advance copies lying on the table. There was nothing left to drink after that, and the books were ruined — but as it turns out, it *was* a good omen. I'd like to thank everyone who was involved with that forerunner of this publication, which has had an amazing response. *The New Astrology For Women* is bigger and better of course (hey, you knew I'd say that) but it wouldn't have happened at all if Helen Littleton at HarperCollins and Sophie Lance at Hickson Associates hadn't given it the world's fastest green light. Thanks, too, to Karin Catt and Katie Mitchell for their amazing contribution to the visuals — I could have sworn the eye on the spine in the Barnes and Noble 5th Avenue store followed me around the bookshop the last time I was in there! On the editorial side of things, I should also like to thank Anne Reilly and Heather Jamieson, and Peter Guo for his typesetting marathon. Thanks to Gavin Hammond and Prue Rushton, too, for proofreading. On the computer boffin side of things, I should also like to thank James Williams at Tags Multimedia in Sydney, and in London, the brilliant chaps at Electric Ephemeris. A lot of my magazine, newspaper and internet work over the last two years has also triggered some of the new sections in this book. Heartfelt thanks to *The Daily Telegraph*, *Cosmopolitan*, *Orange*, *New Woman*, *Dolly*, *Elle* and *ninemsn* for giving me a chance to experiment, and for making my columns and features look so good. Finally, readers around the world, friends, ex-boyfriends, neighbours, landladies and family members have all thrown their two-bob's worth in. Feel free to demand a bottle of amazing self-opening Bollinger the next time you see me.

Jessica Adams
McMahons Point 1998

FIRST words

YOUR STAR SIGN PACKAGE

Your Sun sign

Most women know their star sign automatically. This is actually your Sun sign — the constellation that the Sun was passing through on the day you were born. The Sun describes what is important to you, what you identify with, what you feel proud of, and what you become an expert on. So — taking Madonna as an example (hell, why not!) if you have a Leo Sun, your pride is important to you, you identify with well-known or successful people, you feel proud of your leadership abilities and you become an expert on creativity and ideas.

Your Sun sign is every magazine and newspaper astrologer's great standby, but only for this reason: their editors only give them one line of space to identify each sign. So, born on 1st April? There you are, under Aries, categorised as a 21st March—20th April person.

However, other planets are just as crucial in making up the complex person that is you. I dream of having twenty pages of a magazine to myself each week, just so I can print all the other information about Moon, Mercury, Venus and Mars signs. Unfortunately, while Madonna is still taking up most of the space at the back of the magazine, it's not going to happen.

Why are these other planets so important? Basically, because they accurately describe the other bits of you.

Your Moon sign

The Moon sign is very different from your Sun sign and the odds are also high that this sign will be in a different planet from your Sun sign. Another part of you is filled in once you discover your Moon sign. And because this planet describes your house or flat, your feelings about food, and the things that make you feel comfortable, it has a completely different feeling to your Sun sign.

According to her 16th August 1958 birthday, Madonna has the Moon in Virgo. Her house is impossibly neat (have you seen that photograph of all her shoes 'filed' on shelves?). When it comes to food, she's a famously pure, or healthy, eater. What kinds of things make Madonna feel comfortable? Having everything perfect, eating macrobiotic soup, working hard and looking at her neatly filed shoes. We'll leave Madonna right there for now, by the way. But it's interesting to see how two very different sides of her are already nicely pinpointed by her Sun sign and Moon sign.

Your Mercury and Venus signs

The planet Mercury describes another side of you again, and in many cases, another sign (although it's reasonably common to find people with a matching Sun and Mercury sign). Mercury indicates the way you learn, the way you write, the way you talk and the way you communicate.

The sign that Mercury happened to be in on the day you were born imprints you with yet another set of qualities. Or — if your Mercury sign is the same as your Sun sign or Moon sign — it will crank up those Sun or Moon qualities.

Venus is extremely important, because it is a female planet. The Greeks and Romans, who passed on much of what we know about astrology today, saw the goddess as all boobs, roses and love potions, and, although this may sound bizarre in the 1990s, the meaning of Venus — female power, femininity, beauty — is exactly the same. I have found that women tend to live out their Venus sign every bit as — or sometimes *more* — strongly than their Sun sign. You know those women who appear to be a typical Aries, say, or a typical Taurus? They usually have Venus and the Sun together in the same sign.

Some women won't double up at all. If this is you, it means yet another sign to fit into your personal birthday package.

Your Mars sign

Mars describes the things that make you angry. It also pinpoints how you get moving, what kind of opponent you are and what kind of sport suits you best. Mars is the planet which is associated with assertiveness and strength, too.

SEE YOURSELF IN 3-D

Some clients I have worked with have found this confusing. 'But what am I?' they wail. 'Am I a Scorpio, a Virgo, a Libra, a Sagittarius, a Pisces, or *what*, you crazed woman?'

The correct answer is: you are a Scorpionic–Virgoan–Libran–Sagittarian–Piscean type. And that's the way it should be. Women are contradictory, complex, multi-faceted and multi-talented creatures, and your personal package of signs explains it all. Of course, there are certain days, in certain years, when all five planets are passing through the same constellation at once. You may end up having just one sign to yourself, and will be a dynamite expression of it, by the way. Instead of being 3-D, or 4-D, or 5-D, you'll just be 1-D. Kylie Minogue is a 1-D Gemini (don't worry, they do alright for themselves).

Women with a 1-D sign profile are the exception, however. Mostly, by the time you have looked up your Sun, Moon, Mercury, Venus and Mars signs, you will have discovered quite a few sides to yourself. Unless you've had your chart done before, you won't even know they were there.

GOOD PICK-UP LINES

If I ruled the world, people would no longer slink up to each other at parties and say, 'What's your sign?' Instead, they would wander around with stickers on proclaiming GEMINI–LEO–AQUARIUS TYPE, and the world would be much more efficient. (I think the standard of pick-up lines would improve, too.)

One of the greatest discoveries women make is that their Mercury sign, or their Moon sign, has been dictating their entire life and times. It's true — many women do seem to feel more comfortable with one sign in the package than the others, and push it as far as they can take it. At this stage, I find women who have *never* believed in astrology suddenly raving about it. Food-loving nurses with Cancer Moons suddenly understand why they are food-loving nurses. Hyperactive jockeys with an Aries Mercury suddenly understand why they are hyperactive jockeys.

YOU ASTRO PROFILE

Flip straight to the chapter called Working It All Out at back of the book (page 473) to find out your Sun, Moon, Mercury, Venus and Mars signs, then fill them in here:

MY SUN IS IN   _____

MY MOON IS IN   _____

MY MERCURY IS IN   _____

MY VENUS IS IN   _____

MY MARS IS IN   _____

Now you're ready to make the most of *The New Astrology For Women*.

PLANETS in aries

Read this section if you have your Sun, Moon, Mercury, Venus or Mars in Aries.

YOUR ARIAN SIDE
Energetic ★ Unafraid ★ Competitive.

USING ARIES

This is a fantastic sign to have in your astro-package, because it helps you to assert yourself to get what you want. An Aries planet which is being used properly can turn a dream into a reality. Your Aries Sun, Moon, Mercury, Venus or Mars can be used to push yourself towards what you most desire. It's a goal-oriented, fearless sign and having it as part of your overall chart make-up is like having a tiger in your handbag. It also helps you in those situations where you must defend and protect yourself. And along with the tiger in the handbag, there is a set of red designer armour in there!

ARIES ACTION WOMEN

Whatever interests or enthusiasms are described by the other signs in your profile — or by your Rising sign — Aries will crank up the energy behind them. This planet accelerates, boosts and ignites. It is rather like having an outboard motor attached to some part of you providing the muscle and adrenalin necessary to do whatever you have to — or choose to — do. You may have planets in other signs which describe various passions and interests.

Forget women who run with the wolves. Your Aries planets guarantee you'll run with virtually anything. If this side of you is strongly developed, you'll probably be one of the very few women who can develop a passion for male sport as well. Two strands of the Aries myth lend themselves to sport: firstly, strength, and secondly, a true spirit of competition. Whenever I think of Aries Sun.

Speed and sweat

Lisa Curry-Kenny — Swimmer — Mars in Aries
Martina Navratilova — Tennis champion — Moon in Aries
Jane Flemming — Athlete — Mercury in Aries
Betty Cuthbert — Athlete — Sun in Aries
Kerry Saxby-Junna — Walker — Venus in Aries
Sue Barker — Tennis champion — Sun in Aries
Gabriela Sabatini — Tennis champion — Sun in Aries
Jennifer Capriati — Tennis champion — Sun and Mercury in Aries
Clare Francis — Yachtswoman — Sun and Mercury in Aries
Sonja Henie — Ice skater — Sun and Mercury in Aries
Naomi James — Yachtswoman — Venus in Aries
Zola Budd — Athlete — Venus in Aries
Valentina Tereshkova-Cosmonaut — Venus in Aries
Beverley Buckingham-King — Jockey — Mercury in Aries
Karen Lunn — Golfer — Sun, Mercury and Mars in Aries
Kirstie Marshall — Skier — Venus in Aries
Michelle Martin — Squash player — Mercury in Aries
Lisa Ondieki — Marathon runner — Mars in Aries
Karin (Dunne) van Wirdum — Swimmer — Sun in Aries
Margaret Dupont — Tennis champion — Sun in Aries

One of the basic things I notice about clients with planets in Aries is that they always feel better after they've walked things off, or, in the words of one Mercury Aries woman, 'sweated things out'. You don't have to be a Jane Flemming to live out this sign in your life, but you will find that everything seems to come together better when your body is being stretched.

SUN in aries

You identify with

Champions ★ Self-made women ★ Heroes ★ Heroines ★ Winners ★ Fighters ★ Sports stars ★ Military maids ★ Pioneers ★ Sex bombs.

You're an authority on

Speedometers ★ Assertiveness skills ★ Training shoes ★ Winning ★ Career strategies.

Your career Top Ten

You need: 1) Your independence; 2) Lawyers or arbitration committees! 3) A gym, track or pool nearby; 4) People to argue with; 5) Your own workspace; 6) Short days; 7) Rewards for coming in on deadline; 8) A fast set of wheels; 9) People who operate at your speed; 10) Competition and rivals — it spurs you on.

Expressing your Arian side

If you have the Sun in Aries then, somewhere inside you, you contain an Aries. If your Arian side is well developed, you will probably also have people with Aries planets in your life. If this section doesn't accurately reflect what you're all about, you may want to read the chapter headed Walking Your Planets (pages 175–183).

THE VERSUS FACTOR

Aries planets create you-versus-them situations more frequently than any other sign. Some Aries-influenced women consciously enter into fights, and some don't ask for them, but seem to get them anyway. Your Aries Sun, Moon, Mercury, Venus or Mars will often land you in two-way contests or three-way triangles, and the following scenarios are especially common:

Husband versus wife	Friends versus friends of friends
Mother versus daughter	Nation versus nation
Father versus daughter	Neighbour versus neighbour
Husband versus wife versus mistress	Team versus team
Husband versus first and second wives	Employer versus boss
Lover versus ex-lover	Brand versus brand
Business partner versus business partner	Business versus business
	You versus the world!

in aries

What you need

Sporty, outdoors or fitness pursuits ★ A dynamic role at work ★ Friends who will argue with you ★ Friends who will forgive you ★ Absolute equality with men ★ A cause.

The Moon in Aries home

Eventually, your guests will trip over your skis, your trainers, your wet bathers or your 'serious' walking boots. The worst case scenario with the Moon in Aries home is a kitchen full of angry notes between family or household members. Women with an Aries Moon who live alone even manage to leave angry notes for their pets! When you renovate or decorate, you do it in half the time that everybody else does, but you tend to start off enthusiastically, then lose interest. You're always dashing in and out.

The Moon in Aries cook

You do it better than everybody else, as your competitive side comes out when you're cooking for an audience. You are an impatient cook, and spend a lot of time staring at the oven timer and sighing heavily. Don't cook soufflé — it's just not going to work. You eat fast food, often get home delivery and cook a lot of

10-minute pasta. You eat when you're stressed or on the run, too, which is not such a good idea.

Expressing your Arian side

If you have the Moon in Aries then, somewhere inside you, you contain an Aries. If your Arian side is well developed, you will probably also have people with Aries planets in your life. If this section doesn't accurately reflect what you're all about, you may want to read the chapter headed Walking Your Planets (pages 175–183).

MARS — ARIES' RULING PLANET

Aries is one of the least acceptable signs in our society, because its ruling planet, Mars, is so brutal. Mars was the God of War and represents pure aggression. In mythology and astrological tradition, he is dripping with blood and hungry for battle.

The socially acceptable face of Aries is sport and organised war machinery — the Army, the Navy, the Air Force. Also, sanctioned places where aggression, attack and defence can be played out — like the police force, politics and the legal arena. Corporate aggression is okay, too. If you are strongly Aries-influenced these general areas and themes may have already played a part in your life. Still, it is unusual for little girls to be told that scrapping in the playground is a fabulous idea, that becoming a general is the way to go, and that tough girls are good girls.

Society as a whole has always had a problem with women who have Aries planets. Its preference is generally for nice women, but I really don't think the word 'nice' is what your Arian side is all about. Strong, tough, assertive, feisty and fearless are adjectives which are much closer to the mark.

If you try to pretend that your Aries planet isn't there, it will squeeze in through the back door. Then, in what appear to be circumstances beyond your control, you have to face all manner of stresses, irritations, bitchfests and snarling relationships — all of which seem to take ages to resolve.

These long-running snarlfests are a total negation of what your Arian side is all about. Arian fury should be honest, plain, obvious and both aired and finished with as quickly as possible. It also needs to go back to its *true* source. Complications seem to arise for Aries-influenced women when they either: a) Ignore the original source of their anger, and end up venting their spleen on inappropriate targets around them, or b) Stretch out the purity of quick fury into something niggling and time-consuming — like nagging, sniping, passive aggression or secret bitching sessions.

 in aries

The Mercury in Aries student
Impatient ★ Prefers to be Dux, or Number One in class or sport ★ Mercury in Aries girls enjoy arguing the point with teachers, or getting stuck into class debates.

Your communication style
Assertive.

Your letters
You send postcards.

You think like
Boadicea.

You talk like
It matters.

The Mercury in Aries voice
Strong.

Your tactics
Aggressive.

Expressing your Arian side
If you have Mercury in Aries then, somewhere inside you, you contain an Aries. If your Arian side is well developed, you will probably also have people with Aries planets in your life. If this section doesn't accurately reflect what you're all about, you may want to read the chapter headed Walking Your Planets (pages 175–183).

HANDLING ARIAN ANGER

I don't think any astrologer would recommend that an Arian type should just march over and bop someone on the nose — or indeed, throw a frying pan at them. But to pretend that you were not born with an Arian side, and have no connection with Mars, God of War, could end up making life very complicated. Perhaps unhealthy, too, as diluted anger becomes stress, and anger turned back in on the body has been known to reveal itself as illness.

There are many ways to deal with the inevitable battles or mini-wars that affect your Arian side. One way is to write it all down. Paula Yates — a Moon, Mercury and Venus Aries, did this to great effect when going through the Bob Geldof–Helena Christensen–Michael Hutchence Press saga. Vita Sackville-West was another famous Arian type stuck in a love triangle. Hers was between her female lover, Violet, and Violet's male fiancé, Denys. Vita was famous as a writer and spectacular gardener, in that order, but her diaries are one of the most interesting thing about her: Here is her Venus in Aries side, cutting loose in September 1920:

> I *now hate him* (Denys) *more than I have ever hated anyone in this life, or am likely to; and there is no injury I would not do him with the utmost pleasure.*

Denys lived to see another day (Vita can't have had too many frying pans available) but her furious diary entries highlight this fact about your Arian side: you can write your rage — or paint it, or play it out in the pool, or just take care of it by hissing from a distance. Two Aries Suns — and enemies — Bette Davis and Joan Crawford, did a wonderful job of this when they filmed *Whatever Happened to Baby Jane?* In one scene, Bette's character had to kick Joan's. Crawford said 'I'm not doing it. I don't trust Miss Davis. She's going to kick my teeth in.' Those making the film said she was probably right.

There will be times when you must *genuinely* attack or defend, though, in which case your Arian side will be very useful, maybe even life-preserving. Finally, forget the personal: your Arian 'Tank Girl' side is a fantastic plus for whichever good cause or group goal you lend it to. It's your Aries planets which make the difference between sitting on the couch worrying about things, and actually being motivated enough to do something about them. Chrissie Hynde, an Aries Moon, uses it to project her leather-pants image, but also to battle for animal rights.

Here's a list of well-known women whose Aries planets have led them into some *personal* Battles Royal:

Joan Crawford (Sun and Venus in Aries) and Bette Davis (Sun in Aries)
Doris Day (Sun in Aries) and Martin Melcher
Chrissie Hynde (Moon in Aries) and McDonalds
Candice Bergen (Mercury in Aries) and Dan Quayle
Shannen Doherty (Sun in Aries) and Aaron Spelling
Vita Sackville-West (Venus in Aries) and Denys Trefusis
Whitney Houston (Moon in Aries) and Bobby Brown
Sarah Ferguson (Moon in Aries) and Buckingham Palace

 in aries

You love

Action Men ★ Strong Women ★ Winning fights ★ Looking sexy ★ Challenging apathy ★ Racing around ★ Pushing people into bed ★ Pushing people out of bed ★ Heart-stopping spectator sports ★ Muscles in tight pants ★ Adrenalin ★ Sexy sports cars ★ Getting your way ★ Watching your rivals crumble ★ Doing your face and hair in five minutes ★ Potent perfume ★ Impact sports ★ Impact wardrobes.

You loathe

Wimps ★ Weeds ★ Waiting for sex ★ Waiting for traffic lights ★ Losing ★ Giving in ★ Being last.

Expressing your Arian side

If you have Venus in Aries then, somewhere inside you, you contain an Aries. If your Arian side is well developed, you will probably also have people with Aries planets in your life. If this section doesn't accurately reflect what you're all about, you may want to read the chapter headed Walking Your Planets (pages 175–183).

MARS in aries

The best revenge is
Winning.

Sporting Aries
Aggressive or fast team sports — and any activity where you compete against your personal best.

Your battle tactics
You are potentially the most alarming warrior maiden in the zodiac. If you are seriously taking your Mars for a walk, then you could become quite physically angry and aggressive. A punchbag at the gym may be necessary — or perhaps one of those blow-up clowns that bounce back when you pelt them. Your tactics are probably made up on the spot, because battles with you tend to be fast, potent and an enormous drain of energy.

What kind of opponent are you?
Swift ★ Energetic ★ Assertive.

Expressing your Arian side
If you have Mars in Aries then, somewhere inside you, you contain an Aries. If your Arian side is well developed, you will probably also have people with Aries planets in your life. If this section doesn't accurately reflect what you're all about, you may want to read the chapter headed Walking Your Planets (pages 175–183).

SELF-STARTERS
A tremendous number of women with Aries planets succeed in their own businesses, or in fields where they are pretty much left to their own devices. If you have the Sun, Moon, Mercury, Venus or Mars here, you have enough energy, courage and confidence to make it on your own. The Aries number is One. It also rules the

first house of the horoscope wheel. Being number one, and doing it by yourself, is a constructive way of channelling your aggressive Aries planets.

Some of you run one-woman shows inside larger organisations (I knew an Aries Moon matron once, who practically had her own company on the fourth floor of the hospital where she worked.) It's also very common for Aries-influenced women to set up under their own names or to be strongly identified on a first-name basis with their clients or customers. If you have an Arian side, people tend to relate to *you* first, and what you have to offer becomes entwined with your personality. Your name leads the product or service.

Here are some Aries-influenced women who have famously gone out on their own:

Jan Chapman — Sun and Mercury in Aries
Yvonne Allen — Sun, Moon and Mercury in Aries
Mariana Hardwick — Moon in Aries
Elle Macpherson — Sun and Mercury in Aries
Eve Mahlab — Venus in Aries
Maggie Beer — Moon in Aries

SPIRITUAL REDHEADS

If you have a planet in Aries, and strongly identify with the sign, then you are virtually a spiritual redhead. Mars, the ruler of Aries, has long been associated with the colour red. It's interesting to see how this colour turns up in the lives of the Aries-influenced, too. Some of you are almost auburn — or almost auburn again. The fates may become your personal hairdresser if you are born with an Aries planet, or a strong Mars signature in your horoscope. You may develop a thing about red cars, red lipstick or red flowers, as well. It doesn't matter what colour your hair is, though — you may still seem like a redhead if you are strongly Arian.

Born to be red

Linda Evangelista — Mercury in Aries
Vivienne Westwood — Sun in Aries
Sarah Ferguson — Moon in Aries
Shirley MacLaine — Mercury in Aries
Geena Davis — Mars in Aries

Priscilla Presley — Venus and Mars in Aries
Juliette Lewis — Mars in Aries
Toyah Wilcox — Venus in Aries

ARIES MYTHS

Scarlett O'Hara

The sassy, independent, and occasionally aggressive heroine of *Gone with the Wind* is one of many fictional Aries women (Lucy van Pelt in the *Peanuts* cartoons is another). Scarlett's most famous feud was with Rhett Butler, but her cinematic spats are many and varied. Throughout the film, she is continually seen in competition with other women — most famously, her Southern Belle rivals at the auction where Rhett bids for her, and against the third corner in a classically Aries love triangle — Melanie, wife of Ashley. Her name also contains the famous Arian allusion to red. Her style is very Arian — impatient, brave, tough and full of pioneering spirit. If you need to take your Aries planets for a walk, hire the video, see the film on the big screen, or read Margaret Mitchell's book. The author shared Arian qualities with her heroine and had planets in the other two Fire signs — Leo and Sagittarius — in real life, women with these signs in their astro-package often hook up together, too.

PIONEERING SPIRIT

Aquarius-influenced women tend to be ahead of their time, but Aries allows you to be right *on the edge* of the first wave. (With planets in both signs, incidentally, you'll permanently be in touch with tomorrow.) This sign gives you a charge signal that can lead you into some pioneering areas: never too far ahead of the trend, but always on top of it. Your Arian side enjoys being first, or being involved with the first wave of anything. This side of you likes to race off in new directions as quickly as possible.

It's partly your competitive side that dislikes being left behind, but it's also a genuine desire to champion new ideas or new trends, explore new territory and lead the field. Your Aries Sun, Moon, Mercury, Venus or Mars is interested in opening up new areas. In fact, the word *new* has a hypnotic effect on most Arian types. This side of you is unafraid, and enjoys risks: this tends to make you an innovator. Other signs in your astro-package may be slower or more cautious, but your Aries planets will always push you forward. You were probably *living* affirmative action even as governments were inventing a word for it. Women with Aries planets typically dislike being last to catch on, or the last to know.

And this is one of the reasons Aries-influenced women are so often identified with equality, breaking the glass ceiling or advancing women's progress. It may, or may not be, the ethical questions surrounding feminism and equality that concern you, but you are unlikely to tolerate being last in any race, or the last to follow any new idea. The fact that you are a woman is irrelevant. The pursuit of the *new* is the thing that stimulates you, and if that means crashing through the occasional gender barriers as you race forward, you could probably care less. Anything that slows you down — including discrimination — just won't be taken seriously.

TOUGHER THAN TOUGH

Your Aries planets lend you a toughness that does your image no harm at all. It's a kind of jodhpurs-and-leather-boots swagger, and it exists no matter what you're wearing. I suspect Aries-influenced women could wander around in pink frilly caftans and still look tough. Mars, the ruler of Aries, was also known as Gradivus, or The Strider. The ancients associated your sign with striding out into battle. Many women project their striding Arian side straight into their wardrobes, and live their lives in pants or jeans. More importantly, they tend to stride and swagger through life itself. Here are some tougher than tough 'striders':

Karen Blixen — Moon in Aries
Erica Jong — Sun in Aries
Gloria Steinem — Sun in Aries
Grace Jones — Moon in Aries
Chrissie Hynde — Moon in Aries
Diana Ross — Sun in Aries
Aretha Franklin — Sun in Aries
Paula Yates — Moon, Mercury and Venus in Aries
Candice Bergen — Mercury in Aries
Melissa Etheridge — Venus in Aries

A SENSE OF SELF

The words 'me' and 'I' are strongly associated with Aries, because this sign rules House One of the horoscope, where women develop a sense of self. Aries gone mad can be notoriously self-centred for this reason. Handled properly, though, an Aries planet can be wonderfully assertive. Most of you who have developed your Arian side will have no problem using the 'me' word or the 'I' word. Women who sing or write songs for a living tend to lean hard on this Arian sense of self to push their personalities across.

Aries in her own words

You Don't Own Me — Lesley Gore, Mercury in Aries
R.E.S.P.E.C.T — Aretha Franklin, Sun in Aries
I Want to be Free — Toyah Wilcox, Venus in Aries
Stand up for Your Love Rights — Yazz, Mars in Aries
Shut up and Kiss Me — Mary Chapin Carpenter, Moon in Aries
Stop Your Sobbing — Chrissie Hynde, Moon in Aries

THE CLASSIC ARIES

Katharine Hepburn

Born on 12th May 1907, Katharine Hepburn had only one planet in Aries — Venus — but lived her life through this sign to an incredible degree.

Aries action women Katharine Hepburn and John Ford were passionate golfers and their time off set was spent in competitive golf rounds at the California Country Club. According to Ford, their golf bets included this one: that if he won, and Katharine lost, she would have to forfeit her usual comfortable attire of slacks and a shirt and turn up to the film studio 'dressed like a woman'.

The versus factor Katharine's longtime rival and adversary was Louise Tracy, wife of Spencer — a classic Arian story of wife versus mistress. Her other famous battle was against the House Un-American Activities Committee in Hollywood.

Handling Arian anger As a child, Katharine was notorious for beating up bullies. As an adult, she channelled her anger into battles with the film studios, and into the women's movement. At 65, she was still suing MGM.

Spiritual redheads As well as embodying the qualities of her sign, Katharine was also the genuine article and from birth, was known as Redtop to her family. Red was one of her favourite colours. She was also in the running for the role of Scarlett O'Hara, which eventually went to Vivien Leigh. One of her later roles was in the film *Sylvia Scarlett*.

Self-starters Katharine found her own career as an actress against her father's will.

Pioneering spirit Most of her life was spent as a pioneer — she became a symbol of the New Woman in films, and popularised sportswear, pants and jodhpurs before they became fashionable. For a real insight into Aries' pioneering style, though, watch Katharine Hepburn in *The African Queen*.

Tougher than tough Apart from her infamous pipe-smoking on the set of *Mary of Scotland*, Hepburn was also famous for her 'golf-course stride' and her uncompromising nature.

A sense of self Katharine got this from her mother, who once said, 'I want her to express her true self, fully! We never suppress her.'

ARIAN SYMBOLS

If you have the Sun, Moon, Mercury, Venus or Mars in Aries, then either Carl Jung's synchronicity, or the fates, could land these themes or signposts in your life and times:

Rams ★ Mars ★ Crimson ★ Scarlett O'Hara ★ Red ★ Redheads ★ Rouge ★ The Airforce ★ The Army ★ The Navy ★ Amazons ★ Athletes ★ Matches ★ Competitions ★ Danger ★ Races ★ Speedways ★ Motorbikes ★ Sports cars ★ Formula One ★ Champions ★ Fighters ★ Heroes ★ Heroines ★ Sportsmen ★ Fights ★ Speed ★ Adrenalin ★ Pioneers ★ One ★ Accidents ★ Scars ★ The Head ★ Guns ★ Maid Marian ★ Boadicea ★ Police ★ Sport ★ Gymnasiums ★ Trophies ★ Swords ★ Torches ★ Rivals ★ Competitors ★ Feuds ★ Balls ★ War ★ Warrior Queens ★ Warrior Kings ★ Striding ★ Battle of the Sexes ★ Tomboys ★ Pants ★ Spears ★ Attack ★ Defence ★ Nike ★ Masculinity ★ Fire ★ Fire engines ★ Anger ★ Emergencies ★ High temperatures ★ Fevers.

PLANETS in taurus

Read this section if you have your Sun, Moon, Mercury, Venus or Mars in Taurus.

ARE YOU DOING YOUR TAURUS?

You love beautiful things

You are good at giving and receiving massage

You have your finances — and your value system — sorted out

You are continually finding new pleasure in art or music

YOUR TAUREAN SIDE

Practical ★ Money-conscious ★ Swayed by beauty.

USING TAURUS

If you have the Sun, Moon, Mercury, Venus or Mars in Taurus then you instinctively know the value of things. You may express this in the traditional way, by becoming a collector or an investor, or you may develop your value system to include the things that money cannot buy. For this reason, some of you become conservationists — as you believe nature cannot be bought and sold. Others become world-class bargain hunters, or sharp-eyed collectors. Your Taurean side increases your enjoyment of art, music, food, fashion, jewellery, furniture and beauty. It helps you appreciate quality.

MARKET FORCES

Taurus is intensely practical, understands the market, and knows how to buy and sell at the right time. Self-made businesswomen figure heavily in the Taurus story, and so do thoughtful investors. Taurean-influenced women become expert in areas like commerce and economics — and there are also a few 'women at the top' who have a canny appreciation of their own worth, and value, in the market. Having a planet in this sign does not guarantee a gold-plated existence, but it will help you to recover better from financial lows, and give you a finely tuned understanding of supply and demand. Taurus is associated with the stock market through bullion, and also through bull markets. It is common in the charts of high earners, wealthy investors and small business success stories. The ultimate expression of Taurus and finance? Queen Elizabeth II of England, a Taurus Sun.

 in taurus

You identify with
The natural world ★ Musicians ★ Businesswomen ★ Collectors ★ Connoisseurs ★ Hedonists ★ Artists ★ Idealists ★ Ethical investors.

You're an authority on
Beautiful things ★ Moral values ★ The Market ★ Selling out versus making money ★ Valuables.

Your career top ten
You need: 1) Career stability; 2) An attractive work environment; 3) Plants; 4) No pressure deadlines; 5) A comfortable chair; 6) Long gourmet lunches; 7) Wood, wool and cotton around you; 8) A ban on muzak; 9) Good-looking clients, colleagues or employers; 10) An expense account.

Expressing your Taurean side
If you have the Sun in Taurus then, somewhere inside you, you contain a Taurus. If your Taurean side is well developed, you will probably also have people with Taurus planets in your life. If this section doesn't accurately reflect what you're all about, you may want to read the chapter headed Walking Your Planets (pages 175–183).

SWAYED BY BEAUTY

Madonna, a Taurus Mars, collects the paintings of Frida Kahlo, a Taurus Moon. With a planet in this sign you may pursue beauty through the visual arts, or develop a strong response to painters, sculptors, craftspeople, illustrators or designers. Germaine Greer, who has a Taurus Moon, is best-known as the author of *The Female Eunuch* — showcasing her Aquarius Sun. She is also, however, the author of *The Obstacle Race: The Fortunes of Women Painters and Their Work*. The Taurean connection to visual beauty comes from Venus, your ruler. The Taurus Moon Carrie Fisher once said, 'I don't want life to imitate art, I want life to *be* art,' which pretty much sums up the aesthetic concerns of your sign. The other sign ruled by Venus — Libra — is also strongly represented in art galleries and studios, and among collectors and designers.

Artists, sculptors, designers

Annemieke Mein — Venus in Taurus
Bridget Riley — Sun in Taurus
Frances Mary Hodgkins — Sun in Taurus
Estelle Pankhurst — Sun in Taurus
Eileen Diss — Sun in Taurus
Fiona Foley — Venus in Taurus
Carla Zampatti — Sun in Taurus
Prue Acton — Sun in Taurus
Frida Kahlo — Moon in Taurus
Paloma Picasso — Mercury and Venus in Taurus

 **in taurus**

What you need

Security and certainty — unless you give up your money for an ideal, you'll opt for home ownership every time ★ A beautiful garden ★ Collectible furniture ★ Original art ★ Home insurance ★ Beautiful bargains ★ A financial safety net ★ A personal code of values ★ Above all, perhaps, a good accountant.

The Moon in Taurus home

If you rent, you'll forget it isn't yours, and feel very uncomfortable when you have to move. For most of you, the best feature of your house or flat will be the piece of paper that says it's actually yours. You like beautiful natural fabrics and double your pleasure if you can decorate with furniture or curtains at a bargain price that are well-made, built to last and easy on the eye. Even if you have a high-rise flat, you'll still find somewhere for a pot plant. Most of you opt for nature in abundance where you can.

The Moon in Taurus cook

You recycle the fruit and vegetables into a compost bin if you have a garden, and save your plastic bags. You're a fine chopper and a careful slosher — you don't believe in wasting ingredients. Above all, you dislike borrowing, and lending, food. You love gourmet ingredients: balsamic vinegar, virgin olive oil, fresh strawberries and Belgian chocolate. You tend to stick to the recipes you know and love, and don't mind spending hours stirring, blending or basting. You relate to food in a sensual way, and think of good restaurants as storehouses for aphrodisiacs.

Expressing your Taurean side

If you have the Moon in Taurus then, somewhere inside you, you contain a Taurus. If your Taurean side is well developed, you will probably also have people with Taurus planets in your life. If this section doesn't accurately reflect what you're all about, you may want to read the chapter headed Walking Your Planets (pages 175–183).

THE NATURAL WORLD

Venus, your ruling goddess, went back to nature when she fell madly in love with Adonis. Perfume, hairbrushing and gazing on precious metals (her favourite pastimes) were replaced by rambling expeditions through the woods and hills. Dressed like the huntress Diana, the lovesick Venus suddenly transferred her love of beauty to the natural world, and it was there that Adonis found her, with her dogs by her side.

If you have a planet in Taurus, then you may find the story of Venus reflects your two sides quite accurately. One is fond of *things* and objects, and fragrance and clothes. The other — once she is fully in love — prefers to run wild. Your passion may be for an Adonis of your own, or a vocation. But it is common for women with the Sun, Moon, Mercury, Venus or Mars in this sign to find their wilder, natural side when lust for life overtakes them.

 in taurus

The Mercury in Taurus student

Practical, sensible and methodical ★ You take your time and prefer to go for the hard facts ★ You do well in the Venus-ruled subjects: art, music, business, economics.

Your communication style

Slow but sure.

Your letters

Written with *your* pen.

You think like

A builder.

You talk like

A thinker.

The Mercury in Taurus voice

Sensual.

Your tactics

Stubborn.

Expressing your Taurean side

If you have Mercury in Taurus then, somewhere inside you, you contain a Taurus. If your Taurean side is well developed, you will probably also have people with Taurus planets in your life. If this section doesn't accurately reflect what you're all about, you may want to read the chapter headed Walking Your Planets (pages 175–183).

MUSIC AND TAURUS

Women whose horoscopes show planets in Taurus or Libra (the signs ruled by Venus), or a strong Venus signature are often musically talented, and are always strongly drawn to music. Among the musically inclined, of course, dancers also feature (Margot Fonteyn was a Taurus Sun). Here are some Taurus-influenced women who have taken their talent and passion for music into their careers:

Debbie Harry — Venus and Mars in Taurus
Tina Weymouth — Moon in Taurus
Madonna — Mars in Taurus
Belinda Carlisle — Mars in Taurus
Jane Wiedlin (Go-Gos) — Sun in Taurus
Barbra Streisand — Sun in Taurus
Kate Pierson (B52s) — Sun and Mercury in Taurus
Suzi Quatro — Mercury and Venus in Taurus
Alison Moyet — Venus in Taurus
Janet Jackson — Sun in Taurus
Carly Simon — Venus and Mars in Taurus
Kate Bush — Mars in Taurus
Ella Fitzgerald — Sun in Taurus
Cher — Sun in Taurus
Tammy Wynette — Sun in Taurus
Grace Jones — Sun in Taurus
Siouxsie Sioux — Moon and Mercury in Taurus
Enya — Sun in Taurus
Dame Nellie Melba — Sun in Taurus
Nina Hagen — Mars in Taurus
Elizabeth Fraser (Cocteau Twins) — Mars in Taurus

VENUS in taurus

You love

Lovers who are materially — or spiritually — rich ★ Natural beauty ★ Music ★ Paintings ★ Beautiful clothes and jewellery ★ Collectors' items ★ The oldest kind of plants ★ Men with a strong value system ★ Luxury hotels — especially if someone else is paying ★ Massage — a must; essential oils are an option, petrochemicals are a no-no ★ Everything that is beautiful, valuable and rare — you're a conservationist at heart.

You loathe

Commercial tackiness ★ Vinyl chairs ★ Cheapskates ★ Ecological vandalism.

Expressing your Taurean side

If you have Venus in Taurus then, somewhere inside you, you contain a Taurus. If your Taurean side is well developed, you will probably also have people with Taurus planets in your life. If this section doesn't accurately reflect what you're all about, you may want to read the chapter headed Walking Your Planets (pages 175–183).

KNOW YOUR GODDESS

Venus owns two signs of the zodiac — Taurus and Libra. She expresses her passion for love and beauty through both signs, but in different ways. In Libra, the emphasis is rather more on partnership and marriage. In Taurus, money and ownership play a larger part and there is more emphasis on love and money. Having the Sun, Moon, Mercury, Venus or Mars in Taurus is rather like having the goddess Venus sitting on your shoulder. In the interests of knowing her a little better, here are the main myths and themes associated with her:

Venus values beauty

Paintings and statues depicting Venus show her in many different forms, but they are all classically beautiful. As the Venus de Milo she has wavy hair, a perfect profile — and no arms. But the goddess wears her groin-level toga like a designer dress. Sandro Botticelli has painted her like a modern supermodel in The Birth of Venus, which shows her rising from a clam shell with flowers floating around her, and being offered yet another ancient designer dress ready to be worn. Uma Thurman, who played Venus in the film The Adventures of Baron Münchhausen, is a Sun Taurus.

 in taurus

The best revenge is
Being rich enough to do what you want.

Sporting Taurus
Stamina sports.

Your battle tactics
Your ultimate weapon is just having more money or resources than everyone else. You can also use your female charm or sexuality as a weapon. You take your time and plan your strategies, and can wait until the end of time if you have to. Like a bull, you snort and paw the ground, but take so long to charge that your opponents panic and lose their concentration.

What kind of opponent are you?
Endlessly patient.

Expressing your Taurean side
If you have Mars in Taurus then, somewhere inside you, you contain a Taurus. If your Taurean side is well developed, you will probably also have people with Taurus planets in your life. If this section doesn't accurately reflect what you're all about, you may want to read the chapter headed Walking Your Planets (pages 175–183).

.

FINDING A VALUE SYSTEM
Non-material values are arguably the most sophisticated expression of a Taurus planet. This does not negate your understanding of market forces, or your eye for all that is beautiful and 'priceless'. Taureans often transcend money and materialism to settle on something bigger, though.

For some of you, this is your professional integrity. Taurean types often struggle with the idea of selling out. Madonna (Taurus Mars) sang Material Girl, but by forming her own company, she has found the power to veto projects that she doesn't believe in.

In other cases, Taurean types put a higher price on human values — commonly, human lives. 'I wouldn't touch a leper for a thousand pounds,' said the late Mother Teresa, a Taurus Moon, 'yet I willingly cure him for the love of God.'

If you have a planet here, you may typically find that you follow both roads. One part of you is the instinctive collector and owner — money-minded, swayed by beauty and longing for security. The other part of you has a highly sophisticated understanding of a different kind of marketplace. Here, you are trading in other values: the price of a rainforest, the cost of saving a life, or the value of your own credibility and integrity.

What price reputation? Your Taurus planets probably understand this issue quite well. Many Taurus-influenced women are well known for dealing in an alternative value structure that has absolutely nothing to do with money or materialism. *Priceless integrity* is the domain of Taurus, above all other signs. Getting there seems to involve a lot of trial and error, but when your Taurean side has fixed a price on the things that cash cannot purchase, it's exceedingly hard to go back.

If life is an auction, then it's this Taurean side of you that refuses to sell out to the highest bidder: you leap over money into a value system that is personal and precious to you. It doesn't mean that you lose your Taurean awareness of money — far from it. But if you choose this 'elevated' Taurean pathway, then you'll also have an awareness of quite a different value system. Destiny says you'll be obliged to choose, however.

For love, not money

Mother Teresa — Moon in Taurus
Audrey Hepburn — Sun in Taurus
Monica Dickens — Sun in Taurus
Florence Nightingale — Sun in Taurus
Josephine Butler — Sun in Taurus
Elizabeth Fry — Sun in Taurus

THE TAUREAN BULL

The ancient astrologers could have chosen any symbols for their constellations. In all honesty, the stars that make up the Taurean Bull could just as easily make up the Taurean Aardvark or the Taurean Ferret. The symbolism of the Bull suits your Taurean side rather better, though. The ancient astrologers noticed that people born when the Sun appeared to be passing through this part of the sky were slower to move, and more stubborn than most. Today, astrologers notice the staying power and persistence of women who have a planet in this sign. I remember having a tug-of-war with a Sun Taurus once. We both claimed the same pair of stockings in the laundrette (she hung in longer, and won, of course).

Your Taurean side slows you down, and the image of the bull describes this steady, powering side of you quite potently. If you have speedier signs in your astro-package such as Aries, Gemini or Virgo, you may find that you have a problem with timing. To really tap into Taurus, walk up to the fence and gaze at the next bull you see in a paddock. That ambling style, those dug-in heels, that slow watchfulness ... it all changes, of course, when the bull charges. Your Taurean side can be awfully slow to react — and to act — but it is quite forceful when a decision has been reached.

STAYING POWER

Your Taurean side has a steady, relentless quality that is very hard to beat. The steadiness and slowness of Taurus results in a stubborn refusal to give in or give up. Women with planets in Taurus have proven, over the years, that they are in it *for the distance*. The bounce-back qualities of the sign are justifiably famous, and only a Capricorn planet makes you a better long-term stayer. Here are some famous Taurean stayers:

Queen Elizabeth II — Sun in Taurus
Joan Collins — Moon in Taurus
Michelle Pfeiffer — Sun in Taurus
Shirley MacLaine — Sun in Taurus
Meryl Streep — Moon in Taurus
Diana Ross — Moon in Taurus
Karen Blixen — Moon in Taurus

Shirley Temple Black — Sun in Taurus
Golda Meir — Sun in Taurus
Candice Bergen — Sun in Taurus
Priscilla Presley — Sun in Taurus

LOVE AND MONEY

Inevitably, love and money will be entwined issues if you have a Taurus planet. The connection with money comes from the Second House of the horoscope, which Taurus rules. Your planet/goddess Venus supplies the love, and issues around both seem to follow Taurean types around.

In the first place, vocational or career choices are based around 'for love or money' decisions. In close relationships, though, the Venus–Taurus issues really ignite. There is often a wealth gap between Taurean-influenced wives and their partners. Or the issue may be this: money can't buy you love. Some of you opt for relationships where money and lifestyle matters just seem to follow both of you around. Separations and divorces involving women with Taurus planets (Princess Diana is one example) often involve money and possessions to an extreme degree. Every time you fall in love, or make love, Venus walks in. As an archetype, a goddess and a planet, she will present questions about the extent to which the financial and material world should intrude on romance and passion. That part of the marriage vow that reads 'for richer, for poorer' was definitely written by a Taurean.

TAURUS MYTHS

Elizabeth Bennett

The heroine of Pride and Prejudice has many Taurean traits. She loves music. She falls in love with paintings. She develops endless reserves of patience. Also importantly, in the pursuit of love, she is slow to give in, or give up. She must choose between love and money twice in Jane Austen's book: firstly, with the obnoxious Mr Collins, then with Mr Darcy at his most unloveable. When Darcy develops some values and becomes desirable, she finds herself winning both love and wealth simultaneously. Some of the Venus myths surround her, too: she is always being placed against female rivals — sometimes her sisters, sometimes other women who are also pursuing Darcy. Like the goddess, when she falls in love, she runs wild: Elizabeth is associated with rambling, running and horses as much as she is associated with beauty.

THE CLASSIC TAURUS

Joanna Lumley

Born on 1st May 1946, Joanna Lumley — the star of both *Absolutely Fabulous* and *The New Avengers* — has the Sun in Taurus.

Market forces In her autobiography, *Stare Back and Smile*, Joanna writes: 'It runs in the family: the more grotesquely unnecessary and expensive something is, the fewer reasons we can think of for doing without it.' (She was buying a Rolls Royce at the time.)

Swayed by beauty Joanna collects paintings and drawings by the artist John Ward.

The natural world She is a keen walker and environmentalist.

Music and Taurus Joanna actually married a conductor — Stephen Barlow.

Know your goddess Apart from a career as a model (see Venus dresses to inspire love) Joanna was also a single parent to her son before marrying Stephen Barlow (see The mother–son relationship).

Finding a value system Well known for charity work, Joanna also has strong views on the distribution of wealth and social services. Even at the age of twelve, she wrote to the English Chancellor of the Exchequer suggesting that he should double the value of the pound so that everyone in the country could become rich!

The Taurean bull From Purdey to Patsy, her staying power has been typically Taurean.

Love and money 'I often wonder if I have done everything wrong,' she writes in *Stare Back and Smile*. 'Should I have got married, for decency's sake (and maybe divorced later)? ... Should I have given up acting and found a more secure, less potentially rewarding job near home ...?' In the end, as most Taurean types do, Joanna seems to have found both love *and* money.

TAUREAN SYMBOLS

The rule of synchronicity decrees that Taurean themes, symbols, ideas and icons may turn up in your life in important ways. If you have the Sun, Moon, Mercury, Venus or Mars in this sign, you may want to check this list:

The Bull ★ Venus/Aphrodite ★ Incense ★ Flowers ★ Fabric ★ Pearls ★ Apples ★ Rivals ★ Mars ★ Love ★ Cupid ★ Diana the Huntress ★ Girdles ★ Hair ★ Beauty ★ Jealousy ★ Worship ★ Fashion ★ Cosmetics ★ Perfumes ★ Two ★ Money ★ Possessions ★ Values ★ Sales ★ Trade ★ Economics ★ Commerce ★ Stock markets ★ Bull markets ★ Bullion ★ Antiques ★ Art ★ Collectors ★ Poverty ★ Wealth ★ Church mice ★ Doves ★ Myrtle ★ Roses ★ Dogs ★ Shopping ★ Earning ★ Selling ★ Selling out ★ Commercialism ★ Equity ★ Budgets ★ Currency ★ Barter ★ Exchange ★ Beauty contests ★ Mothers and sons ★ Shepherds ★ Paris ★ Helen ★ Ethical investment ★ Bankers ★ Gold ★ Platinum ★ Silver ★ Vulcan ★ Blacksmiths ★ Steel ★ Metal ★ Craft ★ The Arts ★ Aesthetics.

PLANETS

in gemini

Read this section if you have your Sun, Moon, Mercury, Venus or Mars in Gemini.

ARE YOU DOING YOUR GEMINI?

You love the telephone

You travel whenever you can, even for brief getaways

You write for pleasure or profit

You've worked out precisely why sibling issues are so important to you

---

YOUR GEMINIAN SIDE

Well-informed ★ Witty ★ Forever young.

USING GEMINI

Your Sun, Moon, Mercury, Venus or Mars in Gemini is your intelligence quotient. Use this side of you at any time you are required to outsmart the opposition or articulate what you mean to say. Your Gemini side can make bimbos of us all! This sign is also your popularity passport. Use the famous Gemini wit, and you will charm or distract absolutely anybody into absolutely anything. Your Geminian side also brings a passion for reading which you can enjoy from childhood to old age.

DOUBLE IDENTITIES

These women, with the Sun, Moon, Mercury, Venus or Mars in Gemini also have the double identities of Castor and Pollux, the heavenly twins. If you have a Geminian side, you may attract nicknames or alter egos, or change your name to suit yourself.

Norma Jean Baker — Marilyn Monroe — Sun in Gemini
Frances Gumm — Judy Garland — Sun in Gemini
Priscilla White — Cilla Black — Sun in Gemini
Genevieve Alison-Jane Moyet — Alf — Sun in Gemini
Barbara Streisand — Barbra Streisand — Mars in Gemini
Sheena Orr — Sheena Easton — Venus in Gemini
Cherilynn Sarkasian La Pierre — Cher — Venus in Gemini
Susan Dallion — Siouxsie Sioux — Sun in Gemini
Bessie Simpson — Wallis Simpson — Sun in Gemini
Robyn Smith — Robyn Archer — Sun in Gemini
Julie Lush — Julie Anthony — Moon in Gemini
Gaynor Hopkins — Bonnie Tyler — Sun in Gemini
Mary Louise Streep — Meryl Streep — Mercury, Mars in Gemini

I have never met a woman with planets in Gemini who was not known by another name at some stage in her life. I have a friend with a Gemini Sun and Mercury who was christened Jane, but she has also been called everything from Millie to Zoid to Intellectual Cow at various times in her life!

If you have Gemini planets, you may find that you are quite happy about the name your parents gave you, but everybody else feels moved to re-christen you as quickly as possible. It's almost as if you really have been split into one or two sets of twin personalities, and each time someone different sees one of these multiple versions of you, they give you a different name.

Some Geminian women change their names for professional reasons. Some of you may not feel entirely comfortable with your given name, so you make an adjustment. With the right name, you can end up with quite a variety of alternative labels.

If you have friends who also have Gemini planets, a whole chain of nicknames and alter egos can develop between you. If you have quite a few Gemini-influenced people in your social circle then when you all get together outsiders won't have a clue what or whom you are talking about!

in gemini

You identify with

Writers ★ Talkers ★ Reporters ★ Teachers ★ Switchboard operators ★ Couriers ★ Messenger girls ★ Newsagents ★ Students ★ Travellers.

You're an authority on

Sibling relationships ★ The neighbourhood ★ News ★ Words ★ Writers ★ Loose talk ★ Journeys ★ Facts.

Your career Top Ten

You need: 1) Intellectual challenges; 2) Space for private phone calls; 3) Endless variety; 4) A platform for your written abilities; 5) Good talkers and listeners; 6) Mobility — a good car, bus service or taxi account; 7) Your own noticeboard; 8) The biggest diary known to humankind; 9) Intelligent clients or employers; 10) Courses and seminars tied to your work.

Expressing your Geminian side

If you have the Sun in Gemini then, somewhere inside you, you contain a Gemini. If your Geminian side is well developed, you will probably also have people with Gemini planets in your life. If this section doesn't accurately reflect what you're all about, you may want to read the chapter headed Walking Your Planets (*see* pages 175–183).

SIBLINGS AND TWINS

Your Geminian side can also be expressed through a sister or brother figure, or real-life sibling issues. Brothers or sisters may have a huge impact on your life if you were born with Gemini planets, or you may find the fates throw you someone who acts as your symbolic twin, or other half.

Many women with Gemini planets have platonic, sisterly relationships with men for this reason. It is common for women with Gemini planets to report that someone in their life is 'just like a brother' or 'just like a sister', reflecting the myth behind the sign. After Zeus had sex with a mortal, Leda, the poor woman gave birth to twins, Castor and Pollux, brothers to Helen. Important brother and sister figures, real or substitute, are very common in the lives of strongly Geminian women. For better or worse, this is the sign of the sibling.

If your Geminian side is strongly developed, it may be hard for you to think of yourself, or your life and times, without immediate reference to a brother or sister. Astrologers who are also qualified psychologists invariably ask about brothers and sisters if a Gemini-influenced client turns up for counselling. Sometimes, the issue is that there was no sibling at all, and psychologists find it has influenced the whole family dynamic.

The myth of Castor and Pollux also describes cousins, and your Gemini planets may bring strong issues around the children of your mother's and father's siblings.

Sometimes Gemini planets lead not only to friendships which are brother–sister or sister–sister, but to marriages and serious relationships with a 'twin' figure. Jackie Kennedy-Onassis had a Gemini Venus. She married John F. Kennedy, they became known as Jack and Jackie. Two years ago, I attended the wedding of a Gemini Sun friend — she was marrying her cousin. If you have the Sun, Moon, Mercury, Venus or Mars in Gemini, you won't have too far to look to find a 'twin' brother or sister.

Heavenly twins

The well-known sisters listed below could hardly be called heavenly twins, but the ancient myth of Castor and Pollux has modern parallels with these Geminian types. In the myth, Castor was killed in war, while Pollux survived. The heartbroken Pollux told Jupiter he would exchange his own life for his twin's. Jupiter generously offered this deal: he would bring Castor back to life, but only on alternate days. On Castor's 'off' days, Pollux would take his place. If you have Gemini planets, your relationship with a sister or 'twin' figure may involve all kinds of complex issues, reflecting the complicated relationship of the twins in the original story. You may live parallel lives, you may be rivals, there may be a difficulty if both of you occupy the same position or place in life, or there may well be a deeper connection.

Of the siblings teamed up here, some are well-known rivals while some just can't be interviewed without an immediate question about their brother or sister.

Kylie Minogue — Sun in Gemini — and Danni
Joan Collins — Sun in Gemini — and Jackie Collins
Margaret Drabble — Sun in Gemini — and A.S. Byatt
Mandy Salomon — Sun in Gemini — and Melanie
Gladys Knight — Sun in Gemini — and Brenda
Deniece Pearson — Sun in Gemini — and Doris, Lorraine, Stedman and Delroy
Ann Wilson — Sun in Gemini — and Nancy
June Carter — Sun in Gemini — Helen and Anita
Laverne Andrews — Mars in Gemini — Maxine and Patti
Lee Radziwill — Moon in Gemini — and Jacqueline Onassis

 **in gemini**

What you need

People ★ Books and magazines ★ Radio and TV ★ Pens and paper ★ A mobile telephone ★ Above all else? Variety, change and constant talk and opinion-sharing.

The Moon in Gemini home

Your house or flat will have a nerve centre that looks a bit like your version of Communications HQ. Everything in the Moon in Gemini place leads back to the telephone eventually. You read *everywhere* — in the bath, in bed, and while you're stirring potatoes. Moon in Gemini women stick up postcards from friends, and have post-it notes and scribbled reminders stuck in the most unlikely places.

The Moon in Gemini cook

The part of cooking you most enjoy is nipping round to your favourite local shops, where you can pick up gossip or bump into people you know. You're a kitchen talker. Guests arrive and spend half the night yelling, 'What did you say?' as you attempt to carry on long conversations while simultaneously stirring vats of spaghetti sauce. You like quick food, and are one of those women who rip recipes out of magazines.

Expressing your Geminian side

If you have the Moon in Gemini then, somewhere inside you, you contain a Gemini. If your Geminian side is well developed, you will probably also have people with Gemini planets in your life. If this section doesn't accurately reflect what you're all about, you may want to read the chapter headed Walking Your Planets (pages 175–183).

LANGUAGE IS A VIRUS

Singer and performance artist Laurie Anderson (Gemini Sun) had two hits. One, 'O Superman', was largely based around an answering machine (typically Gemini) and the other, 'Language is a Virus', sums up the wordy, verbal obsessions of the sign. Your Geminian side is the one that inspires you to make up names or nicknames for other people (or objects). Mercury, your ruler, is associated with *naming things* and many women who have Gemini planets seem to delight in fixing humans, animals, or even cars with a title.

Your Geminian side may be the one that lets you create catchphrases, or pick them up. Most Gemini-influenced women have a pet phrase or expression that family or friends associate with them. Words just seem to stick with Gemini, and if you have planets here you will continually supply those around you with your aural 'signatures' and quotable quotes. Crosswords, dictionary games, Scrabble, diaries, journals, poems, letters, postcards, books, memos, post-it notes, sign language, switchboards, telephones, pagers and puns are Gemini's domain, too.

Gemini famously gives you a *way with words* above all other things, and a love of language. Your place in the astrological tribe is to articulate, refine, polish and play around with your language of choice. For this reason, your Geminian side may be equally entertained by scripts, song lyrics, poetry, fiction, prose, non-fiction, or journalism. If new words or slang start to float around you, the chances are you either started it, or some other Gemini-influenced female is spreading the verbal virus. Gemini planets help you to pick up foreign languages more easily, too. Just as you can transmit information, you also seem to absorb it effortlessly. No wonder the Geminian self-education process is lifelong. Fleetwood Mac's Stevie Nicks has the Sun and Mercury in Gemini and has famously kept tour diaries for years — bound in velvet (of course).

Quotable quotes

Women with Gemini planets have become associated with these memorable phrases:

'These boots are made for walking' — Nancy Sinatra
'Diamonds are a girl's best friend' — Marilyn Monroe
'Girls just wanna have fun' — Cyndi Lauper
'It's my party and I'll cry if I want to' — Lesley Gore
'We are not amused' — Queen Victoria
'You can never be too rich or too thin' — Wallis Simpson

 in gemini

The Mercury in Gemini student

Horribly intelligent ★ Good at English, Speech and Drama, Debating or Languages ★ You gossip in class or pass notes, but get a stunning report anyway.

Your communication style

Chatty.

Your letters

Witty, but they run off the end of the page.

You think like

A reporter.

You talk like

A professional.

The Mercury in Gemini voice

Clear.

Your tactics

Cunning.

Expressing your Geminian side

If you have Mercury in Gemini then, somewhere inside you, you contain a Gemini. If your Geminian side is well developed, you will probably also have people with Gemini planets in your life. If this section doesn't accurately reflect what you're all about, you may want to read the chapter headed Walking Your Planets (pages 175–183).

DOUBLES AND MULTIPLES

Linda Goodman was one of the first astrologers to notice Gemini's tendency to double up on things. Her observations, which she made in the late sixties, still hold true today. I have clients and friends with Gemini planets who have a kind of 'multiple choice' lifestyle which results in these doubles and multiples: remember, too, the original Gemini myth actually described three siblings *and* a bad case of double identity, so if you have Gemini planets you could end up with multiples. My mother, who has Mars in Gemini, has owned about 40,000 Mini Vans since the day I was born.

Here are some more real-life multiples I've come across belonging to Geminian types:

Two identical teapots	Five nicknames
Two passports	Three television sets
Six pseudonyms	Two fax machines
Four jobs	Eight identical black poodles
Two sexual preferences	Four telephones
Two houses	

If you have planets in Gemini, you may also be doubling up on *life itself*. Some women, who have two or three planets in the sign, actually seem to split themselves into different people, pursuing different lifestyles, countries, social circles and professions simultaneously. Dual passports, or dual citizenship, is another example of Gemini's tendency to double up. I have known several Gemini-influenced teachers who always seemed to have *two* subjects, spread over *double* periods. Your Geminian side is a natural juggler.

 **in gemini**

You love

Reading ★ Scribbling ★ The English language ★ Witty comedies ★ Intelligent men ★ Amusing girlfriends ★ Gossip ★ Wrinkle cream ★ Naming things — especially animals or babies ★ Long, flirtatious phone calls, faxes or e-mail ★ Re-reading the same books and actually *bothering* with the lyrics inside CD covers. You even read the labels inside clothes ★ Most of all, being *smart*.

You loathe

Bimbos ★ Dumb-dumb sports ★ Boredom ★ Plane delays ★ Phone disconnections.

Expressing your Geminian side

If you have Venus in Gemini, then somewhere inside you, you contain a Gemini. If your Geminian side is well developed, you will probably also have people with Gemini planets in your life. If this section doesn't accurately reflect what you're all about, you may want to read the chapter headed Walking Your Planets (pages 175–183).

TRAVELLING LIGHT

Gemini is strongly associated with short journeys — the kind where you can boomerang back to your original starting point very quickly. Gemini's ruler, Mercury (also identified with Hermes) spent a lot of time zipping around with winged sandals, but never really went very far. If you are strongly Gemini, your life may be full of short hops, either for professional or personal reasons.

Long overseas hauls are more suited to women with Sagittarian planets (incidentally, if you have these, too, you'll never stop moving!). Your Geminian side inclines itself to city–country hops, interstate journeys, neighbourhood circuits and short treks to other countries. Flight attendants with Gemini planets always seem to stick to short hauls. And I know a vast number of women in the media with Gemini planets who spend their lives in the backs of taxis! (Gemini rules taxi drivers and couriers, too.) The more your

Geminian side dominates your life, the more likely you are to divide your time (the twins again) between two or more destinations.

Gemini planets incline their owners towards the neighbourhood above all other things, perhaps because that is originally where Mercury felt at home. There is often a lively, local feel in the lives of strongly Geminian women, and the sign has traditionally been associated with neighbours. The soap opera *Neighbours* originally became popular with two Gemini Suns, Kylie Minogue and Jason Donovan, in the leads. If your Geminian side is active, you may be quite involved with your neighbours, or have a definite network locally. You will tend to identify with, and feel at home with, the few kilometres around your home.

 in **gemini**

The best revenge is
Talking people to death.

Sporting Gemini
If you have to, you'll wear a Walkman.

Your battle tactics
You tend to lie when all else fails, but will also formulate the Fiendishly Cunning Plan. You play your enemies like a game of Scrabble (incidentally, word games bring out your competitive side like nothing else).

What kind of opponent are you?
Articulate.

Expressing your Gemini side
If you have Mars in Gemini, then your Geminian side is as much a part of you as the Sun or Moon. If your Geminian side is well developed, you will probably also have people with Gemini planets in your life. If you don't identify with this section, you may want to read the chapter called Walking Your Planets (pages 175–183).

FOREVER YOUNG

The heavenly twins have always been drawn as pubescent, and the ancients never updated the image. In an old illustration of the twins hanging on my wall, they look exactly like two copies of the young Marilyn Monroe, a Gemini Sun. Your Gemini planets contribute to the side of you that is young at heart, and this may play itself out in your appearance, or in your attitude towards life.

There is something perpetually youthful about Gemini planets, and whenever women with Gemini planets troop in for consultations with me, I always guess their birth year wrong. Sometimes I get the entire decade wrong.

There are those who just never seem to get any older physically (the lucky few) and, more commonly, a whole group of women with Geminian sides who can hold their own with people born twenty or thirty years later. Your Gemini planets will keep you curious about life, and interested in everything going on around you, well into your senior years.

Mercury, of course, had to be fit, active and mentally alert to fulfil his function as Messenger of the Gods. Your Gemini side will contribute to good legs and a fast, updated brain for as long as you let it. Women with Gemini planets become great readers, talkers and walkers when they retire, which is entirely appropriate for this sign. When you're in your teens and twenties, you'll zip around with a mobile phone or a pager, a laptop computer or a pile of postcards in your handbag. You may have the Sun, Moon, Mercury, Venus or Mars in Gemini, but wherever it falls, you have something lively, active and bright to contain.

TRICKY WOMEN

The original twins, Castor and Pollux, were decidedly tricky. Twins tend to be like that, too — especially if they are identical. Your Gemini planets incline you towards jokes, cunning, juggling, sleight of hand and truth-twisting. Quite a few women with Gemini planets have a history of shoplifting, forgery, tall tales, graffiti, terrible practical jokes and outrageous lying! I really know of no other astrological factor which is associated so strongly with clever tricks, sneaky moves and 'fiddling' in every sense of the word. Maybe it's understandable — Gemini rules the fingers and the wits, and the temptation to use both simultaneously is typical of the sign — especially in youth.

BUYING AND SELLING

Mercury, the ruler of Gemini, was the Italian god of commerce and your Geminian side is adept at either finding bargains, or running a sales pitch. Some women use this side of themselves to good advantage during the June sales, others do it for a living. If you're having a garage sale, set up with another Gemini-influenced person. You should get excellent results. Seriously commercial Geminian types often have a special flair for business.

GEMINI MYTHS

Lois Lane in Superman

Having the double 'L' in her initials is only part of the legendary Ms Lane's Geminian status. She is also dealing with real-life twin figures — the bespectacled Clark Kent and the pectorally well-endowed Superman. Her job as a reporter for the *Daily Planet* surrounds her with intelligent people, plenty of short journeys around town, and a telephone and typewriter — all Geminian essentials. She's forever young, too. Created in the 1930s, Lois has remained twentysomething for decades. Her Geminian catchphrase must be, 'Clark, you're never around when you're needed.' Clark Kent, too, is a Gemini, but he probably has Aries Rising as his life journey is all about heroic missions!

GEMINIAN HUMOUR

Behind the best comedy lies a Gemini planet (note the *Absolutely Fabulous* connection in the list below). Part of your Geminian inheritance is an extremely sharp sense of humour. One of the first lessons the girl with a Gemini Sun, Moon, Mercury, Venus or Mars learns is this: people listen harder to you if you're funnier. Many Gemini-influenced women are brilliant mimics

(Meryl Streep, with Mercury and Mars in Gemini, is one of them.) You'll either 'do' a voice to make your point, or use silly accents for selected parts of your sentence. If you develop your Geminian side, you may end up being as lethally amusing as the women below.

Victoria Wood — Mars in Gemini
Jennifer Saunders — Venus in Gemini
Joanna Lumley — Venus in Gemini
Ruby Wax — Moon in Gemini
Candice Bergen — Venus in Gemini
Sandra Bernhard — Sun in Gemini

Patricia Routledge — Moon and Mars in Gemini
Nora Ephron — Mercury and Venus in Gemini
Kathleen Turner — Sun in Gemini
Penny Marshall — Mars in Gemini

THE CLASSIC GEMINI
Anne Frank

Born on 12th June 1929, Anne Frank — one of the world's most famous diarists — had the Sun and Mercury in Gemini. Her life was short, as she died in Belsen concentration camp in March 1945. In an odd way, like another tragic Sun Gemini, Marilyn Monroe, she *has* remained forever young — at least in the public imagination.

Double identities Anne originally wanted to call herself Anne Aluis, and later, Anne Robin. When the Nazis recorded her name, they did so as Anneliese Frank. The world knows and loves her as Anne Frank. She famously invented pseudonyms for all the real people mentioned in the diary. She nicknamed her father Pim.

Siblings and twins One of Anne's books, recovered from the Secret Annexe where she hid with her family, was actually called *The Twins & Tabiffa*. Her real-life sister Margot was a central character in the diaries.

Language is a virus Anne's diary has been published in 55 languages and more than 20 million copies have been sold — with many quotable quotes.

Doubles and multiples Today, Anne's diaries have been sorted into three versions — a, b and c. She used two types of handwriting — printed and cursive.

Travelling light Anne's Geminian 'neighbourhood' shrunk dramatically when her family went into hiding but she wrote about the other Annex tenants as if they were locals just a few streets away. It's common for women with Gemini planets to have a community, neighbourhood or *Melrose Place* feel to their lives.

Buying and selling Anne's diaries contain meticulous notes on war coupons, food prices and the family's wartime trades.

Gemini humour Anne's 'brochure' for the Secret Annex, passed on to other Jews going into hiding there, contained descriptions of the unique 'low-fat diet' and the running water supply — 'on various inside and outside walls,' Anne joked.

GEMINIAN SYMBOLS

If you have planets in Gemini, these keywords, ideas and related themes may turn up in your life with above-average frequency. It's one way that your own Geminian side may be fed back to you:

Diaries ★ Short-hand ★ Stamps ★ Letters ★ Scrabble ★ Quicksilver ★ Mercury ★ Brothers ★ Sisters ★ Three ★ Hermes ★ Thoth ★ Typewriters ★ Dictionaries ★ Messages ★ Couriers ★ Taxis ★ Birds ★ Nicknames ★ Names ★ Doubles ★ Multiples ★ Abbreviations ★ Puns ★ Mimics ★ Twins ★ Cousins ★ Parrots ★ Lyres ★ Liars ★ Fingers ★ Hands ★ Nerves ★ Secretaries ★ Tape recorders ★ Journalists ★ Editors ★ Novelists ★ Languages ★ Pens ★ Keyboards ★ E-mail ★ Megaphones ★ Photocopiers ★ Forgery ★ Notes ★ Schools ★ Colleges ★ Buying ★ Selling ★ Carrier pigeons ★ Pagers ★ Braille ★ Alphabets ★ Wit ★ Imitations ★ Messengers ★ Translators ★ Speech ★ Vocals ★ Thieves ★ Crossroads ★ Merchants ★ Signs ★ Sign language ★ Vocabulary ★ Thoughts ★ Opinions ★ Telegrams ★ Telephones ★ CB radio ★ Mass media ★ Talkback radio ★ Defamation ★ Accents ★ Voicemail ★ Diction ★ Speech therapy ★ Prose ★ Peter Pan ★ Initials ★ Desks ★ Memos ★ Aerials ★ Pen names ★ Documents ★ Handwriting ★ Pseudonyms.

in cancer

Read this section if you have your Sun, Moon, Mercury, Venus or Mars in Cancer.

ARE YOU DOING YOUR CANCER?

You're totally in touch with the part that childhood and home plays for you

Turning a house into a home is a mission of love for you

You've found at least one human or animal in your life to protect and nurture

---

YOUR CANCERIAN SIDE

House-proud ★ Clan-conscious ★ Sympathetic.

USING CANCER

There are two Cancerian symbols which you can use at various times of your life. Having the Sun, Moon, Mercury, Venus or Mars here means you can play the part of Diana, the Huntress — or the more traditional Earth Mother. Many women with planets here swap both roles. One part of you is a homemaker and clan keeper, while the other is much wilder and more independent.

THE MOTHER ROLE

The word *mother* resonates with Cancer-influenced women for all kinds of different reasons. Some of them are positive reasons, some of them are more complicated, and some of them are downright difficult. Mary Beth Whitehead has the Moon in Cancer. Your Sun,

Moon, Mercury, Venus or Mars in Cancer describes how you feel about being a mother, and how you feel about your own mother — and the role of women as mothers in general. If you decide to go ahead and have a child, it will be a bigger deal for you than for most other women. If you skip parenthood, then similarly, it's going to be a very big deal.

I think it's accurate to say that your Cancerian side will be *family-conscious*. There will be very little that you do which can take place without reference to your family, to your place in the clan and to your relationship with those people. Along with the word mother (which is also contained in the word *grandmother*) the other word which seems to spark with Cancer-influenced women is *clan*.

Some astrology books have described Cancer Sun women as stove-bound, baby-sprouting, soup-making matriarchs. Having a planet here does make you family-conscious, yes, and certainly extremely sensitive to the notion of mother–child relationships. Your own maternal instincts, though, will be strongly influenced by your particular experience of the family set-up, and this is one of the most complicated areas of Life as an Astrologer Knows It. All we know when you walk in the door with your birthday on a piece of paper is this: if we barge in with insensitive comments about your family, your mother, or your feelings about children, we are likely to lose a client. Like, yesterday!

For every woman with a Cancer Sun, Moon, Mercury, Venus or Mars with three children at school and another on the way, there is one who has a problem with the notion of motherhood. For this reason, the women listed here are clan-conscious, rather than famously maternal.

Of course, some of them are powerful matriarchs: but most are just intricately involved with their families and clans because destiny has intervened. Emmeline Pankhurst is a good example of this: born on 14th July 1858, she was a Cancer Sun, and the mother of Christabel, Sylvia and Adela, who all became part of the suffragette movement. Emmeline herself was the daughter of a radical mother. Her daughter Adela emigrated to Australia eventually, and contributed to winning women the vote there.

Clan conscious

Princess Anne — Venus in Cancer
Princess Margaret — Moon in Cancer
The Queen Mother — Venus in Cancer
Rose Kennedy — Sun in Cancer
Emmeline Pankhurst — Sun in Cancer
Jessica Mitford — Mars in Cancer
Judy Garland — Mercury and Venus in Cancer
Nancy Reagan — Moon in Cancer
Nancy Sinatra — Moon and Mars in Cancer

INTERPRETING CANCER

Women with planets in Cancer who have a problem with the traditional image of child-bearing hips and pots and pans prefer it when the notion of motherhood is analysed a little more thoroughly. Cancer has described different maternal roles at different stages in history. Once it may have been about endless baby-popping and apron-tying, but today Cancer's maternal feelings encompass a variety of different roles. You will probably recognise an aspect of yourself here, yet all of these roles are also aspects of modern motherhood. They may be applied to your own family, if you have one, or to the world outside your front door:

Nurse ★ Doctor ★ Psychologist ★ Counsellor ★ Chef ★ Sports coach ★ Courier ★ Taxi driver ★ Entertainer ★ Mediator ★ Switchboard operator ★ Waitress ★ Cleaner ★ Interior decorator ★ Accountant ★ Security guard ★ Vet ★ Storyteller ★ Home renovator ★ Teacher ★ Nanny ★ Electrician ★ Plumber ★ Nutritionist ★ Caterer ★ Tailor ★ Masseur ★ Party organiser ★ Defence Minister.

All of these roles, in Cancerian terms, are done for love. And they are accomplished *protectively*. As with all things associated with this sign, the accent is on caring and caretaking. You may be a traditional mother taking on a variety of these modern roles, or you may take on responsibility for others, in which case you may gravitate towards a career where you are caring for others in a wider sense, or towards interests which extend to others' welfare. This will be particularly obvious if you have more than one planet in Cancer, or a strongly placed Moon in your chart, too. Having a planet here guarantees you'll always drop into these, or similar, roles at various times in your life. The Cancerian thing is *looking after other people*. Maria Montessori had Mars in Cancer.

in cancer

You identify with

Two roles, taken in turns: firstly — mothers, good cooks, home-makers and those in the caring professions. Secondly — independent, spirited and active women. At various times in your life you will be both Moon Mother and Diana the Huntress.

You're an authority on

Female friends ★ Female anger ★ The home ★ The natural world ★ 'Hunting' on a professional level ★ Feminine indulgences ★ Children ★ Mothers ★ Family relationships.

Your career Top Ten

You need 1) Time out for the hairdresser; 2) A limit on your travelling time; 3) Something to pay the mortgage — or the decorator; 4) A caring role; 5) Emotional satisfaction; 6) Women around you; 7) People who need you, on the most basic level; 8) A decent selection of cafes or restaurants nearby; 9) Somewhere to run wild occasionally; 10) Space to make private phone calls.

Expressing your Cancerian side

If you have the Sun in Cancer then, somewhere inside you, you contain a Cancer. If your Cancerian side is well developed, you will probably also have people with Cancer planets in your life. If this section doesn't accurately reflect what you're all about, you may want to read the chapter headed Walking Your Planets (pages 175–183).

THE HUNTRESS ROLE

Diana, the Huntress, is the Cancerian alter ego. She has been painted with the Moon, your symbol, in her hair, a greyhound by her side and a bow and arrow in her hand. Her company was mostly female — in the form of nymphs. (Cancerian types usually run with a pack of girlfriends, by the way.) She was a virgin goddess, too, reflecting one of the basic truths about your wilder side, and your destiny may be played out as single, celibate or solo in spirit.

Diana ruled the valleys which grew with cypress and pine trees. In these valleys, she had a sacred cave, which describes the 'haven and home' symbolism of this sign. The myth tells us that she was returning home for a long bath when Actaeon accidentally stumbled into the cave, and saw her naked. She blushed, picked up an arrow and shot him. He immediately turned into a stag, and his own dogs turned on him. Savage revenge for an innocent mistake!

This Cancerian myth describes the self-possession of your Diana side, and also your capacity for anger. The huntress part of Cancer is just as important as the caring, nurturing side. With the Sun, Moon, Mercury, Venus or Mars in this sign you inherit a fierce 'ownership' of your own space — and your own body and sexuality. You are also a match for any man who impinges on that personal space.

If this myth has already reminded you of another famous, very modern, blushing Shy Di, you may want to read more about the way the Huntress myth resonated for Princess Diana at the end of this section. In your own world, a Cancer planet offers you a considerably more self-contained and defiantly single identity than previously supposed. I have noticed that it is the times that Cancer-influenced women *do without men* that call forth their wilder Diana side in a more obvious way. Emma Peel, the independent, high-kicking heroine of The Avengers, is played by Diana (there's that name again) Rigg, a Cancer Sun.

in cancer

What you need
Security ★ Your own home ★ A family, or substitute family ★ A sense of place ★ Privacy ★ Female friends ★ Feminine self-indulgences ★ Old photo albums ★ Trees ★ Animals ★ Something to nurture or care for.

The Moon in Cancer home

This is where life begins and ends, as your house or flat is the centre of everything you need. You need a signed document to say that the place is yours, above all other things, as the insecurity of renting is not really your ideal. Peaceful surroundings, or a door that slams on the outside world, are very important. The bathroom is full of potions, lotions, luxuries and gadgets, and only the kitchen comes up for the same kind of attention. Girlfriends are always dropping in, and you need somewhere nearby to go rambling or running around in.

The Moon in Cancer cook

You either inherit family recipes, or create classics which are then passed on through the clan. Your mother always seems to be floating over your shoulder when you cook, too! You're good at doling out food for the 500, and shine at those 'gathering of the clan' functions. You're especially fond of food you grew up with, or associate with your homeland. You're a nostalgic cook.

Expressing your Cancerian side

If you have the Moon in Cancer then, somewhere inside you, you contain a Cancer. If your Cancerian side is well developed, you will probably also have people with Cancer planets in your life. If this section doesn't accurately reflect what you're all about, you may want to read the chapter headed Walking Your Planets (pages 175–183).

FOOD AND DIET

The Moon rules Cancer, and this planet is associated with food and eating issues by astrologers. You may express this in different ways. Some of you are expert cooks, some of you just love food. Others have difficult issues around eating, and dieting, and food consumption: if this sounds like you, an astrologer will look at the position of the Moon in your personal horoscope for initial clues.

Most of you are enthusiastic cooks, or natural entertainers, have a fine appreciation of good food, and some of you even make a career out of it: a strong Moon or Cancer emphasis in a horoscope usually describes a natural cook. Dorothy Hodgkin, the woman who told the world what was in vitamin B12 (and won a Nobel Prize) was a Cancer Mars. Gina Lollobrigida, who led an advertising campaign for an Italian supermarket food brand, is a Cancer Sun. Jean Marsh, who wrote the popular TV series, *Upstairs Downstairs*, is a Cancer Sun. You may be served or serving, but a Cancer planet usually increases your interest in the end product.

Gourmets and gourmet writers

Victoria Alexander — Venus in Cancer
Gay Bilson — Moon and Mars in Cancer
Rita Erlich — Moon in Cancer
Beverley Sutherland Smith — Sun in Cancer
Delia Smith — Mercury, Venus and Mars in Cancer

 in cancer

The Mercury in Cancer student

You tend to form study habits — both good and bad. You like subjects about *people*, first and foremost: the humanities or people-related sciences will appeal most.

Your communication style

Soft.

Your letters

Full of reminiscences — and clan news.

You think like

A woman.

You talk like

Someone's sister or mother.

The Mercury in Cancer voice

Gentle.

Your tactics

You use old tricks.

Expressing your Cancerian side

If you have Mercury in Cancer then, somewhere inside you, you contain a Cancer. If your Cancerian side is well developed, you will probably also have people with Cancer planets in your life. If this section doesn't accurately reflect what you're all about, you may want to read the chapter headed Walking Your Planets (pages 175–183).

THE HOME ENVIRONMENT

Because both your goddesses — the Moon Mother, and Diana the Huntress — are associated with the home, it's not surprising to find that this is a huge issue for women with planets in Cancer. Having the Sun, Moon, Mercury, Venus or Mars in this sign increases your interest in, and enjoyment of, your own place. It may give you a concern for the housing or accommodation given to other people, too — Baroness Ryder, founder of homes for the disabled in England, is a Cancer Sun. Lois O'Donoghue, who has both Moon and Venus in Cancer, has contributed greatly to the building of Aboriginal hostels in Australia.

Women who earn their livings in real estate, the hospitality industries, architecture, interior design and building often have a Cancer planet. Ramona Koval, an expert in environmental design, is a Cancer Sun. Leona Helmsley, the notorious Queen of the New York hotel trade, has the Sun and Venus in Cancer.

One of the biggest concerns of Cancer Sun Emmeline Pankhurst was the Married Women's *Property* Committee, formed as part of her battle for women's rights. It took a Cancer Mars, Ella Stack, to help rebuild Darwin in Australia after Cyclone Tracy.

You don't have to work in the area of property to like it, though. Most of you with a Cancer planet are perfectly happy to stand in front of real estate agents' windows, or cart home DIY equipment from the hardware shop on the weekend. All of you seem to adore turning empty houses or flats into havens. This is an intensely home-oriented, shelter-seeking, cave-retreating sign. And like Diana the Huntress, your favourite room may well be the bathroom.

 in **cancer**

You love

Your home ★ Your country ★ Clan or household companionship ★ People you've known for years ★ Memories ★ Security ★ Decorating ★ Hibernating occasionally ★ Mothering people or looking after them ★ Hotels you know like the back of your hand ★ Romance ★ Sentimental memories ★ Coming home after a long trip away ★ Being complimented on your cooking ★ A sense of history or place.

You loathe

People who don't eat what you cook ★ Family arguments ★ Being forced to move house.

Expressing your Cancerian side

If you have Venus in Cancer then, somewhere inside you, you contain a Cancer. If your Cancerian side is well developed, you will probably also have people with Cancer planets in your life. If this section doesn't accurately reflect what you're all about, you may want to read the chapter headed Walking Your Planets (pages 175–183).

YOUR HOMELAND

My country, right or wrong, is a phrase that seems particularly appropriate to Cancer planets. Your ancestry may be Aboriginal, Irish or fifth-generation Australian, but a strong sense of homeland seems to come with the territory. A deep sense of roots, history and belonging is necessary for your Cancerian side, which may beam out strong messages about your culture, origins or nationality to people who meet you. This is never more obvious than when you are far from home, or a long way away from your roots.

The Cancer Sun, Moon, Mercury, Venus or Mars has these themes in order of priority: my people, my homeland, myself. It's an intensely tribal thing, even if your 'tribe' happens to be living in the middle of deepest, darkest Manchester in a high-rise flat! Not surprisingly, Cancer planets lend an incredible patriotism, and a strong identification with familiar slang, customs, food and cultural preferences. Identifying with your roots in this way could influence everything from your favourite recipes to the kind of accent you speak with. It may influence you on election day, or when you switch on the television to watch the news.

The Australian politician Jocelyn Newman, a Cancer Sun, is one of the few women in the public forum to take an interest in national defence. The singer Kate Bush, with a Cancer Venus, wrote the song 'England My Lionheart'. If you have a Cancer planet, your origins or roots seem to follow you around.

I have noticed that there are a few women with Cancer planets who cannot bear the idea of living in their own country (sometimes for painful reasons) yet create a sense of belonging elsewhere. They become flag-wavers or enthusiasts for other people's homelands, cultures and beliefs. Strange but true — but then your Cancerian side will always need roots, even if they are borrowed from elsewhere.

The black American entertainer Josephine Baker, a Cancer Venus, found her second homeland in France, where she worked for the French Resistance in World War Two; Sheena Easton (Mars in Cancer) is perennially Scottish; Aretha Franklin, a Cancer Moon is well known for her own version of 'The Star Spangled Banner'. No matter where Cancer Mars Dolly Parton tours, Nashville seems to travel with her. And you can take Sandra Bernhard (Mars in Cancer), the comedian, out of New York — but not the other way around.

Some of you with a Cancerian side are so interested in your origins that you turn your attentions to history, or family trees. Some, like Cancer Venus Jacquetta Hawkes, become archaeologists. Alexandra Hasluck, a Cancer Venus, became a historian.

in **cancer**

The best revenge is
A mood swing.
Sporting Cancer
You burn off energy doing housework, gardening or home repairs. You like outdoors pursuits with a bath afterwards!

Your battle tactics

You drag in members of the clan to fight on your side (your own family, or your substitute family of friends). If you're up against a man, you may stress your positive female qualities — when you're in a rage, you can be like a man's worst mother or nanny nightmare!

What kind of opponent are you?

Defensive.

Expressing your Cancerian side

If you have Mars in Cancer then, somewhere inside you, you contain a Cancer. If your Cancerian side is well developed, you will probably also have people with Cancer planets in your life. If this section doesn't accurately reflect what you're all about, you may want to read the chapter headed Walking Your Planets (pages 175–183).

CHILDREN AND TEENAGERS

Those of you who do feel comfortable expressing your family-conscious, child-conscious side often gravitate towards areas where you can do something to reach children and teenagers in a practical way. The author of the Famous Five and Secret Seven series (and the infamous Noddy books), Enid Blyton, was a Cancer Venus, and so is the children's writer Joan Aiken.

Hazel Hawke, a Cancer Sun, has been involved in many professional caring roles, and the Children's Television Foundation is on the list. Margaret Reynolds, a Cancer Sun, established Kindergarten Headstart. Kaye Webb, a Cancer Mars, founded a publishing empire just for children — Puffin Books. Audrey Hepburn, a Cancer Mars, was a roving ambassador for UNICEF and worked for children all over the world. Princess Anne, a Cancer Venus, is a long-time supporter of children's charities.

The Australian writer Christina Stead, A Cancer Sun–Mercury, produced a first novel titled *The Man Who Loved Children* — a book about a father who creates a special language so that he can communicate with his children. The founder of hospitals and orphanages, St Francesca Cabrini, was a Cancer Sun.

Frida Kahlo, the Mexican painter who was unable to bear children, made them a central focus of many of her paintings. The last word should probably go to Meryl Streep, a Cancer Sun, who told *Vanity Fair* magazine: 'I had three children and that's a lot like making a movie. There's a lot of the same worries. Will it have legs? Will it go wide? How will it do domestically and what if it goes foreign?'

CANCERIAN MYTHS

Mary Poppins

Mary Poppins adopted a clan — or perhaps they adopted her — when she landed, via umbrella, in the home of a London family. Her 'spoonful of sugar helps the medicine go down' technique is typically Cancerian, and so is her insistence on early bedtime. Her Moon Mother side is obvious, but her wilder Huntress side comes out when the umbrella is lifted by wind (and when she tangles with a chimney sweep). Not only does she take care of children, she also helps the family father get in touch with his inner child — truly an accomplished Cancerian feat!

KNOW YOUR NYMPHS

Diana the Huntress, one of your goddesses, was famous for her company of nymphs. If you have the Sun, Moon, Mercury, Venus or Mars in Cancer you may also have a few nymphs (or nymphettes) in your pack. The Cancer Mercury–Venus Robyn Archer is well known for her production *The Pack of Women*.

The ancient myth reveals that Diana's nymphs were responsible for her javelin, quiver, bow, robe and sandals. Crocale, the most skilful of all the nymphs was also Diana's hairdresser. Nephele and Hyale had the enjoyable task of looking after Diana's bathroom. Cancerian types have sporty nymph friends, and more classically feminine nymph friends. Some of them are hairdresser and shoe shop aficionados, others may be into the gym or the great outdoors, even if they're not actually handing you a javelin!

Cancerian types tend to have one, sometimes more, all-female packs around them. Jennifer Saunders, a Cancer Sun, even created an entire TV show — *Absolutely Fabulous* — around an all-female star cast. Your Cancer planets like a clan feeling, and many of you seem to seek it through the company of nymphs!

THE CLASSIC CANCER

Princess Diana

Born on 1st July 1961, Princess Diana had the Sun and Mercury in Cancer.

The Mother role Mother–child relationships were particularly important in Diana's life. Her second name, Frances, was her mother's. After her parents divorced, she also lost her real mother and gained a stepmother. She was, of course, the mother of the 'heir and the spare' to the English throne.

The Huntress role Diana not only had the name of Diana the Huntress, she also showed an aggressive and defensive side to male photographers who attempted to intrude on her personal space. Her wilder side — the part of her that ran solo, or with her 'pack of nymphs' girlfriends — was also important. In a strange piece of synchronicity, the Goddess Diana was also the patron of none other than a warrior named Camilla!

Food and diet Food and eating issues for Diana were difficult but, bulimia aside, she also found help from Susie Orbach, author of *Fat is a Feminist Issue*.

The home environment Diana was well-known for her concern with the homeless, and her defence of women affected by domestic violence. She once worked as a house cleaner for her sister and, when young, signed up as a charlady with an agency called Solve Your Problems.

Children and teenagers Diana began her working life enrolled with Knightsbridge Nannies, taught ballet to children, and worked at the Young England kindergarten. She was a favourite of children around the world.

Know your nymphs Diana usually had a circle of female friends around her. In her early, apartment-sharing days, her fellow nymphs were Carolyn Bartholomew, Anne Bolton and Virginia Pitman.

CANCERIAN SYMBOLS

With a Cancer planet in your life, some of the following themes, ideas and words may have a special part to play. They may turn up in any context, too.

The Moon ★ Crabs ★ Four ★ Houses ★ Flats ★ Homes ★ Property ★ Cooks ★ Chefs ★ Mothers ★ Doctors ★ Nurses ★ Children ★ Babies ★ Teenagers ★ Families ★ Patriotism ★ Family ★ Trees ★ Shelters ★ Caves ★ Diana ★ Hunters ★ Cribs ★ Prams ★ Domesticity ★ Food ★ Health ★ Diet ★ Nutrition ★ Milk ★ Breasts ★ Pregnancy ★ Matriarchs ★ History ★ Roots ★ Family planning ★ Fertility ★ Birth ★ Midwives ★ The Red Cross ★ Dogs ★ Bows and arrows ★ Archery ★ Baths ★ Nymphs ★ Blushing ★ Female friends ★ Cleaners ★ Nannies ★ Babysitters ★ Care ★ Adoption ★ Healing ★ Feeding ★ Nurturing ★ Architecture ★ Building ★ Cypress ★ Pine.

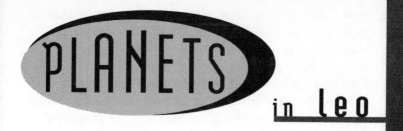

PLANETS in Leo

Read this section if you have your Sun, Moon, Mercury, Venus or Mars in Leo.

ARE YOU DOING YOUR LEO?

You're proud of who you are, and what you're doing with your life

You have an outlet for expressing yourself (some may call it showing off!)

You have a position of leadership somewhere

You walk tall

YOUR LEONINE SIDE

Confident ★ Creative ★ Dignified.

USING LEO

Your Sun, Moon, Mercury, Venus or Mars in Leo are very useful when life calls for something impressive. Your Leonine side makes it easier for you to approach life in a confident way, and it helps your self-esteem. Leo planets are also invaluable when you need to out-class the opposition. Something about your Leonine side intimidates others very easily and in the right time and place this 'class act' can be helpful. Leo's other bonuses? Brainwaves and ideas. This is the sign which gives birth to schemes, dreams and projects.

RANK AND PRIVILEGE

Since the time of Richard I, Coeur de Lion, in 1189 AD Leo has become a popular symbol of monarchy, and Leo's connection with royal rank and privilege survives through republicanism, communism and anarchy. Courtney Love, widow of Kurt Cobain, lead singer of Hole, Queen of American Punk and much given to wearing a tiara, has Mercury in Leo.

If you have planets in this sign, there may literally be some royal or aristocratic link in your life. Evonne Cawley has Leo planets and was made a Member of the British Empire by the Queen. Barbra Streisand has Leo planets and is a Royal Command performer. I have clients with Leo Moon planets who can trace OBEs, royal chefs, Scots aristocrats and mediaeval courtiers in their family trees. In the United States and in Argentina, the Leonine connection also works towards the president. Bill Clinton has the Sun in Leo. Monica Lewinsky, believe it or not, has both the Sun and Venus in Leo. Nancy Reagan has the Moon there. Dawn Steel, the former President of Columbia Pictures — who has since sadly passed on — was born on US President Bill Clinton's birthday, and was part of a two-way Leo mutual admiration society with him. Then there's Geraldine Ferraro, who has the Moon in Leo. Evita Peron had the Moon in Leo and to finish the sequence, Madonna, who has Evita's film role, has the Sun in Leo. The Lion can also point towards the prime minister in any nation — both John Howard and Janette Howard have the Sun in Leo in Australia. Annita Keating — another First Lady — has Venus in this sign.

The symbolism is the same — it stands for rank and privilege, divine leadership and all that those things entail. Your planets in Leo incline you towards the world of the special, the exclusive and the elite. In Hollywood, this means superstars. In London, this means Buckingham Palace. In swimming pools and stadiums across the land, Leo leads to gold medals and the company of winners. Very commonly, women with Leo planets have a connection to people in the world of film, television, music, sporting success, politics, radio or media — which is where the new Kings and Queens come from. They shift you towards the Gods, in theatrical terms. The upper echelons of the establishment, and the top ranks of corporate life, are also Leo's domain.

Leo points towards the special, the starry, the important, and the well-known. I knew a Moon–Venus–Mars Leo client who lived in a retirement village and she proved the adage that wherever Leo is found, she moves towards the centre. My client was dating the star of all their local amateur dramatic productions and was on the steering committee of their catering association!

You may win your Leonine rank and privilege by your own ambition, leadership abilities or earning power. You may be voted, approved or elected to a certain position, or may purchase your castle, crown and throne by using your creative abilities or leadership skills. Leo shines. That is its ultimate function.

You identify with
Leaders ★ Performers ★ VIPs ★ Stars ★ Social lionesses ★ Queen bees.

You're an authority on
Leadership ★ Children ★ Babies ★ Youth ★ The creative process ★ The entertainment world ★ Above all else, *yourself*!

Your career Top Ten
You need: 1) Space for your soaring ambition; 2) A leading role; 3) Special privileges and perks; 4) An important title; 5) Centre stage; 6) Recognition for your achievements; 7) Your own office; 8) An impressive business card; 9) Someone else to do the menial tasks; 10) Glory — reflected or personal.

Expressing your Leonine side
If you have the Sun in Leo then, somewhere inside you, you contain a Leo. If your Leonine side is well developed, you will probably also have people with Leo planets in your life. If this section doesn't accurately reflect what you're all about, you may want to read the chapter headed Walking Your Planets (pages 175–183).

PRIDE AND DIGNITY
The Sun rules Leo in astrology, and it is associated with the Ego. If you have planets in this sign, then you will express yourself with

considerable pride in at least one department of your life, and probably more. The Sun in Leo encourages you to be proud of yourself. The Moon in Leo urges you to take pride in your home. Mercury in Leo puts you on your dignity when you write, sing or speak. Venus in Leo makes you proud of your appearance. Mars in Leo produces a haughty, dignified strategy when life challenges you.

This really is the sign of invisible height, and wherever Leo planets fall in your chart, you are likely to live your life from a slightly elevated perspective. Your Leonine side expresses itself proudly and with dignity because of the link with female royalty. It has always been necessary for Queens to appear proud and dignified to inspire the confidence of the people — and to intimidate pretenders to the throne, and rival powers. This is the origin of Leo's pride, and it actually derives from a very real feeling of insecurity and fear, although you will seldom be conscious of it.

Your Leo planets will express themselves with dignity very convincingly, but there is usually some perspiration under the crown. Many women with Leo planets have told me that it feels automatic and natural to approach life in a dignified way — but they are also aware of the performance that goes with the territory. This may be another reason why Leo is associated with creativity and entertainment. Every modern queen is an actress at heart (otherwise, how does one face the TV cameras on Christmas Day, my dear?) and if you have planets in this sign, you will come to know this 'stagey' feeling in your working life, and perhaps in your private life as well.

The writer Nancy Mitford, who had the Moon in Leo, wrote *The Sun King* and *Noblesse Oblige*. More tellingly, she always preserved what other people saw as a 'perfect shopfront', even when facing marital breakdown and illness. During the Second World War, the Queen Mother (Sun in Leo) put on a brave face by remaining at Buckingham Palace for the duration of the Blitz. Wherever you find Leo planets in your own life, you will also find that perfect shopfront or brave face. Leo Queens are the kind of monarchs who face the guillotine with their heads held high. Elevated posture, elevated views, elevated speech and an elevated nose (!) are all deeply Leonine.

LEO'S ROYAL BLOODLINE

Princess Margaret — Sun in Leo
Princess Anne — Sun in Leo
The Queen Mother — Sun in Leo
Queen Elizabeth II — Moon in Leo
Princess Beatrice — Sun in Leo
Prince Phillip — Moon in Leo

 in **Leo**

What you need

The spotlight ★ A child — or a brainchild ★ Special treatment ★ Luxury ★ Authority ★ Loyalty ★ A leading role ★ Five-star accommodation ★ First-class tickets.

The Moon in Leo home

Your house or flat is designed for parties, children or creativity (or perhaps all three). There is usually a playroom in a Moon in Leo home, and it may be a 'nursery' for various hobbies, interests and talents, or — if you have children — the real thing. Leo Moon homes always contain something grand, impressive, rare or expensive. You are house-proud and really need a palace or a castle. Chairs matter, too — the throne symbol!

The Moon in Leo cook

You are a creative cook and really come into your own when you are trying to impress people. In a perfect world, cooks and maids would do it all for you, but Moon in Leo women don't mind washing up afterwards if they receive well-chosen compliments when it's all over. You prefer impressive menus and are quite a confident cook. You'll end up with Alessi or Wedgwood eventually!

Expressing your Leonine side

If you have the Moon in Leo then, somewhere inside you, you contain a Leo. If your Leonine side is well developed, you will probably also have people with Leo planets in your life. If this section doesn't accurately reflect what you're all about, you may want to turn to the chapter headed Walking Your Planets (pages 175–183).

THE CHANEL CONNECTION

The Leonine links in the life of Coco Chanel are full of mysterious synchronicities. And it's fitting that the Chanel label still symbolises VIP status today — very Leo! To begin at the beginning, Mademoiselle Gabrielle 'Coco' Chanel (Leo Sun) designed the pink suit Jackie Kennedy (Leo Sun) was wearing on the day the President was assassinated. Two decades later, Madonna (Leo Sun) was also wearing Chanel designed by Karl Lagerfeld (Leo Mercury). Claudia Schiffer (Leo Mars) is a favourite Chanel model, too. Marilyn Monroe (Leo Rising) recently became the face of Chanel No. 5 (the Leo number) in perfume advertisements. Coco is buried in Lausanne, beneath a tomb carved with *lions*.

There are many other Leonine words and images in her life: the Chanel men's fragrance L'Egoiste (Ego is certainly Leo's domain), the name of Coco's orphanage — Sacred Heart of Mary (Leo rules the heart, Mary is a royal name), one of her first clients, Elizabeth, the Queen Mother, and a later one — Metro Goldwyn Mayer — whose logo — of course — is the lion. Many of her clothes are held (where else?) at the Victoria and Albert Museum in London — including a very famous evening dress and cape worn by Mrs *Leo* D'Arlanger. If you have Leo planets, your life and times may not be quite as laden with symbols as Chanel's, but you may appreciate her perfume, or her little black dress nevertheless.

 in **leo**

The Mercury in Leo student

Too proud to admit she is wrong ★ A creative thinker ★ Prefers to lead class debate ★ Holds confident opinions ★ Dislikes teachers who practise humiliation tactics — or ignore her.

Your communication style
Confident.

Your letters
Stylish.

You think like
A queen.

You talk like
You mean it.

The Mercury in Leo voice
Luxurious.

Your tactics
Regal.

Expressing your Leonine side
If you have Mercury in Leo then, somewhere inside you, you contain a Leo. If your Leonine side is well developed, you will probably also have people with Leo planets in your life. If you don't identify with this section, you may want to read the chapter headed Walking Your Planets (pages 175–183).

LEONINE LUXURY
Embellishment, decoration and self-expression accompany your Leonine side. This is partly because ancient monarchs really had to be myth-builders. To build an aura around a monarch, symbols, images and designs must be constructed — rather like those surrounding religious icons. To protect the sacredness and power of the monarch's position; personal seals, stamps and coats of arms must be made. Precious jewels must be worn, robes must be sewn and gold must be hammered. Your Leo planets incline you towards the luxurious. In physics, a lux is a unit of illumination, which is pretty much the effect your Leonine side is looking for. Like gold, luxury shines and glows.

The act of personalising something to suit oneself — or of choosing the rare and exclusive — is inherently Leonine. The art of being widely imitated is also woven into the sign. All of this influences your Leonine side to pursue style — which is really just another word for distinction. Invariably, clients I have seen who are strongly expressing their Leo planets seem to have tremendous flair. There is a preference for putting a stamp or a seal on things — and this may be done by adopting a memorable trademark style, or by doing things more dramatically, creatively or distinctively than usual. It was pilot Amelia Earhart's Leo Sun which made her wear luxurious silk scarves in the cockpit.

As the ruler of Leo, the Sun illuminates whatever it touches, and it becomes important to have something to show, display or express. If you have planets in Leo, it is never enough to wear the ordinary, display the everyday, own the commonplace, say the mundane or achieve the indifferent. To express yourself in a way which sets you apart, but also inspires imitation or admiration, is the essence of Leo.

 in Leo

You love
The rare, the special and the luxurious ★ Being famous for fifteen minutes ★ Knowing people who are famous for fifteen minutes ★ Privileged treatment ★ Attention ★ Compliments ★ Praise for your talents ★ A leading or organising role ★ Space to display, perform or hold court.

You loathe
Being ignored ★ Feeling invisible ★ Feeling poor ★ Drab clothes ★ Dull art ★ Second best.

Expressing your Leonine side
If you have Venus in Leo then, somewhere inside you, you contain a Leo. If your Leonine side is well developed, you will probably also have people with Leo planets in your life. If this section doesn't accurately reflect what you're all about, you may want to read the chapter headed Walking Your Planets (pages 175–183).

THE CREATIVE IMPULSE

Leo rules the Fifth House in astrology, which is where babies are conceived and born, children are raised and great ideas are also delivered and nurtured. If you have planets in Leo, then you need to grow some kind of seed, and what that seed becomes will be entirely reflective of your genetic make-up, your bloodline and the environment you inherit.

On the most obvious level, this seed will be a child — or you may adopt a child. But the creative impulse is so strong with Leo planets that it is never enough for a Leo-influenced mother merely to conceive and give birth to a baby: the creative process may still be going on during the child's adolescence. Leo mothers enjoy the bending, shaping and guiding process that parenting involves. They also take particular enjoyment in the drawings, stories and scribbles of their offspring.

There are many women with Leo planets who are childless by choice or circumstance, and their creative impulse goes into a very different kind of conception, birth and nurturing. These are the women who begin with a blank sheet of paper, an empty desk, a bare garden or house, a vacant stage, a bare table or a blank canvas.

Productivity, ideas and performance tend to be cyclical. Your Leo planets will make you profoundly aware of ideas being 'born' or 'delivered'. If you choose to be a parent, you will also have the heightened awareness of conception, gestation, incubation, birth and nurturing that comes with the territory.

I have seen many non-Leonine clients over the years who experience five years of Leonine existence when a planet crosses through their Fifth House — ruled by Leo. At this time they become pregnant, or find a brainchild. They create from their bodies, their brains or their hands, and experience everything from morning sickness to post-natal depression, from maternal attachment to birth announcements. This has applied to clients who are creating small businesses, patchwork quilts, paintings — and women who are becoming mothers for the first time.

Essentially, your Leo planets represent that side of you which has the urge to enjoy yourself and reproduce. That may be why women with a strongly developed Leonine side either make a vocation out of love and motherhood or, alternatively, out of all that their brains or bodies can express. Your Leonine side is about the child or the *brainchild*, and your Leo planets will never let you forget it.

 in Leo

The best revenge is
Feeling superior.

Sporting Leo
Gold medal sports like running or swimming.

Your battle tactics
Royal sulks ★ The Miss Piggy head-fling ★ Theatrical and dramatic fury ★ Staging is everything to a Mars in Leo woman. You may also get other people — friends, minions, outsiders — to wage the war — rather like the Queen ordering in her troops.

What kind of opponent are you?
Proud ★ Confident.

Expressing your Leonine side
If you have Mars in Leo then, somewhere inside you, you contain a Leo. If your Leonine side is well developed, you will probably also have people with Leo planets in your life. If this section doesn't accurately reflect what you're all about, you may want to read the chapter headed Walking Your Planets (pages 175–183).

LEONINE AUTHORITY

The Sun, Leo's ruler, is associated with authority and leadership qualities in astrology. Wherever you have a planet in this sign, you will find a side of you that is convinced it can captain the team, steer the meeting or head up the business.

If you are strongly Leo-influenced you may become head of your own company, or take a position of influence and importance in someone else's. I was a waitress years ago, and worked alongside a Leo Sun. She was seventeen, had a very professional-looking ponytail, and — most importantly — *looked like she knew what she was doing*. They didn't have a position called Weekend Staff Manager before she arrived, but the café owner quickly created one. I expect she's running her own restaurant today somewhere.

Is the well-documented authority of a Leo planet born or made? Probably both. Little girls with a Leo planet seem to remember the times they do well and are praised, and ignore the occasions where they fall down. Your planets in Leo will move you swiftly away from failure or disappointment. This quote, from a Moon Leo woman, is typical: 'If I can't do it brilliantly then I'm not going to do it at all.' Your Leonine side is interested in being complimented, shining and being acknowledged by other people. It takes confidence to believe that you are capable of taking over or taking the lead, and I think that Leo-influenced women develop this confidence by a very natural kind of positive thinking.

At some stages of your life, this may manifest as vanity. Be careful — Leo planets have a way of blotting out so much of the reality when it's distasteful that you could develop an unrealistic view of yourself. Queens lose their heads (or their tax havens) when they lose touch with real people, real issues — and above all — their own failings and faults.

I've heard this story many times from women with Leo planets: 'One day I thought I had it all, and the next day I didn't.' If Leo is very strong in your life, you may experience the classic fall from grace that accompanies this sign. In America they call it a come-down and in England they call it a come-uppance. It sometimes seems cruel and unfair — just bad luck. But Leo planets can also invite a fall from grace by promoting confidence in you, at the expense of a reality function. Remember — Marie Antoinette was executed, Queen Elizabeth was forced to pay tax!

LEONINE MYTHS

Lady Penelope

The puppet heroine of *Thunderbirds*, Lady Penelope Creighton-Ward, has a family crest, aristocratic heritage, a family mansion, a chauffeur and a pink Rolls Royce. She is also a British secret agent, working for Queen and country. Sylvia Anderson, who created Lady Penelope and her costumes (and provided the character's voice in the original series) was kind enough to confirm to me that Penelope was indeed 'born' between July and August, making the character a Leo Sun. We met at a book launch, and I think Sylvia was genuinely concerned for my mental health when I breathlessly rushed up to ask, 'When is Lady Penelope's birthday?' As I expected, the glamorous puppet is most definitely a Leo, and as Sylvia is an Aries Sun, even their Sun signs are compatible! Penelope's wardrobe is full of French couture (luxury), she was Head Girl at her school (authority) and she's a part-time fashion journalist (creativity). Very Leo, very Lady Penelope!

MYTH BUILDING

Do myths occur naturally around Leo planet women, or do they create the myths deliberately? Your Leonine side attracts stories, gossip and 'legendary' anecdotes about you, but only you can say if you consciously encouraged the story, or found it had just woven itself around you. Your Leonine side is a brilliant editor. It cuts out the drab bits, censors the clumsy scenes and omits the ordinary, the awful or the less-than-glorious.

A toothpaste advertisement shown on Australian television in the seventies reminds me of this trait in Leo types. An air hostess was being interviewed: 'How's your love life?' the voice asked. 'Wonderful,' the air hostess enthused, 'London, Paris, New York ...' The voice persisted. Finally, the air hostess admitted her love life was terrible (no doubt because of her appalling halitosis).

The Sun, Moon, Mercury, Venus or Mars in Leo *likes* myths. Something mysterious, something a little special, something that seems like a smug secret or a reason to shine. Misery, failures, embarrassments, humiliations, poverty and disappointments do not go on display because they spoil the act. Perhaps the myths around you come from this. It certainly creates mystery and curiosity, and when this happens, myths follow.

With planets in this sign, you can literally make yourself up. (You don't believe this? Find your resumé or CV. Your Leo planet will have left its signature somewhere on page three ...) You may not even realise you are doing it. Either way, when you exit the room, people will say, 'Did you know that she ...?'

THE CLASSIC LEO

Jacqueline Kennedy Onassis

Born on 28th July 1929, Jackie had the Sun and Mercury in Leo. Known popularly as Queen of Camelot, her life reflects these Leonine themes:

Rank and privilege In India they dubbed her Durga, Goddess of Power. When she went to Paris, half a million people chanted, 'Vive Jacqui! Vive Jacqui!' Her official title was First Lady. Her sister-in-law Eunice Kennedy observed that 'Jaclean rhymes with queen'. Her own husband believed she had 'too much status and not enough quo'.

Pride and dignity 'It was dignity, not novelty, that Mrs Kennedy wanted,' said fashion designer Oleg Cassini. At JFK's funeral, French President Charles de Gaulle was moved to say this of her: 'She gave an example to the whole world of how to behave.'

Leonine luxury *Women's Wear Daily* dubbed Jackie 'Her Elegance' and she favoured Chanel, Balenciaga and Givenchy and redecorated the White House.

The creative impulse Leo planets give you 'brainchildren' or children — Jackie had both. She worked as a photojournalist for the *Washington-Times Herald*, and later at the Viking and Doubleday publishing houses.

Leonine authority Whether working as a Doubleday editor or First Lady, Jackie led all the way.

Myth building Dark sunglasses were her choice, and Camelot may have been good PR from the White House. But Jackie's myth occurred *naturally*.

LEONINE SYMBOLS

If you have planets in Leo, the ideas, symbols and icons in this list may be woven into your life story. This is the poetic part of astrology at work, or the more mysterious side of the art.

The Sun ★ The Lion ★ Gold ★ Fire ★ Orange ★ Queens ★ Kings ★ Cats ★ Sunflowers ★ Crowns ★ Orbs ★ Sceptres ★ Thrones ★

Ermine ★ Leopardskin ★ Tigers ★ Fleur de lys ★ Babies ★ Children ★ Teenagers ★ The heart ★ Apollo ★ Ego ★ Creativity ★ The Fisher King ★ Sovereigns ★ Chiefs ★ Presidents ★ Prime ministers ★ Politicians ★ St Mark ★ Traditional royal names: Anne, Elizabeth, Victoria, Catherine, Mary, Jane, Alexandra, Margaret ★ The Father ★ Tiaras ★ The spine ★ Coats of arms ★ Crests ★ Fur ★ Manes ★ Marigolds ★ Five ★ Stars ★ Polo ★ Gilt ★ Authorities ★ VIPs ★ Five stars ★ First class ★ Courts ★ Rings ★ Jewels ★ Spotlights ★ Mirrors ★ Metro Goldwyn Mayer ★ Mythology ★ Winston Churchill ★ Hollywood ★ The Stage ★ Ceremony ★ Limelight ★ Velvet ★ Costume jewellery ★ Soundtracks ★ Drama ★ Queen Nefertiti ★ Queen Cleopatra ★ Empires ★ Pomp ★ Ceremony ★ Princes ★ Princesses ★ Glory ★ Suntans ★ Red carpets ★ Nobles ★ Aristocrats ★ Cinemas ★ Theatres ★ Music venues ★ Palaces.

PLANETS in virgo

Read this section if you have your Sun, Moon, Mercury, Venus or Mars in Virgo.

ARE YOU DOING YOUR VIRGO?

You're in touch with health, fitness and body issues

You enjoy detailed work or interests that challenge your brain

You're a reader, or a writer

You can't leave any project unfinished or less than perfect

YOUR VIRGOAN SIDE

Body-conscious ★ Hard-working ★ Well-informed.

USING VIRGO

This is an interesting sign to find your Sun, Moon, Mercury, Venus or Mars in. Virgo is connected with both the body and the mind, and it gives you the potential to perfect either of them. Mercury, the planet associated with Virgo, lends you a gift for communication, analysis and understanding that only Gemini can equal. Ceres, the 'virgin' symbol associated with Virgo, is the goddess of the body and all natural things. She will ground you firmly in the body when it looks as if your mind is taking over, and having this sign in your astro-package gives you a feel for the practical issues of life as well as all the head exercises.

VIRGOAN WORDPLAY

Your ruler, Mercury, spent most of his time as a translator, interpreter, researcher, scriptwriter and speechmaker. Your Virgoan side has passed on this talent for word-play, and many Virgo-influenced women enjoy stretching the English language like a piece of elastic. My friend Barbara is a Sun Virgo. She actually invents new words which her husband refers to as 'Barbara-isms'.

Your Virgoan side enjoys naming things, and although you generally practise on people you know (like Gemini types, you are good at inventing nicknames) you will find your own name for anything else within a 100-kilometre radius. Everybody and everything has to be called *something* in the Virgoan world — houses, the cat with the strange ears who lives in the next street, plants ... Something about Mercury also means that others end up naming you, too — Virgoan types are often called different things by different people. I know two journalists who have planets in Virgo and Gemini and their whole *life* is nicknames.

in virgo

You identify with
Writers ★ Teachers ★ Students ★ Dietitians ★ Aerobics instructors ★ Yoga gurus ★ The head of Mensa ★ Workaholics ★ Media people.

You´re an authority on
Words ★ Vitamins ★ Illness ★ Muscles ★ Communication ★ The education system.

Your career Top Ten
You need: 1) Routine, routine, routine; 2) Productivity bonuses; 3) A water cooler; 4) Your own space in the fridge; 5) Ergonomic chairs; 6) A designer filing cabinet; 7) Colleagues with high standards; 8) Space for your writing skills; 9) An organised workspace; 10) The best cleaner in town.

Expressing your Virgoan side
If you have the Sun in Virgo then, somewhere inside you, you contain a Virgo. If your Virgoan side is well developed, you will probably also have people with Virgo planets in your life. If this section doesn't accurately reflect what you're all about, you

may want to read the chapter headed Walking Your Planets (pages 175–183).

DELIVERING THE MESSAGE

Virgo thrives on information, communication and the world of words. Only planets in Gemini and Sagittarius are as deeply concerned with knowledge (if you have these in your astro-package, too, you may as well decamp to a library or radio station and live there).

Getting the message across correctly is a chief concern of Virgo. Your Virgoan side is there to question, record, nod, contradict, agree, check — and then transmit. There is a strong sense of dedication and responsibility surrounding your messenger role. It's not enough to write it, or say it, casually. Information is never just flicked with a towel when Virgo is behind it — you assess information critically. Whatever is passed on by your Virgoan side to others has to be researched, checked, double-checked and *word perfect*. (An amazing number of Virgo-influenced women surround themselves with computers, by the way — all, no doubt, using WordPerfect software.)

Many of the world's greatest writers, educators and media figures have Virgo planets for this reason. So do many women who act as messengers and information agents for those in the communication, education and information industries — and women who are the informal news services for their families and friends. Some of your interests and abilities will be defined by the other signs that are in your birth package. The talent for getting it all across, though, is definitely Virgo's domain. Whatever field you find yourself in, you will often find fate asks you to be the courier or reporter who kicks the information across.

Virgoan bestsellers

Shirley Conran — Sun in Virgo
Fay Weldon — Sun in Virgo
Antonia Fraser — Sun in Virgo
Janet Frame — Sun in Virgo
Mary Stewart — Sun in Virgo

Jackie Collins — Mercury and Venus in Virgo
Dorothy Parker — Sun in Virgo
Shirley MacLaine — Moon in Virgo
Agatha Christie — Moon in Virgo

MOON in Virgo

What you need

Pure food, without additives or toxins ★ White sheets ★ Lead-free petrol ★ A job you worship ★ Order and organisation ★ Books ★ Pens and paper ★ A doctor or health adviser.

The Moon in Virgo home

You create order out of clutter. You know exactly where everything goes, and enjoy sorting it all out. People move your bathroom things into new places, and you just move it all back again. I'm afraid Madonna (a Moon Virgo) files her shoes on specially made shelves. Will you go that far? Maybe. You like having bits of nature around you, even if you live in an urban setting. The Virgoan essentials? Vitamins, white things, herbs.

The Moon in Virgo cook

You like piling everything up on the chopping board, like an illustration from a Five Food Groups chart. Here are the onions, here are the mushrooms, here are the organic lettuces ... Your kitchen is a shrine to neatness and order and you feel physically ill when the rubbish collectors go on strike. You're a good breadmaker, even if you don't know it. Your herbs are *fresh*.

Expressing your Virgoan side

If you have the Moon in Virgo then, somewhere inside you, you contain a Virgo. If your Virgoan side is well developed, you will probably also have people with Virgo planets in your life. If this section doesn't accurately reflect what you're all about, you may want to read the chapter headed Walking Your Planets (pages 175–183).

BODY MAINTENANCE

To understand your Virgoan connection with the body, consider the story of Ceres, who is your ruling goddess. After Ceres' daughter, Proserpine, was kidnapped by Pluto, she went on a heroic quest to find her again. Part of the quest involved healing a little boy with a fever. After giving him the kiss of life, she mixed poppy juice in his milk to cure him, and massaged his arms and legs until he recovered. This provides the modern links with diet, health and massage that Virgo has today. Ceres also held responsibility for herbs and grains in the ancient world: when women with Virgo planets today toast wholemeal bread or throw herbal teabags into the pot, they are issuing homage to Ceres.

Virgo planets do often conspire to create the classically health-conscious or body-conscious woman. You may develop an interest in health and healing, or a strong connection to your own body. Along with the typical Virgo-influenced clients I see (mineral water, yoga and vitamin B girls) I also know a few who are interested in recreational drugs. Body-consciousness with Virgo does not always take the form of a mineral water habit or a penchant for massage. Ceres' use of opium — the source of illegal, as well as legal, drugs — has something to say about this.

Virgo planets know about poisons and toxins, botany and biology, the sea and the air, the soil and the plants, the blood and the bones. Your experiences with illness, or more serious crises within your body, will be turning points in your life, because they bring your Virgoan side into sharp focus. Often, the woman with a Virgo Sun, Moon, Mercury, Venus or Mars is superbly body-conscious because illness has made her that way. Similarly, if you are intimately involved with the body issues of other people then life will never really be the same again. New rituals, discoveries and routines will be born. Inevitably, your Virgoan side will lead you back to the body every time.

If you have Virgo planets, you will eventually develop the ability to 'read' your body and understand the equation that leads you to peace of mind and mental equilibrium — or to low energy and personal downtime. You may also be able to do this, quite shrewdly, with those around you — even animals — especially when they are suffering.

It is the *intelligent handling of the physical* that defines Virgo. Your own body is the initial practise ground for this, but eventually it may extend to others as well. Even a Virgo with a junk food habit will be able to tell you the fat content of the junk, the effect she expects it to have, and the kilojoule conversion rate!

The Mercury in Virgo student

Literate ★ Good with details ★ You hand in impossibly neat projects — leave it to the other signs to put coffee rings on the back of their essays ★ You are modest, but worryingly intelligent ★ You pick up on your teachers' mistakes.

Your communication style

Informative.

Your letters

Neat.

You think like

A critic.

You talk like

A modest expert.

The Mercury in Virgo voice

Unfussy.

Your tactics

Tricky.

Expressing your Virgoan side

If you have Mercury in Virgo then, somewhere inside you, you contain a Virgo. If your Virgoan side is well developed, you will probably also have people with Virgo planets in your life. If this section doesn't accurately reflect what you're all about, you may want to read the chapter headed Walking Your Planets in this section (pages 175–183).

THE NATURAL WORLD

Increasingly, as the planet is affected by more and more imbalances, your Virgoan side will become affected by what goes on *around* the body, too. This is very much a part of the story of Ceres. In the myth, she is so angry at losing her daughter that she causes cattle to die, breaks the ploughs, pours on too much sun, creates terrible floods of rain and destroys every seed in the ground. Your Virgoan side is intimately connected to the earth, no matter if you live in a high-rise apartment block with only a cactus on the window ledge for company. Part of your Virgoan inheritance is a profound understanding of the natural world. If a Jacques Chirac comes along to pollute that natural world, your Virgoan side — through Ceres — is the part of you that will be most affected.

Many women who have Virgo planets are concerned with environmental and ecological issues as they specifically affect the atmosphere, the sea, the food chain or the ozone layer. Lynette Thorstensen from Greenpeace is a Virgo Venus, and the amazing Dr Helen Caldicott is a Virgo Mercury and Venus. Your garden is important to you if you have planets in Virgo, but the world is the biggest garden of all.

VENUS in virgo

You love
Reading ★ Writing lists ★ Passing on what you know ★ Showing off your IQ — modestly ★ Massages ★ The telephone ★ Handsome health or fitness professionals ★ White shirts ★ Organised wardrobes ★ Smart female friends ★ You also enjoy short-haul flights and zipping around town ★ Mercury, your ruler, was always on the move ★ The biggest Venus in Virgo passion? A lover who drops vitamins in your mouth with a teaspoon.

You loathe
Dirty fingernails ★ Chaos ★ People less bright than you ★ No-option menus ★ Filthy flatmates.

Expressing your Virgoan side
If you have Venus in Virgo then, somewhere inside you, you contain a Virgo. If your Virgoan side is well developed, you will probably

also have people with Virgo planets in your life. If this section doesn't accurately reflect what you're all about, you may want to read the chapter headed Walking Your Planets in this section (pages 175–183).

THE WORK ETHIC

Virgo's dawn-to-dusk reputation comes from the nature of rural life, which Ceres — your goddess — controlled. Women farmers, for example, had to get up with the sun, deal with the family, the crops and the animals, then get up and do it all over again the next day. At the mercy of nature's deadlines, these women practically never had the luxury of a holiday.

If you have a planet in Virgo, you need to monitor this aspect of the sign quite carefully. Ceres has an extremely good understanding of equipment, the work ethic and hard labour. However, she was by nature a workaholic and a calendar-watcher! In the myth, we discover that her kidnapped daughter was only returned to her for six months of each year, so the goddess was always peering in her celestial Filofax.

The other crucial point about Ceres is that she was absolutely tireless. She was looking for her daughter when Aurora brought the sun up, and still looking when Hesperus brought the stars out. When the goddess actually decided to rest, she did not allow herself the luxury of a decent sleep in a good hotel, but sat on a stone in the wind and rain for nine days and nights. Inheriting this sign in your astrological package is something that needs careful consideration. Part of it is certainly about finding value and pleasure in what can be achieved by letting the clock and the calendar dictate your efficiency and productivity. However, there are many women with a strong Virgoan side who find that routine takes them over, or that the work ethic becomes their whole life.

You will see your Virgoan side most strongly when you begin your first full-time job, choose to embark upon motherhood for the first time, or even tackle unemployment for the first time. All these experiences seem to drag Ceres out of hiding, and one of the most important things you will do in your life is establish exactly the kind of work ethic *you* wish to live by.

MOTHERHOOD AND VIRGO

Ancient myths have a strange habit of resonating in the present. If you have Virgo planets, your story may resemble the story of Ceres in any of the following ways.

The uneasy compromises between a mother, daughter and son-in-law

Ceres' daughter, Proserpine, was desired so badly by Pluto that he carried her off, leaving Ceres in absolute misery. When Ceres discovered her daughter had actually *married* Pluto she could stand it no longer, and asked Jupiter to bring Proserpine back. He refused to do this, but agreed to this compromise: Proserpine shall spend half the year under the ground with her husband, and half the year on the Earth with her mother (thus giving us the seasons).

Playing mother-substitute

The little boy Triptolemus finds his second mother in Ceres. He has a real one, of course, but she is powerless to educate him or heal him, and it is Ceres who mixes the milk and opium that cures him, massages his limbs back to life and resuscitates him. Later on, she personally educates and trains him. Along with the story of mothers and daughters that accompanies Virgo, it is also worth noting that Ceres was a substitute mother to *other people's children*.

At the time of her death, Mother Teresa, a Virgo Sun, had quite literally become the 'mother' most recognised in India: in England, this role was taken up by the Virgo Mars Royal, the late Princess Diana. Strongly Virgoan types make extremely good babysitters and childminders, and universal aunts.

MARS in virgo

The best revenge is

Listing someone's faults.

Sporting Virgo

Yes, but how clean are the changerooms?

Your battle tactics

Only a Gemini Mars is as cunning as you. You can be a horribly tricky enemy, and enjoy plotting and scheming. You are brilliant at identifying your opponent's failings and weak spots, and either yelling them out, or silently capitalising on them.

Expressing your Virgoan side

If you have Mars in Virgo then, somewhere inside you, you contain a Virgo. If your Virgoan side is well developed, you will probably also have people with Virgo planets in your life. If this section doesn't accurately reflect what you're all about, you may want to read the chapter headed Walking Your Planets (pages 175–183).

STUDENTS AND TEACHERS

Your Sun, Moon, Mercury, Venus or Mars in Virgo makes the student–teacher relationship in your life particularly important. Not only is your ruling planet associated with listening skills, memory and understanding, your ruling goddess, Ceres, was herself a teacher. After curing the sick boy Triptolemus, she instructed him in agricultural science and horticulture, which he then passed on to other humans. She was one of the *original* teachers, all of which makes your own experiences with learning and education important.

Your Virgoan side is a great advice-giver and source of knowledge, and you may do this formally or informally. You may find you literally have students and protégées at various stages of your life, or you become — apparently by accident — a kind of instructor or guide for the very young — or just the totally ignorant!

Your experiences as a student become particularly important because of this. Your Virgoan side lends itself to an informal self-education process that goes on long after you've officially left the classroom or the lecture hall. Your personal experiences with teachers will describe how much you do, or don't, enjoy it. But the issue of education, learning, knowledge-gathering and information-processing is always huge with Virgo-influenced women.

VIRGOAN MYTHS
Miss Jane Marple

There are actually several mythical Virgos in the books of Agatha Christie (see over) but the fiendishly intelligent and extremely orderly Miss Marple is the most impressive. When she isn't snapping up bargains at the Army & Navy Stores, she is compiling lists (a very Virgoan activity) of murder suspects. She has Virgo's cunning (she pretends to be a fluffy old lady) and also Virgo's sibling issues — Jane Marple is alienated from her brother, but close to her sister. She is also a substitute mother to her nephew, Raymond. She is a tireless letter writer, reliant on gossip and very much part of her village. A mythical Virgo, in fact. Her professional knowledge of pharmaceuticals and the human body would make the goddess Ceres proud.

ORDER AND ORGANISATION

Virgo rewards thoughtful organisation. Ceres, your goddess, places a high value on women who know how to sort and separate: in her temple, the women who win Ceres' approval are those who wander in off the street and clean up the rakes and sickles, and pile up all the corn and barley in a systematic way.

In your own life, it is the filing, sorting, weighing, cleaning, judging, filtering, classifying, marshalling, cataloguing and tidying that counts. I have heard an awful lot of women with a Virgo planet groan when they hear this. It does — on the surface — sound fairly dull. Some spectacular things can occur when Virgoan types create order out of chaos, though.

A WORLD IN MINIATURE

Virgo planets are strongly associated with the village or neighbourhood, and the local community. Mercury, your ruler, ruled roads and crossroads, the local markets and trading centres. Your Virgoan side is very much a part of its *local* community and I have seen this literally be as small as a friendly apartment block, but never bigger than the newsagent, the chemist and the traffic lights on the corner! Because your ruler, Mercury, is also chatty by nature, a lot of Virgo-influenced women seem to build up a natural network among their neighbours or the local community.

SHOPPING AND TRADING

The ruler of Virgo, Mercury, is also strongly associated with shopping, swapping, buying, trading and bartering. Having a planet in this sign is extremely helpful if money talk is part of your personal or professional life. It also leads to the famous 'eye for a bargain' that your zodiac twin, Gemini, shares with you. If you have planets in both signs, then your bargain-hunting abilities are multiplied. Virgo planets also lend a considerable talent for trading and selling. Of all the signs, Virgo and Gemini have the greatest success at the local bazaar.

SIBLING ISSUES

Turning to the Mercury myth, astrologers find a god who stole from his own brother, then was forgiven by him — after that, they became best friends. If you have brothers and/or sisters, then some classical Mercury issues may come up. Whatever is stolen, literally or symbolically, by a sibling, may be a very big deal indeed. Your Virgo planets incline you to repeat the original myth, though, which describes how Mercury amused and entertained his brother so much that the two siblings were reconciled. How has the Virgo–Mercury myth played itself out in your own life?

THE CLASSIC VIRGO
Agatha Christie

Born on 15th September 1890, Agatha Christie had a Virgo Sun that she used at every stage of her life.

Virgoan wordplay Agatha Christie used a pseudonym, Mary Westmacott, when writing romances. She also relished giving the characters in her books appropriate and sometimes ironic names, christening one detective after the classical hero Hercules (a man of immense size) and another Ariadne (after the woman who helped Theseus find his way out of the Minotaur's labyrinth).

Delivering the message Not only did Agatha write 78 crime novels, around 150 short stories, six straight novels, 19 plays and four non-fiction books, she has been translated into 104 languages!

Body maintenance Agatha's first jobs were in hospitals — firstly as a nurse, and then as a dispensing pharmacist. Even after becoming successful, she claimed she would have been happy to remain a nurse. She refused to drink alcohol throughout her life.

The natural world Agatha Christie was a passionate gardener and her gardens at Greenway, where she lived, are now open to the public.

The work ethic Even Christie described her writing career as 'a sausage machine'.

Motherhood and Virgo Agatha's own mother had an adoptive mother, who became an 'Auntie-Grannie' to her. Her mother was against her first marriage.

Students and teachers Agatha Christie's informal education was provided by her second husband, archaeologist Max Mallowan.

Order and organisation Hercule Poirot and his secretary, Miss Lemon, are classic Christie Virgoan characters; her endless lists of suspects are also deeply Virgoan.

A world in miniature Agatha enjoyed the local village as much as her creation, Miss Jane Marple.

Shopping and trading Christie was a natural 'dealer' — both with literary and real estate agents.

Sibling issues Madge Miller Watts, Agatha's sister, was also a writer. It was Madge's challenge to Agatha to write a mystery that began her career. Agatha saw them as friendly rivals.

VIRGOAN SYMBOLS

If Virgo has a place in your life, you may find that these symbols, themes and ideas provide links in your life and times. Many of these are similar to your twin sign, Gemini, as you both share Mercury as a ruler.

Virgins ★ Mothers ★ Daughters ★ Healing ★ Health ★ Seeds ★ Opium ★ Milk ★ Wheat ★ Corn ★ Harvest ★ Ceres (Demeter) ★ Six ★ Mercury (Hermes) ★ Communication ★ Language ★ Writing ★ Speech ★ Commerce ★ Merchants ★ Travellers ★ Libraries ★

Neighbours ★ Illness ★ Poppies ★ In-laws ★ Speeches ★ Computers ★ Letters ★ Postcards ★ Memos ★ Short-hand ★ Pens ★ Tricks ★ Thieves ★ Roads ★ Crossroads ★ Shops ★ Sales ★ Brothers ★ Sisters ★ Nature ★ Agriculture ★ Soil ★ Climate ★ Rainfall ★ Medicine ★ Cures ★ IQ tests ★ Lists ★ Order ★ Cleaners ★ Servants ★ Ritual ★ Routine ★ Sorting ★ Classification ★ Method ★ Publication ★ Teaching ★ Learning ★ The voice.

PLANETS in libra

Read this section if you have your Sun, Moon, Mercury, Venus or Mars in Libra.

ARE YOU DOING YOUR LIBRA?

You make room for romance in your life

You have a strong feeling for colour, texture, design, shape or form

You're happy to play the role of peacemaker

You feel good about your attractiveness and appearance

YOUR LIBRAN SIDE

Diplomatic ★ Attractive ★ Fair.

USING LIBRA

Your Sun, Moon, Mercury, Venus or Mars in Libra can be used at any time you need to charm people into submission! Libra is the public relations sign, and if you have a planet here, you have a natural ability to make the peace or win people over. Libra planets also intensify your enjoyment of music, art, design and beauty. Libra's ruling planet, Venus, is associated with incense, perfume, doves and robes. Having a planet in this sensual sign increases the pleasure frequency!

PARTNERSHIPS

If you have planets in Libra, then the world of partnerships and relationships becomes unusually important to you. Your Libran side is about co-operation, compromise and balance. In France, the sign is actually known as 'Balance' and if you have the Sun, Moon, Mercury, Venus and/or Mars in Libra, then your romantic relationships will be the first big balancing acts of your life.

The ultimate expression of Libra is a successful partnership, and having one or more planets in this sign encourages you to pursue it, either through business ventures or professional double-acts, or through marital or de facto relationships.

On a wider scale, your Libran side may inspire some very personal views on men, women, equality, justice and the whole damn thing. Libra really is the barrister, and the barometer, of human relationships.

SUN in libra

You identify with

Lovers ★ Wives ★ Partners ★ Peacemakers ★ Artists ★ Designers ★ Makers of the Law ★ Defenders of Justice ★ Above all, perhaps, you identify with women!

You're an authority on

Aesthetic concerns — colour, form, shape, texture ★ Social, political or ideological issues — always revolving around justice, fairness and equality ★ Inevitably, Sun in Libra women end up becoming authorities on relationships as well.

Your career Top Ten

You need 1) A pleasant work environment; 2) Fair treatment in the workplace; 3) Equal opportunity policies; 4) A social angle on work relationships; 5) A position that gives you authority without compromising your popularity; 6) A career that is in tune with the times; 7) The freedom to dress according to your taste; 8) A working life that does not contradict your principles; 9) Rewards for your diplomatic skills; 10) Enough time out for your love life.

Naturally, if you work for yourself, you can arrange all of the above. If not, try to find a Libra-friendly career.

Expressing your Libran side

If you have the Sun in Libra then, somewhere inside you, you contain a Libra. If your Libran side is well developed, you will probably also have people with Libra planets in your life. If this section doesn't accurately reflect what you're all about, you may want to read the chapter headed Walking Your Planets (pages 175–183).

CROSSING BOUNDARIES

Libra planets make it difficult to fly solo, because they describe an alliance between two sides. It is common for strongly Libran women to marry across their social class, across their nationality, across their background or across their status. Why? Because Libra wants the perfect formula that will make two radically different species appear to be equal. Also, perhaps, because the Libra inside you needs the challenge of differences in order to understand what equality and balance are really all about.

I have a Libra Sun–Mercury client who has been married for 40 years. He is an introvert, she is an extrovert. He is into cars, she is into art. He likes action films, she prefers comedies. She views the marriage as a work of art in its own right, and believes that 'different but equal' is the story of their married success. To the outside world, they are definitely a unit. 'It consists of me, him and us,' she says, 'but nothing would exist without the us part.'

Using patience, trickery, subtlety and native intelligence, your internal Libra will ultimately balance the scales, and particularly in romantic relationships. The Libra inside you is interested in getting the red needle in the partnership to wobble in the middle — not to swing violently from left to right. The process of partnership is often as meaningful as the end result for Libra. Perhaps for that reason, strongly Libran women seem to gravitate towards relationships or marriages where their partner comes from a different world.

The same principle exists in the professional partnerships formed by women with Libra planets. If you have the Sun, Moon, Mercury, Venus or Mars in this sign, it is easy for you to fall into a double-act. Libra really translates as the ampersand, or the 'and' in your life. It describes two parts of a whole. Commonly, what makes the alliance so interesting in its own right is the fact that it is clearly bridging some kind of gap. This is the source of the 'different but equal' message spelled out by the sign.

LIBRAN BALANCING ACTS

These women — who all have the Sun, Moon, Mercury, Venus or Mars in Libra — have notably formed romantic relationships across all kinds of barriers:

Sarah, Duchess of York — commoner/Royal — Sun in Libra
Dawn French — white/black — Sun in Libra
Whoopi Goldberg — black/white — Mars in Libra
Iman — black/white — Moon in Libra
Linda McCartney — American/English — Sun and Mercury in Libra
Jessica Mitford — English/American — Mercury and Venus in Libra
Lulu — Scottish/Australian — Mercury and Venus in Libra
Nicole Kidman — Australian/American — Mars in Libra
Susan Sarandon — older/younger — Sun in Libra
Olivia Newton-John — older/younger — Sun in Libra
Agatha Christie — older/younger — Moon in Libra

Women with planets in Libra are also responsible for some of the world's most successful professional partnerships:

Siobhan Fahey — Shakespear's Sister — Venus in Libra
Tracey Thorne — Everything But The Girl — Sun in Libra
Nerys Hughes — *The Liver Birds* — Mercury in Libra
Jayne Torvill — Torvill & Dean — Sun in Libra
Dawn French — *French & Saunders* — Sun in Libra
Penny Marshall — *Laverne & Shirley* — Sun, Mercury, Venus and Mars in Libra
Julie Walters — *Wood & Walters* — Moon in Libra
June Whitfield — *Terry & June* — Mars in Libra

What you need

Peace, harmony and co-operation ★ A place for everything that is aesthetic or easy on the eye ★ Above all else? Loving relationships.

The Moon in Libra home

Your house or flat tends to be a setting for your social life above all other factors. Appearances will be unusually important and you may spend a long time selecting the colours, shapes and textures you prefer. Typically, you are less interested in the structure or foundations than the colours or design of the guest towels. A mansion designed for good manners is really your dream home.

The Moon in Libra cook

Beautifully presented food, gracefully handed over, is your style. You prefer restaurants where chefs are artists, and find it hard to resist the romanticism of low lighting and foreign menus. You're a tactful cook, always finding ways to let your guests off the culinary hook. Who caters for vegetarians, carnivores, dieters and chocaholics without flinching? A Moon in Libra woman.

Expressing your Libran side

If you have the Moon in Libra then, somewhere inside you, you contain a Libra. If your Libran side is well developed, you will probably also have people with Libra planets in your life. If this section doesn't accurately reflect what you're all about, you may want to read the chapter headed Walking Your Planets (pages 175–183).

THE AMPERSAND SIGN

Many women with Libra planets seem to slide into partnerships where two names merge into one, and are connected only by an ampersand. Nicole Kidman's Libran side has helped her turn into Tom & Nicole. Jayne Torvill's Libran side has helped create Torvill & Dean. This does not take away your independence or identity. However, there will be times in your life when you must also weigh up the differences between you, the other person involved and the partnership itself, which often seems to become as complicated and as real as a third person in its own right.

Jane Austen, who had the Moon in Libra, never married but spent her entire career writing about engagements. In her most famous novel, *Pride & Prejudice* (there's that ampersand again!), she described the chemistry between the proud Mr Darcy and the prejudiced Miss

Bennet in a way that sums up the capacity of Libra to create partnerships and marriages which are so complex, so colourful and so intricate that they become entities in their own right. If you have planets in Libra, it is very likely that you have created your own Jane Austen novels from the various alliances, romances, double-acts and duets in your own life.

 in libra

The Mercury in Libra student

Diplomatic in class debates ★ A preference for studying in pairs or groups ★ An intense dislike of teachers who practise favouritism or prejudice.

Your communication style

Smooth.

Your letters

High on etiquette and well presented.

You think like

A woman.

You talk like

A diplomat.

The Mercury in Libra voice

Refined.

Your tactics

Soft sell.

Expressing your Libran side

If you have Mercury in Libra, then somewhere inside you, you contain a Libra. If your Libran side is well developed, you will probably also have people with Libra planets in your life. If this section doesn't accurately reflect what you're all about, you may want to read the chapter headed Walking Your Planets (pages 175–183).

AESTHETICS AND VISUALS

Libra is associated with the visual arts, fashion, beauty, design, packaging, presentation and, above all, taste. This common theme seems to run through the lives of most women with planets in Libra. In the Libran universe, appearances really do count.

Venus, the ruler of Libra, also rules beauty. By association, this means the art you prefer to look at, the colours you prefer in your home, the opinions you hold about fashion and the kind of face you want to present.

Planets in Libra lend themselves to expression through colour, form, shape, design and texture. If this sign really is strong in your chart, then you may personally become a kind of modern Venus in your own right — adored by men and admired by other women. There are plenty of Libran women who are well-dressed, beautifully packaged, and quite literally born beautiful. There are also quite a number who have a passion for texture, colour, design and shape. Libra is certainly over-represented in the beauty, art, fashion and design-based industries! Elizabeth Tilberis, the stylish Editor-in-Chief at US *Harpers Bazaar* magazine, has Mercury in Libra.

 in **libra**

You love

Your social life ★ Good taste ★ Marriage ★ Paris ★ Romance ★ Beautiful landscapes ★ Colour ★ Music ★ Art ★ Looking fabulous ★ Peace and justice ★ Good manners ★ The art of seduction ★ Women ★ The female arts ★ Equal partnerships ★ People who are socially easy.

You loathe

Violence ★ Aggression ★ Cultural voids ★ Yobbos ★ Bad hair days ★ Exploitation ★ Blatant injustice.

Expressing your Libran side

If you have Venus in Libra then, somewhere inside you, you contain a Libra. If your Libran side is well developed, you will probably also have people with Libra planets in your life. If this section doesn't accurately reflect what you're all about, you may want to read the chapter headed Walking Your Planets (pages 175–183).

FINDING A BALANCE

Your planets in Libra are there to help you develop your taste, to increase your appreciation of beauty, and to encourage you to build partnerships. Most importantly, Libra planets are also there to help you build bridges. This sign abhors imbalance and injustice. Why should rabbits be used in laboratory experiments because they were born in the animal kingdom and not the human one? Why should working-class children receive a different education to upper-class children? Why should one country reserve the right to invade another one? Why should the First World exist at the expense of the Third World? Why do whites receive more opportunities than blacks? Why should women be treated differently to men? Why aren't fat women and thin women equal? These are all essentially Libran questions, although you will find your own way of framing them. It's really a matter of finding the particular injustice that rankles most.

I suspect women with planets in Libra only come into their own during times of war, because that is precisely the moment that diplomats and peacemakers are required. Today, women with planets in Libra turn their attention to other battles. Racism, class warfare, animal exploitation and sexism are just some of them. Wherever there is prejudice, bias, unfair treatment or discrimination your Libra planets will jump in. Your Libran side has a sharp eye for a flaw in the system, and it will seem natural for you to try and restore balance, order and harmony. Some women with Libra planets have told me they cannot bear to look at prejudice, bias or discrimination in the world, as they find it physically ugly and offensive. This is also typical of Libra, which tends to see things in an aesthetic, visual way. Whatever offends the eye with you is likely to be the same thing that offends your sense of fairness and justice.

 in libra

The best revenge is
Looking good.

Sporting Libra
Anything graceful with a gorgeous outfit!

Your battle tactics
Get allies on your side ★ Use the legal system to work for you, and if not, resort to your own version of justice ★ Take the high moral ground.

What kind of opponent are you?
Charming.

Expressing your Libran side
If you have Mars in Libra then, somewhere inside you, you contain a Libra. If your Libran side is well developed, you will probably also have people with Libra planets in your life. If this section doesn't accurately reflect what you're all about, you may want to read the chapter headed Walking Your Planets (pages 175–183).

WAR AND PEACE
Not every woman with planets in Libra becomes involved in political or ideological battles, although many do. However, if you are expressing yourself at least partly through this sign, you are unlikely to ignore the unfair, the ugly and the brutal in this life.

The difficulty for you, with planets in Libra, is to find a way to protect your principles without ending up in a fight. Occasionally, it will be possible to do this. Being intensely female, charming and attractive are potent weapons in their own right, and many women with Libra planets use them. The real test for Libra-influenced women is to weigh up the cost of battle against the price of peace.

In a perfect world, it would be sufficient to sweetly point out the injustices, give a nice smile and hope that human intelligence will prevail. Inevitably, there comes a point when even a peaceful protest will not do, and it is at this point that the famous Libran ability to weigh and measure will appear.

If you are expressing your Libra planets quite strongly, you may already be aware that you have diplomatic skills and a talent for negotiation. Libra is interested in finding the common ground, not the differences. If you are really living this sign, then a lot of your energy will go into peace treaties, bargains, deals and double-acts.

The Libra inside you is a charmer, a peacemaker and a diplomat. However, it is also true to say that your Libran side is prepared to put on armour when all else fails — *especially* if your sense of justice is offended. Your first preference is to find a useful ally. Forming alliances is natural if you have planets in Libra. If all else fails, you will resort to conflict as a last option. Classically, you will be more prepared to fight if someone else is on your side or wedded to your cause, and a great deal of energy goes into these kinds of mergers.

If the price of war is the price of peace, then your planets in Libra will ultimately decide if you must pay it. This applies in your private life, in your career, or, in a wider context, in causes and principles you believe in. If it really does seem to be right, then your Libran side may well have to decide to fight for it. Campaigns of one kind or another are a common theme with strongly Libran women — but peace and balance are always driving the decisions. As the Moon in Libra politician Golda Meir said, 'A leader who doesn't hesitate before he sends his nation into battle is not fit to be a leader.'

War maidens

The following women — who have the Sun, Moon, Mercury, Venus or Mars in Libra — have all fought in or been associated with these battles:

Margaret Thatcher — Falklands War — Sun, Mercury and Mars in Libra
Jessica Mitford — Spanish Civil War — Mercury and Venus in Mars

Eleanor Roosevelt — Second World War — Sun in Libra
Golda Meir — Israeli War — Moon in Libra
Joan of Arc — French War — Moon in Libra
Jennie George — Vietnam War — Moon in Libra

LIBRAN MYTHS

Katherine in *Henry V*

In Shakespeare's play, the French Princess Katherine is fated to marry England's King Henry as part of the peace settlement between the two countries. She is the perfect Libran bridge between two worlds. Were she not beautifully packaged and diplomatic, she would not be considered a good peace offering by Henry, but she is quickly accepted. The fashionable, feminine, charming Katherine agrees to the marriage not only in the interests of forming a romantic partnership, but also in the interests of a diplomatic accord between the two sides, France and England. If you have planets in Libra, the symbolism of Katherine's story in *Henry* V may also reflect aspects of your own life and times.

FEMALE PRINCIPLES

Along with Taurus, which is also ruled by Venus, Libra is the most intensely female of the twelve signs. If you have planets in Libra, you will not give up your womanhood lightly, even if you do find yourself moving in the world of men. Destiny says that many Libra-influenced women end up in all-male environments, or break ground — as a female — in a male-dominated area.

For some, this sense of womanhood means perfume, lipstick and heels. For others, being defiantly female means choosing to incorporate the traditional strategies of the wife or girlfriend — charm, negotiation, conflict resolution — into professional life.

Helen Reddy, who has Mercury, Venus and Mars in Libra chose to belt out a song titled 'I Am Woman' which subsequently became an anthem for the feminist movement. Margaret Thatcher, with the Sun, Mercury and Mars in Libra, chose to define her female principles simply by being the first English prime minister ever to be seen (publicly) in a frock.

Some Libra-influenced women use love, care and feminine intuition in their working lives as an acknowledgement of female principles. For you, with planets in Libra, a lot depends on how you define femininity and womanhood. It may be wearing white lace lingerie under your business suit, putting flowers in your office, or simply refusing to play it like a man even if you're moving in a male environment. Women with planets in Libra who spend time together invariably send one of two strong messages to the world: either very girly or strongly feminist. Both are compatible with the nature of Venus, your ruler. For some, Venus is a ballerina or a dancer. For others, the extreme femininity of the sign lends itself to soft feminism — the kind that is also acceptable to men.

THE CLASSIC LIBRA

Anita Roddick

Born on 23rd October 1942, the Body Shop's Anita Roddick has the Sun, Mercury, Venus and Mars in Libra. Her life reflects these classic Libran themes in a very pure way.

Crossing boundaries When Anita married Gordon Roddick, she found herself wedded to her opposite. 'I was as loud and brash as he was quiet and introspective,' she says in her autobiography, *Body and Soul*.

Partnership She counts her husband as both her business and life partner.

The ampersand sign The *and* in Anita Roddick's life comes from this quote in *Body and Soul*: 'Gordon and I operate on the partnership principle — he does his bit, and I do mine, but we do it together, with a common purpose.' Note the *and* in her book title, too!

Aesthetics and visuals Anita's career is obviously about beauty. But the Libran concern with aesthetics and appearance also influences everything the Body Shop is all about — from the trademark green shopfronts to the design of the packaging.

Finding a balance Anita's stance against animal testing is one example of the Libran peacemaking process between different worlds (animals and humans). Her well-known involvement with Third-World trade is another example of balancing. Finally, her status as a woman in a largely male business world — and her decision to sell 'beauty' products to men — creates a balance between *genders*.

War and peace Anita has been a member of the Campaign for Nuclear Disarmament and Ban the Bomb. Her campaigns for the environment continue.

Female principles Anita writes: 'I think all business practices would improve immeasurably if they were guided by 'feminine' principles — qualities like love and care and intuition.'

LIBRAN SYMBOLS

If you have planets in Libra, some of these keywords, symbols, people and themes may turn up in your life in obvious — and surprising — ways. Check the list below for Libran synchronicities in your own life.

Venus ★ Scales ★ Balance ★ Apples ★ Art ★ Perfume ★ Oils ★ Hair ★ Make-up ★ Paint ★ Clothes ★ Love ★ Romance ★ Passion ★ Young women ★ Design ★ Values ★ Gaia ★ Beauty ★ Marriage ★ Weddings ★ War ★ Peace ★ Enemies ★ Seven ★ Pictures ★ Image ★ Equality ★ Dance ★ Partnerships ★ Lingerie ★ Clothing ★ Serenades ★ Courtship ★ Justice ★ The Law ★ Harmony ★ Cupid ★ The United Nations ★ Counsellors ★ Decoration ★ Two ★ Aesthetics ★ Roses ★ Incense ★ Doves ★ Treaties ★ Allies ★ Campaigns ★ Flowers ★ Packaging ★ Taste ★ Relationships ★ Appearances ★ Love songs ★ Softness ★ Ink ★ Colour ★ Brushes ★ Pearls ★ Diplomacy ★ Popularity ★ Fabrics ★ Textiles ★ Pleasure ★ Artists ★ Hairdressers ★ Beauticians ★ Designers ★ Models ★ Lawyers ★ Barristers ★ Solicitors ★ Judges ★ Advocates ★ Advisers ★ Mediators ★ Diplomats ★ Dressmakers ★ Fashion agents ★ Husbands ★ Wives ★ Crafts ★ Picture frames ★ Interior decorators ★ Mannequins ★ Costumes ★ Meditation ★ Accessories ★ Bells ★ Pacifists ★ Graphics ★ Manicurists ★ Girdles ★ Patterns ★ Public Relations ★ Marriage counsellors.

PLANETS

in scorpio

Read this section if you have your Sun, Moon, Mercury, Venus or Mars in Scorpio.

> ### ARE YOU DOING YOUR SCORPIO?
> You get wholly involved with people and projects, or not at all
> You respect intense emotion, from passion to pain
> You're in touch with your sexuality at the deepest level
> You understand that being human is all about acknowledging the taboo stuff

YOUR SCORPIONIC SIDE

Passionate ★ Intense ★ Powerful.

USING SCORPIO

Your Sun, Moon, Mercury, Venus or Mars in Scorpio gives you depth and intensity. You can channel this into the goals which are most important to you, with powerful results. Single-minded passion is Scorpio's domain, and having a planet in this sign makes it simple for you to express yourself powerfully and with enormous focus. Controlled obsession for the goals which matter most will not only bring them closer, but also with results that deepen your understanding of life.

ALL OUR DARK SIDES

Scorpio is about taboo subjects, above all other things. Pluto, the ruler of Scorpio and the Underworld, was a dark monarch who rode on black horses. If you have planets in Scorpio, then for professional reasons, or intensely personal reasons, you will come into contact with all our dark sides.

Oprah Winfrey, with the Moon and Mars in Scorpio, has used her television show to bring many taboos into the light — including her own sexual abuse and survival of incest. Television producer Penny Chapman has a Scorpio Venus: some of her best-known ABC productions include dramas about taboo subjects — *Brides of Christ*, *Seven Deadly Sins*, *The Damnation of Harvey McHugh*.

Marianne Faithfull, a Scorpio Venus, wrote in her autobiography, *Faithfull*: 'For the past few years I've been performing Kurt Weill's *Seven Deadly Sins*. Perfect for me, not simply because I've committed them all . . .' Marianne's life has taken her into some of our society's biggest taboos: heroin addiction, bisexuality, the occult and suicide. But does this necessarily mean that every woman with a Scorpio planet pursues the dark side?

Sometimes the dark side just happens to Scorpio-influenced women of its own accord. Consciously, you may be pursuing the most uncomplicated life: living in the light, and apparently a million miles away from Pluto's black horses. Then one day, you wake up with the sinners — or the sinned-against — on your doorstep. This has happened to several opera singers, who wander around in a most un-Scorpionic existence, then find themselves *living* the Scorpionic life on stage. Faust or Orpheus come to claim them, and Scorpio wakes up for a few days. There are so many glimpses of death, the devil, heaving bosoms and straining codpieces in opera that it couldn't fail to be deeply Scorpionic on some level!

The composer Helen Gifford, who has Mars in Scorpio, wrote a piece called 'Regarding Faustus' in 1976. Dame Joan Sutherland has both her Sun and Venus in Scorpio. Heather Begg, the resident principal mezzo soprano with the Australian Opera has Venus in Scorpio. You do not have to have a planet in Scorpio to be in opera — but it helps. I suspect that a Scorpio planet would be useful in a career in heavy metal as well. I'll let writer Kathy Lette have the last word — she has the Sun in Scorpio and told *Harpers & Queen* magazine: 'I have a star sign everybody hates. As soon as I mention the fact that I'm a Scorpio, it's as though I've admitted I'm the Fuhrer's plaything.'

in **scorpio**

You identify with

Powerful people ★ Femme fatales ★ Survivors ★ Healers ★ Confidantes ★ Dark horses ★ Women of Passion ★ Torch singers ★ Sexual dynamos.

You're an authority on

Any taboo subject — sex, death, race, power or money ★ The dark side ★ Human survival.

Your career Top Ten

You need: 1) A locked filing cabinet; 2) A silent number or private phone line; 3) A little black book; 4) Informants; 5) A powerful or influential position; 6) People you can trust; 7) Intense challenges; 8) Room to change direction; 9) Respect for your privacy; 10) Goals you are passionate about.

Expressing your Scorpionic side

If you have the Sun in Scorpio then, somewhere inside you, you contain a Scorpio. If your Scorpionic side is well developed, you will probably also have people with Scorpio planets in your life. If this section doesn't accurately reflect what you're all about, you may want to read the chapter headed Walking Your Planets (pages 175–183).

INDECENT OBSESSIONS

Colleen McCullough, author of *An Indecent Obsession* and *The Thorn Birds* and also the First Man in Rome series, is a Scorpio Mars. In her books you can find priests doing what they not ought to, and Ancient Romans ripping off their togas. The most important question for your Scorpionic side will always be this one: at what point does obsession become indecent on your terms? Scorpio Moon Cynthia Paine — England's most famous brothel madam —

has some interesting views on this subject, but every Scorpio-influenced woman's view of sex is unique.

In the original Pluto myth, we find the dark lord hit by Cupid's arrow, and overwhelmed by his passion for Proserpine. In some books, he is her 'ravisher', and in others he is her rapist. This is a powerful and dark myth which surrounds Scorpio. The theme is continued when we learn that Proserpine has given in to her appetites and eaten Pluto's forbidden fruit. The twin ideas of 'wrong' obsession, and sexual appetite, tend to follow Scorpio around. If you have a planet here, then it is in the area of sexuality that your first contact with your Scorpionic side will emerge.

 **in scorpio**

What you need
Intensity ★ Passion ★ Dramatic and powerful music ★ Emotional purges ★ Mystery ★ Secrets ★ Sexuality with depth ★ A walk on the wild side ★ Mutual obsession ★ Above all — privacy.

The Moon in Scorpio home
Your house or flat is one of those places where everything leads back to the bedroom. People wandering through will pick up emotional traces in your books, or in your CD collection. You have little boxes and locks and special drawers, and what isn't hidden there is pushed under the bed. Depending on the state of play with family members, flatmates or neighbours, your home will either crackle with atmosphere, or be drenched in the strangest vibrations!

The Moon in Scorpio cook
You like the sensuality of food, and get a great deal of enjoyment from the oral component of cooking and eating! Scorpionic cooks can become quite manic about their recipes and usually have to be dragged away from their culinary masterpieces. You are passionate about your favourite flavours and scents. You also tend to cook for love, or prepare food or drinks with a view to sex. In your dreams, you have a 9½ Weeks kind of kitchen to play in.

Expressing your Scorpionic side

If you have the Moon in Scorpio then, somewhere inside you, you contain a Scorpio. If your Scorpionic side is well developed, you will probably also have people with Scorpio planets in your life. If this section doesn't accurately reflect what you're all about, you may want to read the chapter headed Walking Your Planets (pages 175–183).

HUMAN SEXUALITY

Some of you will meet your Scorpionic side through your careers. I know a Sun Scorpio woman who works with gay men in an AIDS ward, for example. Some of you may meet Scorpio directly, in the most difficult way, through your own experience of the unacceptable face of human sexuality. However you experience human sexuality, it is part of the Scorpionic inheritance to drag taboos into the light — if only for your own benefit.

Actresses who have Scorpio planets seem to trade on the sign's association with indecent obsessions. Scorpio Sun Julia Roberts played a prostitute in *Pretty Woman*. Scorpio Sun Demi Moore played a stripper in *Striptease* and a 'purchased' woman in *Indecent Proposal* (there's that 'indecent' word again). Scorpio Sun k.d. lang took a leading role in the fringe film *Salmonberries*, a drama which deals with lesbian passions. *Vanity Fair* editor Tina Brown (Scorpio Sun, Mercury, Venus) put k.d. lang on the cover of her magazine — being shaved by Cindy Crawford.

Scorpionic sexuality reflects the deeper issues — nothing that can be dismissed as shagging and bonking, but the intensity of our entire sexual underworld. Prostitution, lesbianism, male homosexuality, sexually transmitted diseases, AIDS and HIV, rape, sexual abuse, incest, sadism and masochism, masturbation, tantric sex, impotence, sexual addiction, whips, chains and strippers with pythons are all fair game for Scorpio's domain! If you have planets in Scorpio, then in astrological terms you are one of the very few women who are qualified to address this 'underworld'.

The writer Helen Garner who has a Scorpio Sun, Mercury, Venus and Mars was sacked as a schoolteacher in 1972 after discussing sexual issues with her classes. Today, she writes about the problematic issues which surround sexual harassment.

It is not easy to live out a Scorpio planet if you are a woman. Unfortunately, one of the ways some of you come into contact with it is by dealing with a real-life Pluto issue — the myth of male darkness may become real to you. Astrologer Donna Cunningham, who holds a Master's degree in Social Work, wrote a book called *Healing Pluto Problems* based on her own experiences with women who have planets in Scorpio and who have followed this road.

The theme of *sexual appetites* and *forbidden fruit* also seems to resonate with Scorpio-influenced women. In the myth of Pluto and Proserpine, we discover that she can only be released from her husband–abductor if she can prove that she ate none of his food during her time with him. One pomegranate was to prove her downfall, and in Thomas Bulfinch's book, *Myths of Greece and Rome*, we hear that Proserpine had 'sucked the sweet pulp from a few of the seeds' — precisely six — enough to lock her up with Pluto for half the year for the rest of her life!

The k.d. lang song 'Constant Craving' expresses this side of the Scorpionic appetite particularly well. If you have a planet in this sign, you may experience both sides of the Pluto story — acting out Proserpine's role (hungry for forbidden fruit) as well as her dark husband Pluto's (feeding forbidden fruit to others). Some women with a Scorpio planet do this 'feeding of the forbidden' in a professional way — as sexual advice columnists — like Bettina Arndt, who is a Scorpio Moon. Remember the legendary rumour about Marianne Faithfull, Mick Jagger and the Mars Bar? Her Scorpio Venus seems to have propelled her into the ancient myth of sexual appetites in the most eccentric way! Christie Ann Hefner, who has the Sun in Scorpio, is Hugh's daughter and also won presidency of Playboy Enterprises. Truly forbidden fruit for a woman, even if she is a Hefner. Marie Stopes, that pioneer of the most taboo sexual and contraceptive issues for women, had Mercury and Venus is Scorpio. Then there's that other pioneer in taboo sexual issues Billie Jean King, who has the Sun in Scorpio too. Finally, how can anyone forget that *Cosmopolitan* sexual revolutionary, Helen Gurley Brown — or indeed her Scorpio Moon?

 in scorpio

The Mercury in Scorpio student

Penetrating research is your trademark. You like subjects which revolve around human passion and survival — everything from literature to psychology — or head straight for the 'serious money' subjects.

Your communication style

Secretive.

Your letters

Invisible ink preferred.

You think like

A secret agent.

You talk like

Mata Hari.

The Mercury in Scorpio voice

Sexy.

Your tactics

Concealed.

Expressing your Scorpionic side

If you have Mercury in Scorpio then, somewhere inside you, you contain a Scorpio. If your Scorpionic side is well developed, you will probably also have people with Scorpio planets in your life. If this section doesn't accurately reflect what you're all about, you may want to read the chapter headed Walking Your Planets (pages 175–183).

RACE AND COLOUR

For as long as racism and bigotry continue to be taboo issues in society, Scorpio planets will seek out the awkward, uncomfortable issues around them. Many of the women on this list are involved with Aboriginal or African–American issues. Others are concerned with racism on other levels. Our collective dark side, ironically enough, often surfaces in questions about black skin and white skin. It is no accident that the planet Pluto was also given its name in 1930, just as race hatred was on the rise. If you have a Scorpio planet, your experiences with race or colour will trigger many of the questions in you that polite society would prefer to forget about. If race or colour are the 'dark horses' of modern life, then it is unlikely that your Scorpionic side can simply allow them to run away without closer inspection.

These Scorpio-influenced women are well-known for their concern with questions of race and colour:

Mum Shirl — Sun, Mercury and Venus in Scorpio
Whoopi Goldberg — Sun in Scorpio
Marion Hansen — Sun and Venus in Scorpio
Isabelle Adams — Sun and Mars in Scorpio
Rosalie Medcraft — Sun, Moon and Mercury in Scorpio
Muriel Patterson — Mars in Scorpio
Oprah Winfrey — Moon and Mars in Scorpio

VENUS in scorpio

You love

Mystery ★ The dark side ★ Sexual taboos ★ Secrets ★ Power ★ People who rise from the ashes ★ Erotic intensity ★ Obsession ★ Intrigue ★ Knowing the unmentionable ★ Turning the key in the lock ★ Black lingerie ★ Tangled sheets ★ Long, unbroken eye contact ★ Thrills and chills ★ Investigative astrology ★ Dragging censored topics into the light ★ Breathing heavily ★ Biting your lip.

You loathe

Nice, clean girls — or boys — next door ★ Superficial smiles ★ Hypocrisy.

Expressing your Scorpionic side

If you have Venus in Scorpio then, somewhere inside you, you contain a Scorpio. If your Scorpionic side is well developed, you will probably also have people with Scorpio planets in your life. If this section doesn't accurately reflect what you're all about, you may want to read the chapter headed Walking Your Planets (pages 175–183).

SECRETS AND MYSTERIES

Why is your Scorpionic side so famously secretive? Some astrologers argue that it lends you the power, or control, that you seek in life: rather like the playground chant of, 'I know something you don't know,' it gives you considerable influence!

There may be something in this. Knowledge is power, and your Scorpionic side does have an ability to draw out sensitive information from other people without ever revealing too much of yourself in return. This in itself makes you a rather powerful figure, although not every woman with a Scorpio planet is conscious of her behaviour patterns.

There is another explanation for your secretiveness, and that is the intervention of fate. Destiny singles you out for intense experiences which really cannot be tossed around like so much gossip. Consequently, you get into the habit of censoring large parts of yourself, and by a chain reaction, become discreet or silent on other matters, too. Agatha Christie, a Scorpio Venus, is famous for disappearing rather mysteriously during her marriage breakdown. Murder writer P.D. James also has Mars in Scorpio.

On a lighter level, many women with Scorpio planets have a huge appetite for mystery — especially in books and films. Joan Lindsay, who wrote Picnic at Hanging Rock, was a Scorpio Sun. Planets here give you an appetite for ghosts and disappearances, murder and magic. Pluto's world was always night. And Scorpio is strongly associated with everything that takes place from midnight to dawn — including the late-night horror shift, and the slow tread of the vampire.

Women who are strongly Scorpio-influenced are often familiar with the occult, and have a slightly 'witchy' feel or appearance about them. I have also known a few girl-next-door Scorpio Suns and Moons who fulfil the sign in other ways by reading Gothic romance under the sheets. Part of Agatha Christie's success was her Virgo side — but her Scorpio Venus provided the blood and midnight chimes that made her a legend.

 in **scorpio**

The best revenge is
Death.

Sporting Scorpio
Anything involving sweaty, sexy bodies.

Your battle tactics
You plot and manipulate behind the scenes, and draw on secrets and confidences to find your opponent's weak point. Other people's sexual vulnerabilities are a key strategy point for some. In other cases, you power-trip people to hell and back!

What kind of opponent are you?
Obsessive.

Expressing your Scorpionic side
If you have Mars in Scorpio then, somewhere inside you, you contain a Scorpio. If your Scorpionic side is well developed, you will probably have people with Scorpio planets in your life. If this section doesn't accurately reflect what you're all about, you may want to read the chapter headed Walking Your Planets (pages 175–183).

SERIOUS MONEY
Scorpionic money is the kind one dies for, the kind that is hushed up or kept confidential, the kind that carries power, splits families, breaks marriages or runs deep. It is *power* money, at its most basic level, and really not the same money at all as Taurean cash — which goes on perfume, wine and pearls. Scorpionic money has nothing to do with the shopping centre, it is about sex, power or death, or all three.

Your Scorpionic side will draw you into the world of serious money by hurling you into the professional side of it, or by walking you through its personal implications. Invariably, when clients come to see me with a big Scorpio (Eighth House) cycle going on, they will inherit money from a dead relative, enter into binding financial agreements with their husbands or partners, be involved in hush-hush stock market deals, or find themselves surrounded by bankers and taxmen and lawyers!

The more complex side of money is your domain. (If you have planets in Taurus, too, then finances will be a major part of your life.) With Scorpio planets, you will find that serious money leads you on a trail to your other Scorpionic qualities. A woman with a Scorpio Mercury found this side of herself came into sharp focus when she tackled a complicated divorce. She suddenly saw money in a completely different light. There are women with Scorpio planets (and money) who marry men with nothing. They become sharply aware of issues like power and control in connection with finance. There are a few female bankers and stockbrokers around with a complete understanding of the legend that Scorpionic money is hush money. Often, too, Scorpionic wealth is buried — or underground.

DEATH AND DYING

Civilised society is most comfortable handling death inside the walls of life insurance offices and quiet, enclosed hospitals. Any discussion of Scorpio has to include death, though — and not only because Pluto ruled the Realms of the Dead in mythology.

Women with Scorpio planets or Pluto chart signatures have a deep understanding of death and dying issues. Elisabeth Kubler-Ross had Pluto next to her Sun on the day she was born. Whoopi Goldberg (Scorpio Sun) worked in a morgue. Any discussion of Scorpio and death also has to include the afterlife as well. This sign is deeply concerned with questions about heaven and hell, spirits and resurrection, death and rebirth. No wonder so many writers and actors with Scorpio planets gravitate to tales of ghosts, murder and the Church. No wonder so many women in the caring professions end up working with *life and death* situations, courtesy of their Scorpio planets.

In the myth, it is a three-headed dog with snaky hair who guards Pluto's realms of the dead. It takes a great deal more than that to frighten your Scorpionic side away, though. Something about this sign is pulled towards — or pulled into — these issues. More than any other sign, Scorpio seems to know and understand them.

SCORPIO TRANSFORMS

Your Scorpionic side is rather like the phoenix. You die, symbolically, and are then reborn from your own ashes after being transformed. Most of you will have experienced this process between the years 1984–1995, as Pluto passed over your Scorpio Sun, Moon, Mercury, Venus or Mars. It will have affected you as follows:

Scorpio Sun

An identity crisis — which, depending on your birthday, may have hit in the eighties or the nineties. A feeling of being stripped down to the core and then rebuilt. The results today? A completely different sense of self.

Scorpio Moon

You appear to have gone through an emotional purging session. Family, house or flat crises have coincided with the most intense period of soul-searching and change. You are not who you were, but it's over now!

Scorpio Mercury

Changes of attitude and opinion — a complete mental transformation — have been the most obvious developments in either the eighties or nineties. The way you communicate may have changed as well.

Scorpio Venus

All the familiar issues of the Pluto and Proserpine story may have been experienced in your own life for the years that Pluto crossed over your Venus. Many of you may well feel that you have risen from the ashes.

Scorpio Mars

Dealing with anger — and your own need to attack or defend — has been a potent source of change and transformation in your life. You may have dealt with your own warrior side, or faced it in the behaviour of other people.

One of the reasons you seem to carry such a depth charge around with you is this: you've been through crisis, survived and *changed*. Perhaps it is these qualities that attract you to others going through intense experiences and transformations, or maybe they gravitate towards you because of the signals they read that you cannot see!

Scorpio-influenced women seem to find themselves around people who are in crisis, on the edge, or bravely facing tremendous healing in their lives. Some of you do this because you seek it out. But I have known just as many women with a Scorpio Sun, Moon, Mercury, Venus or Mars who find themselves placed there by fate. I know a Scorpio Venus nurse who works with children who are blind. They trust her because she has been through her own underworld and survived. Whenever people go through great changes and a rebuilding of the inner or outer self, a Scorpio-influenced guide is invaluable.

FEMALE POWER

Scorpionic power generally seems to channel in two distinct ways with women. Some of you find it by forming friendships, close relationships or marriages with extremely powerful people. You receive your influence by proxy. Another group of you with the Sun, Moon, Mercury, Venus or Mars in Scorpio trade on your sexual charge and female identity — and combine it with career skills or financial acumen.

Women with Scorpio planets are sometimes a magnet for people with money, power or influence of their own. Sometimes you seek this out quite deliberately. At other times, these people just seem to 'happen'. There are many Scorpio-influenced women who are powers behind their partners' thrones.

SCORPIONIC MYTHS

Lady Macbeth

Shakespeare's Lady Macbeth has female power in abundance. Her story also sums up all our dark sides — sex, mystery, obsession and death. *Macbeth* is a tale of taboos on all fronts, and Lady

Macbeth is the supreme femme fatale, holding invisible controls. The Underworld in the play is not unlike the Hades of Pluto and Proserpine, with its ghosts who walk, and maddened horses. Lady Macbeth is a tragic Scorpio, whose crisis leads to a dark transformation — from woman to madwoman. Despite the tragedy, there is still something passionate, intense and awe-inspiring about Shakespeare's version of the Scorpionic female.

THE CLASSIC SCORPIO

Anne Rice

Born on 4th October 1941, Anne Rice, the author of *Interview with the Vampire*, is a Scorpio Mercury and Venus.

All our dark sides 'The fourth vampire volume in the Vampire Chronicles,' says Rice, 'is really about the ruthlessness, the evil, in us all.'

Indecent obsessions 'Vampires don't have sex,' Rice says, 'they transcend gender.'

Human sexuality 'I would go to the Supreme Court to fight for the right of a little woman in a trailer park to read pornography — or write it, if she wants to,' Rice says.

Race and colour 'You live in a town like Dallas, you see what real bigotry is,' she told *New Orleans Magazine*.

Secrets and mysteries 'I grew up in a world where people believed in the miraculous,' she says.

Serious money In 1993 Rice signed a publishing deal for the extraordinary sum of US$17 million.

Death and dying 'I lost my mother when I was 14. My daughter died at the age of 6. I lost my faith as a Catholic,' Rice says. 'When I'm writing, the darkness is always there. I go where the pain is.'

Scorpionic transformation 'Darkness never really goes away once you've seen it,' she believes. 'You learn to see the light in the darkness. In fact, once you've seen the darkness, the light is brighter.'

Female power 'I believe absolutely in the right of women to fantasize what they want to fantasize, to read what they want to read,' Rice says. She is no power behind her husband's throne, but in her own right is one of the world's most powerful novelists.

SCORPIONIC SYMBOLS

If your Scorpionic side is a major part of your life, some of these symbols and themes may have personal relevance for you:

The Scorpion ★ Eight ★ Pluto ★ Proserpine ★ Hades ★ Sex ★ Death ★ Black ★ Blood ★ Transformation ★ Power ★ Money ★ Ghosts ★ Resurrection ★ The phoenix ★ Night ★ Darkness ★ Taboo ★ Sin ★ Censorship ★ Control ★ Invisibility ★ Intensity ★ Caves ★ Atomic power ★ Sewers ★ Purges ★ Obsession ★ Indecency ★ Italy ★ Catholicism ★ Murder ★ Mystery ★ Obscenity ★ Near-death experience ★ Spirits ★ Faust ★ Orpheus ★ Eurydice ★ The Underworld ★ Survival ★ Healing ★ Secrets ★ Witches ★ Mummies ★ Vampires ★ Lust ★ Crime ★ Revenge ★ Passion ★ Depth ★ The occult ★ Gothic ★ Sabotage ★ Rebirth ★ S & M ★ Homosexuality ★ Lesbianism ★ Temptation ★ Seeds ★ Forbidden fruit ★ Dark horses.

PLANETS in sagittarius

Read this section if you have your Sun, Moon, Mercury, Venus or Mars in Sagittarius.

> ## ARE YOU DOING YOUR SAGITTARIUS?
>
> You travel or explore whenever you can possibly get away
>
> You are committed to a strong sense of meaning or purpose in your life
>
> You exercise your sense of humour wherever possible
>
> You are continually learning and educating yourself

YOUR SAGITTARIAN SIDE
Adventurous ★ Funny ★ Knowledgeable.

USING SAGITTARIUS
Drag out your Sagittarian side when a difficult or trying situation needs to be broken up with a joke. Next to Gemini, this sign is strongly associated with a talent to amuse. Your Sun, Moon, Mercury, Venus or Mars in Sagittarius is also about the printed word, knowledge and learning. If you make space for Sagittarius in your life, you may become one of the best-read and most knowledgeable women in the zodiac. Finally, Sagittarius is associated with all that is global and international. Having a planet in this sign will well and truly give you the big picture and a wide perspective which can only make your journey easier.

SAGITTARIUS AND SIZE

Women with Sagittarius planets have a preoccupation with size. Not just being too fat or too thin — which you might expect in our fat-phobic society — there is also height (too tall, too short) to consider, and then the individual size of each body part. This sign has size issues to deal with because your symbol, Chiron the centaur, looks so uncomfortable with a human upper body, and a horse's hindquarters below. Everything is out of proportion.

Sagittarius-influenced women often have issues about their own, or other people's, bodies to deal with. If this sign is especially strong in your chart, you may always have felt as if bits of you were too tall, too short, too fat, or too thin. You may also be sensitive to other people around you being giants or midgets, skeletons or beachballs. More than anything else, Sagittarius planets lend themselves to thinking about *proportions*. It may be one of the challenges of this sign to learn that there is really no such thing as average. Some women who have Sagittarius planets — Kate Fischer and Maggie Tabberer are some obvious examples — profit by their generous proportions. Most Sagittarius-influenced women understand that size is a sensitive subject, not only for themselves but for other people, too.

SUN in **sagittarius**

You identify with
Explorers ★ Adventurers ★ Funny women ★ Idealists ★ Philosophers ★ Gurus ★ Academics ★ Female judges ★ Politicians ★ True believers.

You're an authority on
At least one 'ology' or 'ism' — and sometimes more than one. You're an expert on other countries, cultures or beliefs, too.

Your career Top Ten
You need: 1) Long holidays; 2) Work-related travel; 3) Long-distance connections; 4) People who laugh at your jokes; 5) The big picture; 6)

 118

Space to take a few gambles; 7) Continual opportunities for expansion; 8) People who share your enormous vision; 9) Amusing colleagues or clients; 10) Permission to go over the top once in a while.

Expressing your Sagittarian side

If you have the Sun in Sagittarius then, somewhere inside you, you contain a Sagittarius. If your Sagittarian side is well developed, you will probably also have people with Sagittarius planets in your life. If this section doesn't accurately reflect what you're all about, you may want to read the chapter headed Walking Your Planets (pages 175–183).

COMEDY AND HUMOUR

The Sagittarius planets which lead to a preoccupation with size also give you a talent to inflate, exaggerate and over-emphasise — and also to play things down in a deadpan way. Dramatic situations become tiny. Trivia becomes over the top. In plain English, this is comedy.

In situation comedy, the funniest characters are usually the ones who are larger than life. Extreme and excessive, over-the-top characters. If you have a Sagittarian side, you also possess a talent for amusing people. By over-stressing the trivial and underplaying what is serious, you create comedy. You can stretch a joke, keep a straight face, or wave your hands around to make a point.

Crazy mirrors in amusement arcades have the same effect — by squeezing people thinner and blowing them up larger. It's common to find women with Sagittarius planets who have this same ability to play around with the proportions of things — the emphasis in a story, for example. Some Sagittarian-type women seem to specialise in talking in exclamation marks and capitals and italics. Sometimes your Sagittarian side means to be funny, sometimes you just *are* — effortlessly. Here are some women who have used Sagittarian humour in their careers:

A talent to amuse

Bette Midler — Sun in Sagittarius
Kaz Cooke — Sun and Mercury in Sagittarius

Pamela Stephenson — Sun in Sagittarius
Mary Tyler Moore — Moon in Sagittarius
Dawn French — Venus in Sagittarius
Goldie Hawn — Mercury in Sagittarius
Tracy Ullman — Mercury and Mars in Sagittarius
Diane Keaton — Mercury in Sagittarius
Judi Dench — Sun in Sagittarius
Meg Ryan — Mars in Sagittarius
Jamie Lee Curtis — Mercury and Venus in Sagittarius
Julia Louis-Dreyfus — Moon in Sagittarius
Janine Turner — Sun in Sagittarius

 **in sagittarius**

What you need

Wide open spaces ★ Freedom to come and go ★ Weekend getaways ★ Overseas hauls ★ A philosophy, belief system or sense of meaning ★ People who share your sense of humour ★ Family, flatmates, or even a pet who makes you laugh out loud.

The Moon in Sagittarius home

You definitely need a room with a view, and can become edgy if you feel too locked in. Bits and pieces from your travels or periods of wanderlust end up in drawers and on shelves. You need something cross-cultural, imported, exotic or different around you to remind you of the world beyond your window. Bags, rucksacks or suitcases are never very far out of reach, and your bookshelves are crammed with the most mind-expanding non-fiction you can find. You really *need* an answering machine.

The Moon in Sagittarius cook

You're optimistic and like taking gambles. Exotic and imported ingredients are irresistible, but if you're running around too much to cater in-house, you'll send out for Asian, Indian or possibly Outer Mongolian. You have a thing about serving size — too much? too little? — but you're a genius at campfire cooking and barbecues. You like exchanging the kitchen ceiling for the stars and the results are delicious. Smorgasbords suit you — if everyone helps themselves, that frees you up completely.

Expressing your Sagittarian side

If you have the Moon in Sagittarius then, somewhere inside you, you contain a Sagittarius. If your Sagittarian side is well developed, you will probably also have people with Sagittarius planets in your life. If this section doesn't accurately reflect what you're all about, you may want to read the chapter headed Walking Your Planets (pages 175–183).

TRAVELLERS AND EXPLORERS

Sagittarius rules the Ninth House in astrology. In the Middle Ages, the Ninth House described foreigners and exotic, unseen places. After NASA played golf on the Moon in the 1960s, the Ninth House also started to describe extra-terrestrial places. Until you actually get offered a ticket up there, though, your interests may remain with Europe and Asia if you are based in Australia, and just about anywhere if you are one of the roaming Sagittarian types.

If you have planets here you may end being a lifelong traveller, or work in a field where ISD dialling codes become part of your life. You may stay put (for financial reasons) or work in a less than adventurous career. However, you will get your global 'fix' by subscribing to the Internet, watching SBS or reading foreign writers. Sagittarius planets really do not like the neighbourhood, the corner store and the local scene. They incline you towards the world of the unexplored and exotic, the ethnic and cosmopolitan. There are many Sagittarius planet women around with passports which look like abstract artworks, they are so overlaid with stamps. And if Sagittarius is strong in your chart, you may always have your bag packed ready to go, or a suitcase flung under the bed. In a small, small town it is always the Sagittarius-influenced woman who is first to jump on the first available bus out of there.

The Great Outdoors is also part of Sagittarian territory. This sign needs to *literally* look beyond the horizon. If you have planets in this sign, you may be a four-wheel driver, a long-distance walker, a keen sailor or an unstoppable climber. You may enjoy the endless horizon that appears over the ocean at sunset, or the suggestion of pure space that is found in the desert.

If you can possibly fly to it, walk towards it, swim around it, jump off it or drive ahead of it, then you probably will. When your Sagittarian side catches sight of vast, open spaces, it doesn't really matter if you're looking at the local golf course or the ski fields of Europe — the response is the same. British Airways, predictably enough, was incorporated on 13th December 1983, which gives the airline the Sun in Sagittarius. Apart from a lust for global roaming, BA also displays that other Sagittarian characteristic — comedy on tap. I don't know about you, but on my last Los Angeles–London flight it was Mr Bean and Monty Python all the way.

If your Sagittarian side is particularly strong, you may emigrate, work in a field which involves a lot of interstate or international juggling, or 'adopt' somewhere suitably far-flung or exotic. I know one Sagittarius Moon woman who has claimed France for her own. I also know a Sagittarius Mars client who has conducted a love affair with Italy for 20 years and flings fettuccine at the walls as if her last name was Lollobrigida. She was born in Taree, by the way. Writer Helen Demidenko-Darville's passion for the Ukraine is well known: she has Venus and Mars in Sagittarius.

It is in the nature of the sign to be interested in other cultures, other customs and other perspectives. World citizens and international bright young things really can't afford to be xenophobic. It's common to find women with a Sagittarius planet shaping careers where the adjective 'international' becomes part of their job description. Sagittarius's association with size also lends itself to this all-encompassing view of the world. But even if you're not that ambitious, the big picture will be an important part of your mindset. I once knew a woman with a Sagittarius Venus who lived on a farm. She ordered *National Geographic* by subscription, tuned in regularly to the BBC World Service and spent all her free time planning the next trip into town!

 in **sagittarius**

The Mercury in Sagittarius student
Knowledgeable in a broad way ★ An eclectic and scatter-gun approach to learning ★ Occasionally you'll play the class joker ★ You like subjects which give you the big picture — History, the Humanities, Philosophy.

Your communication style
Entertaining.

Your letters
Hilarious.

You think like
A Wise Woman.

You talk like
An optimist.

The Mercury in Sagittarius voice
Elastic.

Your tactics
Make 'em laugh.

Expressing your Sagittarian side
If you have Mercury in Sagittarius then, somewhere inside you, you contain a Sagittarius. If your Sagittarian side is well developed, you will probably also have people with Sagittarius planets in your life. If this section doesn't accurately reflect what you're all about, you may want to read the chapter headed Walking Your Planets (pages 175–183).

THE MEANING OF LIFE
When I was studying philosophy one of our courses was actually called 'The Meaning of Life'. When the rather brilliant prof. asked the members of the class what they thought it was, someone stuck

their hand up and said, 'A Monty Python film'. Sagittarius *is*, however, strongly associated with the search for a belief system, a sense of meaning and some kind of faith. As an astrologer, I have yet to meet a woman with a Sagittarius planet who is content to wander around in a meaningless universe. Demented though it may sound, having a planet in this sign *will* send you looking for The Meaning of Life, sooner or later.

Along with Pisces, this is the sign most associated with conventional religion. For every one of you who finds your meaning or moral order in set religions, though, there is one who looks for something less structured. I have had Sagittarius-influenced clients who have taken up meditation as part of their inner search, touching on Eastern philosophy. Some have found meaning in life after experimentation with LSD, which they believe has helped them see the universe differently. Belief systems are intensely personal things. Tina Turner (Sagittarius Sun) crawled out of a violent and verbally abusive marriage to Ike Turner after she found Buddhism. The comedian Dawn French (who, incidentally, played a woman of the cloth in the television series *The Vicar of Dibley*) is a Sagittarius Venus and a Christian.

Your Sagittarian side will not let you accept a void. Jupiter, your ruler, lorded it over the heavens and anything 'up there' is part of Sagittarian territory, too. The idea that we are all here for no purpose, that life is a chaotic, random mess and that suffering is without purpose seems to horrify Sagittarian types. It may take you years to find your own sense of meaning (Bette Midler, a Sagittarius Sun, became a born-again believer late in life). Alternatively, you may grow up having a strong personal philosophy, and I have known women with Sagittarius planets to borrow 'bits' of philosophy and religion to make sense of it all.

For some women with Sagittarius planets, the only code or philosophy which fits is the one contained in the constitution or inside the law. Elizabeth Evatt, who has Mercury and Mars in Sagittarius, was Australia's first judge in the Family Court, and president of the Australian Law Reform Commission. Somewhere, somehow, your Sagittarian side also has to find a code by which to live, or a philosophy by which to stand or fall.

 in **sagittarius**

You love

Travel ★ Exploring ★ Well-travelled people ★ Other countries and cultures ★ Being outdoors ★ Activities with an endless horizon — sailing, swimming, walking, surfing ★ Courses ★ Books ★ Lifelong learning ★ Having a bet ★ Taking risks ★ Romantic adventures ★ A room with a view ★ People who hold ideals and beliefs as strongly as you do ★ Comedy and humour.

You loathe

Small-town attitudes ★ People who don't see the joke ★ Being tied down ★ Routine.

Expressing your Sagittarian side

If you have Venus in Sagittarius then, somewhere inside you, you contain a Sagittarius. If your Sagittarian side is well developed, you will probably also have people with Sagittarius planets in your life. If this section doesn't accurately reflect what you're all about, you may want to read the chapter headed Walking Your Planets (pages 175–183).

THE PRINTED WORD

Sagittarius is associated with the mass media, education, mass communications, and all aspects of the printed word. Having a Sagittarius planet is a little like having a library of the best fiction and non-fiction locked inside your head, and when you are not planning your next trip, you will probably be curled up with a book. Fate may send you in directions where the printed word is the biggest part of your life, and your other planets — and your Rising sign — will give more information about this.

Alternatively, you may just be one of those well-read women the rest of us are happy to sit next to on planes. Sagittarius planets seem to pick up information as a professional librarian does — in a kind of broad, interdisciplinary way. Jupiter, the ruler of Sagittarius, governs anything with the word *mass* in front of it. It connects your sign to the big, global picture.

Australia's two most successful media proprietors are a Sagittarius Sun and Sagittarius Moon respectively — Kerry Packer and Rupert Murdoch. Elisabeth Murdoch, Rupert's mother, and a kind of matriarchal figure in the mass media, is a Sagittarius Mars. Alongside Gemini and Virgo, Sagittarius is the sign which repeats more than any other in the world of mass communications.

Even those of you who choose not to stay in the formal education system carry on a kind of informal education throughout your lives. A friend of mine with four out of five planets in Sagittarius left school at 16, but is permanently on courses and workshops. Your Sagittarian side has a horror of the classic small-town mentality, and for this you can thank Chiron, the wise centaur, and Jupiter, the God of all nations. I met a Sagittarius Sun telephone operator the other day. When she wasn't 'plugged in' to Germany, Belgium, Canada or Hong Kong, she was reading a magazine on her knee. I think that sums up one aspect of your Sagittarian side perfectly. Most of you have heads like libraries.

 in **sagittarius**

The best revenge is
A lecture.

Sporting Sagittarius
You love most outdoor activities.

Your battle tactics
You are a natural crusader, and when you are on the attack or defence, will take a morally superior, crusading stance. You'll lean hard on a belief system, philosophy or ideology to back up your point. You exaggerate your opponent's faults!

What kind of opponent are you?
Over the top.

Expressing your Sagittarian side

If you have Mars in Sagittarius then, somewhere inside you, you contain a Sagittarius. If your Sagittarian side is well developed, you will probably have people with Sagittarius planets in your life. If this section doesn't accurately reflect what you're all about, you may want to read the chapter headed Walking Your Planets (pages 175–183).

A MATTER OF PRINCIPLE

Sagittarius rules moral principles, and ethical principles, but above all, it rules the *law* — as it applies to your own life. If you have the Sun, Moon, Mercury, Venus or Mars in this sign then destiny says you will have to involve yourself with moral questions as they are defined by judges and politicians.

Some women with a strongly Sagittarian side do go on to become solicitors, barristers, judges, politicians and trade union officials. But a peculiar thing happens for any Sagittarius-influenced woman: every so often, between the joking, the travelling and the reading, it all comes to a screeching halt *on a matter of principle*.

Some barristers do use this tactic in court: they turn over the judgement to others by using these words: 'Matter for you'. This is, of course, not the whole story. What seems right is seldom a matter for the individual, it is also a reflection of what someone in a wig — or someone in Parliament — decided 20 years ago. The Bible (written by the early disciples) is still the book on which those in court must take their oath, and to a large extent it still informs many of our laws and commandments today. Barbara Thiering, the author of *Jesus the Man*, is a Sagittarius Venus.

You will bite on this simple fact several times in your life: someone *else's* word is law. Some women with Sagittarius planets meet this in the course of their working lives, some meet it through their love lives, or family experiences. Some of you end up believing that the law really is an ass, others find something very pure in it.

Your Sagittarian side may become triggered quite sharply if you find yourself having to run things through a legal department, or being on jury duty, or tackling other points of law. Similarly, any experiences you have with religion will drag out your inner Sagittarius. She, above all other sides of yourself, has to define what justice really is. Also, perhaps, what is moral and ethical, fair and correct. If you want to destroy your own dinner party in five minutes flat, invite a group of women with Sagittarius planets in their charts to talk about politics, religion or the constitution! Nevertheless, the Sagittarian pool of talent in society always produces the liveliest debates, and it is from this pool that our ideas about what is wise, correct and just seem to come.

Astrologers give religion and the law over to Sagittarius because of your ruler, Jupiter, who administrated the entire cosmos. Any woman who has Jupiter dominating her chart — or a strong Sagittarian side — will be concerned, above all else, with *the rules* and what they mean. Now that the mighty planet Pluto is travelling through Sagittarius, power lawyers are cropping up all over the place. Robert Currey, of London's Astrology Shop, picked it up first — come on down legal eagles and super-wives Hillary Clinton and Cherie Blair.

legal eagles

Mary Gaudron — Justice, High Court of Australia — Moon and Mars in Sagittarius

Ann Mallalieu — QC — Sun in Sagittarius

Elizabeth Evatt — Senior Deputy President, Australian Industrial Relations Commission — Mercury and Mars in Sagittarius

Political thinkers

Cheryl Kurnot — Sun and Mercury in Sagittarius

Anna Booth — Sun and Venus in Sagittarius

Petra Kelly — Sun in Sagittarius

Sonia Gandhi — Sun in Sagittarius

Sallyanne Atkinson — Moon in Sagittarius

Margaret Trudeau — Moon in Sagittarius

Franca Arena — Mars in Sagittarius

Betty Boothroyd — Moon in Sagittarius

Blanche D'Alpuget — Venus in Sagittarius

Glenda Jackson — Moon in Sagittarius

Jane Fonda — Sun and Venus in Sagittarius
Vera Brittain — Mercury in Sagittarius
Lillian Russell — Sun in Sagittarius
Caroline Kennedy — Sun in Sagittarius
Edna Ryan — Sun in Sagittarius

ETERNAL OPTIMISTS

Jupiter, the ruler of Sagittarius, is also known as Jove in ancient mythology. From this comes the word *jovial*, which my trusty, coffee-stained *Thesaurus* defines this way: 'merry, joyous, joyful, sparkling, mirth-loving, waggish, jocular, witty, gay and frivolous'. It also suggests kittenish and rackety, but I'm not sure how you feel about that. Having a planet in this sign is like having a recorded message in your head saying 'Never surrender'. Even when you're feeling black, your Sagittarian side will come through and find that famous *sense of meaning* or *philosophy of life* which turns negatives into positives. It's not accurate to say that every woman with a Sagittarius Sun, Moon, Mercury, Venus or Mars is a rackety old kitten, but you are certainly eternal optimists.

SAGITTARIAN MYTHS
Maggie O'Connell

The person who flies the local plane in the cult American television series *Northern Exposure* is Maggie O'Connell, played — ironically — by a Sagittarius Sun, Janine Turner. The fictional Maggie is a frontier woman, unafraid of guns and a skilled bush pilot. She also happens to be the town mayor. If you've never seen the programme before and if you really want to see Sagittarius in full flight, Maggie O'Connell is your woman. Eternally optimistic (five of her lovers have died, and she is still looking for number six) she is incapable of taking anything too seriously.

THE CLASSIC SAGITTARIUS
Nancy Mitford

Nancy Mitford, author of the largely autobiographical novels *The Pursuit of Love* and *Love in a Cold Climate*, was born on 28th November 1904, with the Sun and Mercury in Sagittarius.

Sagittarius and size 'We had a tape measure,' writes Nancy in *The Pursuit of Love*, 'and competed as to the largeness of our eyes, the smallness of wrists, ankles, waist and neck, length of legs and fingers, and so on.'

Comedy and humour 'I see my childhood (and in fact most of life) as a hilarious joke,' Nancy once told her mother.

Travellers and explorers A longtime Francophile, Nancy eventually moved to Paris and lived there until her death. She later became a literary translator.

The Meaning of Life The two 'isms' in Nancy Mitford's life were, firstly, Fascism, and after she rejected that, Socialism (she helped find homes for Republican refugees from the Spanish Civil War).

The printed word Nancy was a bestselling author and journalist. She was also a lifelong reader and letter writer. And she worked in a London bookshop for many years.

A matter of principle Born into a family of variously composed of Communists, Fascists and Nazi sympathisers, Nancy's whole life became a matter of principle.

Eternal optimists This is Nancy light-heartedly discussing her own funeral arrangements in 1963: 'Have you got any thoughts on the tomb?' one of her sisters wrote. 'Large and showy, with angels and a long inscription saying how lovely I was and greatly missed,' replied Nancy.

SAGITTARIAN SYMBOLS

If you have the Sun, Moon, Mercury, Venus or Mars in Sagittarius, some of these ideas, symbols and themes may bounce off your life and times in important ways:

Chiron ★ Centaurs ★ Jupiter (Jove) ★ Aeroplanes ★ Nine ★ Size ★ Humour ★ Travel ★ Philosophy ★ The Law ★ Education ★ Academia ★ International organizations ★ The World ★ The Heavens ★ Passports ★ Ships ★ Foreign ports ★ Explorers ★ Politics ★ Religion ★ Horses ★ Gambling ★ Casinos ★ Polo ★ Cartoon characters ★ Maps ★ Globes ★ Justice ★ Wisdom ★ Multiculturalism ★ Imports ★ Exports ★ Height and weight ★ Legs ★ Legislation ★ Rules ★ Defence ★ Beliefs ★ Laws of the Land ★

Broad Horizons ★ Courses ★ Seminars ★ Foreign affairs ★ Foreign accents ★ Foreign languages ★ Luggage ★ Bulk ★ Mass ★ Mass media ★ Volumes ★ Libraries ★ Academies ★ Encyclopaedias ★ Trips ★ Mind expansion.

PLANETS in capricorn

Read this section if you have your Sun, Moon, Mercury, Venus or Mars in Capricorn.

> ### ARE YOU DOING YOUR CAPRICORN?
> You have amazing ambition and are prepared to work
> to see it fulfilled
> You have older people, or respected role models,
> around you
> You understand that nothing happens in this life
> without self-discipline
> You respect hierarchies and structures

YOUR CAPRICORNIAN SIDE
Ambitious ★ Patient ★ Reliable.

USING CAPRICORN
This sign helps you take the job seriously, and no matter what else may be going on in your life, things will always come back to your job! Your Capricorn Sun, Moon, Mercury, Venus or Mars lends you ambition, organising ability and patience. It makes you resourceful, and in control. It gives you, above all other things, a reality check. It's an aid to accomplishment, no matter how high you aim.

A SENSE OF DIRECTION
What does it take to become a director — of anything? Capricornian qualities seem to lend themselves to leading positions. All the women listed here have shown a strong sense of direction, albeit in

The new astrology for women

radically different fields. Some of them have directed films, others have directed galleries. Some took over campaigns, others directed restaurants and businesses. Wherever you choose to aim your personal ambitions, your Capricornian side will help your sense of *direction* along the way.

Gillian Armstrong — Director, *My Brilliant Career* and many other films —
Mercury and Venus in Capricorn
Betty Churcher — Director, National Gallery of Australia — Sun, Venus and
Mars in Capricorn
Deborah Tabart — Director, Australian Koala Foundation — Sun, Moon and
Mercury in Capricorn
Jane Campion — Director, *The Piano* — Mars in Capricorn
Diane Keaton — Director, *Heroes* — Sun and Venus in Capricorn

 in **capricorn**

You identify with

Organisers ★ Directors ★ Bosses ★ Workaholics ★ Traditionalists ★ Older people ★ People in history books ★

You're an authority on

Age ★ Experience ★ Structures ★ Traditions ★ Taking the controls ★ Handling inhibitions.

Your career Top Ten

You need: 1) A realistic job description; 2) The big picture; 3) Order and organisation; 4) Proper methods; 5) Continual work; 6) High status; 7) Regular promotion or bonuses; 8) Control; 9) Space to delegate to others; 10) A solid professional structure.

Expressing your Capricornian side

If you have the Sun in Capricorn then, somewhere inside you, you contain a Capricorn. If your Capricornian side is well developed, you will probably also have people with Capricorn planets in your life. If this section doesn't accurately reflect what you're all about, you may want to read the chapter headed Walking Your Planets (pages 175–183).

MY BRILLIANT CAREER

Sometimes, looking at the career paths of Capricornian types, it's difficult to imagine how they got here from *there*. If you have a planet in this sign, you stand a better than average chance of pole-vaulting way, way above the place you started from.

There are many Capricorn-influenced women who have rags to riches life stories. And there are those who have seemingly achieved the impossible — gone from actor to director, or from small-town girl to Big City Empress.

The rare combination of frank ambition, combined with the persistence and shrewdness of this sign, often produces women of remarkable achievement. It's the beginnings in the lives of Capricornian types which matter as much as the endings:

Capricornian beginnings

Julia Roberts, Mars in Capricorn A single-parent family in Smyrna, Georgia, then a job selling running shoes in the Athlete's Foot shop in New York.

Diane Keaton, Sun and Venus in Capricorn Her father was a municipal engineer, and she grew up in suburban Santa Ana. She made her way to New York and future fame by winning a scholarship.

Dorothy Parker, Moon in Capricorn A single-parent family in New York (her mother died in Dorothy's infancy) then a job writing captions for photographs in *Vogue* magazine for $10 a week.

Kate Moss, Sun in Capricorn From ordinary London schoolgirl to the goddess of Paris and Milan. Kate was discovered at an airport, coming back from a family holiday.

Edith Piaf, Venus in Capricorn As a teenager, Edith Giovanna Gassion was said to have been sent into the streets to sing for money by her father. She eventually became the most famous singer of her time.

Sharon Stone, Mars in Capricorn Her father is a tool-and-die maker and had a sixth-grade education, and her mother quit school in tenth or eleventh grade, according to Stone. Her first job? Modelling.

 in **capricorn**

What you need

People who are as organised as you are ★ A feeling of control, at home and at work ★ Family, flatmates, lovers or friends who know the form ★ A job where you can truly achieve ★ Friends or contacts in high places.

The Moon in Capricorn home

At heart, you're a home owner, not a renter. You need those firm foundations, and the prospect of throwing everything into a removal truck every few years makes you depressed. You like good, solid construction and like it if you can see the plans. You're modest about your house or flat, but anybody can see the place is the result of amazing hard work on your part. You like a workspace at home, too, and because you so often bring things home with you, will develop one part of your living space as a kind of floating desk or office.

The Moon in Capricorn cook

You try harder if someone amazing is coming to dinner, but you're always organised. You're a cautious cook — you stick to recipes you know, or give everything a run-through before a big dinner party. You're loyal to certain brands and products, and won't switch easily. You have one or two tried and true things which you *always* make, and have a wonderful knack of getting other people to help you, when they're not entirely sure that's what they've been doing!

Expressing your Capricornian side

If you have the Moon in Capricorn then, somewhere inside you, you contain a Capricorn. If your Capricornian side is well developed, you will probably also have people with Capricorn planets in your life. If this section doesn't accurately reflect what you're all about, you may want to read the chapter headed Walking Your Planets (pages 175–183).

GUIDES AND MENTORS

With a Capricorn planet, you like attaching yourself to people who can teach you something. The figure of the guide or mentor is crucial to women with a Capricorn Sun, Moon, Mercury, Venus or Mars. During the course of your life, you may find that it is one remarkable, much older 'destiny figure' who turns things around for you — or you may collect all sorts of guides, mentors, teachers and helpers along the way.

Part of the reason for this is your ruler, Saturn. This planet — and archetype — is the wise elder. When Diane Keaton was unemployed, she nearly gave up on her dreams of an acting career and went back home. It was Grammy Hall, her grandmother, who told her to go back and try again. She did, and the rest is history. Keaton's other mentor, of course, is Woody Allen.

Your guide may be male or female, but this person will inevitably be more experienced than you. You may feel that you have a lot to live up to with them, or that you must test yourself as you struggle to meet their standards or expectations. It is seldom an easy process, but then Saturn, your ruler, has never been known for producing easy learning experiences. For Dorothy Wordsworth, the guide was her brother, the poet William Wordsworth. The singer Ruth Brown, with Venus and Mars in Capricorn, had Duke Ellington — who discovered her. Capricorn Sun Annie Lennox had the older, and more experienced, musical survivor Dave Stewart.

Frequently, Capricornian types have a series of mentors or guides throughout their lives: Cher, a Capricorn Moon, has had several — including Oscar-winning actress Meryl Streep, with whom she worked on *Silkwood*. A few years later, Cher had an Oscar of her own, for *Moonstruck*. Writer, Dorothy Parker, a Capricorn Moon, also had many mentors, including Frank Crowninshield, who chose her as his protégée on both *Vogue* and *Vanity Fair* magazines. Susanna Hoffs, a Capricorn Sun, met ⚥ (formerly known as Prince) — among other mentors — when he wrote the hit 'Manic Monday' for her band, The Bangles.

 **in capricorn**

The Mercury in Capricorn student

Organised — and you'd rather ask for an extension than hand in something that looks sloppy. You work extremely hard and like subjects where there is a right answer and a wrong answer. You can procrastinate, but you're shrewd, too.

Your communication style

Cautious.

Your letters

You never run off the page.

You think like

A wise old woman.

You talk like

A shrewd operator.

The Mercury in Capricorn voice

Patient.

Your tactics

Methodical.

Expressing your Capricornian side

If you have Mercury in Capricorn then, somewhere inside you, you contain a Capricorn. If your Capricornian side is well developed, you will probably also have people with Capricorn planets in your life. If this section doesn't accurately reflect what you're all about, you may want to read the chapter headed Walking Your Planets (pages 175–183).

THE GETTING OF WISDOM

Henry Handel Richardson, a Capricorn Sun, wrote *The Getting of Wisdom* (later made into a film) which perfectly describes part of this sign's legacy to you. Having the Sun, Moon, Mercury, Venus or Mars here puts you on a learning curve. Destiny says you often have to do it the hard way. Your Saturn Return in particular (see 'Your Future') is going to have a major impact on you. Saturn rules Capricorn, so if you have a Capricorn planet, this period, around your late twenties and early thirties, is really going to resonate with you.

Some of you seem to gain strength from hardship. Having suffered, you learn — and fast. Jean Beadle, a Capricorn Sun, was born in 1868. She eventually became a magistrate, but not before an early life which saw her working in a clothing sweatshop, looking after a widowed father and supporting her husband while he was on strike. In later life she came out on the side of both miners and women sweatshop workers, and ended up as part of the *extremely* respectable Perth Establishment.

Dolly Parton came from a large family and real poverty to international fame and enormous wealth. Maggie Tabberer, a Capricorn Mercury-Venus has also done things the hard way: faced with single parenthood, she had no alternative but to work — and work hard. She has created an amazing life from a tough set of options. She is also one of the few ex-models to have created a fashion business empire — and more! Kim Basinger, a Capricorn Moon, had to file for bankruptcy in 1993 after losing an $8.1 million lawsuit — but she shows no signs of giving in, or giving up.

Having a planet in Capricorn does not automatically qualify you for one of those 'We were so poor, we lived in a cardboard box on the middle of the road' types of stories. Nor does it mean that life has to be just one long and difficult haul. On the contrary, what it does do is give you a kind of freedom. When you hit a bad patch, your Capricornian side will feel more comfortable with it, more prepared to handle it — and more interested in the challenge — than any other part of you.

I have often noticed that clients with a Capricorn planet seem to turn struggle into success. It is when they hit a low of insecurity, or real-life practical problems, that the process begins, as their Capricornian side wakes up and rallies round. With a planet here, you are in the unique position of being able to use your hard-won experience to fuel something bigger and altogether better for yourself. Things which leave other women feeling helpless actually become a source of strength for you, and this in itself is a kind of protection, as well as a kind of freedom.

Drew Barrymore, a Capricorn Mars, was a child star and high school dropout who started drinking at the tender age of nine, and taking drugs at the age of ten. After checking in to Rehabilitation, she then starred in *Fifteen and Getting Straight*, a TV drama about drug abuse, and then wrote her own autobiography, *Little Lost Girl*. In 1993 she won a Best Actress Golden Globe. From there to *here*: it's a classic Capricornian saga.

VENUS in capricorn

You love
Serious, experienced lovers ★ Everything that has a place in the past — classical or traditional values or styles, for example ★ Sophisticated or worldly tastes ★ The status that comes from success, or the right kind of social standing ★ Women who are dignified, steady and cool ★ Classic black, brown and navy clothes. The chances of seeing you in a hot pink boob-tube chewing gum? About ten million to one.

You loathe
Himbos and bimbos ★ Trendy-Ugly fashions ★ Dole bludgers ★ Pointless one-night stands.

Expressing your Capricornian side
If you have Venus in Capricorn then, somewhere inside you, you contain a Capricorn. If Your Capricornian side is well developed, you will probably also have people with Capricorn planets in your life. If this section doesn't accurately reflect what you're all about, you may want to read the chapter headed Walking Your Planets (pages 175–183).

UTTERLY PROFESSIONAL
On the job, a Capricorn planet helps you to be utterly professional. The same traits, though — reliability, commitment, common sense

— are also likely to filter through into your private life. There is something wonderfully sensible, earthed and true about Capricornian types, and it is these women who help the rest of the zodiac maintain a sense of standards!

Some women loathe having a planet in Capricorn. They feel it's too boring, too staid or too hungry for success. In the greater astrological tribe, though, Capricorn's values and strengths are desperately needed. Without your mature approach, your love of hard work and your cautious good sense, a great many things would begin to fall apart. Lean harder on your other signs if you have decided you really want something a little more adventurous, dramatic or colourful. Then channel your Capricornian side back in to provide the staying power and common sense you are going to need to get there from here.

 in **Capricorn**

The best revenge is
Sacking someone.

Sporting Capricorn
You like goals that encourage you to achieve your personal best.

Your battle tactics
You can be a really formidable fighter, because you have the patience and persistence of a feline. You formulate a plan in a calculating way, then strike when the timing is absolutely right. You can be remarkably icy when something angers you and you prefer a practical plan every time. Under attack, you defend yourself by using whoever, or whatever, can help you.

What kind of opponent are you?
Dog-eat-dog.

Expressing your Capricornian side
If you have Mars in Capricorn then, somewhere inside you, you contain a Capricorn. If Your Capricornian side is well developed,

you will probably also have people with Capricorn planets in your life. If this section doesn't accurately reflect what you're all about, you may want to read the chapter headed Walking Your Planets (pages 175–183).

WOMEN GROWING OLDER

Because Capricorn is ruled by Saturn, the Lord of Time, the issue of being the right *age* for anything is a particularly big one for you. Ita Buttrose, who is a Capricorn Sun, felt this very keenly when she started her own magazine — *Ita* — for older women. Dorothy Parker, a Capricorn Moon, wrote about this in 1944, in an article titled 'The Middle or Blue Period'. As Parker so succinctly put it: 'It's that word *middle*. Any phrase it touches becomes the label of the frump; middle of the road, middle class, middle age. If only you could leap these dreary decades and land up in the important numbers. There is chic to seventy, elegance to eighty.'

Clients with Capricorn planets have often told me they feel too old when they are young (sixteen going on forty) and then too young when they are growing older. But — here's something to look forward to — Capricornian types grow into their 40+ years far more comfortably than the rest of us seem to.

The writer George Eliot, a Capricorn Moon, published her most famous novels — *The Mill on the Floss* and *Middlemarch* in her forties and fifties. Strangely enough, Capricorn Sun Marlene Dietrich had her biggest hit with a song called 'Too Old to Cut the Mustard' but as an icon in her eighties and nineties, nothing could have been further from the truth.

QUOTABLE CAPRICORN

'I want everything. Not that I want everything right now, but I do want everything.' — **Nastassja Kinski, Mars in Capricorn.**

The job of Women's Affairs Adviser to the South Australian Government took 'a skin like a rhinoceros, the cunning of a fox, diplomacy, a sense of humour and physical strength because if

I collapse they will say it's because I'm a woman'. — **Rosemary Wighton, Sun in Capricorn.**

'I'm happy to age because I think it's appropriate to my personality. Everybody has their age, and I think I'm moving into the age I've always been — which is about 40.' — **Sharon Stone, Mars in Capricorn.**

'I do believe we're never given more than we can deal with. In some other human cycle there was a more fragile me that was spared the bullshit.' — **Julia Roberts, Mars in Capricorn.**

'How on earth can I plead helplessness when I must be so efficient?' (The acceptance of *responsibility* is very much part of the Capricornian story.) — **Barbara Hepworth, Sun and Venus in Capricorn,** a sculptor acclaimed after her death as 'the greatest woman artist in the history of art'.

'My own experience of myself is that I write quite slowly, and painstakingly ... I guess what may be different about me is that I work every day, for long hours. I stay with it.' — **Joyce Carol Oates, Moon in Capricorn.**

'Working nine to five, what a way to make a living ...' — **Dolly Parton, Sun, Mercury and Venus in Capricorn**.

CAPRICORNIAN MYTHS
Tess McGill, *Working Girl*

You don't have to have seen the film to appreciate the Capricornian myth. Tess McGill is a steady, serious secretary whose boss, Katherine Parker, won't give her the respect she deserves. Tess is shrewd enough to come up with great business ideas anyway — and ambitious enough to pursue them when Katherine is away. Jack Trainer is an older mentor figure and, incidentally, her employer's lover. Through him, she finds a way to make her career brilliant after all — and picks up the pieces with precision when the vindictive Katherine Parker returns. It's a classic there-to-here Capricornian story!

A SENSE OF STRUCTURE

Two well-known female sculptors — Barbara Hepworth and Hilarie Mais — also both happen to be Capricorn Suns. I've also known Capricorn-influenced osteopaths and spinal injury nurses. Stones and bones, which give us our structure in life, have a deep connection with Capricorn. With this sign, there is a great respect for sturdy structures which have stood the test of time. Other parts of you may be more maverick than this, but your Capricornian side wants to know that there is some semblance of order out there; that things are just as they should be.

Having a planet in this sign helps you to understand hierarchies. Not only professional hierarchies, but also the social strata around you. Without trying too hard, you will probably understand where everyone fits in just by looking at them. Women I have known with a strongly developed Capricornian side who move through the Establishment, or the glitterati, have an instinct for the social pecking order, and social propriety. You not only know what's what, you also know who's who. Most of you are determined to respect that structure, and some of you may become a part of it. Others stay on the outside, but still keep a shrewd eye on the form.

SERIOUS YOUNG INSECTS

You may have planets in other signs which are lighter or wackier. Having a Capricornian side, though, means having a distinctly serious side. This sign slows you down and steadies you. You can bring this out whenever you need to — to prove to others that you mean business, to make the right impression on more conservative people, or to persuade those around that order must be restored.

The flipside of occasionally being a serious young insect is that it can tip you over into serious pessimism — negative thinking. Being cautious, careful, controlled and seeing the hard realities, not the champagne corks, is okay in proportion. However, I have seen enough Capricorn-influenced women dropping in for chart readings over the years to realise that this famous propensity for seriousness can also lead to depression and worry.

If you have the Sun, Moon, Mercury, Venus or Mars in other signs, you can use them to help lift yourself out of the Capricornian glooms when you need to. You may like to re-read those sections, and make an effort to take the planets in those signs for a walk when your Capricorn planets become too much. It's quite common for women with a Capricorn planet to also have something in

Sagittarius or Aquarius, for example: these signs will push the humour back in and help you to adjust things.

'I'm prone to periods of unhappiness,' Cher (a Capricorn Moon) told an interviewer once. 'I'm not an extrovert, I'm quite introverted and I can be really morose. Not for long periods but sporadically.' She leans hard on her more flippant, forever-young Gemini Venus to get herself out of those kinds of doldrums.

Other Capricorn-influenced babes who were prone to bleakness include Dorothy Parker and Janis Joplin. The passage of time seems to make it easier for you to handle and understand your serious side. Just don't take it too seriously ...

THE CLASSIC CAPRICORN

Cindy Crawford

Born on 20th February 1966, Cindy Crawford has Venus in Capricorn. This is her story:

A sense of direction 'I see myself as the president of a company that owns a product, Cindy Crawford, that everybody wants,' she says.

My Brilliant Career Cindy's father worked at various times in a pizza parlour, as an electrician and as a glazier. He separated from his wife when Cindy was in high school. Her first job? Detasseling corn in fields during the school holidays. Her first ambition? Becoming American President.

Guides and mentors Richard Gere, her ex-husband, has been one of several teacher figures. Commenting on the relationship after it began, photographer Herb Ritts said, 'He's changed her. He's a mature, intelligent guy. Anybody older, you learn if you're open to it.' Of the marriage, Cindy has said, 'I did learn a lot. I also learned that I didn't know as much as I thought I knew.'

The getting of wisdom Cindy's early life saw the death of her younger brother from leukaemia, and her parents' separation. These experiences, and more, seem to have grounded Crawford and given her a more serious set of values.

Utterly professional 'A model's career is like an athlete's,' Cindy says. 'You've got ten years to make it.'

Women growing older 'When I start seeing wrinkles and things drop, I want to have enough other interesting things going on that it doesn't matter,' she told an interviewer. 'When I'm 40 I won't be Cindy Crawford any more in terms of this strange icon-thing that happened.'

A sense of structure 'If I'm giving 100 percent, I expect everyone else to,' she says.

Serious young insects Asked by British *Vogue* if she was happy, Crawford replied, 'Sometimes. Yes, I think I have a good life. I don't expect to be happy all the time. Life is hard. But I feel loved, and have good friends.'

CAPRICORNIAN SYMBOLS

With the Sun, Moon, Mercury, Venus or Mars in Capricorn, you may find you tune in to some of these symbols, themes and ideas:

Saturn ★ Ten ★ Ambition ★ Ice ★ Structure ★ Stone ★ Rock ★ Sculpture ★ Bones ★ Skeletons ★ Pyramids ★ Directors ★ Bosses ★ Employers ★ Age ★ Experience ★ Old age ★ Senior citizens ★ Mentors ★ Guides ★ Tradition ★ Classics ★ Organisation ★ Patience ★ Caution ★ Fear ★ Black humour ★ Watches ★ Clocks ★ Time ★ Calendars ★ Goats ★ Professionals ★ Foundations ★ Industry ★ Maturity ★ Commitment ★ Waiting rooms ★ Colds ★ Cold temperatures ★ Consistency ★ Discipline ★ Ladders ★ Timing ★ Earth ★ Work ★ Mountains.

PLANETS in aquarius

Read this section if you have your Sun, Moon, Mercury, Venus or Mars in Aquarius.

YOUR AQUARIAN SIDE

Unusual ★ Independent ★ Well-intentioned.

USING AQUARIUS

Your Sun, Moon, Mercury, Venus or Mars in Aquarius is an exciting option to have in your astro-package. This side of you will help you to break new ground, explore some highly experimental territory and convince all those around you that you are part-genius, part-visionary. Your Aquarian side is utterly original and prefers to do its own thing. Make the most of this side of you whenever you need to excel professionally — it is in the nature of Aquarius to have sudden insights and to make innovations and discoveries which will help you to stand out from the pack. It is the things which are most unique about you — even if they are a little eccentric — which you need to feel confident enough to express.

UTTERLY INDIVIDUAL

Without Aquarius, women would not have had feminism. But this sign is linked to highly individual viewpoints of all kinds. If you have planets in Aquarius you are, above all, an extreme individualist. Any debate or discussion about social change or 'the future' has to have you somewhere in the middle of it, yet as it is in the nature of the sign to be answerable only to itself, there will be times when you are utterly out on your own. It is your Aquarius planets which strive for something which is brilliantly clear, honest and true — but principally *for you*. There are women with Aquarius planets who are radical conservatives, and there are women with Aquarius planets who are radical radicals.

For many women with Aquarius planets, the decision to be their own woman, or follow their own unique course is easy. Inside, they know they are right. Life only becomes difficult when eyebrows are raised, objections are made and people become threatened.

Aquarius is a sign that often makes people feel uncertain, or unsafe. One of the biggest challenges for you is finding a way to accommodate your own unique ideas, opinions, life and values in a way that other people can accept. Most of the time, this live and let live approach will work successfully. However, it is in the nature of this, the maverick eleventh sign, to be stubborn. Aquarius — like Leo, Taurus and Scorpio — is fixed. The freedom that you crave to be yourself, and the changes and new ideas that you long for may never happen unless you can find some kind of bridge that will lead you to the rest of the population. Your Aquarian side absolutely detests compromising and faking it, smiling politely and falling into line. But a small amount of this social oil — even a token gesture — will be necessary if your intense individuality is going to be allowed to breathe.

SUN in aquarius

You identify with

Eccentrics ★ Rebels ★ Visionaries ★ Radicals ★ Humanitarians ★ Renegades ★ Innovators.

You're an authority on

Friendship ★ Networking ★ New ideas ★ Your own opinions ★ The future ★ A better world.

Your career Top Ten

You need: 1) Freedom to be eccentric; 2) A flexible routine — or no routine; 3) Special rewards for your flashes of genius; 4) An ethical workplace; 5) Honest work relationships; 6) Your own dress code; 7) Long lunches with friends; 8) An Apple Newton or IBM Thinkpad; 9) Fabulous equipment; 10) A measure of craziness.

Expressing your Aquarian side

If you have the Sun in Aquarius then, somewhere inside you, you contain a Aquarius. If your Aquarian side is well developed, you will probably also have people with Aquarius planets in your life. If this section doesn't accurately reflect what you're all about, you may want to read the chapter headed Walking Your Planets (pages 175–183).

AHEAD OF YOUR TIME

I have always liked the story of Marjorie Lawrence, an Australian soprano who was born in 1907 with the Sun, Mercury and Venus in Aquarius. Crippled in her thirties, she always appeared in operas sitting down on a chair. She made history by once going on stage on horseback, and in 1949 launched the career of an Aboriginal tenor, Harold Blair. Several decades before we even thought of having a Year of Indigenous People or a Year of the Disabled, Marjorie Lawrence was living the life. And living it to the full.

Your Aquarian side, incidentally, is always living in the future. Sometimes it cannot resist looking into it, either. (If you bought this book, your Aquarius planets may have to take full responsibility: this sign rules astrology.) Mostly, though, Aquarius planets are always a few decades ahead, and quite unknowingly.

My friend Prue has an Aquarius Sun and Mars. She sniffs trends about three years before they happen. Aquarius planets are very useful if you are in a career where you must be sensitive to the *Zeitgeist*, the spirit of the time, or the invisible movements, trends and preferences that drive us all on. Your Aquarian side will 'get' things before the rest of the population even knows they are desirable. Bear that in mind that sometimes you will be *too* far ahead of your time. When magazine editor Ita Buttrose helped install a *male* nude centrefold in *Cleo* magazine in the 1970s, she was actually establishing a radical tradition that would still be common in women's magazines twenty years later. If there is anything your Aquarian side is particularly good at doing, it is establishing these kinds of 'radical traditions'. You can do it in your home, in your personal life, at work or at play.

IN A MAJORITY OF ONE

A good definition of eccentric. At this point I am going to have to involve Dame Edna Everage in the discussion. Her male alter ego, Barry Humphries, is an Aquarius Sun. But Barry has channelled pure Aquarius through his beloved Dame. There is no other titled, gladioli-waving, transsexual celebrity on television apart from her. In fact, although I have no idea when Dame Edna was 'born' I am so convinced she has Aquarius planets I have included her as the Mythical Aquarius in this section.

On to other majorities of one: a nineteen-year-old pianist who also has wild hair, a peculiar operatic voice, an obsession with the Bront's and a strange habit of dancing around woods in a red leotard. It's not unusual for Aquarius planets to show themselves in adolescence, when general strangeness and rebellion is virtually expected: maybe that's why Kate Bush, with her Aquarius Moon, affected the world so profoundly. Another majority of one is even more eccentric. Joyce Mayne has been a professional tap dancer (on roller skates), a writer, a television personality, an astrologer, a horse racing tipster and — her best-known achievement — Director of Joyce Mayne Retailers. One more majority of one: an outspoken Aboriginal woman with a row of studs in her ears and a pair of custom-made running shoes designed in the colours of her native flag. I like Cathy Freeman's surname, too — it couldn't be more Aquarian if destiny had chosen it!

THE SOLO JOURNEY

The strongly Aquarian woman often literally takes a solo journey — living by herself, travelling by herself, working by herself or taking a lone stand. Kay Cottee — with the Sun, Mercury and Venus in

Aquarius — sailed solo, non-stop and unassisted around the world. Your Aquarian side will often have you travelling the same way, either short-term or long-term. Sometimes your Aquarian side will make this choice quite consciously. You follow the single life, or the solo path, because your strong need for freedom and independence allows you to see that happiness is not necessarily about clinging to the clan (or a man) indefinitely. Sometimes your Aquarius planets will put you on this solo voyage when you would honestly prefer not to take it. Repeatedly, I have heard this from women with Aquarius planets: whether they choose time alone, or apart, or whether they have it forced upon them, solitude is always a route to discovery.

WOMEN WHO DON'T

Your Aquarian side expresses itself most strongly through what you don't do. If you're Jocelynne Scutt, a Moon Aquarius, then you *don't* accept honours from the monarchy. If you're Sandie Shaw, a Mars Aquarius, then you *don't* wear shoes. Here are some other Aquarian refusals I've jotted down over the years (some of them still make me laugh):

Not driving	Not having a TV set
Not eating meat	Not carrying change
Not collecting the mail	Not cooking
Not using washing-up liquid	Not wearing a watch
Not wearing underwear	Not having sex
Not wearing lace-up shoes	Not paying parking fines
Not wearing anything red	Not admitting to being female

The things that your Aquarian side actually *does* do are probably just as personalised. I know an Aquarian type who carries an alarm clock in her handbag — and no, she is not a dotty old lady. Another Aquarius Sun washes her underwear by wearing it in the shower, and I know an Aquarius Mercury who pretends to be the RSPCA when people she doesn't know ring her up!

THE ISSUE OF CHANGE

Your Aquarian side can be quite perverse. It can desire change when hardly anybody else sees the need for it, and absolutely *refuse* to change if there is a sense that you are being pressured or forced. You are a reformer at the same time that you are quite a stubborn defender of your own position. Once you have made up your mind to be an Aboriginal supporter, a Republican, an Anti-Republican, a Radical Celibate or a member of the Flat Earth Society ... well, that's it. Having placed your vote on Our Common Future, you are unlikely to allow yourself to be forced into an alternative position.

You may also find this happening to you: you turn sharp right (or left, or sideways) and then other people start following you, whereupon you swing around dramatically in another direction. I really believe this is not conscious perversity. Your Aquarius planets often seem to be responding to some mysterious signal the rest of us cannot see or hear. And it's impossible to resist it.

Aquarian feminism

Feminism is the best example of that mysterious Aquarian perversity. Some of you with planets here are absolutely feminists of the Old School. Some of you think many of the feminists got it wrong. Mostly, women with Aquarius planets do pick up on the basic aspects of feminism — freedom and independence are really what it's about, and Aquarius craves these. Think of Geena Davis (Mercury in Aquarius) in *Thelma and Louise*. Remember the perversity, though? You'll find just as many fellow Aquarian types who will happily argue about the finer points until one of you falls over. Anyway, here's the contingent:

Germaine Greer — Sun in Aquarius
Gloria Steinem — Venus in Aquarius
Anne Summers — Moon and Mars in Aquarius
Carmen Callil — Moon in Aquarius
Ann Sherry — Sun in Aquarius
Emily Bennett — Sun in Aquarius
Louisa Lawson — Sun in Aquarius
Georgina Sweet — Sun in Aquarius
Simone de Beauvoir — Venus in Aquarius
Betty Friedan — Sun and Mercury in Aquarius
Erica Jong — Venus in Aquarius

 in aquarius

What you need

A room of your own ★ Freedom ★ Machines that go *ping* ★ Strange hobbies ★ Your funny little ways ★ Independence ★ Mad clothes ★ Men who treat you as an equal — or superior.

The Moon in Aquarius home

You have the most peculiar domestic set-up in the zodiac. Even Aquarius Moon homes which appear to be quite normal are based around something very … slightly … odd. It's hard to generalise about your house or flat, because this sign is so intensely individual. However — whatever your friends or family have, you don't want. Whatever the home and lifestyle shows tell you to do, you won't. The basic rule with the Aquarian home is that you need lots of space to yourself, and freedom to come and go.

The Moon in Aquarius cook

You tend to shock people on a regular basis, either because your kitchen set-up is not what they expected, or because you produce food on the table which they frankly hadn't dreamed of seeing *even* under the effect of hallucinatory drugs. You can be a shockingly good, or shockingly awful, cook. But you do like new gadgets and whizzy equipment that looks like it should be in the galley of the Star Ship *Enterprise*.

Expressing your Aquarian side

If you have the Moon in Aquarius then, somewhere inside you, you contain an Aquarius. If your Aquarian side is well developed, you will probably have people with Aquarius planets in your life. If this section doesn't accurately reflect what you're all about, you may want to read the chapter headed Walking Your Planets (pages 175–183).

EXPERIMENTAL THINKERS

Let me tell you: I've been on the Internet and it's crawling with Aquarian types. This sign leads you where all the experiments and new ideas are forming. That's why women with Aquarius planets in the 1920s and 1930s headed straight for Psychology and Anthropology, and why today you'll be lurking around the Self Help shelves of the bookshop (new theories? brilliant!) the New Age cafes, the Computer Superstores or the Science section in the library.

Your Aquarius planets reach into the atmosphere and pick out whatever is strange, new — even shocking — and definitely 'out there'. Most of women behind the great discoveries and developments have an Aquarius planet — or Uranus, its ruler — dominating their chart. Ada Byron, the inventor of the first mechanical calculator (and the Godmother of the computer) had Uranus, the ruler of Aquarius, *everywhere* in her horoscope. It's natural for you to be different, and to innovate wherever you can. Frequently, you'll dive into new technology to be able to do your own thing. It's not so much the wires and the bytes that are sexy to your Aquarian side, it's the fabulous things they can do.

If you have planets in this sign, you may become a regular Lieutenant Uhura or ignore the technical bits and leap straight into playtime. Incidentally, your Aquarian brothers tend to be into the classical 'male' sciences (and science-fiction) side of things. You may do this, but on the whole I have found Aquarius-influenced women prefer the 'female', people-oriented sciences — Psychology and Sociology . Still, anything with a hypothesis, an experiment and a conclusion will probably do!

 in **aquarius**

The Mercury in Aquarius student
Original ★ Subject to flashes of brilliance and Eureka!-styled lightbulbs over the head ★ Good with computers ★ Not good with stuffy, boring or overly bossy teachers.

Your communication style
Unique.

Your letters
Strange and with handwriting that is unmistakeably you.

You think like
A mad genius.

You talk like
A mad genius.

The Mercury in Aquarius voice
One of a kind.

Your tactics
You like to shock.

Expressing your Aquarian side
If you have Mercury in Aquarius then, somewhere inside you, you contain an Aquarius. If your Aquarian side is well developed, you will probably also have people with Aquarius planets in your life. If this section doesn't accurately reflect what you're all about, you may want to read the chapter headed Walking Your Planets (pages 175–183).

TOTAL FREEDOM
I have known several women involved with Amnesty International who were February Sun Aquarians. The principle of freedom is part of what you are all about. Some of you will push for this freedom for other people — sometimes for other living things. Other Aquarius-influenced women tend to concentrate on their own personal freedom and independence. Janis Joplin (Aquarius Mercury and Venus) sang 'Freedom's just another word for nothing left to lose', which sums it up.

Women with Aquarius planets tend to worry when things look unfair — when one group is treated in a second-rate way because of their appearance, race, class, sex or even their species. Your Aquarian side becomes horrified at the idea of anything being trapped or confined or hampered. There are many Aquarius-influenced feminists precisely because the pre-Pankhurst female was the most obviously trapped species in the world. As feminism swings backwards and forwards, so do its Aquarian supporters. But there are many women with Aquarius planets who battle racism and apartheid for exactly the same reason — a loathing of any situation which *forces* those concerned into accepting limitations, rules and barriers. Something about that seems to make Aquarius itch. Your Aquarian side will often ask: 'Why can't I?' and 'Why shouldn't they?' and 'What's stopping us?' Your Aquarian side has a very good track record in the field of social change, by the way: This sign is remarkably well represented in the ANC, in UNESCO, in the Civil Rights movement and in the Red Cross. This side of you is concerned with *choice*. On a personal level, you reserve the right to choose your options, and where others are concerned you also tend to feel their right to a choice particularly strongly. This basic respect for freedom is one of the reasons why Aquarius-influenced women have become so strongly associated with humanitarianism. The late Princess Diana had the Moon in Aquarius. On one level she demanded to *choose* her royal 'good causes' and on another level, she gravitated towards AIDS patients, the homeless and women living with domestic violence — people who appeared to have no choices or basic freedoms.

 **in aquarius**

You love

New ideas ★ Eccentric people ★ Freedom ★ Independence ★ Unique clothes or art ★ Original men ★ Unusual women ★ Being your own person ★ Shocking boring or stuffy people ★ Coming up with your own theories ★ Tailoring your job to suit yourself ★ Being alone ★ Being with a loose group of friends ★ Being surprised ★ Surprising others ★ The New Age ★ Playing with hi-tech buttons ★ Tapping into the future ★ Radical options for society.

You loathe

Rules ★ Routines ★ Limits ★ Ruts ★ Restrictions ★ Pointless traditions ★ Boredom ★ Stale ideas.

Expressing your Aquarian side

If you have Venus in Aquarius then, somewhere inside you, you contain an Aquarius. If your Aquarian side is well developed, you will probably also have people with Aquarius planets in your life. If this section doesn't accurately reflect what you're all about, you may want to read the chapter headed Walking Your Planets (pages 175–183).

BORN TO SHOCK

Even when you don't mean to, you end up leaving all around you reaching for the brandy and groping for a chair. It is almost a rule with Aquarius-influenced women. You *will* shock your family or friends one day, and perhaps for quite a few days in the future after that. The word 'suddenly' or the phrase 'out of the blue' will make a lot of sense in the context of your life.

Your Aquarian side will encourage the most surprising decisions, the most unlikely possibilities and, sometimes, the most shockingly sudden events. Uranus, your ruler, is associated with lightning. If you have ever watched a storm in its entirety, you will have seen something of your Aquarian side played out in the sky. Lightning may literally strike, not just once, but several times, in your own life and times. In a word, you get zapped. There will also be occasions when things do not happen *to you*, but you seem to happen to *them*. After a few decades of being around you, I believe those who know you well will hardly be surprised at what you do or say any more. 'You've decided to give yourself up to an inter-galactic alien breeding scheme? How wonderful for you.'

 in **aquarius**

The best revenge is

Expect it when you least expect it.

Sporting Aquarius

You don't look like anyone else on the team.

Your battle tactics

You surprise people ★ Your ploys are to strike when they have been lulled into a false sense of security or to do something really weird ★ There's a refusal to conform ★ Aquarian babes don't play by the rules of the game — you make up your own ★ You're stubborn ★ You can be downright peculiar ★ There's lightning around when you go into battle.

What kind of opponent are you?

Perverse.

Expressing your Aquarian side

If you have Mars in Aquarius then, somewhere inside you, you contain an Aquarius. If your Aquarian side is well developed, you will probably also have people with Aquarius planets in your life. If this section doesn't accurately reflect what you're all about, you may want to read the chapter headed Walking Your Planets (pages 175–183).

AQUARIAN MYTHS

Dame Edna Everage

Dame Edna Everage is a man. She was born, as Barry Humphries, on 17th February 1934, giving her an Aquarius Sun and Venus. She shocks her audience by refusing to let celebrities like Jane Fonda into the building, and arranging booby traps for minor members of the Royal Family. She is, for obvious reasons, in a majority of one. She is an Australian in England, a man in a woman's frock, a superstar in the suburbs, and a housewife on prime-time television. She appears to have jettisoned her husband Norm long ago in her quest for independence, and — apart from her bridesmaid, Madge — defiantly travels solo. She was certainly 30 years ahead of Priscilla, Queen of the Desert!

ON THE OUTSIDE

The writer Janet Frame has an Aquarius Mars, and describes the traditional feeling of loneliness associated with this planet in many of her books. For her, it came partly from being an outsider. With frizzy red hair and bad teeth — and a prodigious talent — she never really felt at home during her youth in New Zealand. She felt even less at home when she was diagnosed as mentally ill — never conventional enough to fit in with the 'sane' world, but never truly loopy enough to be mad.

Her example is extreme, but your Aquarius planets may well show you this classic scenario: everyone seems to be speaking one language or sharing one reality and you don't understand, or fit into, any of it. Your Aquarius planets will tend to guide you into situations where you are separated from the majority in a very clear way. Here are some examples:

Country mouse in the city
Beautiful in a family of plain sisters and brothers
Dyslexic at school
Black in a white legal firm
Lesbian in a straight family
Punk in a religious family
Stranger in a strange land

From time to time, your Aquarian side will place you firmly, but gently, in a world where you are immediately and obviously quite different. It may help to know that there are other women wandering around with an Aquarius Sun, Moon, Mercury, Venus or Mars who have felt their outsider status just as strongly. The irony of all this? You love having friends and belonging to a loose tribe or network. With your fair, friendly style, a cool and easy popularity among a large and casual series of connections is ensured. It's just that, from time to time, you really will be stuck on the outside looking in, either because you have chosen that role, or because it has been chosen for you by what the Ancients called Fate.

By the way, so many astrologers have planet in Aquarius that it's not surprising that ancient art/science has been on the outer for so long. Now that we are crawling into The Age of Aquarius, astrology is now decidedly in, of course — but it may never be totally accepted.

If your Aquarian side is strongly developed, you won't care. And just think of the benefits — having a planet here gives you a natural, instinctive feeling for stargazing. My friends Emma and Sophie, in London and Sydney respectively, are the best non-astrologers I know. Both have planets in Aquarius.

THE CLASSIC AQUARIUS

Germaine Greer

Possessing more Aquarian factors in her chart than most women will ever be born with, Germaine Greer is a brilliant example of Aquarian womanhood.

Utterly individual Even seventies feminists who revere Greer can't agree with all her opinions.

Ahead of her time Around a decade after *The Female Eunuch*, England found its first female PM.

In a majority of one Australian in England. An academic woman in sixties Australia!

The solo journey Apart from her housekeeper, Greer apparently still lives alone. Her position on feminism has also isolated her from both sides!

Women who don't She didn't wear a bra, for a start.

The issue of change Strangely enough, Germaine Greer literally wrote about the Change in her book on menopause.

Experimental thinking *The Female Eunuch* is acknowledged as the start of late twentieth-century women's liberation.

Born to shock Did *you* burn your bra or attempt to taste your own menstrual blood?

Total freedom The name of the cause that made Greer famous is women's *liberation*, above all other things.

AQUARIAN SYMBOLS

If you have planets in Aquarius, these keywords, ideas and concepts may turn up from time to time. If this planet is strongly influencing your horoscope, your life and times may bounce around these themes with a strange kind of regularity.

Lightning ★ Electricity ★ Inventors ★ Innovation ★ Freedom ★ Liberation ★ Uranus ★ Eleven ★ Friends ★ Groups ★ Tribes ★

Clubs ★ Associations ★ Madness ★ Wires ★ Shocks ★ Eccentrics ★ Change ★ Choice ★ Rights ★ Radicals ★ Rebels ★ Outsiders ★ Genius ★ Invention ★ Originals ★ Anarchy ★ Perversity ★ Computers ★ Technology ★ Science ★ Psychology ★ Anthropology ★ Zoology ★ Experiments ★ Hypotheses ★ Pandora ★ Prometheus ★ Water-bearers ★ Legs ★ Limbs ★ Waves ★ New Age ★ New Men ★ New Feminism ★ Causes ★ Struggles ★ Outcasts ★ Equality ★ Avante-garde ★ Campaigns ★ Astrology ★ Air ★ Circulation ★ Brilliance ★ The Star ★ Futures ★ Tomorrow ★ Extremists ★ Revolutionaries ★ Humanitarianism ★ Surprises ★ Trailblazers.

PLANETS in pisces

Read this section if you have your Sun, Moon, Mercury, Venus or Mars in Pisces.

ARE YOU DOING YOUR PISCES?

You escape from the world through poetry, music, art, film or literature

You listen to your dreams and take them seriously

You regularly serve huge dollops of sympathy, sensitivity and soul — to people or animals

You're in touch with something spiritual, special, spooky, saintly or unseen

---

YOUR PISCEAN SIDE

Sensitive ★ Imaginative ★ Kind.

USING PISCES

Your Sun, Moon, Mercury, Venus or Mars in Pisces helps your visual imagination. You can use this in your career, but also when you are picturing personal goals. Pisces planets help the art of positive visualisation, and many women who are influenced by this sign seem to do it quite instinctively. In many ways, you don't use Pisces at all — it just washes over you. But your understanding of life will deepen as a result of having this sign in your chart. To begin with, you will always understand compassion better than the rest of us ...

RESCUE MISSIONS

Pisces rules the feet in astrology and you put yourself in other people's shoes. As a result you're hopelessly sentimental and easily moved and are frequently involved in helping others. The traditional Church is important to many Piscean-influenced women, and so are alternative religions and philosophies. You also identify with a sense of oneness with us all. It took a Pisces Mercury — Chaka Khan — to sing 'I'm Every Woman'. Then there are those of you who are neither Christian nor Buddhist, but unable to be anything but selfless.

This side of Pisces comes from your ruler, Neptune, which dissolves boundaries and increases your sensitivity. You 'just know' what is going on in other people's heads, or behind an animal's eyes and you really *feel* for them. The leap of the imagination that is required to identify with all creatures great and small is part of the Piscean package. Women with Pisces planets do seem to have a special regard for other creatures — even dinosaurs! It was Doris Day (Pisces Mercury) who said, 'It's a crime to kill an animal to make a fur coat.' Pisces Sun Cindy Crawford said she'd rather go naked than wear fur. Penny Figgis, Vice President of the Australian Conservation Foundation, is a triple Pisces. Jane Goodall, who famously lived with chimpanzees in Gombe, Nigeria, is a Pisces Mercury. Joy Adamson, who shared her life with lions, is a Pisces Venus. The Pisces Sun poet Pam Ayres often writes about animals — usually in the first person!

SUN in pisces

You identify with

Dreamers ★ Artists ★ Musicians ★ Photographers ★ Saints ★ Mystics ★ Fictional characters ★ Actors ★ Martyrs ★ Poets ★ Healers.

You're an authority on

The human condition ★ Animals ★ Dreams ★ Imagination ★ Mysteries ★ The Arts ★ Sacrifice.

Your career Top Ten

You need: 1) A space and a place to dream alone; 2) A charity collection tin on the front desk; 3) Low pressure — or better still, no pressure; 4) A gentle atmosphere; 5) Subdued lighting; 6) Flexible hours so that you can escape when you have to; 7) Sensitive handling of sick leave or holidays; 8) Something to draw and doodle on; 9) Rewards for your imagination; 10) Birds on the windowsill, or a stray animal to feed.

Expressing your Piscean side

If you have the Sun in Pisces then, somewhere inside you, you contain a Pisces. If your Piscean side is well developed, you will probably also have people with Pisces planets in your life. If this section doesn't accurately reflect what you're all about, you may want to read the chapter headed Walking Your Planets (pages 175–183).

FANTASY AND REALITY

Your Piscean side does not see the real world as other people see it. This may be literal — your eyesight may be out — but the distortion can also take place behind your eyes, and there are many Pisces-influenced women who have perfect eyesight but enjoy a kind of coloured slide show going on behind each iris!

The pictures or films running in your head can be remarkably useful if you are in a field where imagination is necessary. If you are working in a strictly practical job, and surrounded by strictly practical people in your private life, you may need consciously to find a place, and a space to dream and escape. If not, Pisces may help you to excuse yourself from practical reality by inviting vagueness, lateness or daydreaming. At its most extreme, this 'slipping away' syndrome can result in drug or alcohol dependency for some — and even prescribed drugs can fall into this category.

Drugs and alcohol typically produce one of two polarised reactions from strongly Piscean women. Some of you avoid them because of the alarming effect they have — the rest of you enjoy them in moderation, and love the effect, as the Piscean inner cinema or slide show becomes more colourful. I have had many Sun, Moon, Mercury, Venus or Mars clients wandering through the office who have a penchant for serious vodka, marijuana, or valium.

Betty Ford was born with both the Moon and Venus in Pisces. There are just as many who are terrified of drugs or alcohol and will not use them on these grounds: the inner cinema just becomes too extreme. A friend of mine, an artist and triple Pisces, was given painkillers once and hallucinated so wildly that she imagined sandwiches on a plate that did not exist!

If you have a Pisces planet, you may already have found ways to incorporate fantasy into your reality. You may discover this by losing yourself in photography, films, music, art or fantasy. Perhaps you enjoy diving into a swimming pool or gazing at fish through a glass mask. Or you may have found a professional or after-hours pursuit which allows you to see pictures in your head or chase — quite literally — a 'fantasy' career.

Pisces planets have a reputation for being elastic with the truth. When others demand the 'bare facts' or 'raw truth' something in you just wants to soften the story or even slip away altogether. The classic vagueness — and sometimes quite conscious evasiveness — that surrounds Pisces is a pretty mild 'wobble' on reality. When your unconscious is saying, 'Enough reality already, someone get me out of here!' it takes a great deal of insight to see what is actually going on. This Piscean part of you is especially clever with white lies, sometimes for the highest possible motives.

Something most women with a Pisces Sun, Moon, Mercury, Venus or Mars must face is this: at some point your reality will clash with other people's. For Carrie Fisher (Pisces Mars), Billie Holiday (Pisces Mercury, Venus, Mars) and Drew Barrymore (Pisces Sun, Venus) this played itself out in addiction problems — they were so addicted to their own inner cinemas, and the substances that created them, that those in the real world considered they needed treatment. Neptune, the ruler of Pisces, is a common signifier in the charts of women who have drugs or alcohol in their lives.

Above all, perhaps, a Pisces planet gives you enormous sensitivity — to everyday atmospheres, but also to the pain or problems in the world around you. In much the same way that sensitive skin is layered with cream and protected by cotton wool, a Pisces-influenced woman needs to find some kind of layer and protection against the pain in the outside world. Finding a sense of meaning, or a sense of spirituality, will become increasingly important as you go through life. In common with those who have Sagittarius planets, you cannot bear to live in a void.

The album 'Raw Like Sushi' by singer Neneh Cherry (Pisces Sun, Mercury and Mars) pretty much sums up your sensitivity. For some of you, this will develop into a galloping psychic awareness. For others, it will result in these familiar Piscean experiences:

'I forget who I am for a few minutes. I actually seem to get inside the other person's head.' (Christine, Pisces Venus)

'I get into conversations and find myself picking up on things that the other person hasn't mentioned, but are uppermost in their mind.' (Gwynn, Pisces Sun)

 **in pisces**

What you need

Music ★ Poems ★ Romance ★ Art ★ Escapes ★ Dreams ★ Psychic friends ★ Creative interests ★ People or animals to care for ★ Plenty of time ★ Fantasy ★ No pressure.

The Moon in Pisces home

Your creative efforts, or those of artists or photographers you admire, will be important features of your house or flat. Some of you may have books on spiritual matters on the shelves. Other books will reflect your favourite escapist interests. You like whimsical bits and pieces around you, too. You definitely need fantasy in your reality! The Pisces Moon home is usually decorated in an inspired and imaginative way. If you can, you'll live near water, or have a pool or pond. All creatures great and small — in the garden, or indoors, will make a difference to you.

The Moon in Pisces cook

If you're okay about wine and spirits, you'll either throw them into the recipe, or have a glass while you cook. Those of you who are teetotallers (and there are a few) will still pour in essences, oils and vinegars — this sign rules liquids. At best, you are the classic 'hunch' cook, at worst, you are chaotic and prone to losing vital ingredients — like the cutlery. You enjoy having music playing in the background while you clean or cook, too. You're inspired by glossy food illustrations.

Expressing your Piscean side

If you have the Moon in Pisces then, somewhere inside you, you contain a Pisces. If your Piscean side is well developed, you will probably also have people with Pisces planets in your life. If this section doesn't accurately reflect what you're all about, you may want to read the chapter headed Walking Your Planets (pages 175–183).

PISCEAN CHILDHOODS

Your Piscean side probably found a place to breathe in your childhood, above all other times in your life. At an age when fairy tales are read aloud, picture books seem true, pets are cared for and imaginary friends made up, Pisces-influenced little girls seem quite well catered for. There is also the familiar world of Doctors and Nurses (rescuing people, dolls and animals) and the fantasy world of the Tooth Fairy, Santa Claus and the Easter Bunny.

If you feel your childhood wasn't that colourful or happy, your Piscean side may have helped you escape by encouraging daydreams or long wishing sessions. The inner life of a Piscean-influenced child is often very rich, and can sometimes make an effective substitute for reality. Women with Pisces planets have passed on these childhood experiences as particularly important and special to them:

Imaginary friends
Reading books to escape sadness
Believing in fictional or imaginary characters
Vivid dreams — still remembered today
Raising money for charities
Animal friends who are almost human
Dressing up dogs and cats
Curiosity about God and heaven
Creating outfits from the dressing-up box
Finger painting
Nonsense rhymes

 **in pisces**

The Mercury in Pisces student

Dreamy ★ Imaginative ★ Good at making up excuses ★ Vague with facts or figures ★ Artistic ★ Brilliant at mimicking the teachers or other kids ★ An ability to soak up favourite subjects without being conscious of it.

Your communication style

Sympathetic.

Your letters

Works of fiction, prose or poetry!

You think like

A psychic.

You talk like

The person you're talking to.

The Mercury in Pisces voice

Gentle.

Your tactics

Dodgy.

Expressing your Piscean side

If you have Mercury in Pisces then, somewhere inside you, you contain a Pisces. If your Piscean side is well developed, you will probably also have people with Pisces planets in your life. If this section doesn't accurately reflect what you're all about, you may want to read the chapter headed Walking Your Planets (pages 175–183).

SAVIOURS AND VICTIMS

If you have a planet in Pisces, then at various times in your life you will feel moved to save, help or rescue people whom you see as victims. Identifying with all that is vulnerable, suffering, in trouble or defenceless in the world is a common Piscean experience. Writer Jilly Cooper has the Sun in Pisces and once told a magazine, 'I'm a typical Pisces: terribly disorganised, and I cry at anything. I'd make a terrible nurse as I can't stand seeing people in pain.' You may spend time in the helping, healing or caring professions for this reason, or find yourself in situations in your domestic or personal life where you must perform the role of what we commonly know to be a saint! You may, or may not, be a religious or spiritual person. But the ancient images and archetypes associated with these areas may resonate with you:

Martyred saints	Karma
Sinners saved	Nirvana
Sacrificial lambs	Redemption
Do unto others	

At what point does a Piscean type cease being a saviour, and turn into a victim? And is it a happy and healthy state of affairs to be a martyr to anything? This is one of the most baffling areas of Piscean experience, and astrologers often find themselves grappling with the contradictions. The two fish in the Piscean glyph do not swim in opposite directions for nothing. The contradictions in the victim–saviour patterns that you will experience in your lifetime are rather like those fish.

Confusion — a very Piscean word — is the common result of these discussions, which are basically ethical in nature, and will make far more sense to you on a personal level than words on a page ever will! Perhaps it is true to say that you may find it useful to analyse your own ideas about what a victim is, what a martyr is and what a saviour should be doing. The word *victim*, in its own way, is quite a potent and powerful six-letter word. One of the issues that I find useful discussing with strongly Piscean clients is *survival*. This seems to be the key to many Piscean dilemmas. Perhaps it is because of this: at the point that a victim turns into a survivor, he or she also becomes a healer for others.

 in **pisces**

You love

Poetry ★ Song lyrics ★ Real-life romantic fantasy ★ Healing emotional or real wounds ★ Sensitive men ★ Spiritual women ★ Inspired artists or photographers ★ Giving your time, energy or money ★ Anything which allows you to turn off, relax and float ★ Most of all, perhaps, a unity between all things — men, women, animals, kids, babies ★ Drifting happily into romantic fantasy, exotica or erotica when life falls short — it can seem almost real!

You loathe

Boring practicality ★ Cruelty to people or animals ★ Sceptics ★ Cynics ★ Philistines.

Expressing your Piscean side

If you have Venus in Pisces then, somewhere inside you, you contain a Pisces. If your Piscean side is well developed, you will probably also have people with Pisces planets in your life. If this section doesn't accurately reflect what you're all about, you may want to read the chapter headed Walking Your Planets (pages 175–183).

THE NON-MATERIAL WORLD

Aretha Franklin (Pisces Mercury) sang 'I Say A Little Prayer' and quite a few Pisces-influenced women seem to know exactly what she meant. You may also be a meditator, a lifelong wisher, a mantra chanter or even a spell-caster. Pisces describes the unseen and the non-material world. There is something deeply mysterious — and basically 'sensed' — about this area of Piscean experience. Annie Lennox, who has Mars in Pisces, is a famous supporter of Buddhism. Joan of Arc had the Moon in Pisces, and Shirley Maclaine has Venus in Pisces — one way or another, both have heard voices.

The blind and deaf Helen Keller, a Pisces Moon, spent most of her time in a world which was literally unseen by others. In this letter to a friend in 1899 (published in her autobiography,

The Story of my Life), she describes 'seeing' statues of mythological figures. 'Venus entranced me,' she wrote. 'She looked as if she had just risen from the foam of the sea, and her loveliness was like a strain of heavenly music.' To Helen Keller, imagination was sight. Running her fingers over a sculpture, she saw her own reality.

What you *perceive* as part of your Piscean experiences may be a result of your sixth sense, or a sense beyond that. You may be one of the Pisces-influenced women who also sees ghosts, registers the spirit within yourself, knows God, or experiences lucid dreaming. You may *feel* atmospheres, or simply sense the *Zeitgeist*, the spirit of the time, which manifests itself in the invisible trends and changes in the wind which affect us all. Piscean hunches can be highly accurate and quite profitable.

Above all, your Piscean side has an extreme sensitivity to all that cannot be measured, charted, or tested in a laboratory. Sometimes it is impossible for strongly Piscean experiences to be articulated, just because they lack this measurable, material quality.

Many Pisces-influenced women feel drawn to the esoteric, mysterious side of astrology, and have little interest in sceptics demanding proof and data. Some of the best astrologers I have known have Pisces planets because they bring intuitive gifts to the field. They also have a rare ability to sympathise and empathise with their clients, and to feel their way around a chart.

If you are strongly Piscean, and there are no Earth signs — Taurus, Virgo, Capricorn — around your birthdate, then you may find you need to earth yourself, because the influence of the non-material world may very well take over. Going out of your way to sink your hands into the soil or put your feet on the ground is one way of doing it. The symptoms of Pisces gone mad? Unpaid bills, professional or domestic chaos and a general feeling that the practical details of life are eluding you. Of course, there are Piscean types who can happily live in this kind of world — the neighbourhood children will benefit from being read some wonderful stories and the local cats never go hungry — but this life is not for everyone, and some of you seem to go to enormous lengths to counteract it. Making lists and trying to stick to them appears to be quite popular!

 in **pisces**

The best revenge is
Deception.

Sporting Pisces
Ocean, sauna or spa.

Your battle tactics
Walking around with a pained expression on your face and doing your Noble Martyr bit usually fixes your opponents ★ Being a good liar or a natural actress when you need to be ★ Slipping in and out mysteriously — before people are sure what has happened, all around have been fooled.

Expressing your Piscean side
If you have Mars in Pisces then, somewhere inside you, you contain a Pisces. If your Piscean side is well developed, you will probably also have people with Pisces planets in your life. If this section doesn't accurately reflect what you're all about, try reading the chapter, Walking Your Planets (pages 175–183).

MAGICAL MYSTERY TOURS
Somewhere between Helen Keller and the Beatles, I think, the elusive, mysterious spirit of Pisces may be nailed down.

Magical mystery tours are certainly going to be a big part of your life. Because Pisces seeks to be transported from the real world, music — psychedelic, classical, soft or exotic — holds obvious appeal. Then there is the option of sitting in a cinema in the dark in the middle of the day, creating fantasies on paper, losing oneself in poetry and holing up inside an art gallery.

The following are some Pisces-influenced women who seem to express all that is magical, mysterious or wonderfully escapist through their music, writing, acting or art:

Anaïs Nin — Sun in Pisces
Elizabeth Barrett Browning — Sun in Pisces
Audrey Hepburn — Moon in Pisces
Sarah Bernhardt — Moon in Pisces
Holly Hunter — Sun and Moon in Pisces
Vita Sackville-West — Sun in Pisces
Miranda Richardson — Sun in Pisces
Susan Norrie — Moon in Pisces
Kate Greenaway — Sun in Pisces
Shirley MacLaine — Venus in Pisces
Nastassja Kinski — Venus in Pisces
Mary Quant — Mercury and Mars in Pisces
Jilly Cooper — Sun in Pisces

PISCEAN MYTHS
Cinderella

Most people know the story of Cinderella, but it contains so many Piscean themes and symbols that it's worth retelling here. A victim of her ugly sisters' cruelty, Cinders martyred herself in their interests as a household slave until the day her Fairy Godmother appeared. Already, our heroine is having Piscean hallucinations of the first order, but as is so often the case with this sign, her fantasy was actually her reality as well. Mice were turned into horses (she loved animals, of course) and a saviour appeared in the form of a Handsome Prince. In dazed, confused and chaotic Piscean fashion, Cinderella lost her glass slipper as she fled the ball. Just when it looked as if a life of saintly domestic martyrdom was on the cards again, she was saved a second time. Kind to the end — even to her tormentors — she lived happily ever after. Which, incidentally, is the only appropriate ending for Pisces.

NEPTUNE'S SACRIFICES

The myth surrounding Neptune, your ruler (also known as Poseidon) involves several images of sacrifice. Black bulls and horses were thrown into rivers for the god, and Neptune was occasionally given human sacrifices as well.

When astrologers look at Neptune in a personal horoscope, they associate sacrifice with the area of life occupied by that planet. Neptune in the Fourth House, for example, describes a sacrifice made in connection with one's family, and perhaps one's homeland or house. In the Second House, Neptune describes giving up money and possessions.

With the Sun, Moon, Mercury, Venus or Mars in Pisces, both the idea and the reality of sacrifice will be an important part of your story. What has been given up by you, or lost by you, may be totally involuntary, or it could be a fully conscious and personal decision. A Pisces planet, however, lends the sacrifice a kind of depth and richness as well. There is less a sense of things having been mindlessly forfeited or thrown away, as a conviction that the sacrifice makes sense in the context of your whole life.

THE CLASSIC PISCES

Elizabeth Taylor

Born on 27th February 1932, Elizabeth Taylor is a Pisces Sun, Mercury and Mars.

Rescue missions Elizabeth's charity commitments are lifelong. She is best known for the Elizabeth Taylor AIDS Foundation.

Fantasy and reality In Donald Spoto's biography of the star, her mother, Sara, is quoted this way: 'When other teenage girls were reading romantic stories and imagining themselves as the heroine, Elizabeth was *living* her dream world, by acting the role of the heroine — that is, at the studio.'

Piscean childhoods Elizabeth's pets included a mare named Betty and her animal co-stars in the *Lassie* and *National Velvet* films.

Saviours and victims In her relationships there are many saviour–victim patterns. Alcohol and drugs are central to these.

The non-material world Elizabeth was accepted into the Jewish faith in the 1950s. Her near-death experience around the filming of *Cleopatra* is well-known.

Magical mystery tours Magic and mystery have always been part of Taylor's personal and creative lives. With Richard Burton, she shared a love for Yeats, Browning, Eliot and Shakespeare. The venue for her sixtieth birthday? Disneyland.

Neptune's sacrifice Most of all, perhaps, Taylor has famously sacrificed her marriages.

PISCEAN SYMBOLS

Neptune (Poseidon) ★ Fish ★ Twelve ★ Sacrifice ★ Fog ★ Mist ★ Oil ★ Water ★ Pools ★ Drowning ★ Rescue ★ Saviours ★ Saints ★ Nets ★ Dolphins ★ Martyrs ★ Drugs ★ Alcohol ★ Hypnosis ★ Clairvoyance ★ Oceans ★ Seas ★ Rivers ★ Floods ★ Lakes ★ Blindness ★ Eyes ★ Vision ★ Distortion ★ Altered images ★ Haze ★ Deception ★ Lies ★ Photography ★ Contact lenses ★ Illusions ★ Film ★ Surrealism ★ Poetry ★ Escape ★ Oasis ★ Blurring ★ Impressionism ★ Paintings ★ Illustrations ★ Fiction ★ Psychedelia ★ Blues ★ Springs ★ Tridents ★ Horses ★ Waterlilies ★ Liquids ★ Lifesavers ★ Sea monsters ★ Myths ★ Dreams ★ The collective unconscious ★ All creatures great and small ★ God/Goddess ★ Religions ★ Spirituality ★ Ghosts ★ Hauntings ★ Shells ★ Surf ★ Sand ★ Feet ★ Shoes ★ Atmosphere ★ Intuition ★ Virtual Reality ★ 3D ★ Addiction ★ Fantasy ★ Mermaids ★ Glass ★ Glasses ★ Pine ★ Bulls ★ Tunny-fish ★ Harbours ★ Lighthouses ★ Faith ★ Instinct ★ The RSPCA ★ Guide Dogs for the Blind ★ Cameras ★ Turquoise ★ Violet.

WALKING your planets

Very few women manage to use all their planetary energies all the time. You are born with a Sun sign, Moon sign, Mercury sign, Venus sign and Mars sign at your disposal, but anything from your family, to your job situation, to the state of your love life, can switch some of these planets off. The result? A whole chunk of yourself goes missing, and the energies which go with the sign you are rightfully entitled to go missing as well.

How bad is it to go without your Mars, and your Mars sign? This bad — imagine that you are walking down your street, late at night, and an aggressive stranger confronts you. Unless you have your Mars ready to go, you could find yourself without an attack or defence mechanism, without a sign to work for you and without the necessary courage and adrenalin to get yourself out of the situation.

How bad is it to go without your Venus, and your Venus sign? Well, if you're content not to look in the mirror for six months, and if you could care less about loving and being loved, I suppose it's tolerable. Skipping Venus, though, will not only disconnect you from your own appearance, but also disconnect you from the art of charm. Without taking Venus for a walk occasionally, you could be living in a fairly drab, flirtation-free and charmless zone.

The Sun, Moon and Mercury can be bypassed just as easily. This may not be a permanent state of affairs. Indeed, at the opposite end of the spectrum we can sometimes benefit from planet overload. For example, when Venus is working overtime for you, you're never out of the bathroom, you're seducing yourself senseless. During Sun plus times you're gaining confidence and doing well in your career. When the Moon is being given breathing space in your chart you'll cook more, feel more comfortable with family relationships and will find a stronger sense of belonging. Mercury plus times result in career progress or academic success. Mars plus times find you feeling stronger, emotionally and physically.

The whole thing only becomes a problem when the Sun, Moon, Mercury, Venus or Mars go missing for so long that you end up jamming your circuits. Why? Basically because one planet serves the others. If you overload on assertive tough Mars then you desperately need a soft, preening, charming and flirtatious Venus to balance it out. If you do the Moon thing for years — looking after other people, cooking, making homes out of houses — then you desperately need a chunk of the Sun in there to remind you that you are important even when you're not caring for other people.

The idea of Walking Your Planets is to: a) allow the planet to work for you — after all, it has a job to do, and b) capitalise on the *sign* that the planet is in. If you've scanned the section on your Sun, Moon, Mercury, Venus or Mars sign and feel that it isn't a part of you, then hopefully this section will reconnect you.

It can take a while for women to get in touch with all their planets, and the nature of the signs they are in. Once you're there, though, life becomes infinitely more interesting, and *all* the parts of you start to work at the same time.

taking the  **for a walk**

Next to Mars, the Sun is the planet most women seem to lose. The Sun describes how important you feel, how confident you are, how ego-driven you can be, and how special you consider yourself.

This can be a fairly sensitive subject with people, and no wonder: the Sun, after all, is a comment on you and how you feel about yourself. It's a terrible thing for an astrologer to see a woman whose Sun sign has gone absent without leave. If you're not currently identifying with being an Aries, a Taurus, a Gemini or whatever, it usually means that a reasonable amount of your personal pride has gone missing as well.

Women who don't take their Sun sign for a walk usually get other people to do it for them. In other words, if you're not 'doing' your Sun, you'll make a point of finding friends, lovers or gurus who, uncannily enough, seem to symbolise everything you've ever read that your Sun sign is supposed to be.

The Aries Sun woman who drags herself in to see an astrologer without any energy or oomph whatsoever — but with an awfully dynamic set of friends, or an Action Man lover — is one example. The Virgo Sun who is way out of touch with her body, but best of friends with an aerobics instructor, is another one. And the list goes on — Gemini Suns who don't feel comfortable with the art of communication, Leo Suns who think they have nothing special to show off ... either way it's an astrologer's nightmare, and an awful waste of your potential.

SOLVING A MISSING SUN

1. Find a role model who has planets in your Sun sign — a classic Aries, Taurus, Gemini or whatever. Review the section relevant to your Sun sign, and compare it to your role model's life and times. Reading up on women who have done something amazing with the basics of your own sign is a good way to start 'getting' what the sign is all about, and understanding how it is buried in you.

2. If your pride, self-esteem or sense of self-importance is low, you will probably identify the culprits without too much trouble. People who were supposed to build you up, but didn't do the job, are usually at fault — and this one could go back years into your history, or be as recent as last week. If your ego is dented, or on permanent leave, the repair job begins when you identify how, when and where the 'dents' started happening.

3. Realise that your Sun sign is needed in the greater human tribe. Nature works these things out — Capricorn Sun women have a place in the tribe, Aquarius Sun women have a place in the tribe, and so on. Work out what your role is, and get in touch with it by *testing the water* in areas your Sun sign is associated with. Recall the times in your childhood when traces of the sign seemed to come up. Children 'get' their Sun sign very early on, quite spontaneously — it's up to you to retrace the steps.

If you don't relate to the sign your Moon is in, then you may have missed out on being mothered in some way. The Moon describes the people who are supposed to feed you, accommodate you and look after you when you're ill. If you didn't have a particularly motherly mother, or if the mothering process was interrupted, then the Moon may be stumbling in your chart.

Some women find a substitute parent or 'mother' outside their family, or find themselves adopted by people who seem to do all the caring and supporting that a parent could not. This can certainly help bring the Moon back to life, and give the Moon sign somewhere to breathe.

Other classic symptoms of a missing or faulty Moon are: problems with food or cooking or eating, a general problem with how you feel about your body, an inability to feel truly safe in the world, and some difficulty in intimate relationships. The degree to which this occurs will reflect just how blocked your own Moon sign is.

SOLVING A MISSING MOON

1. One of the best things you can do to retrieve a missing Moon — and its sign — is to cook it back into life. This planet rules every aspect of food, from its purchase to the last stages of cooking it and eating it. This may sound somewhat bizarre, but I have found that the more women cook (and the more they take the whole thing seriously) the more their Moon sign begins to show itself in this — and in all other areas of their lives.

2. Achieve a sense of place. If your Moon is in trouble, and your Moon sign is operating on a weak signal, there may also be a problem in feeling 'at home' in the world. Getting a sense of place — in your house or flat — is a good place to start. Then you can take this further, and consciously start thinking about your country — wherever you perceive that to be — and the things you associate with that place. A good Moon wake-up exercise is dream home sketching. You don't have to be good at drawing — just roughly

sketch your ideal home on some paper. Jot down notes on colours, shapes, the setting and what's *inside* the place. Go to as much trouble as you like — in fact, the more energy you put in, the better reception your Moon will start to offer.

3. Look after something — or someone — for a time. To function properly, your Moon must be 'allowed to help you nurture, care and protect. You can do this with the people, animals and plants around you. When you consciously adopt a person, creature or growing thing then you are waking up your Moon sign in a major way. When you take someone chicken soup when they are ill, when you let an animal know it is appreciated and when you raise a plant from a seedling, you will be closer to your Moon — and its sign — than at most other times in your life. Try it — it works!

taking  for a **walk**

Mercury is that part of you which speaks and writes effectively. Having said that, there are many deaf people who are completely in touch with their Mercury signs and excel at sign language. If you feel that your Mercury sign is not really part of you, the chances are high that other things in Mercury's domain are a stumbling block.

The education process is one of them, and if Mercury has gone absent without leave, it is often because of problems at school, college or university. Mercury describes teachers as well as students, and if one of your teachers — or even the entire establishment — did not deliver, then your Mercury sign may have gone missing at about the same time.

Mercury describes how you speak, how you handle telephone calls and how you are in meetings. It also has something to say about your listening skills, and your basic comprehension and understanding. If these areas of your life are causing problems, Mercury may be in trouble. A missing or difficult sibling relationship may also indicate a problem Mercury.

SOLVING A MISSING MERCURY

1. You'll need a pen and lots of scrap paper for this exercise. Basically, it's just about signing your autograph! Try out different ways of making your mark. Try capitals, lower case or cursive. Doodle. Scribble. Forget the fact that this is something you are supposed to put on bank cheques. Just play with your own name. Mercury comes to life through names.

2. Rename yourself. Sit down with a book of baby names, or draw on books or magazines for inspiration. If you had the option of any ten new Christian names, middle names and surnames for yourself, what would you choose?

3. Take the pressure off yourself when you write by using the 'swill draft' technique. This is something an American situation comedy writer taught me years ago. If you have something to prepare for work, for classes or just a letter for the council, do the swill draft first. Tell yourself that your words will basically be pig swill, yet there may be something there you can retrieve. Treat the writing process as a kind of 'blurt' in the first instance, which you then have the luxury of going back and progressively tidying and changing.

4. If there genuinely is a serious problem with your verbal skills, learning skills or written abilities then you will obviously need outside help, and an astrology book cannot do it for you. More common — and less serious — with a missing Mercury sign is this: you don't feel confident about speaking up. There are some fabulous books on this subject, but you can also try reading out loud. Find some kind of text that you like — a novel, lyrics or whatever — and read it a few times. Mercury will wake up and you'll get your missing sign back.

taking  for a walk

Symptoms of a missing Venus are pretty obvious. You may feel cynical about love, flirtation and seduction. You may believe it's not going to happen for you, or that it's really not important to you. The

Goddess of Love has — in this instance — gone AWOL. Venus — or Aphrodite — is as much the goddess of female beauty and adornment as she is the symbol of love. So another missing Venus symptom is probably ambivalence about your hair, clothes, face or the bottles and jars on the bathroom shelves.

I think many women experience a missing Venus at some stage of their lives. You may go through a difficult Saturn cycle, for example, and find it hard to work up any enthusiasm either for love, or for the way you look. If you are pretty much living like this all the time, you may be fine about it. You may have perfectly formed reasons of your own for skipping flirtatious eye contact at parties, and ignoring the basics of female adornment and self-pampering.

If you do want to get your Venus back (and nine out of ten astrologers would prefer you to go looking for her) you may have to get closer to the myth. She is vain. She is beautiful. She adores beautiful things. She has no concept of morality in love — seduction and flirtation exist on their own terms. Frequently, Venus is associated with love gone wrong — but it is never enough to stop her sending Cupid on various dastardly missions. She is a goddess of the most sensual pleasures — doves, incense, girdles and jewels for her hair. She is also capable of forgetting these and running wild when she herself is in love.

SOLVING A MISSING VENUS

Taste and choice are integral to what Venus is all about. Spending time in an art gallery, wandering around and judging the paintings — for your own satisfaction — is a good way of finding Venus again. She is about beauty, and the aesthetic, on all levels. Fine-tuning your own response to what pleases your eye, and your soul, is a gentle and enjoyable way of waking up this planet in yourself — and in your horoscope.

Drawing Venus — even if you think you can't draw — is another wonderful way of finding her again. And this simple exercise has fascinating results. When I get women clients to do this at home, they report that their Venus pictures, oddly enough, resemble some of the themes, symbols and qualities associated with their own Venus sign. The instructions for these drawings are pretty basic: imagine that she is your romantic gopher. You have called her up to go and find lovers for you. Because it is extremely important that she attracts the right kind of person, there are particular visual signals and messages she should be giving out. Try to work these into your drawing. Consider colours, fabrics, lengths and shapes. Consider her body. Pay attention to eyes, lips, ears and hair. Crawl under a rock to do the drawing if you have to, as this has to be an uninhibited process in order to work. Make notes in the margins about the sort of Venus you have in mind. Then, when you are satisfied with your image of the goddess, fold the paper and put it somewhere private. You can repeat this exercise from time to time, adding or changing whatever features or details seem right. Remember — she will only get what you would *prefer* her to get.

taking  for a **walk**

Mars is the planet most women have a problem with. This is understandable — he is the God of War. He describes female rage, female aggression, and all those socially 'difficult' qualities like competitiveness, defiance, pushiness and strength. Until Barbie dolls come with a battery-operated voice that says, 'I know how to look after myself, Ken!' then most women are going to have a struggle fitting Mars into their lives.

The trouble is, we really need Mars. Without this planet, you will be pushed around, forgotten about, and even (worst case scenario) victimised. Taking Mars for a walk becomes important not only because your Mars sign may have gone missing, but also because you need your attack and defence mechanisms if you are going to survive. Also, perhaps, just to get what you want. Your Mars is the most direct way of going from A to Z. If Mars is asleep, or missing, or if he has been shoved out of the way by other people, then getting him back could change your life!

SOLVING A MISSING MARS

As with the Venus-finding exercise, a lot of your Mars-walking begins with a drawing. Nobody is asking you to be Beatrix Potter with watercolours and easel. Just scribble — sketch. The first rule is that Mars can be male, female, animal or mythical beast. All that is required is this: you must remember that Mars is your attacker and defender. What you are about to draw is something you can pull out of the hat when you need to push through, or push forward. Spend as much time as you like dressing Mars up, supplying armour or physical features and working on the weapons or special qualities this creature might be carrying. Let rip with the drawing — it is in the nature of Mars to be spontaneous and fast. Just remember the key words, attack and defend. And add your private notes or special comments if you feel you need to explain more.

Dreams are a perfect place to use your Mars. Once you feel good about the image you have drawn, consider it yours. Should you need Mars to defend you, protect you, or lead you in a dream, you can call upon your image of him. Some women prefer to depict Mars as a woman — a kind of warrior maid. I have also known women to draw Mars as the most unholy, terrifying and gobsmacking monster they are capable of creating!

Taking Mars for a walk also depends on assertiveness skills, and there are many good books and courses which can help. Learning to say no is a good place to start. It's a cliché, but the old 'I understand what you are saying, but I ...' protest is another good Mars exercise. Growling is good, too. I'm not kidding. I was in danger of being assaulted in a park once, and growling did a lot more for me than shrieking ever could (it's easier, too — you don't have to reach for the high notes). Lest your nearest and dearest catches you growling, drawing or practising your *nos*, you may want to take Mars for a walk in private. But do try it.

Missing this planet from your package can affect your energy, health, libido and self-esteem. Without a properly running Mars, the rest of the machine starts to slow down, or get stuck, or move in peculiar and unhelpful ways. Mars is about immediacy, too. Reacting very quickly, *at the source of your stress*, is a time-honoured way of making this planet work properly. Growl, or use your defences, when the moment strikes. That way Mars won't be squeezing in through the back way, causing you problems later.

YOUR

RELATIONSHIPS

BASIC
CONCEPTS

SIGN COMPATIBILITY

If I could have a can of catfood for every time someone asks, 'Is he compatible with me?' I would never have to go to the supermarket again. Astrology *is* a remarkably good detector of compatibility. Sometimes it can be uncanny.

When people ask, 'Are we compatible?' though, what they really mean is, 'Will we get married and stay married?' This is where I have to hand the catfood back. It's just not possible for an astrologer to tell you, unless she is also a psychic.

What this part of the book can do for you is identify some of the areas in which you click with people, and the areas in which you may have some problems.

In the section called Clicking, you can compare your Sun, Moon, Mercury, Venus and Mars signs with those of other people — not only potential husbands, but also friends, colleagues and your chiropractor, if you so choose. Chances are, you'll find strong bonds with the people who are already in your world: and some interesting insights on the people who left it!

MEN AND WOMEN

Why are men and women so mysterious to each other? John Gray (author of *Men are from Mars, Women are from Venus*) might know the answer to that one, but our differences are explained not only by Venus and Mars, but also by the Sun, Moon and Mercury. (Incidentally, Gray's book has nothing to do with astrology — but we astrologers love the title!)

In this section on relationships, you once again look up the positions of the Sun, Moon, Mercury, Venus and Mars on the day of your man's birth — and can then decide which planet sign he seems to be expressing most strongly. One will probably dominate — and it may not necessarily be his Sun sign.

If you've been together for a while, you'll know all the different sides of him extremely well, and will clearly identify his Arian bits, his Geminian bits and so on. Incidentally, Women Who've Split With the Wolves tell me that this part of the book is also particularly helpful for understanding exes. Let's hope so — we need all the help we can get!

The other part of this book is dedicated to the way he sees you. For this, single out his Moon and Venus signs. These are the female planets in astrology, and, in his own chart, they indicate the way he perceives perfect — and not so perfect — womanhood.

If you are in a relationship with this guy, he may be picking up on qualities you have which most strongly resemble his Moon and Venus signs. If they are both identical in his chart (it does happen) you will experience this even more strongly.

For the most part, though, men have a different Moon and Venus sign. Each page is headed Moon–Venus, which indicates this is where is Moon sign *or* his Venus sign may be.

Once you've finished with one planet, look up the other one. Then lock him in a room and torture him by reading it aloud!

WOMEN AND WOMEN

A whole book could be written on lesbian and bisexual relationships and astrology. It's an under-researched and under-represented part of the art. But there are some basic rules for women who prefer women.

Firstly, go back to your own Moon and Venus signs, in the 'You' section of the book. The Moon describes what you need and what makes you feel comfortable. Venus describes what you love and take the most pleasure in. Somewhere between these two planet signs, you will find a little of what you want and need.

Now do the same for your partner, or your most beloved ex. Go back and check her Moon and Venus signs. This is your guide to what makes her feel most at home, most secure and most 'in love', in the classic meaning of the word.

Some gay women have asked me about their masculine side, which they feel quite strongly. Astrologers always get into politically incorrect territory here, as even talking about 'masculine' and 'feminine' qualities can sound a little limiting.

Nevertheless, astrology is about ancient archetypes, and these just aren't politically correct. We still work with the idea that the Sun and Mars are masculine, and describe the side of women that is more aggressive, more confident, more assertive, more authoritative and altogether tougher. If you are seeking something along these lines in your partner, check out your own Sun and Mars signs — and then hers — for insights.

If there really is strong chemistry between you, you will also find that your Moon, Venus, Sun and Mars signs fall into the same groups, or come under the same signs. Explore the section on Clicking for more information. Unfortunately, clicking is no guarantee of longevity in relationships. But if the basic foundations are there, life will be a lot simpler for both of you.

CLICKING with people

THE ASTROLOGY OF COMPATIBILITY

Most magazine and newspaper columnists compare Sun sign to Sun sign when looking at compatibility. This describes how easily you identify with the other person, how well you massage their ego and how proud you feel to have them as a partner.

For the full picture you also need to compare the other planets. The Moon sign of either person has something to say about being parents together, or perhaps buying a house, or agreeing on domestic routine.

The Mercury sign compatibility between you describes listening skills and communication. Venus, the planet of love and seduction, is absolutely crucial — for obvious reasons. Mars offers insights into the sexual compatibility you share and the way you handle anger together.

Not all couples click in every single department. But for a really good relationship — short-term or long-term — I think you need to have basic compatibility between your Sun, Moon and Venus signs. If your Sun feels comfortable against another person's planet, then your self-esteem will be good. You usually find that being around them makes you feel good about yourself. In fact, you feel more strongly *yourself*.

Your Moon sign also needs to be cushioned by your partner's planets if you are going to be able to live together successfully. If your Moon is clicking with your partner's Sun, Moon, Mercury, Venus and/or Mars, then your home life will be easier, domestic issues can be resolved in a more relaxed way and your feelings about parenthood will be supported.

If your partner's planets click with your Venus sign, then the attraction — especially the physical attraction — and the romantic love never disappear. Often, when old flames meet up, it is a perennial Venus sign connection which is keeping the attraction alive, no matter how difficult the original split may have been. There are some married couples and long-term partnerships I have seen where there is no Venus compatibility, but they tend to be rather practical arrangements.

Mars is the planet of potency above all other things. It can produce strong, heated arguments and extraordinarily passionate sex. If your Mars is not agreeing with your partner's planets, expect tension. If your partner's Mars does not click with one of your planets, then part of you may always feel as if you must be on the attack or defence. Needless to say, the sex drive and libido of either person will also be affected. There are many couples around who have a clash between their Mars signs. Other 'click' points between the Sun, the Moon or Venus keep them together, but they have had to find a way around the flashpoint anger and sexual imbalances that occur when the signs aren't agreeing.

WHAT to look for

What you really need is a lot of planets on both sides falling into the same basic sign group: Fire, Earth, Air or Water. Here's the list:

Fire group — Aries, Leo, Sagittarius
Earth group — Taurus, Virgo, Capricorn
Air group — Gemini, Libra, Aquarius
Water group — Cancer, Scorpio, Pisces

Cross-check your Sun, Moon, Mercury, Venus and Mars against your partner's. If you've been together for a while, or if you're madly in love, you should get quite a few clicks in the same group. You also need as many planets between you as possible in the secondary groups:

Fire–Air group — Aries, Leo, Sagittarius, Gemini, Libra, Aquarius
Earth–Water group — Taurus, Virgo, Capricorn, Cancer, Scorpio, Pisces

At this stage, something odd should be happening: you're beginning to find your friends turning up in compatible groups, too. This is an example of the 'circle of friends' phenomenon in astrology, and I'll discuss it in detail at the end of the section.

COMMON factors

Now that you've sorted both your planets into groups, you can decode the nature of the connection:

Planets in Fire: Aries, Leo, Sagittarius

A Fire group connection describes people who are mutually enthusiastic and fired up about life. You help each other to take awfully big adventures. When people with Fire links get together in a group, there will always be plenty of big ideas and big plans under discussion. Fire links also mean you boost each other's confidence. The future is always extremely important to both of you and sometimes the thought of what you will achieve tomorrow is more exciting than what is actually going on in the present. This is a high-energy connection — lots of immediate feedback, lots of bounced ideas, and a huge amount of lust for life.

Planets in Earth: Taurus, Virgo, Capricorn

An Earth group connection describes people who share a down-to-earth approach to life. You'll help each other out in practical ways if you share a link here. When Earth people get together there's a very solid feel — best described as 'We Shall Not Be Moved'. Problems may occur when one of you feels the other is being impossibly stubborn. There may be differences related to money or values as well. This is a particularly mature and stable kind of relationship which may have a great deal of focus on the material — capitalising on life's rewards together.

Planets in Air: Gemini, Libra, Aquarius

An Air group connection is notorious for helping those who have it to run up enormous phone bills. Conversation and the flow of ideas — or gossip — are what keep Air-connected people interested. If you share links here, you can be a little cool with each other (this is not a touchy–feely connection by itself) but the rapport will be based on a meeting of minds. You'll value each other's intelligence. There's a great deal of electricity between you but it may not really ignite physically unless the mental energy is there first. It's common for Air couples to admit that they fell in love with each other's minds first of all.

Planets in Water: Cancer, Scorpio, Pisces

A Water group connection is a very emotional, sensitive link between people. This can occasionally get mushy — or even teary-eyed — but those who have it often feel a 'soul' connection going on. Sharing feelings — by talking about them or by transmitting them silently — is an important part of a Water-based relationship. When you clash, you'll accuse each other of being irrationally emotional! Passions run high in Water-based relationships. Jealousy and possessiveness, dependency and freedom–intimacy issues, are inevitably going to be extremely important.

Planets in Fire–Air: Aries, Gemini, Leo, Libra, Sagittarius, Aquarius

If you share planets here, you'll be an intensely sociable couple, invited out individually and together. Air–Fire partners entertain themselves and others, and there is usually a strong feeling that both of you are on display, or providing some kind of social teamwork. The Air partner — with Gemini, Libra or Aquarius planets — will appear to be the more logical of the two. The Fire partner will find that they feel more enthusiastic about life, and more charged up with ideas and plans for the future, when the Air person is around them. In return, the Air person will feel needed and wanted.

Planets in Earth–Water: Taurus, Cancer, Virgo, Scorpio, Capricorn, Pisces

As a couple, you'll have no trouble getting your mortgage approved, sorting out the practical details of life and creating security. There's a wonderful *emotional* security here, too: the Water partner will feel supported and cushioned by the Earth partner, who may act as a rock, or anchor. In return, the Water partner can offer a great deal of sensitivity, sympathy and emotional support. One of you will appear to be rather more vulnerable or needy than the other. This is a classic 'Lifestyle Building' combination.

ELEMENTS a quick word

If you're into astrology, sooner or later you'll hear the word elements used. It's quite an old term, and it dates from the days when toothless, unwashed astrologers used to hop around their dirty, spider-ridden hovels muttering 'Fire, Air, Earth, Water.' Basically, all you need to know is this. Each sign of the zodiac belongs to an element. As you've just read, Aries, Leo and Sagittarius are fire signs. Taurus, Virgo and Capricorn are earth signs. Gemini, Libra and Aquarius are air signs. Cancer, Scorpio and Pisces are water signs. Traditional wisdom says that fire goes together with fire — and air. It doesn't like water, and it's not very keen on earth. (Well if you've ever tried to light a Girl Guide campfire you'll know all about that.) Earth loves earth — and it's mad about water, too. Just don't throw too much fire or air into the mixture. Air and air go together, and we already know that fire and air are okay. Still, earth and water? No thanks. Finally, water and water go together, and water and earth go together. But, as you've read, water and fire — or water and air — don't really make much sense.

This applies to your ever-lovin' love life as follows. The more signs you and your soulmate share in the compatible element groups, the more comfortable and natural the relationship will feel. Some astrologers will also tell you that it's more fated, more 'chosen' for you by the universe.

Now, whatever you might think of that, it helps to understand the elements and to get a feel for them. As I'm guessing most of you are interested in using the elements while looking at the male of the species, what follows is a quick look at what it all means in terms of the wonderful world of men.

HE HAS THE ELEMENT OF AIR IN HIS HOROSCOPE

He has a dose of Libra, Aquarius or Gemini in his chart. Think people with glasses — John Lennon and Grahame Garden from *The Goodies*. Intelligent. Detached. Cosmo Kramer from *Seinfeld* is airy — they're totally impractical, have mad ideas about things, and are rather excitable. The mad professor archetype is airy. In the Royal Family, consider Prince Charles in his architecture lecture mode. This is what air is all about (spot it in your own chart):

Theories ★ Ideas ★ Mental energy ★ Communication ★ Wordplay ★ Analysis ★ Detatchment ★ Fairness ★ Logic ★ Reasonableness ★ It computes ★ Cynicism ★ Intellectually weighing ★ Connecting — on an information level ★ Articulating ★ The Internet ★ Shallowness ★ Superficiality ★ Coolness.

Air feeds the fire signs without even trying.

Air can't bear earth — too boring.

Air loves more air — let's talk!

Air gets uncomfortable with too much water around.

Still, the whole point of the elements is that they have to be balanced. If you suspect the airy type in your life is way too out of touch with the real world, suggest this exercise:

1   Take off shoes and socks
2   Lie on the grass
3   Imagine roots growing out of the body and into the soil
4   Repeat after me, 'I am earthed.'
5   Then go and do something sensible, like putting up shelves.

HE HAS THE ELEMENT OF FIRE IN HIS HOROSCOPE

Think Paul McCartney — enthusiastic, full of energy, the 'let's do it!' Beatle. He'll have the fire element in his chart if he's got a dose of Aries, Leo or Sagittarius. Think Bill Oddie in *The Goodies*, and Elaine Bennis in *Seinfeld*. In the Royal Family, think about Princess Anne, oomphy horsewoman par excellence. Tension or anger is never far from the surface with fire — it's partly what seems to energise them. You might have some fire in your own chart, in which case read on:

Enthusiasm ★ Leadership ★ Confidence ★ Optimism ★ Energy ★ Intuition ★ The future ★ Adventurousness ★ Gambling ★ Initiating ★ Driving ★ Pushing ★ Questing ★ Pep talks ★ Enterprise ★ Entepreneurialism ★ Belief ★ Just do it ★ Blazing ★ Roaring ★ Impressing ★ Warming ★ Contagious.

Fire needs air — it hangs around people with Aquarius, Gemini or Libra in their charts. Fire can't spend too long hanging around water — it's the wet blanket effect.

Fire relates to fire, and sparks fly.

Fire feels distinctly ill at ease around too much earth.

Chances are, he has other elements apart from fire working for him. But if you feel he's too damned fiery for his own good, make him try this:

1   Remove all clothes
2   Get into a lake
3   Float.

HE HAS THE ELEMENT OF EARTH IN HIS HOROSCOPE

If your bloke has a dose of Taurus, Virgo or Capricorn then he's earth-bound. Ringo Starr, plodding away on the drums, was the earthy side of The Beatles. Think normal, down to earth, and (they love this word in Beverly Hills) REAL PERSON. In *Seinfeld*, the centre of normality is Jerry Seinfeld. Away from TV, Jerry has the Sun in Taurus, so he really does have a dose of earth in his chart. He earns zillions of dollars. He promotes American Express credit cards. Very earthy, very materialistic, very practical. Do you have this in your own chart? Here's what it's all about:

Practicality ★ Down to Earth ★ Material ★ Financial ★ Realistic ★ Work Oriented ★ Building ★ Securing ★ Stabilising ★ Owning ★ Structures ★ Growth ★ Common sense ★ Normality ★ Endurance ★ Long-term planning ★ Reality ★ Anti-Crackpot ★ Anti-Fantasy ★ Pro-Values ★ The collector ★ The builder ★ The solid earner.

Earth provides a solid, rock-like, holding facility for water so people with Pisces, Scorpio and Cancer bits are reassured and attracted.

Earth just doesn't get fire.

Earth feels quite at home with other doses of earth.

Earth prefers to get a bit of distance between itself and air.

Most blokes are a combination of two or more elements. If he's way too earthed for his own good though (sure sign: he's plodding, becoming boring, becoming a breadhead, or slowing down) he might like to do this:

1 Apply overalls
2 Purchase one pot of red paint, one pot of yellow paint, one pot of orange paint
3 Throw it at a canvas
4 Burn canvas.

HE HAS THE ELEMENT OF WATER IN HIS HOROSCOPE

He has signs like Cancer, Scorpio and Pisces in his chart. This is where you'll find Beatle George Harrison — actually a Sun Pisces, and the epitome of the dreamy, meditative, soulful, emotional and spiritual bloke. In *The Goodies*, think about the over-emotional, weepy and poetically patriotic Tim Brooke-Taylor. When you think about water, think about sensivity. And moods, too. George Costanzas is the water part of *Seinfeld*. Chaos is often a trademark of water — so is a total lack of rationality. Without water signs, we wouldn't have photography or prose. Do you have it in your chart?

Here are the key concepts:

Sensitive ★ Emotional ★ Feelings ★ Irrational instincts ★ Vulnerability ★ Empathy ★ Sympathy ★ Tuning in ★ Unreasonableness ★ It doesn't compute ★ Emoticons ★ Women's intuition ★ Therapeutic ★ Cathartic ★ Depth ★ Dreamers ★ Imaginative ★ Altered states ★ Consuming ★ Drowning.

Water doesn't make sense, and frequently doesn't care. Water needs earth to prop it up, so it looks for Taurus, Capricorn, Virgo.

Water and fire just don't work that well.

Water and water cruise together.

Water and air aren't exactly complementary.

Sometimes people can be too watery — in fact, you may wonder where precisely the real world seems to have gone. Here's a possible solution for the over-watery bloke:

1   Purchase gardening gloves
2   Plant potatoes using a step-by-step instruction book
3   When ready, pick potatoes and make potato soup, once again
     using a step-by-step instruction book.
4   Serve at a dinner party — on time.

MORE on elements

It's very unusual to have someone who is purely fiery, watery, earthy or airy. Most people, as you'll gather from reading this book, have a combination of signs (and consequently elements) in their charts. Still, it's amazing how often people will go into phases when all they seem to be doing is acting out the characteristics of fire, earth, water or air in a cartoon-character way.

People often hang elements on celebrities, or fictional characters. And there's something in human nature that can't resist a band, or a TV show, or a film where an interplay of different elements — fire, earth, air, water — are obviously at work.

The Spice Girls have a bit of air in Scarey Spice (weird, glasses, all the signs) and some water from Baby Spice (soft, emotional). Ginger Spice — who actually is a Leo and looks like she belongs in a fire brigade — supplied the fire element. You can do this exercise yourself. Look at the characters in M*A*S*H, the men and women of ABBA or the guys in The Monkees. Any time a collection of people seems to capture the public imagination, it seems to be because everyone has a 'favourite' — in the Sixties, for example, you were either mysteriously drawn to John or Ringo. It was hard to claim both of them at the same time. And it really didn't matter that Ringo wasn't really that earthy underneath, or that John wasn't as airy as he seemed. Fans latch on to the one-dimensional aspects of what they see, hear and read about. If someone famous seems to be oozing a dose of their own element — a bit of down-home earth, or a bit of clever, sarcastic air — it becomes irresistible.

Children even have their own favourite Teletubby — now there's a test for every wannabe astrologer. And even animals can manifest as element archetypes — Skippy always seemed to me to be an air type (very logical — did you ever see the episode where he got behind the controls of a helicopter?) and Flipper is obviously water.

Put it this way: if you want to have a hit these days, you'd better: join a four-piece band with an equal, obvious dose of earth, fire, air and water — and no, I'm not talking about Earth, Wind and Fire.

SIGNS that go clunk

Inevitably, there are signs that don't create comfort, passion, attraction, need or desire. However, they don't create friction either. These are the 'clunk' signs. If you have too many clunks and not enough clicks, you may feel that the atmosphere between you lacks the vibrations you need for a lively, potent and challenging relationship. A few clunks are okay, but too many can be rather flattening. If you also have clunk signs and clash signs between you (see the section on clash signs below) then you may be facing some real hurdles. Anyway, here are the dreaded clunks!

Aries — Taurus	Cancer — Aquarius
Aries — Virgo	Leo — Virgo
Aries — Scorpio	Leo — Capricor
Aries — Pisces	Leo — Pisces
Taurus — Gemini	Virgo — Libra
Taurus — Libra	Virgo — Aquarius
Taurus — Sagittarius	Libra — Scorpio
Gemini — Cancer	Libra — Pisces
Gemini — Scorpio	Scorpio — Sagittarius
Gemini — Capricorn	Sagittarius — Capricorn
Cancer — Leo	Capricorn — Aquarius
Cancer — Sagittarius	Aquarius — Pisces

Remember, you are first checking your Sun, Moon, Mercury, Venus and Mars signs against your partner's. Then make a point of going back and doing it from their perspective.

SIGNS that go clash

One of the most common problems I see as an astrologer is this: couples with planets in a shared Fire–Air group or Earth–Water group, but with too many individual signs that clash. This leads to the familiar feeling that things are generally okay, but there is also a really difficult stumbling block in there. Probably more troublesome than this are signs that aren't clicking together in any group, and don't qualify as a 'clunk' connection either. These are definite clash signs, and will provide a lot of work for both of you. The aim of this section is to point out where the clash might be, and how the two signs concerned may be able to work with the differences.

Aries-Cancer planets

One of you — the Cancer-planet partner — is a great deal more needy, emotional and sensitive. The other — the Aries-planet partner — is far more energetic, enthusiastic and independent. The Cancer-planet partner will instinctively want to protect the Aries-planet partner, and aim for a close, family feel. After a while, the Arian person may feel as if the atmosphere is becoming terribly wet and spongy. If you have other 'click' planet signs, try to use them. The Cancerian person may need to learn not to cling or lean — or shepherd — and the Arian person will have to be super-sensitive as well.

Aries-Capricorn planets

This is a significant difference. The Aries-influenced person tends to live for the future, in a fairly hyped-up and enthusiastic way. The Arian partner will 'feel' things particularly strongly and 'just know' that something is going to be great. This is all somewhat dubious for the Capricorn-influenced partner, who is far more practical and much more cautious about life. There is also a basic timing problem here. Capricorn respects patience and long-term effort. Aries simply can't be bothered!

Aries-Libra planets

This is a tricky one. Both of your planets fall into a Fire–Air group, so there is no doubt that you work together as a couple —

particularly socially. Others see you as a unit — one person appears to be terribly charming, attractive and well-liked, and the other is admirably energetic, motivated and competitive. The basic conflict will be between 'we' and 'me' and the Arian person needs to work extra hard to understand Libra's essential concern for the partnership and for harmony.

Taurus-Leo planets
The Taurus-influenced person will find the Leo planets belonging to the other person too dramatic. The Leonine person, meanwhile, is exasperated by what they see as the boring practicality of Taurus. One of you is full of faith, enthusiasm, self-interest and ideas. The other is rather more concerned with the practical details. Money, income and the personal values of both people based on these factors may become a hard issue.

Taurus-Aquarius planets
This will only make sense if the Taurus-influenced person has learned to put other values above money and material possessions. If not, then the Aquarian partner will have a real problem with the Taurean person's values. One of you is interested in change, the other is not: that is also a huge problem. Taurus planets in a chart instinctively hang on, and hang in. Aquarius planets cannot wait for an exciting new future to begin. This is a difficult conflict.

Taurus-Scorpio planets
At first this seems to make a lot of sense. The Taurean person seems to offer the Scorpionic person a lot of security and common-sense. He or she seems to be a grounding factor. The person with planets in Scorpio is adding a rich seam of passion and feeling to the relationship. What will rock you more than anything else is the stubbornness both of you are capable of. This part of you both is utterly hopeless at compromising.

Gemini-Virgo planets
This is an interesting clash, because you are both intensely verbal or mind-led people, yet will irritate each other, too. The Geminian person will find the person with Virgo planets too pedantic and hung up on the details. You could also sting each other to death, as

both of you have the capacity to throw critical lines or jokey insults around. There may be a strong awareness of intellectual competition, or a great deal of brain input, but not much grunt or heart. You will need a few clicks to compensate for all of this.

Gemini–Pisces planets

This is another challenging combination. The Gemini-influenced person will be terribly witty and sharp, while the Pisces-influenced person seems to take most of the damage — for themselves and the other victims of the Geminian person's comments. The Geminian type will find Pisces drowns them — the atmosphere becomes very sticky and gluggy. To make this work, lean hard on the signs or groups which do click between you. If there aren't enough of them, this one could feel particularly strange!

Gemini–Sagittarius planets

The good things about this clash are worth mentioning. The Geminian person will inspire and 'feed' the Sagittarian person, at least for a start. In turn, the Geminian type senses (correctly) that the other person needs them to feel more alive, and is at their best around them. The problem is basically a mind one. The Gemini-planet person inevitably finds a lot of what the Sagittarian person is on about to be excessive, illogical or just over the top. The Sagittarius-influenced person may feel that Gemini's sharp brain and mouth is holding them back.

Cancer–Libra planets

The Cancer-influenced person doesn't care what people look like when they're sick. The Libran type does. Cancer worries more about what's in and on the plate than the quality of the guests or the dinner service. Libra can't bear any gathering that isn't wonderful. The Cancerian person's planets lean towards the family and the clan. If the Libran person finds anything ugly or discordant about that set-up, then they will drift away discreetly. You need more clicks! The Libran person may seem too cool to the more emotional Cancerian type

Cancer–Capricorn planets

This is another of those 'fatal attraction' combinations, and some astrologers even argue that they are karmic — in other words, you had a past life together with equal amounts of love and difficulty. Whatever the reason, there is a basic conflict here between the need for home and family security, and the need for career, success and ambition. It may be played out by each of you in turn, or the nature of the relationship may make it uncomfortably obvious that every time the domestic side is okay, work will suffer.

Leo–Scorpio planets

The Leo-influenced person will find Scorpio rather too intense and complicated. The Scorpio-planet person will not feel as if their emotional needs are being met. Every time the Scorpio type seeks sexual intimacy and real relationship 'heat' Leo will start to feel uncomfortable. The Leonine person may find Scorpio to be a confusing game-player at worst, and the Scorpionic type will resent the considerable Leonine ego. Use the signs between you that click, and capitalise on them.

Leo–Aquarius planets

You're both in the Fire–Air group, so already other people are giving you signals of approval because you look *right* together — as a couple you seem to balance each other in odd ways. The difficulty here is that the Aquarian person will 'weird out' the Leonine person, while Aquarius has little time for Leo's silly pride and occasional ego benders. Leo rather likes 'the system' or sections of the Establishment because she or he essentially believes in social order, preferably with Leo at the top. Aquarius loathes it.

Virgo–Sagittarius planets

This is an interesting clash between a person who very much likes ritual, daily routine and the practical, reliable elements of life — and someone who just can't understand any of it! The Virgoan person needs their funny little food and body things, and the Sagittarian type wants to do other things with their life. Sagittarius runs on an intuitive trust in the future, Virgo wants to make a list and cross things off as they are confirmed. Hopefully, you'll have a few other clicks in there, too!

Virgo-Pisces planets

The Virgoan type finds something quite wonderful, special and elusive about the Pisces-planet person. And, for a while, this one looks possible, the Virgoan person supplying the dose of practicality and down-to-earth living that the Pisces type needs. In the company of Pisces, Virgo feels healed. The basic problem is the mindset of each. Pisces wants to escape, dream, emote and feel. Virgo wants to remain grounded and practical and pick apart the logic of things.

Libra-Capricorn planets

There are some things in life which are not particularly useful and serve no real purpose. There are some people like this, too. Libra enjoys all of it, but the person with Capricorn planets can't see the point. There is an obvious problem here, but both sides may feel unable to talk about it. It is in the Capricornian person's nature to aim high and be quite goal-driven. The Capricorn-influenced person has an endless fund of common sense, yet may feel Libra is unappreciative, and more into beautiful things or people.

Scorpio-Aquarius planets

The Scorpio and Aquarius planets of both people will start to feel rather peculiar after a while. The Scorpionic person will not understand the Aquarian's fixation with ideas and theories, while their beloved appears to be cut off from the basics of emotion, sweating, seething and all the other things that humans do. Aquarius can seem terribly cold after a while. Scorpio will seem worryingly dark, a little too intense and just a bit too overwhelming for the cool, thoughtful Aquarian side of one partner.

Sagittarius-Pisces planets

The person with Pisces planets is expressing themselves with a lot of feeling, sensitivity and unspoken emotion. Along comes a Sagittarius planet and finds it all threatening. Sagittarius really does not have time nor energy for the world of feelings — nor is it really into the Piscean need for intimacy. The poor Piscean person can be left reeling by the bouncy, footloose style of Sagittarius planets. Use the signs between you that click and capitalise on them.

the 5-minute  MATCH

This is a quick guide to clicking, clashing and clunking. To make it easier, fill in your Sun, Moon, Mercury, Venus and Mars on this page, then write down his. This five-minute planet match is not meant to be grounds for divorce, de factohood or marriage, by the way. In fact, I was thinking of calling this chapter Jessica's Totally Superficical But Undeniably Useful Five Minute Planet Match. Still, if you've just met someone interesting, grab the birthday then get the basic facts!

By combining all the different matches you can find from your planets to the other person's, you'll end up with a quick prescription guide to your relationship. Using the example of Elizabeth Taylor and Richard Burton (surely the most famous 'I love you, I hate you, I love you' couple in the world) you get these results:

She has planets in Aries, Scorpio, Pisces.

He had planets in Virgo, Libra, Scorpio, Sagittarius, Capricorn. Elizabeth Taylor's relationship with Richard Burton immediately sounds like this:

Click, Click, Clash, Click, Clunk, Cosmic, Cosmic, Clunk, Click, Clash, Click, Click, Clash, Click, Clunk, Clunk, Clunk, Click, Clash, Click, Click, Click, Clash, Click, Clunk.

You can divide up the clashes, clicks, clunks and cosmics to check things as well. With Elizabeth and Richard you get this:

Click, Click, Click, Click, Click, Click, Click, Click, Click, Click, Click, Click

Clash, Clash, Clash, Clash, Clash

Clunk, Clunk, Clunk, Clunk, Clunk, Clunk

Cosmic, Cosmic

. . . Well I would have gone for it, wouldn't you?

HE HAS PLANETS IN	Ari	Tau	Gem	Can	Leo	Vir	Lib	Sco	Sag	Cap	Aqu	Pis
Ari	Cosmic	Clunk	Click	Clash	Click	Clunk	Cosmic	Clunk	Click	Clash	Click	Clunk
Tau	Clunk	Cosmic	Clunk	Click	Clash	Click	Clunk	Cosmic	Clunk	Click	Clash	Click
Gem	Click	Clunk	Cosmic	Clunk	Click	Clash	Click	Clunk	Cosmic	Clunk	Click	Clash
Can	Clash	Click	Clunk	Cosmic	Clunk	Click	Clash	Click	Clunk	Cosmic	Clunk	Click
Leo	Click	Clash	Click	Clunk	Cosmic	Clunk	Click	Clash	Click	Clunk	Cosmic	Clunk
Vir	Clunk	Click	Clash	Click	Clunk	Cosmic	Clunk	Click	Clash	Click	Clunk	Cosmic
Lib	Cosmic	Clunk	Click	Clash	Click	Clunk	Cosmic	Clunk	Click	Clash	Click	Clunk
Sco	Clunk	Cosmic	Clunk	Click	Clash	Click	Clunk	Cosmic	Clunk	Click	Clash	Click
Sag	Click	Clunk	Cosmic	Clunk	Click	Clash	Click	Clunk	Cosmic	Clunk	Click	Clash
Cap	Clash	Click	Clunk	Cosmic	Clunk	Click	Clash	Click	Clunk	Cosmic	Clunk	Click
Aqu	Click	Clash	Click	Clunk	Cosmic	Clunk	Click	Clash	Click	Clunk	Cosmic	Clunk
Pis	Clunk	Click	Clash	Click	Clunk	Cosmic	Clunk	Click	Clash	Click	Clunk	Cosmic

THE CLUNK, CLICK, CLASH,
COSMIC GUIDE

What it means

COSMIC — A highly chemical connection, for better or worse. This is going to be one of those relationships which affects you for years to come, whether it lasts or not — it's rare, it's important, in short, it's cosmic!

CLUNK — A bit of nothing, a bit of dead air between you — a distinct lack of vibe.

CLICK — You complement each other, like each other, and maybe love each other when this appears.

CLASH — A bad sticking point in your relationship and you'll feel it fairly quickly.

The Rules

Just listen to the sound your relationship makes — if it sounds like a horsedrawn carriage going around Central Park — click, click, click, click — then you'll probably end up in one, on your honeymoon. You need a bit of clash or cosmic to keep it interesting, though. If it's cosmic, cosmic, cosmic then watch out — if you thought this was going to be a little dalliance for summer, forget it. This relationship will have an extreme psychological effect. Clunk, clunk, clunk? Oh dear. Your conversations may sound like this too. Clash, clash, clash? You two should take up fencing and just get it over and done with.

And Don't Forget

Don't just go on your usual star signs. You need to look at your Sun, Moon, Mercury, Venus and Mars compared to your partner's. You can also use this for work relationships or flatmates — it's a quick way of checking the 'sound' of your particular connection. If it sounds like a Rolls Royce with two wheels missing heading for a lamp-post, you'll get it pretty quickly — Click, Click, Clunk, Clunk, Clunk, Clunk, CLASH CLASH. In other words, jam all the five-minute prescriptions on these pages together and you'll end up with a personalised one-page summing up of the different zodiac factors working between you.

Much better than watching *Perfect Match*, *The Love Boat* or *Blind Date* for tips, don't you agree?

I HAVE PLANETS IN   THEY HAVE PLANETS IN

_____   _____

_____   _____

_____   _____

_____   _____

_____   _____

you have
planets in   ARIES

THE OTHER PERSON HAS PLANETS IN:

Aries: One of you will have no volume control at all — and the other will complain (loudly). Lack of patience and an addiction to tension will be noticeable in one of you. Arguments and physically charged scenes are pretty hard to avoid when your Aries bits and the other person's Aries bits collide.

Taurus: You move through life at different speeds, and you find it much easier to get moving on things than your Taurean partner does. One of you is much more practical than the other. Unless you are clicking on other signs in your mutual charts — like Gemini, or perhaps another planet in Taurus — this is quite tricky

Gemini: Your Gemini partner will fuel a lot of your energy and lust for life just by being around. Things will move quickly with this one, for better or for worse. People will eavesdrop when you are in restaurants together because you have conversations that wouldn't be out of place in *Neighbours* or *Seinfeld*.

Cancer: You'll notice that one partner has a much lower boredom threshold than the other. There will be a definite gap between one person's need for security, and the other's need for challenge. This is a clash-clash point in both your horoscopes and you will need lots of other click signs between you to help out.

Leo: When you rev each other up with enthusiasm you can be quite a dynamic couple. Do expect fights, as one of you is rather ego-driven and the other can't stand being dominated. The person with the Aries side will inspire the person with the Leo bits to go on to bigger and better things, but it's a fiery match.

Virgo: A totally different approach to the basics of life — money, kids, travel, even what you do on the weekends — may be hard to work with. One of you is more spontaneous than the other. You'll notice the differences between you in quite an obvious way, even while you're at the getting-to-know-you stage.

Libra: It all seems amazingly romantic at the beginning, but the success of this relationship depends on the amount of tact, tolerance and compromise one of you can turn on. Aries and Libra are clash points in both your horoscopes, and if there is the slightest hint of unfairness in the relationship it could explode.

Scorpio: Sooner or later one partner will find themselves wondering who's on top of the relationship, and you'll need to work hard to stop relationship politics spoiling romance. The person with the Scorpio side will have very different conflict or battle tactics to the person with the Aries bits so it's tricky.

Sagittarius: Travelling interstate or overseas together will make you or break you. If it makes you, you could be together forever. Humour is your great saving grace. Between you, you also have a classic fire-fire dose of enthusiasm. I wouldn't be surprised if one of you actually froths at the mouth occasionally.

Capricorn: You are both achievers, but work in completely different ways. One of you is far more patient and cautious than the other and it could create real problems. These two points in your charts are really at odds with each other, and you can expect a strong feeling of conflict or differentness between you.

Aquarius: A lot of the issues in this relationship will revolve around space and freedom, but as long as one partner can control his or her temper, this looks quite exciting. The person with the Aquarian planet/s will feed the person with the Aries characteristics — not with scrambled eggs, but with encouragement.

Pisces: You'll notice that one person is much more inclined to live in the real world than the other, and there'll be times when you appear to be on different planets. One of you seems so on the ball, and so full of energy. The other is much more hard to pin down, and may occasionally seem flaky or even out of touch

you have
planets in TAURUS

THE OTHER PERSON HAS PLANETS IN:

Aries: The differences between you can be quite exciting at first, but it's the long haul which will really test you out. Money, possessions and property could be a sticking point. You move at different speeds too. You could hope for a soulmate who was as fast as you, but some part of them just won't get moving.

Taurus: The first few dates will reveal one of the most striking themes of your relationship — the value system you both have, and the extent to which one of you will or won't sell out! Then there are the banal basics of going out together, or living together. Cheap or expensive? And what's cheap anyway?

Gemini: This sometimes works quite well because both partners have a personal planet (like Venus) in each other's sign. If not, one of you will become rather bored and restless. If the other person has a lot of Gemini, and you have a load of Taurus, then you'll often find them too flighty or hung up on non-essentials.

Cancer: You both like to know where you stand, and a nasty break-up with a totally unsuitable, restless type for one of you just makes the current match seem more reassuring. Inevitably, the talk will turn to life's fundamentals early on, as one person obviously has tabs on real estate or domestic issues.

Leo: Lots of astrologers will warn you off this one, because you are both fixed signs and rather stubborn. A mutual love of luxury homes or holidays could keep you together but one of you may pile kilos on. Your Taurus side likes the good things of life — the other person's Leo side makes this practically a priority.

Virgo: You two are the sort of couple everyone clings to in a crisis, because there is something solid and sensible about the two of you. Big career questions for one partner dominate things. So much earth between two people guarantees loads of common sense solutions and straight-down-the-line plans and ideas.

Libra: As you are both ruled by Venus, individual taste in clothes, music or homes really matters — let's hope you agree on some of it. One person is stubborn, the other super-diplomatic. The person with the dose of Libra is more likely to give way in the interests of having a peaceful life, but will it last?

Scorpio: This is a famously difficult combination, but when it works, it does so because you agree on money and lifestyle (essential) and you have a lucky matching Moon or Venus sign helping out. It's important that you agree on finances, and also on your basic values in life. If not expect an extremely difficult ride.

Sagittarius: You both think you know what counts in life, but for one of you it's something rather adventurous or educational, and for the other person it may be far more down to earth. One of you is clearly in touch with dreams, big plans and visions. The other is reliably sensible, and may get rather burdened.

Capricorn: You are both builders by nature, good at putting down roots at work, through your home, or through anything money can buy. There's steadiness, seriousness and success here. A lot depends on the other signs which are at work between you. But if the Sun-Moon-Mercury-Venus-Mars mix works, so might this.

Aquarius: This relationship requires a huge amount of commitment, because while one partner needs lots of changes and new beginnings in life, the other is pretty scared by it all. In fact, the Aquarian-influenced side of the equation could get endless entertainment value from taunting the other with changes.

Pisces: You'll notice a familiar pattern creeping in after a while, but it feels easy and comfortable enough. One of you simply becomes the practical, commonsense anchor — while the other dreams. Despite this, the Taurus and Pisces points in both your charts click together, so there's a sense of flow here.

you have
planets in

THE OTHER PERSON HAS PLANETS IN:

Aries: Your Gemini side feeds the other person's enthusiasm. The more you talk, the more motivated s/he becomes. This is one of those relationships with lots of feedback, phone calls and private jokes. There's an awful lot of energy floating around between you, and even the fights are productive. Some of your, ahem, witticisms, won't help in a fight though.

Taurus: There will be times when one partner seems awfully flippant or superficial about the things that really matter, and more seriously, times when communication grinds to a halt. Your Gemini side likes new ideas, gossip, and bits and pieces you pick up from TV, radio or newspapers. You may not always find you have an audience for all of this.

Gemini: One of you will repeat old childhood patterns learned from a complicated relationship with a brother, sister or cousin. You are, of course, clicking on the same sign, so a natural bond will be obvious. Communication and a shared sense of humour are the basics of this Gemini–Gemini attraction, but a Peter Pan (or Peta Pan) complex may surface.

Cancer: You can't keep things light and on the surface for long. Sooner or later one of you will draw out deeper feelings and emotions from the other and it may feel strange. Your Gemini side has a rather light and breezy way of looking at some aspects of life, love, death, sex, the universe and everything. The Cancer planet person is more sensitive to it all.

Leo: Lots of marriages, de facto relationships and business partnerships are built on people with Gemini and Leo planets on both sides. As a couple you will either be popular entertainers, or sought-after guests. Your Gemini side feeds the other person, and boosts confidence or lust for life. Shared taste in films or videos will really help you bond, too.

Virgo: An amazing meeting of minds is on the cards here, and one book, magazine or newspaper article will bounce backwards and forwards between you for months. The biggest problem with this blend? Your Gemini side is a lot less practical than his/her Virgo side. And it could all get a bit analytical and clinical. Too many theories, not enough grunt.

Libra: It's unlikely you'll fight at all — if you do, other clashing planet signs are to blame somewhere in both charts. You'll spend an awful lot of time talking about The Relationship though. Your Gemini side is pretty good at articulating things, and asking questions. The other person's Libran side loves all the weighing up of pros and cons between you.

Scorpio: After a while, one of you may be confronted by the fact that some covering up or hiding has been going on, as to face each other with your true personalities on show could be hard. Your Gemini side is rather head-driven, and the other person's Scorpio side is rather intense. That can feel wrong on the most basic level, sometimes. Tolerance required.

Sagittarius: A sense of humour is the basis of this relationship, and you make each other funnier, somehow. Gemini and Sagittarius are the two signs that turn up in the charts of professional funny men and women more than any other. However, these signs are also diametrically opposed. Let's hope the tension between you ends up being creative.

Capricorn: If only one of you would lighten up a bit more, and if only one of you could come down to earth long enough to take life a bit more seriously. S/he can't help living out a few ambitions, and is incredibly goal-driven. You can only stand so much of it before you long for a joke to break things up, but don't ever make light of this person's career.

Aquarius: You two were made for e-mail, but if you're not hooked up to a computer you'll just talk long into the night. Grunty, gritty passion may be hard to find but the love is real, it seems, as Aquarius and Gemini planets have an uncanny way of finding each other. A very new age relationship could be the result, and you'll make it up as you go along.

Pisces: Not everything in your relationship has to be spelled out, and one partner could become quite uneasy at the way the other one always misses the silent feelings. Your Gemini side often misses the emotional point, and you'll be amazed at what's actually been taking place inside the thought balloons in the Piscean type's head. Strange communication!

you have planets in CANCER

THE OTHER PERSON HAS PLANETS IN:

Aries: To one of you, the most important thing in life is Me. To the other, the most important thing in life is stability and emotional security. You have a clash to sort out here. There is a basic incompatibility between the restless, striving spirit of one person, and the other's need for a little more security.

Taurus: Favourite home-cooked dishes, or a particular restaurant, becomes a kind of secret couples' code for both of you. Unless your Moon signs look truly horrible, this is a nice, comfortable match. It's certainly an ego-stroking match. Although you'll need some other zodiac plus factors for true commitment.

Gemini: For this relationship to thrive and survive, one partner will need to have lots of separate friends and interests. Otherwise it could begin to feel basically wrong. The family of one partner may be rather a sensitive subject and it's one of those no-go areas for the relationship where jokes won't be allowed.

Cancer: Babies and children — or perhaps stepchildren — will be a huge issue between you. One partner really will take on the parent role in this relationship, too. The childhood and teenage experiences of both people in this relationship will exert quite a lot of influence on the future, as well.

Leo: As long as one partner is accepted by the other one's family — or accepts them — one of the biggest hurdles will be out of the way. It's not problem-free though. You'll need a few more click combinations between you to really fire up as a couple. In fact, that's the key problem here — someone's fire may go out.

Virgo: This relationship comes into its own when one of you falls ill, believe it or not. Security matters enormously to one of you, and that helps to keep things going. If you have lots of other click points between you, this could be quite a secure and stable relationship between two people who seem to match.

Libra: One person has strong and definite views on marriage, de facto relationships, family structures, pre-nuptial agreements or wedding vows. Let's hope you share similar views. The Cancer and Libra bits that are operating between you will cause a lack of harmony and understanding, so it needs work.

Scorpio: Music or poetry may be the only way one of you can express everything you really feel, as emotions run deep on one side in particular. Possessiveness — of each other or the kids — is a factor. There will be times when you feel as if your life is an opera (or a soap opera) but at least it makes you feel alive.

Sagittarius: Not many astrologers will tell you this is a perfect match, but it does happen. One of you reminds the other person of a much loved family member, or a family pattern is repeated. The Cancer and Sagittarius elements operating between you cause odd chemistry — for part of the time it may not feel right.

Capricorn: One of you works ambitiously so you can have an ideal home or family life, but then work gets in the way of that too and one of you pays the price. This issue will repeat, and repeat . . . This is something of a chemical cosmic connection, and you cannot expect things to stay the same between you either.

Aquarius: An unlikely combination. Huge sympathy and understanding from one of you helps, but do be honest. Is this relationship choice a bit of a rebellious statement for one of you? (Please, don't write and tell me, I get enough letters from astrology mad people with Aquarian planets as it is.) You'll need other click points.

Pisces: This relationship will bring out tremendous kindness, sympathy, softness and saintliness in one of you — not just for the other partner, but in a generalised way, too. Tremendously strong feelings about people in the family circle are part of the astro-package. Music will play a part in the partnership.

you have
planets in

THE OTHER PERSON HAS PLANETS IN:

Aries: There is something special here. You pass the baton between you all the time. It may be an idea that gets you going, a sexual proposition or something more mysterious. Keep your egos in check or you'll fight madly, as your Leo side can be rather self-interested, and this person's Aries side can be very 'Me, me, me' as you'll discover.

Taurus: There is a definite clash between your Leo side and the other person's Taurus side. One of you will consider himself or herself to be way, way above some of the things that preoccupy the other one. There's a bit of haughtiness in here somewhere. The unwillingness to give in for the sake of the other person, or the relationship, is damaging, too.

Gemini: There will typically be a very lively, light and entertaining feeling about your evenings when you allow your Leo side and the other person's Gemini side to lock in. Face facts though. One of you just doesn't want to grow up, so one partner may find himself or herself playing adult. Still, this is fun. And often very funny, too. Other people love you.

Cancer: You do have a rather ego-driven side, and this person's Cancerian side is rather good at making you feel loved, appreciated and wanted. At least one pattern in your relationship will become familiar — coach and player. You'll probably be the player, and the Cancerian type will provide the pep talks but it may also work the other way for you too.

Leo: This is a definite click, but managing two Leo elements in a relationship can be challenging because pride is such a big factor. At some stage you will have to tackle issues like one-upmanship, and silly head-tossing or nose-tilting. You know there's an egomaniac loose in the relationship, but is it you or the other Leo type? There's hot chemistry, though.

Virgo: There could be a bit of ego-feeding going on here, but that's okay. The compliments come in a sincere, careful and detailed way, and one of you just loves that. Silly pride will cause differences, as the other person's Virgo side can be a bit too whiney, picky and critical, and your Leo qualities won't tolerate being judged or looked up and down, it seems.

Libra: This relationship would go nowhere if one person was not unbelievably proud of the other, so let's hope it stays that way. Sharing friends and looking good together matters too. With your Leo side and the other person's Libra side, you could come up with a very sociable double-act. You have tremendous PR skills and seem to be a good couple!

Scorpio: A bit of game-playing is not uncommon when you become involved with a Scorpio but it may take a while to show itself. Both of you could be guilty of this, so watch it. There are major questions about who has the upper hand in things, who is the driving force, and who — at the end of the day — is top dog. It's all hidden at the start, though!

Sagittarius: You both have a natural lust for life, and when you team up, you pep talk each other into bigger and better things. Matching planets in Sagittarius usually produce a strong explorer streak in one or both people, so somehow overseas travel becomes more important, or educating oneself, or discovering the world, becomes a bigger issue.

Capricorn: Someone has an impressive job, title or qualification and it does make a difference, somehow. Try to have conversations which don't feature the 'Me' or 'I' word so much, though! It's important that there's more going on between you than just a helping hand on the old social status or career ladder. Do you click on other planets too?

Aquarius: One person will be stubborn, annoyingly insistent about his or her views, beliefs or tastes, which will cause problems as they seem so hard to comprehend for the other partner. Your Leo side is strangely drawn to the other person's Aquarian side, but unless you have other planet signs helping you, it may feel rather too cold for one of you eventually.

Pisces: The success or failure of this depends on the extent to which one of you is relying on his or her imagination to build it up. The other person's Piscean side can be a bit too vague and wafty for you, as you have a rather gutsy, fiery and enthusiastic streak. Different energy levels between you will be noticeable.

you have
planets in  **VIRGO**

THE OTHER PERSON HAS PLANETS IN:

Aries: You could easily fall into an arrangement where one of you is always trying new things and having adventures, while the other one mops it all up, or sits there and worries. There is a tremendous difference between one person's concern for doing things properly, and the other's disregard for the details.

Taurus: One of you knows the value of a good accountant, and it's amazing how this will make a difference to things! Spend two years building the foundations of love and it could last forever — but it really will hinge on the other click points between you. Other people find a wealth of common sense operating here.

Gemini: Two natural communicators seem to have found each other with this relationship, but one person is much more into details and organisation, while the other one just laughs it off. There are communication clashes and misunderstandings here, so watch out. You'll need back-up from other signs.

Cancer: There's a natural understanding here, and you won't have to work at it. One of you expresses his or her love in practical ways — around the house, for example. When one person is ill, the whole relationship seems to come into its own. Mind you, that's not a reason for developing serial flu — just a bonus.

Leo: One partner seems so loveable that his or her unbelievable ego or arrogance can be tolerated — for a while, anyway. You'll need to take turns at being Ms or Mr Special too. You will need some other click points between you to give this relationship any kind of mileage, as there is a basic lack of harmony here too.

Virgo: Your house or flat will have a slick, pulled-together look and so will you! Endless worry will plague one of you, while the other seems calmer. Don't sweat about the small stuff, otherwise you could get a reputation for feeding each other's neuroses and you'll never be invited to a dinner party ever again.

Libra: Fortunately, one partner decided long ago that he or she would do anything for a quiet life, and this will often save you. Sharing similar tastes — in clothes, music or homes — helps. One person seems prepared to bend and compromise, which is useful. Still, you'll need other click points to help you.

Scorpio: For one person, the quality and duration of the sex will become a bit of a relationship barometer. Just make sure all the other things are weighed up between you too. One person will be noticeably more emotional than the other in this relationship, but there is something sweetly supportive about the blend too.

Sagittarius: One of you takes on adventures and challenges that the other person could never imagine doing, and that's a turn on. You do have big differences in habits or outlooks though. A dose of Virgo and Sagittarius in two charts is a bit of a clash point and you'll need other astro-factors working in your favour too.

Capricorn: One person puts their ambitions, career or goals just a fraction below the importance of the relationship. As long as you both look at it that way, this could be a happy marriage or other kind of commitment. You will, of course, need back-up from other signs in your mutual astro-package as well.

Aquarius: It's unusual to find you two together, so perhaps you have clicks in other areas. Fortunately, you both consider each other intelligent, and logical answers may save things. There is an amazing difference between the common sense, practical and earth-bound approach of one of you compared to the other.

Pisces: You fall into roles very quickly, and it's important that you swap them occasionally or one person will begin to feel very boxed in. Take turns at playing the saviour or rescuer. This is a clash point in your mutual charts, and there's no avoiding it. You'll need help from other compatible factors too.

you have
planets in

THE OTHER PERSON HAS PLANETS IN:

Aries: This relationship could benefit from one of you taking a self-assertiveness course, and the other enrolling in something like yoga or meditation! Always dramatic, never dull. However, there is a basic difference here, as one of you feeds off sparks flying, while the other finds it unnerving.

Taurus: One of you is so completely turned on by the way your partner looks, or dresses, that it could keep you going for years. Money will be a bit of a sticking point sometimes. You'll need to work at this one, as one person is much more inclined to stick with the known and the familiar, which may get boring.

Gemini: This relationship brings out unbelievably good manners and old-fashioned romantic chivalry in one of the people concerned — no wonder your friends think it's good for both of you. Having a dose of Gemini and Libra working for you is a fantastic astro plus-factor. If there are other pluses it could work well.

Cancer: While one partner would rather pick up a relationship self-help book or explain things away with a theory, the other one believes in blood, sweat and tears. A learning experience — how can I put it any other way? To make this one feel truly right and comfortable, you'll require other astrological plus factors.

Leo: You'll know it's good when you catch your partner having a small boast about you at a party. This relationship is about pep talks and ego-feeding. Hopefully for both of you. One partner is also rather good at bending and flexing, which is just as well, as there will be the occasional two-act drama.

Virgo: One person seems to find peace of mind a lot more easily than the other, hopefully setting an example. If this one lasts it will do so because one of you is so tactful or compromising. These two signs don't exactly create wonderful chemistry, so it's likely to be other astro-factors that are stirring up heat.

Libra: It can be rather boring if someone never expresses a controversial opinion, or never takes a hard line on anything. That could easily happen in this love match, so watch it. At the same time, if you are clicking on Libra together there's a mutual love of good design or good music, which is a plus.

Scorpio: This could be extremely sensual if your Moon signs or Venus signs agree. If not, the sex will fade as one of you realises just how much grittier and more passionate he or she is. One partner is also inclined to be light and easy about life, whereas the other becomes much more intense and worked up.

Sagittarius: This could take off when one of you travels, leaving the other one behind, or when you both decide to buy a plane ticket together. If your Moon signs agree it could last forever — primarily because one partner finds commitment such an important thing that he or she is prepared to work for it.

Capricorn: It will take a while, but eventually one partner could start to have doubts about the way the other one handles certain work or business situations. This will need effort. Having these two signs in your relationship is a bit like feeling you know someone — and then you don't. Can you lean on other factors?

Aquarius: The big saving grace of this relationship is your mutual ability to stand back from very emotional or confronting situations and reason them out. It could be good. There is a lot of air in this combination, and air is the element which prefers logical reason over big, dumb emotion. A major plus factor.

Pisces: It's funny how one of you always romanticises things, but painting aspects of the other person or the relationship a certain way can sometimes tide it over too. There is something not quite right about this side of the partnership. Call it a basic difference in the way you both see the world.

you have
planets in SCORPIO

THE OTHER PERSON HAS PLANETS IN:

Aries: One of you has the capacity to really wound or damage the other person, and these sorts of rifts can be hard to mend. It will take a long time for real trust to develop between you. There are big differences here. One of you has a lot more emotion and feeling in his or her make-up than the other, so it's tricky.

Taurus: Which comes first, the future of the relationship, or the insistence by one partner that his or her life should be lived a certain way? This love match will see episodes of stubborness. It's very complex, very difficult and very demanding. You'll need other astro plus factors to make it really flow.

Gemini: You may have very different views on ex partners, old flames, or the threat of flirtatious rivals in the present. One of you could seem heartlessly carefree about it, the other too emotional. You'll be leaning hard on the astro-factors which are actually working for you, but this part of the package won't.

Cancer: This relationship will bring out more passion, tears and depth of feeling in one person involved than either of you have ever seen before, but if your personal charts agree, it's love. Commonsense will go out of the window a million times, as feelings (whoa, whoa, whoa feeeeelings) rule the day here.

Leo: There will be times when sex carries a definite edge, and some of the questions about control and status in the relationship will be thrashed out in bed. Do expect problems though. There is undoubtedly a lot of good stuff here, probably coming from other planets and signs in the package. But egos will clash.

Virgo: Being together has an electrifying effect on one partner, who will start to think about their body more, use it more, and care about it more. If the sex is great, the relationship will be too. If you have other plus factors working for you, then this could actually have staying power. At least it's passionate.

Libra: You will experience shades of Romeo and Juliet in this relationship, but also shades of *Melrose Place*. One of you is a lot more calm and reasonable than the other, it seems. There will be many times when you both feel as if you're missing the boat with each other, or missing the emotional point. It needs work.

Scorpio: Scorpios very rarely marry each other, but it's certain that one of you carries lots of complex sexual issues and feelings into the relationship, and it will count for a lot. Be prepared to watch one person in the partnership accelerate into mega-Scorpio behaviour — licentious, jealous, secretive, intense.

Sagittarius: Unless you can laugh together this could be extremely difficult in the long run. Sharing the same sense of humour will get you over some huge relationship problems. The Scorpio bits and Sagittarius bits working between you will make a terrible clanging noise and it will require patience to sit it out.

Capricorn: Let's just say that this relationship will bring out an obsessive streak in one of you, and leave it at that. The obsession could be work-related or relationship-related. But this is love. If you have lots of other astrological plus factors on your side then this partnership will have what it takes.

Aquarius: You have very different approaches to life. One partner believes that every relationship issue can be thought through, or sorted out by a theory. That attitude leaves the other partner cold. One of you is ruled by his or her feelings. The other one picks everything apart in a rather cool, weird way.

Pisces: You both understand that there are some fated or mysterious aspects about life, love, death or sex that cannot be easily explained. If your Moon signs agree, the sex could be psychic. There is a massive amount of feeling and emotion between you, and one partner finds a release through music, art or books.

you have
planets in

THE OTHER PERSON HAS PLANETS IN:

Aries: The theme song for this relationship should be like a Ramones song: 'Hey ho, let's go!' Heaps of energy is created when you two are together, although the fights can be noisy and nasty. Still, no astrologer in her right mind would tell you that this isn't a big plus factor. Lots of excitement lies ahead.

Taurus: Deciding if you should keep your finances separate, or where your mutual savings should go, could quickly reveal just how differently you feel about what matters in life. There is a fundamental difference in the energy drives, or enthusiasm levels, between you. You'll need help from other astro-click factors.

Gemini: Your differences and dividing lines will repeat on a regular basis over the next few years. Two things will save you. Communication and a sense of humour. The heavens are moving in difficult directions beyond 2000, so challenges lie ahead. Still, if you can make each other laugh, you'll survive.

Cancer: It looks as if one of you has extremely strong feelings, for better and worse, about certain aspects of the family. The other person should never under-rate the importance of this. There is a basic difference in your psychological make-ups, and I'm not talking about blusher. This one will require lots of work.

Leo: When you're in bed together, it's like playtime. At the beginning it must have seemed like a mutual admiration society. For the next few years though, love will mean hard work. Both of you are going through tough relationship challenge cycles. Still, you give each other the most wonderful pep talks.

Virgo: When you get down to tackling the practical basics of living together, you'll really notice the gaps. Even your bookshelves will reveal basic differences between you. Take care. One partner is over the top, given to seeing the big picture, and disdainful of details. The other is much more sensible.

Libra: One person has a clan of friends and this should never be given up, as it actually helps things work between you on a one-on-one level too. Travel will always bring you together. This is a nice, encouraging click point in both your charts. If everything else looks good too, then this one could be a winner.

Scorpio: There could be some interesting differences in beliefs or even ethics between you, and you may not realise it until one of life's big issues — death, sex, money — hits you. This will always be challenging. Unless you share other encouraging factors then you'll often feel you're not quite clicking.

Sagittarius: This is interesting to watch, because one partner will become a little bit deeper and more serious about life under the influence of the other. May–June of any year calls for tolerance. By virtue of the Sagittarius elements here, destiny has set up a bit of an obstacle course. Still, one person makes the other one roar with laughter, and humour is especially close to sex, you know.

Capricorn: Sooner or later one of you will have a big career, lifestyle or business decision and that's when you may realise just how different you really are. Patience is required. Unless you've got loads of other factors in your charts working for you, one person's manic obsession with ambition will grate.

Aquarius: One of you will develop some really fascinating and complex ideas about life, the universe and everything under the influence of the other. Off the wall humour keeps you in lust. You are a most interesting couple and at boring dinners or picnics, it will be you two the others turn to for stories.

Pisces: A birth or death in the family — for either of you — reveals some interesting differences in the way you see things. And neither of you is much good at the practicalities of life. For this one to feel as if it's actually working at a gut level, you'll need plenty of other astrological plus factors.

you have planets in  CAPRICORN

THE OTHER PERSON HAS PLANETS IN:

Aries: Respect will have to be earned in this relationship, as you both have your established ways of tackling life, and one partner may eventually doubt the other person's approach. Having a dose of Aries and Capricorn in both charts is a classic sign of a basic astrological clash. Are your goals in life similar?

Taurus: If one of you has a good solid base, in career, business or home ownership terms, you're more likely to take each other seriously. Together you could be rich one day — and very happy. It does depend on other astro-factors, though. Still, if the overall picture is good you could be awfully secure.

Gemini: For both of you, experiences growing up with a family member are the key to many relationship patterns. For one of you, it's a brother or sister. For the other, it's a father, or father figure. You could psychoanalyse this relationship until the cows come home, but don't forget your sense of humour.

Cancer: As soon as things become serious, you're going to have to decide who's going to take the nurturing, caring role and who's going to get out there and be a success. It could be tough. The relationship could become quite polarised. It needs balance, or one person could feel as if they're living out a stereotype.

Leo: It's doubtful if things would have ever got off the ground in the first place if one of you wasn't special, successful or impressive in some way. Let's hope there's more to it than that, though. There is no point in pretending that Capricorn and Leo factors go together. They don't. Lean on other signs here.

Virgo: When you first get together, plant a tree somewhere. Growing gardens, animals or children will be a happy cornerstone of this relationship. If your other astro-package signs agree, it's a hit. There's a tremendous focus on becoming solid home or land owners, or making sacrifices for true success.

Libra: After a while, one of you will seem so much more serious, hardline or heavy than the other one that things could start to feel quite uncomfortable. It won't be easy. If you have other, more supportive, sign factors working between you, you may find that you lean hard on those and try to get on with things.

Scorpio: Getting naked could have a remarkable effect on the health of this relationship so do it as soon as you get home from work if you have to! With luck, this will last and last. Still, it takes more than luck — a few doses of compatibility from other planets in your mutual astro-package will help.

Sagittarius: The ambitions and goals of one partner will take over now and again. One of you may have a problem with the way this person goes about getting what they want, too. One person will be much more energetic, and let's face it — slightly crazed — than the other. Watch out for emerging signs of boredom.

Capricorn: Do take turns at being silly and frivolous about life, or one specific person will begin to feel older than they really are. Too much maturity and common sense can begin to feel stifling. There is no doubt about the importance of ambition or goal-making in this particular combination, though.

Aquarius: Some of your life together will spill over into the workplace of one person, either via saucy e-mail, or masses of photos in heart-shaped frames on the desk. It won't be easy though. There is a major clash between the mad ideas (and general madness) of one person, and the other person's conservatism.

Pisces: Fortunately the mind-reading skills of one partner will increase as the relationship goes on. Strangely enough, it's when things go wrong that your partnership really seems to blossom. Having Capricorn-Pisces factors working for you is a big plus. Someone will offer a wonderfully supportive shoulder here.

you have
planets in

THE OTHER PERSON HAS PLANETS IN:

Aries: This is a definite plus factor. One of you seems prepared to try absolutely anything, which leaves the other partner full of admiration. There's some manic energy in here occasionally, so channel it into sex or mutual goals, not fighting. The other person's life outside your relationship gives you space.

Taurus: There are some major clash factors going on here. This relationship will reveal just how stuck in their ways one person really is, no matter if it's money, career, friends, family or even basic relationship and sexual habits. A tough call, because your Aquarian side is often slowed down or stifled.

Gemini: This is a fantastic booster for both of you. Wonderful communication leaves other couples wondering how you do it. The success of this high-potential love match depends on one person's ability to continually surprise the other, though. Once again, this is a classic e-mail or internet combination too.

Cancer: Here's an interesing question for you. Who matters more, the friends of one partner, or the family of the other? You two are very different, by the way. Even if you do have some more compatible clicks going on thanks to other planets, it's in your nature to analyse from a distance, but not theirs.

Leo: This relationship will turn one of you into a psychologist. Huge amounts of tolerance and patience will be necessary, as your Aquarian side is not particularly interested in sparing the other person's ego. If one of your theories or ideas about their personality, or the world, gets in the way of their self-esteem it won't bother you!

Virgo: As time passes, it will become pretty obvious that one person is far more tied into the small things of life, while the other person wants a bigger view. Don't let it turn cold, and lean hard on other plus factors between you. You can be quite attatched to your ideas and theories. The other person, less so.

Libra: The chemistry you share seems to bring out some really different, odd, unusual or off-beat traits in one specific partner. This is a brilliant connection to share, and the fact that the other person is so willing to give you the freedom to be yourself — or even be by yourself — is a loveable compromise.

Scorpio: Basic differences between you need a lot of care, or the situation could become messy. One partner must learn to understand, and live with, the other's illogical feelings. Your Aquarian side is capable of taking a long, cool look at anything from orgasms to jealousy. The other person won't understand.

Sagittarius: You do bring out the best in each other. Sure, one of you is a lot weirder by the other person's standards, but there's a similarity in outlooks or interests, too. You could surf island beaches or just the internet together, decide to change the world or change yourselves. A useful planetary click!

Capricorn: When one partner finally reaches the top, in terms of academic success, career achievement or social status, the other will have to handle things very carefully. There's also the little factor of friends — mostly yours, it has to be said. Not all of them are going to impress the other person.

Aquarius: A wonderful feeling of being accepted, or recognised, will exist in this combination. One of you will love the freedom to be as weird or as experimental as they like. You will need more going for you than just this click factor, though, as a pure Aquarius-Aquarius mix may lack a bit of staying power.

Pisces: It would surprise nobody if a friend, family member or paid professional had to be dragged in to tackle some of the most basic and practical tasks for both of you. A tricky relationship, no matter if it exists for romantic reasons or financial and lifestyle reasons. Your emotional temperatures are different.

you have
planets in  PISCES

THE OTHER PERSON HAS PLANETS IN:

Aries: At some point in your relationship, action and initiative will be called for. You must take turns at playing this 'up and at 'em' role, or life could start to look predictable. It would be extremely easy for one of you to play the tempestuous hot-head while the other lets his or her bottom lip quiver.

Taurus: This could be fabulous if your other signs agree. Some wonderful experiences, indulgences and escapes lie ahead for you as a couple. Only money limits imagination here. There's bound to be a big emphasis on the sensual pleasures of being together — wine, spas, good music, and other indulgences.

Gemini: One person in this partnership is wonderful at chatting, or explaining things, but the other person may wonder where all the emotional depth and feelings are. A challenge, which will need to be counter-balanced by other, more positive, astro-factors between you. There are fundamental differences here.

Cancer: If your personal charts are also in sync, this will be a classic love match, full of healing, self-sacrifice, and destined to bring out something saintly and special in you. You make each other feel as if you matter, and that you have something important to offer. If other factors agree, it's love.

Leo: This relationship needs a long, hard two-year reality check before you can truly say that what you think you see in each other is actually there. Avoid quickie engagements like the plague! One of you will be much more sensitive to the other, and may wince when the other person involved seems so out of touch.

Virgo: Feeling waves of sympathy and intuitive understanding wash over you can be a wonderful feeling, but in time the partner who is on the receiving end of all of this may want more. This is a clashing combination, and it comes with certain karmic lessons, if you believe the philosophy of spiritual astrologers.

Libra: You will find that certain romantic songs, films or books can give one of the individuals in this relationship the necessary shot in the arm to keep going — and to keep believing. You will need good, strong support from other signs in your mutual astro-package if this is going to avoid falling into black holes.

Scorpio: If you can both avoid falling into game-playing, or repeating old, bad patterns from your childhoods, then you could transform each other, and the relationship, into pure magic. There is a tremendous amount of feeling, passion and unspoken emotion operating here. Only music can really articulate it all.

Sagittarius: Long conversations about what it all means, and what we're all here for anyway, will become a familiar theme if you stay together. Do expect challenges though. This is a clash point between both your horoscopes, and from time to time life will become quite difficult. Work on communication if you can.

Capricorn: This seems mutually beneficial, unless your Moon signs clash. One partner seems different, special and on another level altogether to the other, who is nevertheless glad to be needed. This is a plus factor for both of you, and the nice thing is the way that one person seems to melt in the other's presence.

Aquarius: You have very different ways of operating, but with a lot of tolerance and deliberate mind-reading on the part of one partner, anything's possible. But do get an accountant. Unless you've got lots of Capricorn, Virgo or Taurus in there somewhere, this will be a saga of impracticality and late bill-paying.

Pisces: You may find that part of your relationship is spent in a victim–rescuer game, or that one person takes on the part of healer/helper. It's okay for a while, but there has to be more. Still, having two Pisces factors in this relationship is pretty special. Life will seem like a poem made flesh.

KARMA and past lives

Do you ever have a 'run' on a particular sign? I have an Aries friend who spent a whole year going out with Librans, and then doing business deals with them. Another friend shudders at the thought of dealing with Virgoans — it's never worked out for her.

I wonder if this is because of some gigantic, universal, astrological system ... A bit like the biggest computer in the galaxy, making sure that we cross astrological lines with other signs at various times in our life, for the purpose of learning something from them along the way as we spiral upwards.

Reincarnation is hard to write about, because it had such a bad name in the Eighties. Cher, Goldie Hawn, Kurt Russell, Richard Burton, Elizabeth Taylor and Leonardo da Vinci, all resident in ancient Egpyt? No thanks. But then I looked at the research. There are now hundreds of cassette tapes and videos floating around universities and research centres worldwide, proving beyond any doubt at all that under hypnosis, an extremely high percentage of volunteers can 'remember' past lives in the most trivial detail. In a second-hand bookshop in country Australia, I made a real find — a book by a Sydneysider, Peter Ramster, called *The Truth About Reincarnation* (Rigby: Australia 1980) with drawings of Egyptian hieroglyphics scrawled by Jenny Green, a Blue Mountains housewife who managed to recall her life in a temple so well that she was using ancient words under trance, and drawing detailed pictures of everyday life. Jenny's drawings, the photograph of her and the actual taped transcripts from her Egyptian 'memories' are wholly convincing.

I gave in and underwent past life hypnosis two years ago. By turns, I was a blonde ice-skater in a red jumper in the 1920s, a very angry, brooding Italian farmhand in the 1700s, a sea merchant trader even longer ago than that, then a genteel housewife in a cartwheel hat, entertaining ladies to lunch in the American South. Watching each life was a little like viewing a short film, but I could also smell the scenery! My American housewife had a garden she was extremely proud of, and the scent of the flowers was quite real in the trance — beyond dreaming. She was also a chain-smoker. When I came round, my throat was actually burning. Bizarre.

After that, I wrote a story on Buddhism for *Vogue*, and met a monk who had been the babysitter to a boy lama who seemed to him to be two going on fifty. This child was not like other children — his concentration span was incredible, and the monk told me he would break into words of wisdom in between baby talk.

But where does this leave astrology? Jeanne Avery has written a book called *Astrology And Your Past Lives* (Fireside:New York 1987) where she argues that Saturn is the planet which describes what you went through last time round, and what you have to learn this time round. As anyone who has been through her Saturn Return knows, there is a sensation of heavy learning — and maybe karma — as you slog through the long process of finally growing up at age 30. For more information, see the section on Saturn Returns in this book.

Avery considers the house placement of Saturn, and the aspects (patterns) it makes with other planets when she goes into past lives. This is quite in-depth astrology, though, and to really get the most from her book you will need your full chart done. Still, if you want to know why you may have inherited the particular Saturn Return you ended up with, this is an eye-opener.

The idea that a soul can choose a body does lend itself to astrology, in quite an obvious way. Let's say that you've just spent your last three or four lives in poverty, having no knowledge of money, and little chance to develop a value system based on anything other than survival. In order to evolve, you're going to need to deal with cash this time around — so your soul waits until the time, place and date lend themselves to a horoscope with lots of Taurus planets, and — wham — you're born (or rather, born again).

If you take this idea further, it's possible that you're also 'choosing' (by virtue of your horoscope) the signs which will click, clunk and clash with you. You have something to learn from all of them, after all — the boss who sacked you, the man you move in with, the sister who gives you a blood transfusion . . . and so on.

If you're into the idea of entertaining a million impossible ideas before breakfast, you might be interested in this view of sign-to-sign karma.

YOU KEEP MEETING ARIANS

They're going to teach you about the fine line between being selfish and self-interested. They're going to show you that anger in itself isn't a bad thing, it depends on how you deal with it. They're going to instruct you in the fine art of being first in the queue. You'll learn about your own capacity to be self-assertive, and how to push without being pushy.

YOU KEEP MEETING TAUREANS

They're going to teach you about your own value system — money versus everything else. They're going to show you how wonderful beautiful objects and possessions can be. They're going to instruct you about money management, one way or another. You'll learn a great lesson about what you will — and definitely won't — sell out for.

YOU KEEP MEETING GEMINIS

They're going to teach you how to be a good and appreciative listener, but also how to talk — or write. They're going to show you that life actually makes sense if you analyse it, discuss it and read about it. They're going to instruct you in the art of short-distance travel. You'll learn a great lesson about what other people's siblings mean to them.

YOU KEEP MEETING CANCERIANS

They're going to teach you that family really does matter, one way or another. They're going to show you what it means to completely identify with one's roots, origins, heritage or nationality. They're going to instruct you about motherhood and parenthood, in specific ways. You'll learn a great lesson about your own family feelings here.

YOU KEEP MEETING LEOS

They're going to teach you what it means to be proud of yourself — or, conversely, to lack self esteeem. They're going to show you how fantastic it is to express yourself, in personal ways, through creative ideas, hobbies, interests or projects. You'll learn a great lesson about pride and dignity — and how you can avoid taking it too far, as well.

YOU KEEP MEETING VIRGOS

They're going to teach you about your body, your health and your well-being. They're going to show you that the body-mind connection can't be ignored. They're going to instruct you in the fine art of paying attention to detail. You'll learn a great lesson about perfectionism, and how doing a job well doesn't necessarily mean becoming manic about it.

YOU KEEP MEETING LIBRANS

They're going to teach you about the aesthetic pleasures in life — flowers, art, tone, texture, colour. They're going to show you how important it is to hang on to civilised human behaviour, even when things become tough. They're going to instruct you in diplomacy. You'll learn a great lesson about compromise, and why it's easy to take it too far.

YOU KEEP MEETING SCORPIOS

They're going to teach you that living life on the surface really isn't living at all. They're going to show you what being human is really like — and that includes all the hidden, complex and 'unacceptable' stuff. They're going to instruct you in the fine art of focus. You'll learn a great lesson about what taboos actually mean — to yourself and other people.

YOU KEEP MEETING SAGITTARIANS

They're going to teach you that life is basically absurd, and consequently even the worst things have a Woody Allen twist.

They're going to show you how important it is to travel and see the world. They're going to reveal how crucial it is to have something to believe in, and something to find meaning in. You'll learn why excess never works.

YOU KEEP MEETING CAPRICORNS

They're going to teach you that climbing patiently to the top is not some naff yuppie concept — it's actually the foundation on which all life is built. They're going to show you what it means to be professional — and unprofessional. You'll learn a lot about the fine line between pessimism and realism. You'll learn what it means to be mature.

YOU KEEP MEETING AQUARIANS

They're going to teach you what individuality actually means. They're going to show you how important it is to live in the future first, the present second, and the past last. They're going to reveal how exciting and liberating it feels to be utterly yourself. You'll learn a lot about doing your own thing without doing other people down.

YOU KEEP MEETING PISCEANS

They're going to teach you about the joys of escaping reality. They're going to show you what it's like to live in a world where being real, sensible, normal and logical isn't actually the big priority. They're going to instruct you in the difference between fantasising and lying. You'll learn a lot about compassion, and kindness and the art of self-sacrifice.

How can you tell if there's some past-life connection going on? Here is what my spies tell me:

- The first time you meet, it all feels very familiar and comfortable.
- One look, and you know you don't like them.

- You owe them money, or they owe you money.
- Just for the hell of it, you always find yourself giving them things.
- They're generous with their time, energy, money or stuff — and yet they don't ask for anything from you.
- After it's over (the affair, marriage, business partnership, relationship) there's some kind of awkward object (anything from a book to a horse) which hasn't been returned.
- Even though this person should be peripheral in your life, destiny keeps pointing them your way, or linking them to you through 'chance' happenings or other people.

As a rule of thumb, don't ever leave things hanging with people. And particularly so, if this is the second or third time you've either gained, or lost, with a particular sign. Ever get the feeling the universe is trying to tell you something? If you have now had problems with six Sagittarians in a row, it may be time to discover more about the sign, from this and other books, and set things straight with as many of those people as you can track down. Similarly, if you always seem to do well with Pisceans (they give you lifts, visit you in hospital or get you jobs) then you may like to start ploughing something back their way.

And finally — shoplifting. If you put this book under your jumper, I may have to meet you in 2200 in an inter-galactic supermarket somewhere and steal your bananas.

RECOMMENDED AND REQUIRED READING:

The Holographic Universe by Michael Talbot (HarperCollins, London 1996) — absolutely brilliant if you're beginning to think there might be something in this past lives thing — or even if you're a convert.

INNER
conflicts

Some relationships — even some first-sight encounters — produce something like an adverse chemical reaction. One woman aptly describes it this way: 'Yes-no feelings. You do, and don't, want to get closer to this person!'

This is often because the person provoking the reaction is reminding you of an inner conflict. As you read through this section, you may have noticed that some of the click, clunk and clash signs are also present in your own chart.

A woman with a Scorpio Sun, Aquarius Moon, Leo Mercury, Leo Venus and Virgo Mars is going to feel the clashing and clunking sides of herself working at cross-purposes a lot of the time. Her Leonine side wants to have the best, to take the lead, to be around the upside of life: her Aquarius Moon doesn't care so much for being socially acceptable or staying at the Ritz — it just wants the freedom to be a little different. Throw in her Scorpionic side, which is terribly emotional and passionate and understands neither of them, and you have a fabulous three-way fist-fight going on inside her.

When this woman meets people (or lovers) with the same signs — Scorpio, Leo or Aquarius — in their charts, she is *really* going to feel the clash. Not just because of the sticking points and differences on the outside, but also because this person is reflecting a very real inner conflict in the woman's own life and times. What you can't get together in yourself, you will not be able to get together in a matching 'clash' or 'clunk' combination.

It takes an extraordinary amount of clarity and detachment to be able to see what is going on when you start to feel the turn-off factor with a partner, a friend or even a complete stranger. If they happen to have a matching sign with you, but it presents problems in your own chart, they will remind you of yourself (good) and have common ground with you (even better) but they will also trigger a basic conflict inside your own personality that has been with you since you drew your first breath.

I'm sorry to drag Princess Diana and Prince Charles into an astrology book (it happened to them all the time) but as they were the world's best-known 'Click–Clash–Clunk' couple, they illustrated this point perfectly.

DIANA AND CHARLES

Diana's horoscope showed: Cancer Sun, Aquarius Moon, Cancer Mercury, Taurus Venus, Virgo Mars. Imagine you were Diana Spencer back in 1981, engaged to the most eligible man in Great Britain. If you had gone to see your crazed local astrologer, you would have heard this: 'Your Taurus Venus clicks nicely with your Sun, Cancer Mercury and Virgo Mars. However, it does clash with your Aquarius Moon.'

The nature of the clash inside Diana? The Taurus Venus — needing practical answers, security, money, possessions and good sound values — and the Aquarius Moon — which likes freedom, lots of change and could care less about money if it meant being a bird in a gilded cage.

Charles' horoscope showed this sequence: Scorpio Sun, Taurus Moon, Scorpio Mercury, Libra Venus, Sagittarius Mars. Let's really stretch the collective imagination at this point and propose that he might also have consulted an astrologer.

'Clash, clash,' she would have said, looking worried. 'Your Scorpio Sun and Mercury are working against your Taurus Moon.' What this means is that Charles' Scorpionic bit was being terribly emotional, passionate and intense, and his commonsense, security-conscious, money-minded Taurean bit was totally bewildered by how much the Scorpionic side will risk for a few feelings. Meanwhile, the Scorpionic bit would have been thinking, 'How boring!'

When preparing both charts, the astrologer would already have been spotting a few clicks, and a few clunks: which you may also have seen. There was a nice feeling between the sensitive, touchy-feely Cancer and Scorpio planets on both sides. There was a fire-air group link between the Aquarius Moon and Sagittarius Mars. There was also a definite clunk between Diana's Virgo Mars and Charles's Libra Venus — not a big issue.

The most difficult problem, though, was this: they both had a planet in Taurus. While this is provided the most resounding click between her Venus (romance, physical attraction) and his Moon (homes and babies) it was also triggering an inner conflict that both of them had. Her Aquarius–Taurus clash, and his Scorpio–Taurus clash were activated when they were together. As a married couple, each reminded the other of things they could not get together in their own lives: there was Diana's freedom-loving, change-loving, enlightened, slightly wacky Aquarian tendency coming up against her change-loathing, shopaholic, Taurean tendency — being around Charles was going to remind her of this. Then consider Charles: Taurus would have been saying, 'Consider the money. Think about the security. What about the vintage wine?' while Scorpio would have been hissing, 'Sex, intensity, passion, emotion!'

The split was especially sad because there were some unbelievably powerful clicks between both Diana and Charles. In the end, it came down to the descriptions of Aquarius, Taurus and Scorpio planets you will read in this book: they both had such different agendas that it may not be surprising that the two human beings who 'owned' the planets set off in different directions. Astrology students out there may want to get out the charts for Prince Philip and Queen Elizabeth, too — their 'click' sign — Taurus — is the same sign which caused so many problems in the marital chemistry of Charles and Diana.

Okay, enough about one of history's most scrutinised couples. Here's the lowdown on your own click signs.

Signs you SHARE

The odds of you and your partner having the Sun, Moon, Mercury, Venus or Mars in an identical sign are fairly low, so if you and your partner have planets in the same sign, then something really special is going on. This may add to the fated, or instinctive, feeling about the match, or the meeting. The odds are high that you are going through the same trends or cycles at the same time — for better or worse!

Remember, it helps if this other person's matching sign is not triggering a clash in your own chart. In other words, if you have a Gemini Sun and Sagittarius Moon (a basic clash) but you meet someone with a Sagittarius Sun, remember that along with the incredible click will come a big reminder of something difficult you cannot get together in your own life and times.

Here's a rundown on what it means to share a sign in common. You'll notice that some of the famous couples I have included as examples have long since split up. This is quite deliberate: the factors which break up a marriage or partnership are far more complex than the 'click' you do or don't hear when you start out together. The example of Charles and Diana supports that. I don't believe that a failed relationship is necessarily proof of a lack of passion or common ground. Most of these successful couples have kept things together, some have not, but I don't think anybody would deny the original bond.

CLICKING ON ARIES PLANETS

Warren Beatty — Sun and Mercury in Aries
Annette Bening — Mercury and Venus in Aries

If you both have planets in Aries, then you will find yourself in an energetic, dynamic relationship. The only problem will be sorting out who gets their own way. These friendships or partnerships seem to zap into life quickly. You are both impatient, and with a Fire connection, have boundless enthusiasm. When things go wrong, each of you will silently accuse the other of being too pushy. You team up best when you are both fighting problems coming from outside.

CLICKING ON TAURUS PLANETS

Madonna — Mars in Taurus
Sandra Bernhard — Venus in Taurus

If you share planets in Taurus, a mutual enjoyment of the sensual things in life will bring you together. Lethal shopping expeditions or long lunches in exclusive restaurants are a common outcome of a Taurus–Taurus connection. If you are both the non-material type of Taureans, you will spend time in the garden or the countryside instead. You can both be terribly stubborn, and if you lock horns, the outcome may take forever to resolve itself. Values — ethical and financial — matter.

CLICKING ON GEMINI PLANETS

Tom Cruise — Mercury in Gemini
Nicole Kidman — Sun in Gemini

These friendships or relationships seem to thrive on little notes and messages, cards and phone calls, faxes, nicknames and e-mail. When you get together the conversation is lively and often funny. When you're feeling less charitable about each other, both of you will bitch that the other is too superficial, lacks soul and has a poor grasp of sensitive issues and feelings. When it works? You won't stop talking. This is a terrifically witty combination — it's also highly entertaining for others who will eavesdrop *continually*!

CLICKING ON CANCER PLANETS

Emma Thompson — Moon and Mars in Cancer
Kenneth Branagh — Mars in Cancer

Both of you will know what's really important in life. Sharing intimate feelings, for a start, being sympathetic and caring and being handy with the chicken soup when someone is ill. You will swap stories about family ties with a lot of interest, and your own family stories may be integral to the relationship. When you clash, you will resent each other for being too clingy or too emotional. Both your feelings about parenthood will be a big issue.

CLICKING ON LEO PLANETS

Derryn Hinch — Moon in Leo
Jacki Weaver — Moon in Leo

This could easily turn into a mutual admiration society, as you both enjoy or identify with each other's talents, reputation or achievements. You'll feel proud to know each other, and will encourage each other in various creative or self-expressive pursuits. Having mutual Leo planets in common can be difficult to manage at times, as both of you express yourselves quite proudly: hopefully, your other planets, in other signs, will supply the 'graceful giving up' that is necessary.

CLICKING ON VIRGO PLANETS

Claudia Schiffer — Sun and Mercury in Virgo
David Copperfield — Sun in Virgo

You could be gym buddies or swap notes on vitamins, eating plans or illness symptoms! Endless talk about 'your body, my body' is common. You relate to each other's hard-working style, and even if there is no work connection between you, will often share activities that feel like a labour of love. Your mutual love of good conversation and good books will produce lively dinner parties and result in an unofficial home library.

CLICKING ON LIBRA PLANETS

Susan Sarandon — Sun in Libra
Tim Robbins — Sun in Libra

You could charm each other to death with this combination, and there is often a trademark sweetness about a Libra–Libra connection. There is tremendous equality with this sign, and you will relate to each other's concern with justice and fairness for all. When problems arise, it is often because one of you feels that the other is fence-sitting to avoid ever having to deal with criticism. Arguments will be sidestepped or quickly defused.

CLICKING ON SCORPIO PLANETS

Julia Roberts — Sun and Mercury in Scorpio
Lyle Lovett — Sun and Mercury in Scorpio

This connection stretches about 1,000 kilometres below the surface. A feeling of depth is characteristic of Scorpio–Scorpio people, and you will instinctively feel drawn to each other's tremendous 'soul' and passion. It's an emotional bond, but typically, there will be times when you sense some pretty raw, uncivilised emotions in each other. You may also find each other too intense. Taboo issues will be a big factor in you, and sexuality will be a huge source of relationship highs and lows.

CLICKING ON SAGITTARIUS PLANETS

Bob Hawke — Sun, Mercury, Venus and Mars in Sagittarius
Blanche d'Alpuget — Venus in Sagittarius

This is not an indoors connection. Sagittarius–Sagittarius people are usually sitting on a plane, driving miles into the countryside — or to the sea — or brushing up on their French. Everything can seem like an adventure. Things are always over the top, but at least you'll share some great jokes. This is an enthusiastic, funny, adventurous combination. As you get older, beliefs, philosophies and convictions will matter more.

CLICKING ON CAPRICORN PLANETS

Johnny Depp — Moon in Capricorn
Kate Moss — Sun in Capricorn

Both of you will know What Really Matters in life. There can be a serious streak to a Capricorn–Capricorn connection, and your ability to understand each other's fascination with various goals and ambitions will make you comfortable around each other. This will be a structured relationship, and there will definitely be a sense of mutual progress. It doesn't hurt the status or career goals of either of you — but you'll need other signs in there, too, to liven things up.

CLICKING ON AQUARIUS PLANETS

Woody Allen — Moon in Aquarius
Mia Farrow — Sun in Aquarius

This is a cool, friendly connection — no matter how intimate things become. There is often a mutual interest in things which other people find a little too strange, cutting-edge, new or different to cope with, or a preference for an unusual kind of relationship by others' standards. You typically give each other a lot of space to do your own thing. Your problems with each other will revolve around how eccentric or inaccessible one of you is being. It's no-ties love.

CLICKING ON PISCES PLANETS

Paul Newman — Moon in Pisces
Joanne Woodward — Sun and Venus in Pisces

You sense each other's imagination, whimsy and vision and it's not long before you're swapping fantasies. You are both escape artists, and understand each other's need to inject dreams into reality. There is also plenty of emotion to swim around in with this connection. When you feel like slipping away from each other, it's usually because one of you feels that the other partner is playing the saviour or the victim too much.

your circle of FRIENDS

It happens all the time. You go to a wedding, meet all of your friend's other friends, and ten new names go into your address book. It's a clicking conspiracy!

'The other thing I find,' says an astrologically aware friend of mine, 'is that all my boyfriend's ex-girlfriends have the same signs as me — Taurus, Virgo, Taurus, every time.'

In some places they call this kind of person — your boyfriend's ex-girlfriend — your 'bonk-in-law'. I found it happening to me one day when I casually asked a boyfriend about the Love of his Life (she was two bonks-in-law behind me). She had my Venus sign. She had my Mars sign. I was totally appalled.

When she and I eventually met up, we didn't actually *shut up* for several days. In fact, when the aforementioned boyfriend and I split up, she was the one who ended up getting my Christmas cards three years later.

THE CLICKING CHAIN

If you have nothing else to do on a rainy Sunday afternoon (or if you have planets in Virgo and love making lists) then try this: write out the names and birthdays of everyone you have ever slept with, every friend you have, everybody they have slept with, and then look for the clicks. Better still, look for *the same signs*. You have probably unearthed an Arian Tribe, a Taurean Circle or a Geminian Energy Field.

If you are feeling really fiendish, you can also jot down the birthday of that person who entered the tribe by virtue of their intimate relationship with one of its members, and through a CLASH–CLASH–CLASH combination, managed to make dinner parties impossible for six months afterwards.

Incidentally, if you're advertising in the newspaper for Share Accommodation people, you may prefer to forget all the stuff about 'Must have decent personal habits' and 'Prefer vegetarian'. What you really need is a Clicking Chain of your existing household and a biro. Please include the dog. They have Moon signs, too, and it *does* affect the social ambience.

men with
planets in

Even when the man with an Aries Sun, Moon, Mercury, Venus or Mars is not directly involved in sport, fitness or physical pursuits, he will be watching it or talking about it. In the original Aries myth, Mars, the God of War, ruled this sign. In times of peace, the fighting spirit is channelled through competitive sport. It's not surprising that literary soccer guru Nick Hornby has the Sun in Aries. Most Aries-influenced men like to see a bit of muscle definition. Some of them head for a yoga class or a thrashy session in the pool. Others aim straight for weekend passions and pursuits that are going to result in a defined bicep — or two.

I have known a few armchair-bound men with Aries planets, but they were always tuned to the football. Elton John is an Aries Sun. Biceps are not his thing, but managing a soccer club is. In truth, if the man in your life has a planet in Aries, he really should be out there, *doing* something sweaty. Otherwise, he'll be blocking off a whole side of his personality, and men with this sign in their charts really need a physical outlet for stress. If your Aries-influenced man is the sedentary type, you may want to lob a cricket ball at him occasionally in the interests of his psychological wellbeing (and his biceps). Some of them are athletic supporters, some of them just wear the gear. But ideally, an Aries planet needs a field, court or pool. Tarzan, 'born' on 1st December 1911 in Chicago, has the Moon in Aries. Golf fanatic and well-known London media redhead Chris Evans also has a dollop of Aries in his chart. Call it the leopardskin underpants sign and leave it at that. But underpants with a built-in jockstrap.

Muscles and adrenalin

Ron Barassi — Mars in Aries
Dennis Lillee — Moon in Aries
Greg Norman — Mars in Aries
Wayne Pearce — Sun in Aries
Jackie Stewart — Moon in Aries

Björn Borg — Moon in Aries
Sir Edmund Hillary — Moon in Aries
Linford Christie — Sun in Aries
Sir Jack Brabham — Sun in Aries
Severiano Ballesteros — Sun in Aries

MARS, GOD OF WAR

Aries is ruled by Mars, the God of War. Hitler had Mercury in Aries, Saddam Hussein has Venus in this sign. Basic aggression is at the core of Aries, yet a lot depends on the life and times of the man in question — if it's not acceptable, or even remotely wonderful, to be aggressive in his world, then he'll cut this side of Aries off completely. Still, this core hostility has a strange way of leaking out.

There are many men out there with an Aries Sun, Moon, Mercury, Venus or Mars who are unconsciously aggressive. So they needle you, then claim they don't know why you're upset — or find other ways to provoke. The evolved types play-act their warrior side through sport or a creative outlet. The less evolved types deny having this in-your-face Arian side at all, but end up leaving a trail of fuming people behind them. The most tragically troglodyte Arian types are bullies. Raised in an environment where they were told it was both acceptable and *masculine* to be an invader, raider, gun guru or lout, they end up feeling like men out of time.

The smart ones, like Aries Sun Spike Milligan, take their energy and pour it into worthwhile causes in a non-aggressive, but amazingly energetic way. Assertiveness skills are what it's all about. Many Arian types seem to have them automatically, but there are a few who still need to do a swift exchange, and turn Mars, the God of War, into something a bit more constructive.

There are many different kinds of armies, including the Salvation Army (founded by William Booth, an Aries Sun). There are many different kinds of battles, too — Malcolm X, the American black leader, was an Aries Moon. Robespierre, the French revolutionary leader, was an Aries Moon, and so too was Che Guevara. A man with an Aries planet has a need to declare war on something, but there are worthwhile goals and wasteful goals, and there are any number of ways of handling a fight.

DEFINING MASCULINITY

Being born with an Aries planet is like having a Neolithic caveman chained to your leg. So how do men deal with it? I've found that the more Air planets (Gemini, Libra, Aquarius) a man has, the more difficult it is for him to figure out a way to be a New Man. Equally, the more sensitive Water planets (Cancer, Scorpio, Pisces) there are in his chart, the more he's going to feel split in two. The men with a planet in Aries, but another planet also in an Air sign, can find all that traditional macho masculinity rather dumb. Often, these men end up using their brains to fight their battles or intellectualise their anger. Men with a planet in Aries, but another planet in an emotional Water sign, have to find a way to deal with anger without drowning in it or being overwhelmed by it.

Some Arian types live out the intense masculinity of the sign by literally acting a role — thus, Timothy Dalton (Aries Sun) as James Bond. Many of them like to play around with macho mythology by buying a leather jacket, or a fast set of wheels. Another way to dig up some Arian caveman style is for them to find an especially gentle, soft partner. Some Aries-influenced men go for women who are traditionally female or intensely feminine. The myth tells us that Mars, the ruler of Aries, was the lover of Venus, who ruled both love and beauty. The important part about Aries planets is this: men who have them can, and should, have fun with them. Fooling around with all the he-man stuff is his right and privilege. So give him his ball back! If not, he may end up projecting his Arian side onto you — and it's a tough role to play.

planets in

RHYTHM AND MELODY

What is the single most obvious thing about a man who has planets in Taurus? It has to be his passion for music. I apologise for the length of this list, but any sign which turns up in the Beatles, the Who, the Beach Boys, the Sex Pistols *and* the Rolling Stones has to be worth a closer look.

The Taurean link with modern music — and the Libran link — are attributable to Venus, who rules both signs. The only way men have been able to get anywhere near the Goddess of Love and Beauty since 1950 *and* keep their masculinity is by pursuing music. For a man with Taurus planets to stay sane and happy, Venus has to be accommodated somewhere in his life. Modern music is still the only legitimate place where this ancient goddess gets any kind of attention: in music, a man can dress up, sing about love, sex and beautiful women, and not have tomatoes thrown at him. In fact, beautiful women are more likely to find him attractive: a definite plus for Venus, who likes to keep an eye on the man with the Sun, Moon, Mercury, Venus or Mars in Taurus. If you consider that everything from rock'n'roll to heavy metal has been about love songs, gorgeous women and fabulous wardrobes, the Taurus–Venus–music connection suddenly starts to make a great deal of sense. The best accompaniment for a Taurean seduction? A superb set of speakers.

Taurean album credits

Bono — Sun in Taurus
Roy Orbison — Sun in Taurus
Michael Jackson — Sun in Taurus
Bjorn Ulvaeus — Sun in Taurus
James Brown — Sun in Taurus
Billy Joel — Sun in Taurus
Sid Vicious — Sun in Taurus
Eric Burdon — Sun in Taurus
Stevie Wonder — Sun in Taurus

Bob Dylan — Moon in Taurus
Mick Jagger — Moon in Taurus
Elton John — Moon in Taurus
Jim Morrison — Moon in Taurus
Morrissey — Mercury in Taurus
Bernie Taupin — Mercury in Taurus
Miles Davis — Mercury in Taurus
Paul Weller — Mercury in Taurus
Paul McCartney — Venus in Taurus

Jimmy Barnes — Sun in Taurus
Pete Townshend — Sun in Taurus
Joey Ramone — Sun in Taurus
Joe Cocker — Sun in Taurus
Burt Bacharach — Sun in Taurus
Chris Novoselic — Sun and Mercury in Taurus

Prince — Venus in Taurus
Brian Wilson — Venus in Taurus
Eric Clapton — Venus in Taurus
Angus Young — Venus in Taurus

MONEY AND VALUES

Taurus is associated with money and ownership, but also the need for a value system. Capitalists and Communists alike have planets here — Karl Marx was a Taurus Sun–Moon, Ronald Reagan was a Taurus Moon. It's not enough to say that a Taurus planet produces an astute businessman, a natural accountant or a stock market genius. For every Peter Abeles (Taurus Sun and Mercury) who is interested in trade and mergers, there is a Peter Garrett (Taurus Mars) who has a different value system.

When a Doors song was sold on as a cheesy TV advertisement jingle, it was Jim Morrison (Taurus Moon) who objected most. Taurus planets do lend an amazing awareness of the *price* of things, but it may not always be in dollars and cents. There are many ethical business success stories represented by this sign — the conservationist and restaurateur Peter Doyle, a Taurus Moon, is one of them. There are also a fair number of Taurean types paralysed by this question: Am I selling out? Am I selling my soul? Perhaps that's why so many musicians have planets in this sign. But you will see Taurus in action any time the man in your life has to make a career decision. Things may be there for the taking, but at what price?

If a Taurus-influenced man hits a financial crisis, destiny says that it will have an extreme effect on his value system, his philosophy of life, and the price he puts on the *priceless* commodities of life. Having a lot of money achieves the same effect. Having the Sun, Moon, Mercury, Venus or Mars in Taurus is like having an accountant in one ear, and your conscience in the other. His Holiness Pope John Paul II is a Sun Taurus, and heads one of the richest (religious) enterprises in the world. Juggling this with a Christian value system presents him with a uniquely Taurean dilemma.

If the man in your life has a planet here, it is just part of the overall story. But don't underestimate it. Taurus will always lead him back to the price of things — every, every time. Quite literally, this one is 'for richer, for poorer' but *spiritually* as well as financially. I'll leave it to you to work out the true cost!

Money talks

'What, after all, is money? Can you eat it, drink it — make love with it?' — **Warren Beatty, Venus in Taurus**

'I could've made more money if I'd sold torn T-shirts with my name on them. The Brando T-Shirt would've sold a million.'

'I notice that the width of a Hollywood smile in my direction is commensurate with how much my last picture grossed.' — **Marlon Brando, Venus in Taurus**

'I had a dream. A vision. Of money in the bank. And I said: If I make a big picture that everybody laughs at they'll give me money . . . and when I'm an old man, I'll go visit my money in the bank.' — **Mel Brooks, Venus in Taurus**

'Whether you think Jesus was God or not, you must admit that he was a first-rate political economist.' — **George Bernard Shaw, Moon in Taurus**

men with planets in  GEMINI

Funny, ferociously intelligent and forever young just about sums up Gemini. Men with the Sun, Moon, Mercury, Venus or Mars in Gemini have a way with words, above all other things, and a set of neurons that appears to fire twice as quickly as everyone else's. If the man in your life is strongly Geminian, he will also have a nickname or an alter ego, a 'twin' figure or sibling issue to deal with, and an ageless quality. The Peter Pan syndrome may come from the fact that Gemini-influenced men can't hold a frown for longer than five minutes — or maybe it's just because all the things they love in life emerged when they were in their teens. Few Gemini-influenced men feel inclined to give them up!

ALTERNATIVE NAMES

In the Gemini myth, Castor and Pollux — the heavenly twins — had to play alternate parts. These Gemini-influenced men also live their life with alternative or 'twin' names. Some of them have even ended up with three different titles — their christened name, their working name and their unofficial nickname. If you know a man with Gemini planets, you may have noticed that nicknames just grow up around him. I have a Gemini Sun–Venus friend whose surname is Ferguson, but the telephone directory has him listed under Armstrong. His nicknames, by the way, are different again!

Also known as ...

GEMINI SUN

John F. Kennedy — J.F.K., Jack
David Gordon Kirkpatrick — Slim Dusty
Robert Allen Zimmerman — Bob Dylan
Stephen Patrick Morrissey — Morrissey
Mark Lizotte — Johnny Diesel
Thomas Jones Woodward — Tom Jones
Jeff Fenech — The Marrickville Mauler
Pro Kevin Charles Hart — Pro Hart
Prince — ⚕

GEMINI MERCURY

Brian Peter George St John Le Baptiste de la Salle Eno — Brian Eno

GEMINI VENUS

James Dixon Swan — Barnesy, Jimmy Barnes
Oondamoorroo — Ernie Dingo
Jon Bongiovi — Jon Bon Jovi

GEMINI MARS

Ray Burns — Captain Sensible

SIBLINGS AND DUETS

Some of these Gemini-influenced men are real-life siblings, and some have found a 'twin' half in a duet for professional reasons. As in the original Castor and Pollux myth, sibling rivalry may be part of the package. But the sibling relationship can be productive as well. Gemini-influenced 'twin' friendships are common, too.

GEMINI SUN

Neil Finn — Tim Finn
Paul McCartney — John Lennon
Noel Gallagher — Liam Gallagher
Paul Weller — Mick Talbot
Thomas Chong — Richard Cheech
Galarrwuy Yunupingu — Mandawuy Yunupingu
Mike Willesee — Don Willesee
Michael Leunig — Mary Leunig

GEMINI MERCURY

Paul Murphy — Justin Murphy

GEMINI VENUS

Jimmy Barnes — John Swan

GEMINI MARS

Hector Crawford — Dorothy Crawford
Jimmy Page — Robert Plant

WORKING THE LANGUAGE

If you know a man with Gemini planets, keep a tape recorder handy — and keep all his letters. These men know how to work the language, at all levels. Some of Australia's greatest male writers have planets in this sign. Shakespeare had a Gemini Moon, Venus and Mars.

Even if your Geminian man never makes it to publication, he will still be: a) Endlessly quotable; b) Witty; c) Well-informed; and d) Inventive with language. Some of them speak at warp speed, like my friend Murray. Some, like my friend James, know how to talk backwards.

The Australian contingent

Henry Lawson — Sun in Gemini
Patrick White — Sun in Gemini
David Williamson — Moon in Gemini
Bryce Courtenay — Moon in Gemini
Peter Carey — Moon and Venus in Gemini
Tim Winton — Mars in Gemini
C.J. Koch — Venus and Mars in Gemini

THEY CAN'T BE SERIOUS

Without Gemini planets, the world would have no *Seinfeld* and no *Blackadder*. You can also forget *The Simpsons* (produced by a man with no less than *two* planets in Gemini). The sign is matched only by Sagittarius in the comedy and cartoon industries.

Professional funny men

Chevy Chase — Mars in Gemini
Jim Carrey — Moon in Gemini
Jason Alexander — Moon in Gemini
Jerry Seinfeld — Mars in Gemini
Michael Richards — Venus in Gemini
James L. Brooks — Moon and Mars in Gemini
Bill Cosby — Venus in Gemini
Michael Palin — Mercury and Venus in Gemini
Bob Mortimer — Sun in Gemini
Spike Milligan — Moon in Gemini
Steve Martin — Mars in Gemini
Paul Reiser — Mars in Gemini
John Clarke — Venus in Gemini
Ben Elton — Venus in Gemini
Rowan Atkinson — Moon in Gemini

men with
planets in CANCER

A SENSE OF PLACE

I can imagine that men with Cancer planets might migrate to another country — but forget their accent, their roots, their heritage, their national anthem? It's unlikely — the man with a well-developed Cancerian side identifies, needs, thinks about, or relishes the homeland far too much. These men have an incredible sense of place, and it doesn't really matter if it's True Blue or Scotland the Brave, This Land is Your Land, or God Save the Queen.

In astrology, Cancer rules the Fourth House of the horoscope, which is where people develop their sense of history, and trace their roots. Men with planets in this sign are often strongly identified with their national or cultural roots. Something also seems to happen to strongly Cancerian men overseas — they develop a marked affinity for their homeland. They become *countrymen*. One thinks of them, and their nationality, in the same moment. Strongly Cancerian types really don't like straying too far from home, and if they travel or move, keep their native language and syntax. Singers who stick to their original accents in their songs (no instant Americanese for them!) are frequently Cancer-influenced: Morrissey is a Cancer Venus and Mars. Robert Smith, from the Cure, is Cancer-influenced. Similarly, Cancer-influenced Americans I have known in Australia really hit those NY or LA vowels! Whether they are aware of it or not, Cancerian types are always flying the flag for their country on some level. Remember Jimi Hendrix playing 'The Star Spangled Banner' on an electric guitar? Cancer Moon.

THE CARE OF OTHERS

Gough Whitlam, a Sun Cancer, created Medi*care*. And this word is strongly associated with Cancerian types of all persuasions. If you're wondering why actor Rob Morrow did such a great job of playing Doctor Joel Fleischmann in *Northern Exposure*, you'll be interested to know that he has his Mercury Sun and Cancer to thank. Cancer-influenced men make fantastic nurses, doctors, cooks, babysitters and fathers if this sign is positively developed in their charts. If the sign is not finding a proper place in their personalities, then there is probably a big problem to deal with, which you can trace way back to their family experiences. If something wasn't quite working in the family system of this man when he was a child, the Cancer planet energy may result in someone who seems needier than the rest — hungry for care, rather than able to give it. Most Cancerian types, though, have a fabulously sympathetic quality, which they like to express in a practical way.

A MAN'S PLACE IS ...

... in the home? Most definitely. And often in the kitchen as well. Cancer planets make expert home brewers, chefs, cooks, wine-makers and bread bakers out of most men. Henry Jones, the man behind IXL Jam, was a Cancer Sun. Thomas Angove, the inventor of the wine cask, is a Cancer Mars. Ken Done, the man behind the world's most collectable tea-towels, has Venus and Mars in Cancer. Bernard King is a Moon Cancer. Heavily Cancerian men feel quite comfortable with pots and pans, oils and potions. Maurice Blackmore, the naturopath who founded the health-food shop empire you see today, was a Cancer Mercury and Mars.

HOMES AND CASTLES

If your partner has Cancer planets he may also be a home-maker in the literal sense. This is the brick-laying, land-surveying, extension-building sign. They can rent, but they can't hide. Most men with a Cancer planet want to own their own place or build an empire. The American real-estate mogul Donald Trump is a Cancer Mercury and Venus. Having a planet here is like a homing signal for men, as they often identify their sense of comfort and security with the physical familiarity and stability of a place to call their own. They can be classically house-proud (with planets in Virgo, too, they'll be rabid cleaners, with planets in Leo they'll try to build a palace). They really need a base, if they are typical of their Sun, Moon, Mercury, Venus or Mars sign, and being rootless can have a hazardous effect on their whole way of life. At the other extreme, there are some notoriously reclusive, borderline agoraphobic Cancerian types who pull the drawbridge up and go unseen for days.

FAMILY FEELINGS

This is an emotional sign, strongly associated with the family. For that reason, family issues are deeply emotional issues, and the Cancer-influenced man can try to be logical or utterly rational about it, but feelings will rule the day. When this sign is being channelled easily and just flows through the chart, you will end up with the classic family man. He puts his clan and his children before everything. Even the permanent bachelors will find someone or something to adopt — usually someone else's child, or a lost soul in need of protection. Should you be in a relationship with a Cancer-influenced man whose family feelings are basically cut off, frozen out or alienated, think carefully about it. Something fairly painful must have happened to stop the male maternal instinct, and it is likely to be a super-sensitive subject with your Cancer-influenced partner. The *mother–son* relationship is absolutely crucial for men with a planet in Cancer.

men with planets in  LEO

For a man with the Sun, Moon, Mercury, Venus or Mars in Leo, creative self-expression is vital. You may be Yves St Laurent, Fletcher Jones, Pierre Cardin or Karl Lagerfeld (all Leo-influenced men) and project this side of yourself into the female arts, like fashion. Or you may get your hands on planks of wood and tubes of glue, and disappear into an all-Australian bloke's shed — a shrine to another kind of Leonine creativity. Reg Mombassa, a Leo Sun, designs for Mambo, plays with Mental As Anything and Dog Trumpet, composes for other bands and has his artwork hanging in the Australian National Gallery. It's a long way from the shed — and it may be Leonine creativity gone mad — but Mombassa's style is exactly what this sign is all about.

LEONINE WEEKENDS

Nothing is sadder than a Leo-influenced man who has never tried to express this side of himself. The Leo who 'doesn't do anything really' is usually battling depression, or so out of touch with himself that he appears quite lost to those around him. It is Leo's right and birthright to pour himself into something with confidence and style — even if he does save it for the weekends. For a Leonine man who is really living his life, there is no such thing as 'just' a job, or 'just' an interest, hobby or enthusiasm. Once he has found the right space to be *himself* in, you may as well just let him go off and get on with it. It's a classy version of what he did as a boy — the old 'Hey, Mum! Hey, Dad! Look at me!' routine. But if Leonine talent, style and self-expression is a by-product of sophisticated showing off, then so be it. Here are a few examples of what a Leo planet can do for a man (and the audience).

Leo Sun

George Bernard Shaw
Dustin Hoffman
Robert Redford
Alfred Hitchcock
Mick Jagger
Stephen Berkoff
Alexei Sayle
Robert Plant

Leo Moon

Andrew Lloyd Webber
Peter Ustinov
Paul McCartney
Ringo Starr
Oscar Wilde
Terry Gilliam
David Bowie
James Joyce
Vivaldi

Leo Mercury

Lenny Henry
Michael Jackson
Peter Sellers
Sylvester Stallone
Tim Brooke-Taylor

Leo Venus

Leonard Bernstein
Sir Harry Secombe
Jeremy Irons
Bill Oddie
Trevor Horn
Pierre Cardin

Leo Mars

Frederick Forsyth
Sir Richard Attenborough
Buddy Holly
Bruce Springsteen

ABOVE IT ALL

There is also an incredible dignity which goes with this sign. It has no room for anything common, mean, embarrassingly petty or vulgar. There are certain things beneath a Leo — and, in this day and age, Leonine men simply glide over the trash and the cheapness as if these distasteful parts of their world did not exist. You can try to drag a Leo down to a lower level, or make him part of a less gracious environment. He will never succumb. It's not his style. And he won't make a fuss about it — he'll just look the other way until the world has re-adjusted itself. It's what the Americans call class and the English call good breeding. Having the Sun, Moon, Mercury, Venus or Mars in this sign is a guarantee that at least one side of this man will be expressed in a courtly, good-mannered, practically mediaeval way.

PLAYING TO AN AUDIENCE

It is not enough for a Leo-influenced man to be classy, inspired or commanding. He must have an audience. He can express himself to the bathroom mirror if he wants to, but Leo basically needs some kind of collective 'you' to impress. Awful Leos are showy and pompous for this reason: they grandstand even when there is nothing worthwhile to grandstand about. Leonine men who have developed in the right directions can be showstopping once they truly have something worthwhile to offer, display or give. Usually, it is a little of themselves. Sometimes, it is all of themselves. But nothing done in the name of creativity or self-expression really seems to count for the Leo-influenced man until he has the compliment confirmed, the feedback registered, or the sound of at least two hands clapping in his ears. Winston Churchill (Leo Moon) painted for himself — but appreciated an audience.

TAKING THE LEAD

Leo-influenced men often have an instinctive feeling that they are the right man to take the reins, at the right time. It is not a decision motivated by vanity, although there may be a certain pride in their own accomplishments when their leading role has got them somewhere. Usually, it is the Leonine man's gut feeling about the need for someone, somewhere, to have the courage and the inner conviction to show others the way. Having a planet in this sign puts Leo-influenced men in direct contact with all the old archetypes and myths attached to the symbol. That constellation up there (the smaller and larger lion) could be strung together to mean *anything*. The ancients associated planets passing through this sign with the lion — both a symbol of jungle supremacy and divine kingship. Even modern observation proves them right: planets in Leo incline their owners towards a leading role. It is the sign of the captain, king, prefect, chairman, chief, boss, head, director, manager, prime minister, frontman — the *old school* style of leader, in fact. This list also includes the odd King of the Wild Frontier:

Winston Churchill — Moon in Leo

Nelson Mandela — Mercury in Leo

Napoleon — Sun in Leo

Sir Edmund Hillary — Mercury in Leo

Neil Armstrong — Sun in Leo

Fidel Castro — Sun in Leo

Davy Crockett — Sun in Leo

men with
planets in

Planets in Virgo produce a well-read, well-informed, workaholic and body-conscious man. Men with the Sun, Moon, Mercury, Venus or Mars in Virgo typically have a split between mind and body, though. One side of them would happily live in a wordy, verbal, brain-oriented world and pretend the physical does not exist. The other side is grounded in the body, but still in a very analytical way. Virgoan men can always give you intellectual arguments for vitamins, workouts, skipping nicotine, or avoiding toxins. This does not, however, lead to the image of the Virgo-influenced male as a paragon of good health. Some are, and some aren't — but those who aren't spend a lot of time worrying about it!

BODY-CONSCIOUSNESS

There are many different ways a Virgo-influenced man can get in touch with his body. Some of them throw themselves at gyms and health-food shops. Others enter the health professions. Still more become dietary faddists or enjoy a lifelong cycle of neglect-and-purge. Virgo-influenced men are stuck with an uncomfortable situation — if they are seen to be too concerned with iron supplements and muscular definition, it delivers a message that the body is existing at the expense of the intellect.

The other extreme is equally wrong, though: cigarettes, sloth, alcohol, drugs, sugar and fat offend Virgo's sense of logic. For this reason, it can take a Virgo-influenced man quite a long time to sort out where he and his body fit into the scheme of things. For every Grant Kenny (Mars in Virgo), and every Kieren Perkins (Venus in Virgo), there are also many Virgo-influenced men who have not yet worked out the ultimate Virgoan truth — that food is science, and exercise is mathematics, and health is *smart*. Maybe singer Elvis Costello has the ultimate Virgoan solution worked out — his Virgo Sun leads him to an exclusive London health club, where he apparently spends his time reading all the newspapers next to the pool!

Illness — mild or serious — is the one time that Virgo planets tend to leap forward into full consciousness. The traditional quest for purity and perfection that is associated with this sign seems to take centre stage when the Virgo-influenced body falls down. Episodes of illness or poor health are frequently the stepping stones to the classic Virgoan lifestyle seen later on — one in which every day is dedicated to the understanding that the mind needs to be served by the body, and that the body requires intelligent handling by the mind. Only George Cadbury, a Sun Virgo, could have built an empire around the message that chocolate is good for you!

INFORMATION OVERLOAD

Few signs enjoy absorbing information as much as Virgo. If the man in your life has planets here, he will be a lifelong student, either formally or informally. It is not just the need to know, it is the need to know *exactly*. The Virgo Sun, Moon, Mercury, Venus or Mars man asks, 'Is that the whole story?' every day of his life.

Virgo planets make a researcher of every man, and anything — a recipe book, a magazine, a computer game, a philosophical treatise — becomes fair game for Virgo's mental microscope. This is a nitpicking, fact-checking, detail-loving, mistake-slashing, eye-straining, page-turning sign. Ruled by Mercury, the Messenger of the Gods, and channelled through the Sixth House of ritual and routine, it makes men both perfectly curious, and curiously perfectionist.

Part of a Virgo planet's function is to communicate — and to make connections. Like Gemini, Virgo is associated with the written or spoken word. The mass media, computers, education and academia all have an overload of Virgo in their ranks. This sign worships the right answer, the perfect definition and the best of all possible *words*. Virgo-influenced men enjoy working the language — but playing with it is equally important. This sign produces men who devour books — or radio. Sir Allen Lane, the founder of Penguin Books was a Virgo Sun–Venus. The poet William *Wordsworth* was a Virgo Moon.

MAN AS MACHINE

Virgo rules the Sixth House of the horoscope, associated with the work ethic, routine, ritual, responsibility and duty. If you know a man with planets in this sign, he will express part of his personality through work, which can make him wonderfully productive, but also burn him out in quite a spectacular way. Workaholism is where the famous mind–body split manifests itself first. If a man who has a strongly developed Virgoan side turns into a machine (endless lists of things to do, obligations to keep, weekends to 'use') then the body will intervene. This sign can only live in the head for so long before the rest of the system starts yelling reminders. Virgo-influenced men can be prolific and productive beyond belief, but they need a balance in their lives, too.

The quotable Virgo

'How you sit down and invent a word is one thing, but how you get the world to accept it is very much another.' — **Stephen Fry, Sun, Mercury and Mars in Virgo**

'I've always found I could communicate.' — **Stephen Hawking, Moon in Virgo**

'I see a body as a classy chassis to carry your mind around in.' — **Sylvester Stallone, Moon and Mars in Virgo**

'To keep up with my grooming, I carry a Swiss Army knife so my nails are always in immaculate condition — and I can get a stone out of a horse's hoof as well.' — **Elvis Costello, Sun in Virgo**

 men with
planets in

HOPELESS ROMANTICS

Men with the Sun, Moon, Mercury, Venus or Mars in Libra believe in love. Some of them are marriage celebrants, some of them just celebrate marriage. The wilder Librans skip the ceremony, but like to think you were together in a past life. Ruled by Venus, the Goddess of Love and Beauty, men with a Libran side can be hopelessly romantic. They are also far more at peace when they've found their other half, or match. They see it in these terms too: Yin and Yang, black and white, quiet and noisy, male and female, Beauty and the Beast. Walt Disney was a Libra Moon. When he'd created Mickey, he had to create Minnie.

Whatever a Libra-influenced man believes that he lacks, he hopes to find it in you. The scales describe Libra. One set of qualities must always balance another, and in this symmetry these men find a kind of beauty and order.

Libran-influenced men enjoy the mythology and poetry of romantic love, and will either be traditional romantics ('Let me open that door for you,' and 'Roses — for you,' and 'God, you're beautiful without your glasses!') or ... radical romantics. John Lennon, a Libra Sun, organised a bed-in with the love of his life, Yoko Ono. David Copperfield (Mercury in Libra) could never resist bringing Claudia Schiffer on stage. Bryan Ferry, another Libra Sun, has built a career on being hopelessly romantic. Libra Sun Clive James keeps his marriage private, but his love of beautiful women very public.

Ruled by the Goddess of Love and Beauty, Libra also goes *looking* for Love and Beauty. This is the sigh sign. It's also the swoon sign. Some Libran types welcome feminism, some do not, but it is hard for them to exclude all that is intensely female and romantic from their vision of perfect womanhood. The composer of Romeo and Juliet, Sergei Prokofiev, was a Libra Moon. 'There are no really ugly women,' Libra Sun Brigitte Bardot once said. 'Every woman is a Venus in her own way.' Once a Libra-influenced man believes that he has caught sight of her, he's lost forever — or at least until another romantic vision appears.

Librans in their own words

'To all the girls I've loved before ...' — **Julio Iglesias, Sun in Libra**

'Short in the leg but unbelievably lovely in the face, she looked like the top half of a Botticelli angel.' — **Clive James, Sun in Libra**

'Is she really going out with him?' — **Joe Jackson, Sun in Libra**

'Every little thing she does is magic.' — **Sting, Sun in Libra**

'Unlove's the heaveless hell and homeless home ... lovers alone wear sunlight.' — **e.e. cummings, Sun in Libra**

THE AESTHETIC PRINCIPLE

Libra planets give men an eye for design. Some of them express this professionally, and others express it in their houses and wardrobes. When I interviewed Bob Geldof for a magazine once, he told me with some pride that he had donated his entire punk wardrobe to the Victoria and Albert Museum in London. Libra-influenced men really *care* about the way things look. Architecture magazines make some of them drool, while others disappear inside art galleries and never come back. Strangely enough, their taste always comes back to Venusian principles: symmetry, harmony, curve, line, balance and shape. Let other men grow cabbages: Libran types want roses. Sir Terence Conran, founder of Habitat and the UK's most famous and influential design guru, has the Sun in Libra. Hubert de Givenchy, who designed for Audrey Hepburn, had the Moon in Libra.

WAR AND PEACE

Equality. Justice. Peace. Harmony. All these issues are classically Libran, and inevitably this leads these men into all kinds of battlegrounds. The unpalatable truth for a man with a Libra Sun, Moon, Mercury, Venus or Mars is that in order to achieve peace, he must sometimes get involved in a fight. Unbalanced and unfair situations always throw the Libran type into a dilemma: argue the point, or walk away. Destiny says that he'll occasionally he'll have no choice, and it doesn't matter if the issue is ideological or personal. His Libran side loathes aggression, but it equally detests any situation which is patently unfair or wrong. The preferred option? Always peaceful protest, and skilful diplomacy. Here are Libran types drawn into conflict, but always on the side of peace:

John Pilger — Sun in Libra	Lech Walesa — Sun in Libra
Mahatma Gandhi — Sun in Libra	Sir Joseph Chamberlain — Sun in Libra
Rev. Desmond Tutu — Sun in Libra	Oliver North — Sun in Libra
Dwight D. Eisenhower — Sun in Libra	The Dalai Lama — Mars in Libra

MUSIC AND LIBRA

Along with Taurus, Libra is the most over-represented sign in the music industry. Both signs are ruled by Venus, a goddess who believed in love songs and dressing up. The man with Libra planets is either musically talented, or just completely sold on music. These well-known Libran types can be found in most CD collections:

John Lennon — Sun in Libra

Elvis Presley — Mars in Libra

Marc Bolan — Sun, Mercury
and Venus in Libra

Sting — Sun and Moon in Libra

Paul Simon — Mercury in Libra

Art Garfunkel — Mercury in Libra

Chuck Berry — Sun in Libra

Neil Young — Venus in Libra

Joe Jackson — Venus in Libra

Robert Plant — Mars in Libra

Bryan Ferry — Sun in Libra

Cliff Richard — Sun in Libra

Luciano Pavarotti — Sun in Libra

Bruce Springsteen — Sun,
Moon and Mercury in Libra

Louis Armstrong — Moon in Libra

Chopin — Moon in Libra

men with planets in  SCORPIO

THE DARK SIDE

Pluto, the planet associated with Scorpio, rules the Underworld. The god Pluto also drives black horses. Astrologers associate planets in Scorpio with a deep understanding of the dark side. If the man in your life has the Sun, Moon, Mercury, Venus or Mars in Scorpio then he has to be in touch with the 'Underworld' in his own psyche before he can truly understand it in others. Sooner or later, though, sex, death, God, the Devil, morality, sin, taboo and every other cheerful Scorpionic topic will drift into his world.

The writer Thomas Keneally, who has a Scorpio Mercury, has spent his career exploring all our dark sides — from *The Devil's Playground* to *The Chant of Jimmie Blacksmith* and *Schindler's Ark*. This is not a trivial, nor a superficial sign. It lends a kind of depth and intensity to those who have it. A Scorpio-influenced man may have planets in other, lighter, signs. But one part of him is intensely private and rather serious. Scorpio's primary interest is in *potting the black* (Eddie Charlton is a Scorpio Sun and Mars) and if a great deal of them seems to exist below the surface, it is usually because they believe certain things are not fit for public consumption.

OFF-LIMITS SUBJECTS

Scorpio planets are concerned with taboo. Death and dying is one area most people have a problem with, but this is precisely where Scorpio often goes exploring. The pivotal event in Scorpio Sun Evelyn Waugh's *Brideshead Revisited* is a deathbed scene. Horror writer Stephen King, a Scorpio Mars, concerns himself largely with death and the afterlife. The actor Dan Akroyd, also a Scorpio Mars, is not only famous for his role in *Ghostbusters*, he also has an extensive collection of books on the supernatural. Dylan Thomas, Bram Stoker and Albert Camus were Scorpio Suns. Colin Wilson is a Scorpio Moon, and so was Alfred Hitchcock.

If the man in your life has a Scorpio planet, then he has a huge capacity for understanding the most difficult human issues, and the twin passages of death and dying are high on the list. Many men working in professions tied to the law, or welfare, or medicine have a Scorpio planet expressing this side of them. It is not enough to politely look the other way and change the subject to something nice, because Scorpio is not particularly interested in that. Perhaps for this reason, men with Scorpio planets often seem to attract intense situations, or intense people — or be drawn towards experiences which ask them to go more deeply into life.

Along with death, human sexuality — in all its manifestations — is part of the Scorpionic journey. Two friends of mine, both of whom are Scorpio Suns, work on soft porn magazines. Graeme Murphy, a Scorpio Sun, Mercury, Venus, has taken ballet into places that *Swan Lake* dare not go. Opera is also full of Scorpionic types — perhaps because they are dealing in a medium where rape and death are part of a professional vocabulary.

It can be difficult to discuss Scorpio and sexuality, partly because the original myth surrounding this sign tells us that Pluto's sexual desires were unacceptable. With a Scorpio planet, on a personal or professional level, men must ultimately decide what is acceptable for them and what is not. I have seen several charts belonging to men in the Catholic Church with Scorpio planets. For some reason, Scorpio always inclines people to ask *moral* questions about the nature of human sexuality. Ultimately, there is an awful lot about this area of life which must be dragged into the light.

Prince Charles, a Scorpio Sun, has found that it is essentially *religious* and *moral* questions which follow his private life around. Patrick White, a Scorpio Moon, had the same problem. On a professional level, Scorpio Sun John Cleese has co-written a book called *Families and How to Survive Them* which tackles everything from homosexuality to the Oedipus complex.

No wonder so many Scorpionic types are natural psychologists. They keep secrets, too — either their own, or other people's. The Reverend Chad Varah, founder of the Samaritans, started a telephone helpline for people dealing with everything from sexual assault to suicide. There is something wonderfully honest about Scorpio, which refuses to pretend that the surface we live on is actually the substance as well. Dudley Moore is a Scorpio Moon and this quote belongs to him: 'Masturbation is always very safe. You can not only control the person you're with but you can leave when you want to.' Film director Spike Lee is a Scorpio Moon, too. 'I don't want to imply racism,' he said once, 'but black sexuality makes people uncomfortable.' That's Scorpio, saying the unsayable.

HAPPILY FANATICAL

Having the Sun, Moon, Mercury, Venus or Mars in Scorpio produces an intense focus which can border on happy fanaticism. Scorpio is never 'slightly interested' or 'quite into' things. It dives in, totally oblivious to ringing telephones or other mundane distractions, and gets lost for hours. This has obvious meaning on a sexual level. But you will also find Scorpio Mercury types who are obsessive book collectors and Scorpio Mars types who burn with passion for their cricket team. This sign is all about passion. Having a planet here makes a man passionate, and it really does not matter if that passion is reserved for art (Pablo Picasso), religion (Martin Luther), body-building (Charles Atlas) or astronomy (Carl Sagan). If the scorpio male doesn't burn for his work, he'll burn for something else on his days off.

men with
planets in

I have yet to find a man with a strong Sagittarian side who isn't an explorer of some kind, be he surfer, swimmer, walker, rider, fisherman, diver or pilot. Even those men with a Sagittarius planet who stay glued to the television fantasise about having a rugged-looking four-wheel-drive parked outside the front door. The man with the Sun, Moon, Mercury, Venus or Mars in Sagittarius needs broad horizons. He may be fascinated by the endless 'out thereness' of it all. He can't resist thinking about life at the other end of the globe, or in the cosmos, and loves foreigners (or aliens) as much as he loathes small-town attitudes.

Here are a few Sagittarian types with the global view. The list includes Bob Geldof, who brought the world together through Live Aid, and the explorer Ferdinand Magellan. Lee Trevino's in there, too — the open spaces of the golf course are probably his version of astronomer Carl Sagan's galaxy. The best way to punish a Sagittarian type? Lock him up in a one-bedroomed flat for a week.

MODERN-DAY EXPLORERS

Bob Geldof — Moon in Sagittarius
Tony Wheeler (Lonely Planet) — Sun in Sagittarius
Gus Grissom (Apollo Astronaut) — Moon in Sagittarius
Ray Bradbury (Sci-Fi author) — Moon in Sagittarius
Lee Trevino (Golfer) — Sun in Sagittarius
Carl Sagan (Astronomer) — Moon in Sagittarius
Ferdinand Magellan (Explorer) — Moon in Sagittarius
Neil Armstrong (Moon pioneer) — Moon in Sagittarius

With Sagittarian men, you really have to put the adjective 'international' in front of most of the things they enjoy. Racing driver Alan Jones, with Mercury and Venus in Sagittarius, began his career with the Spanish Grand Prix and then conquered Argentina, France, Great Britain, Canada and the USA. James Hardy (Sagittarius Mercury) is the world champion yachtsman who in 1993 was appointed ambassador for South Australia. Les Murray, SBS television sports presenter and producer, originally from Hungary, and a specialist in World Soccer, has Mercury in Sagittarius. The playwright Louis Nowra, a Sagittarius Sun, invented a game called Geography of Imagination — so perfectly Sagittarian! The Australian ambassador to Spain has Mercury in the sign ... the list is endless. Other global thinkers are the mass-media empire-builders Kerry Packer (Sagittarius Sun) and Rupert Murdoch (Sagittarius Moon).

This sign likes to think big. It looks at reality as a map, not a corner of the street, and enjoys stretching out. To really see a measure of Sagittarian energy, visit the once secret underground War Cabinet rooms in London, where Sagittarius Sun Winston Churchill directed the strategies which were to win World War II. The 'think global, act local' philosophy that is so successful for Sagittarius is embodied in the rows of telephones and coloured pins on maps in these tiny rooms.

TRUE BELIEVERS

There are preachers, legal eagles, political animals, philosophers and true believers on the Sagittarian list. The ruler of this sign is Jupiter, the god who handed down justice, took the long view and saw everything from a privileged position. If the man in your life has the Sun, Moon, Mercury, Venus or Mars in Sagittarius, then he may have a little — or a lot — of the true believer in him. He can become preachy ... occasionally. But a lot of what this man is about comes from the times of crisis that he lives through. From there, he develops his own particular view of the world, even of the planet. Whatever his particular brand of faith, he has to find a sense of meaning in it all, or life is not worth the exercise. He also needs a thought system or set of values to justify his decisions, as destiny says he'll often be put in ethically or morally challenging situations where he must lean, hard, on his beliefs. All these True Believers were born with the Moon in Sagittarius:

MEN OF VISION

John Wesley	Dale Carnegie
Sri Aurobindo	Michel Gauquelin
Werner Erhardt	Carl Jung
Billy Graham	Carlos Castaneda

NATURAL COMEDIANS

The two signs most commonly associated with comedians are Gemini and Sagittarius. If your current or future husband has planets in both signs, make sure you can bear the idea of going to bed with a kitchen stand-up comedian. Sagittarian-styled humour relies on exaggeration for effect, and if you know a man with a Sagittarius planet, you'll grow to appreciate just how completely over-the-top he can be. In a previous incarnation I was a part-time comedy writer and signed up to work for Steve Vizard, an over-the-top comedian with a penchant for oversized ideas which only someone else with a Sagittarius Moon could appreciate. A concrete mixer full of gigantic Lotto balls trekking around Melbourne? No problem. Fake rain inside the studio? Well, if it's going to get a laugh . . . Like many Sagittarius-influenced men, Steve is effortlessly funny. Here's a list of some of the rest:

Woody Allen — Sun and Mercury in
  Sagittarius
Billy Connolly — Sun in Sagittarius
Rowan Atkinson —
  Venus in Sagittarius
Matt Groening — Mars in Sagittarius
Terry Gilliam — Sun in Sagittarius

Mel Smith — Sun in Sagittarius
Bob Mortimer — Moon in Sagittarius
Gerry Connolly —
  Mercury in Sagittarius
James Thurber — Sun in Sagittarius
Noel Coward — Sun in Sagittarius

men with planets in  CAPRICORN

MEASURING TIME

Men with the Sun, Moon, Mercury, Venus or Mars in Capricorn are concerned with the passage of time. They wait years for what they want, dream about having their time again, count the hours and the minutes or form time-related theories.

Ex-Prime Minister Paul Keating, a Capricorn Sun, is Australia's best-known clock collector. Stephen Hawking, a Capricorn Sun, wrote A Brief History of Time. Two Capricorn-influenced writers have both worked watches and clocks into their stories — J.M. Barrie created a crocodile who had swallowed a clock in Peter Pan, and Lewis Carroll invented a white rabbit with a giant watch.

Albert Einstein was a Capricorn Sun. Isaac Asimov is a Capricorn Sun, and so was Johannes Kepler. If you go looking for a Capricorn planet, sooner or later you will hear a cosmic clock ticking. These types are funny about age, too.

HIS FINEST HOUR

Apart from wondering where time began, or how it works, or how much of it is available to them, Capricornian types also live by the calendar. If, like Capricorn Sun Anthony Hopkins, one has to wait decades for fame and fortune — so be it. Men with a strongly developed Capricornian side often gravitate towards careers where they are expected to take an eternity to find success. They enjoy a distant mountain-top to climb to, and are often classic examples of a thirty-year crawl for overnight success!

They are builders by nature. Block by block, brick by brick, Capricorn Sun, Moon, Mercury, Venus or Mars men build. Their finest hour? Usually the one they gave up twenty years earlier, when everybody else was at a party. Developing discipline is part of what Capricorn is all about. Destiny says that remarkably few shortcuts will be available to them, and extraordinary ambition is necessary to fuel this long slog. If the ambition is realistic, then the Capricorn-influenced man will have an extraordinary life. Mel Gibson, a Capricorn Sun actor-turned-director is a good example of this. The worst case scenario? Towering Capricornian ambition built on a non-existent foundation.

SATURN – THE OLD MAN

Saturn, the ruler of Capricorn, is represented as an old man. Any man with the Sun, Moon, Mercury, Venus or Mars will have an 'old man' of his own to deal with. It may be his own father. It may be a senior male authority figure. Elvis Presley, a Capricorn Sun-Mercury, had Colonel Tom Parker to contend with. Nicolas Cage, a Capricorn Sun, has his famous uncle, film director Francis Ford Coppola. Sometimes the link can be so intensely personal that the Capricornian type will not particularly want to discuss it. It is through this 'old man' figure, however, that a Capricorn-influenced man will come to terms with his own manhood. Frank Sinatra Junior, a Capricorn Sun, has the extraordinarily difficult task of being the son of Frank Sinatra Senior.

The star of the American men's movement, Robert Bly, places a great deal of emphasis on father figures and 'elder statesmen' in his ideas on manhood. This Capricorn Sun man is exploring the productive side of this sign, which can lend a man an amazing mentor, or a wise guide.

If something goes wrong, a Capricornian type can find his 'old man' (literally) or a male authority figure becoming a burden, not a reward. Richard Nixon, a Capricorn Sun, had an abusive father. Robert Kennedy, a Capricorn Moon, had a dogmatic father, too. One way for a Capricorn-influenced type to resolve this kind of problem is to seek out an older mentor, or wiser, experienced guide figure. This can be achieved through work, or other interests or activities.

I've had numerous male musician clients who speak in reverential tones about 'Those old blues guys'. Capricorn planets don't mind looking back — way, way back if necessary — for their male mentors. A grandson–grandfather relationship was crucial to the writer and illustrator Maurice Sendak, who said two figures dominated his childhood — 'Mickey Mouse and my severe and bearded maternal grandfather'.

On some level, any man with a Capricorn planet is only asking this: 'Teach me ...' Ultimately, with enough mentors and guides along the way, they themselves will become an 'old man' or a 'Father Time' figure for somebody else.

In their own words

'Dost thou love life? Then do not squander time, for that's the stuff life is made of.' — **Benjamin Franklin, Sun in Capricorn**

'Any Day Now.' — **Ronnie Milsap, Sun in Capricorn**

'Welcome to the House of Fun, now you've come of age.' — **Graham McPherson, Sun in Capricorn**

'One has to be grown-up enough to realise that life is not fair. You just have to do the best you can in the situation you are in.' — **Stephen Hawking, Sun in Capricorn**

men with planets in  AQUARIUS

Aquarian men can try to conform to other people's expectations if they want to, but it seldom works out. After a couple of crisis situations in their lives, they usually wake up to their own need to be different, and by their forties these men are typically living their own lives, in their own way.

It can be extremely difficult to live as a man with the Sun, Moon, Mercury, Venus or Mars in Aquarius. Schoolboys are fed such rigid messages about what they can — and can't — do in this life that it takes a certain kind of bravery to depart from the rules if you were born male. Ironically, it is the departure from convention — or the norm — that Aquarius is all about. Plenty of mad geniuses and brilliant rebels come under this sign. So do men who are renowned for going their own way:

PROFESSIONAL STIRRERS

Stuart Littlemore — Mercury and Venus in Aquarius

Thomas Keneally — Moon in Aquarius

Phillip Adams — Mars in Aquarius

Derryn Hinch — Sun in Aquarius

Rex Mossop — Sun in Aquarius

Richard Neville — Venus in Aquarius

Timothy Leary — Moon in Aquarius

Auberon Waugh — Moon in Aquarius

Barry Humphries — Sun in Aquarius

John McEnroe — Sun in Aquarius

Aquarius-influenced men do not go quietly. They do not necessarily believe everything they are told. They are not particularly interested in being popular and if they can avoid falling into line, they will. Just avoid getting them started on God, Republicanism, the Media, the existence of extra-terrestrials, the New Age, Men's Liberation or censorship. Unless, of course, you prefer all-night conversation to all-night sexual marathons.

FUTURE TENSE

Men with Aquarius planets are ahead of their time, partly because they are profoundly interested in tomorrow. They embrace technology, theories and inventions which seem unusual or 'difficult' in the present, but make remarkable sense several decades later. The Aquarian fascination with the future may manifest in a passion for science fiction, an obsession with science, or the pursuit of astrology.

Robin Williams — Sun in Aquarius

Charles Kingsford Smith — Sun in Aquarius

Stephen Hawking — Venus in Aquarius

William Shatner — Venus in Aquarius

David Duchovny — Moon in Aquarius

Steven Spielberg — Moon in Aquarius

H.G. Wells — Moon in Aquarius

Leonard Nimoy — Venus in Aquarius

George Lucas — Moon in Aquarius

David Duchovny, star of the hit TV series *The X-Files*, managed to write a Ph.D. dissertation, 'Magic and Technology in Contemporary Fiction', before he took on his job. Technology (computers, chips, bytes or satellites) are *huge* with Aquarian types. Give them the machine that goes *ping*, every time. Chris Carter, who created *The X-Files*, has the Moon in Aquarius, just like Duchovny. Gillian Anderson also has the Moon in Aquarius. Now tell me there's nothing in this astrology business. Of course, having an Aquarian side doesn't necessarily make your man an *X-Files* fan — but he'll always be convinced the truth is out there, one way or another. By the way, those two concepts 'Truth' and 'Out There' turn up in Aquarian-styled conversations about once every 40 minutes.

Aquarius planets promote an interest in change and innovation, and 'the shock of the new', and men who have them are less interested in tradition and the status quo and far more excited by the idea of change and reform.

New ways of doing the same things. Better ways of handling traditional ideas. Brand-new concepts to *completely replace* what was there before. Cardiac surgeon Mark O'Brien (Aquarius Moon) designed an innovative heart valve. Graeme Pearman, chief of the CSIRO division of Atmospheric Research, convened a conference called Greenhouse back in 1987, several light years before anybody else in the world had noticed the problem. He has Mars in Aquarius.

Aquarius gets its energy and its inspiration from a place so far out of most people's field of vision that the things the Aquarian type becomes passionate about are frequently missed or misunderstood. Transmat beam, anyone? The Internet? Cable-fax-microwave-home-computers? The world before Aquarius and the world after Aquarius always looks like a radically different place. Consider the impact Rupert Murdoch and his rival, Kerry Packer (both of whom have planets in Aquarius) have had on the mass media.

AQUARIAN FREEDOM

Adolescence is an interesting time for Aquarian men. From there into their early twenties, they are given more legitimate freedom by society than at any other stage of their lives. Rebellion and wildness is almost expected of young males then. And that may explain the unexpected images in Aquarian man's photo albums: 'This is me running around naked on a desert island with a lampshade on my head,' or, 'This is me being dragged away on a protest march.'

Someone, somewhere, is always telling Aquarians to settle down and do the right thing. But when they do, they are invariably unhappy. They don't want somebody else's idea of security or happiness. What they need is a lifestyle and career that will allow them the following things: Friends. Freedom. Flexibility.

This last point — about the stubborn Aquarian insistence on freedom — is extremely important. Part of them wants it on an ideological, principled level. It gets dressed up as the quest for civil liberties — or free enterprise. This lust for self-determination will also work itself out in their personal life, too — so be aware. Aquarian-influenced men need to *be their own man*.

men with
planets in PISCES

Pisces planets are visionary, occasionally vague and highly imaginative. This is not the easiest space for a man to be in the 1990s, so it's important that a man with a Pisces Sun, Moon, Mercury, Venus or Mars finds an outlet.

Pisces is the sign most associated with what can be seen with the mind's eye. The first group of notable Piscean types includes gifted visionaries and artists for that reason. Put a canvas in front of a Piscean type, and you'll see just how differently his vision functions. Give him a camera, and he'll either produce a work of art, or something so unfocussed it looks like art anyway. A blank notebook? An excuse for poetry ...

THE VISUAL IMAGINATION

The art world

Brett Whiteley — Venus in Pisces
Norman Lindsay — Sun in Pisces
Lloyd Rees — Sun in Pisces
Howard Arkley — Venus in Pisces
Leon Paroissien — Sun in Pisces

Renoir — Sun in Pisces
Albert Carel Willink — Sun in Pisces
Michelangelo — Sun in Pisces
Leonardo da Vinci — Moon in Pisces
Camille Pissarro — Moon in Pisces

Photographers and film-makers

Paul Cox — Mercury in Pisces
Philip Noyce — Venus in Pisces
Michael Pate — Sun and Mercury in Pisces
Ron Howard — Sun in Pisces
Rob Reiner — Sun in Pisces

Tony Armstrong-Jones — Sun in Pisces
Luis Buñuel — Sun in Pisces
Robert Altman — Sun in Pisces
Sam Peckinpah — Sun in Pisces
David Putnam — Sun in Pisces

Poetry in motion

Paul Kelly — Mars in Pisces
Robert Adamson — Moon in Pisces
W.H. Auden — Sun in Pisces
Jack Kerouac — Sun in Pisces

Henry Longfellow — Sun in Pisces
Gabrielle D'Annunzio — Sun in Pisces

ALTERNATIVE REALITIES

It is really not enough to say that men with Pisces planets have addictive personalities. Kurt Cobain and Brett Whiteley — both Piscean types — had heroin problems. But most men with the Sun, Moon, Mercury, Venus or Mars in Pisces need to escape into an alternative reality by other means. Certainly, hallucinogenic drugs can function like dressing-up boxes for the Piscean head, and many of them enjoy the blurring, or distortion, that occurs with them.

Alcohol is also widely linked with this sign. Your partner's Pisces planets can find an alternative reality in many different ways, though, and there are just as many Piscean types who are happy to lose themselves in meditation, daydreams, computer games and films. Great Piscean escapes include fishing, diving and swimming for pearls. Troubled Piscean types dive more deeply into substance abuse, or get hooked on cigarette breaks. But they all need a fantasy land.

SYMPATHY AND EMPATHY

I have known vets and cancer therapists with Pisces planets, and a few modern-day saints and healers as well. Pisces is associated with sacrifice — sometimes on a daily level (time, energy or money goes out to others) or occasionally, in a powerful, once-in-a-lifetime way. The wisest, most wonderful Piscean types always do this from compassion. The ability to give something of themselves comes from this issue — in imagining how another person must feel. Many of the quiet achievers and forgotten saints in your town are probably Piscean types. Your man may have planets in other signs which are more self-interested, but his Piscean side basically wants to give it all up, and give of himself. On an ordinary, everyday level this produces the classic Piscean kindness and sensitivity.

Lopsided Piscean types take the concept of sacrifice to an extreme, and end up becoming martyrs who enjoy the moaning and the mooching that goes with the territory. Also, perhaps, planets here can produce the classically dazed and confused individual who believes his whole reason for existing is to be a human dartboard. Rescuing these rare, but lost, Piscean types can end up being a life's mission for some women.

A SENSE OF THE ABSURD

Pisces planets give a man a strong sense of the absurd. I interviewed Kurt Cobain for a magazine a few years ago, and he spent the first five minutes trying to convince me that Nirvana were going to organise a gigantic hypnotic wheel on stage to mesmerise their audience. A whimsical imagination — and a happily overdeveloped sense of the ridiculous — are Piscean trademarks. Their sense of humour is particularly loopy.

Rolf Harris — Mars in Pisces
Dr Seuss — Sun in Pisces
Kenneth Grahame — Sun in Pisces
Ronald Searle — Sun in Pisces
Douglas Adams — Sun in Pisces
Jerry Lewis — Sun in Pisces
Robin Williams — Moon in Pisces

HOW he sees you

HIS MOON/VENUS SIGN

This is the really sneaky part of astrology, but I don't mind sharing it with you. If you want to know how the man in your life sees the woman in his life (which is hopefully you) then you only have to look at his Moon and Venus signs to find out.

These two planets are female, so when they turn up in a man's chart, they describe his feminine side, but also the sort of glorious female qualities he attributes to whoever he happens to be living with, or in love with.

If his Moon and Venus signs happen to be the same, he'll have a very strong, pure image of perfect womanhood. If they're different (which is more common) then a blend of both the Moon and Venus sign will tell you what he's looking for ... or fantasising about.

HIS aries
moon-venus

HIS IMAGE OF YOU

He sees you as dynamic, energetic — capable of a two-hour pillow fight, or at least some decent arm-wrestling. Men with an Aries Moon or Venus project a little of the Amazon onto you, and find it quite comfortable or attractive. If you're tough, strong and independent they'll find it distinctly appealing. With the Moon or Venus in Aries, about 50% of this man finds female *oomph* extremely persuasive.

He'll approve if you spend your spare time throwing balls around, racing up a pool or running around a field. His image of divine womanhood is sweaty and musclebound to a degree. He finds fitness sexy. But if you just like lying on the couch and yelling at TV sports programmes, that will probably satisfy him as well. I know an Aries Moon man whose wife's connections got him VIP seats at cricket matches. He lived in a state of perpetual bliss.

He enjoys the chase, and prefers women who know how to play the game. He finds all that ducking and diving erotic, and the 'will she, won't she' aspect of a relationship feels very good to him. To keep him interested, you may need to be the kind of woman who can move around a lot — like a really good Goal Defence in a netball game. Nothing is worse for him than the anti-climax of knowing that he's got you where he wants you. Other planets in his chart may point to a need for security or predictability, but a major part of him really wants to pursue you, and win you — or, perhaps, be pursued and won. At school this boy probably played Kiss Chase until threatened with expulsion. As a man, the Aries Moon–Venus type enjoys all the tension of sexual hunting.

He likes women who *do* things with their lives. If you're blazing a trail in your career, or in your interests, so much the better. He likes spirited and daring women who know how to assert themselves. At least half of him is probably looking for a spiritual redhead. It doesn't really matter what colour your hair is, though — you just have to be *energetic*.

He feels comfortable in the lead, if he's being honest. So although he'll give you plenty of space to be independent and assertive, you may prefer not to tell him what to do. You are very unlikely to get away with even the smallest piece of dictatorship in this relationship, unless you are prepared for a battle. Some women who become partners of Aries Moon–Venus types find they enter a state of perpetual warfare, and leave when they realise they can never win. The happy ones can deal with the peculiar set-up this man requires, which involves you being as unstoppable and unbeatable as you like — but never, ever, his boss. Even trivial issues — leaving the toilet seat up, wearing dumb sunglasses, forgetting to pick up the dry-cleaning — can become the centrepieces for battles. You just can't tell him what to do. And that's the end of it.

He enjoys seeing you stride off every day, ready to take the world on. He finds it erotic when you tell him about your latest victory. He likes the way you initiate sex, and the way you talk like you mean business on the phone. If he has the Moon in Aries, then he needs new experiences in his life, and that means you have to be a pioneer alongside him. If he has Venus in Aries, then he loves adventures, and you will have to be prepared to take a few.

What makes him notice you first? Probably the way you come straight to the point. He likes the chase, but he'd prefer it ran like a debate, or a paperchase, and not a boring saga of shy glances and awkward blushes. He'll enjoy the company of any women who can spar with him, and one of the things he may remember about your early days together is the way everything felt like a romantic fencing match.

You are a post-post-feminist, of course, or he wouldn't be interested. These men really *believe* in women who do their own thing, and part of them just longs to be run over by an Amazon on a red motorbike. If you happen to have Aries planets, or an Aries Rising sign, you'll genuinely have qualities which fit the bill. If you don't, you'll need a strongly placed Mars in your horoscope (your astrologer can explain this) which will give you that incredible drive, oomph and energy he longs for.

With the Moon in Aries, he'll want you to be a tiger-mother to his children, if you have them. With Venus in Aries, he'll want you to be a tiger in the bedroom. You can never get away with lying back and thinking of your shopping list, incidentally. Sex is like sport to him. Or, more specifically, a wrestling match.

Henry VIII had an Aries Moon, which takes us to the other key part of the sign. When he needs a fight, or feels like the erotic stimulation of a yelling match, he'll blame it on you. King Henry had six wives, and there is no evidence at all to suggest that he thought anyone was at fault but *them*. Fortunately for you, public beheading is now out of fashion. Henry was also a hunter, which tells you something else about this sign. As soon as the hunt is over, the excitement is gone. That's often why relationships with Aries Moon or Venus men seem to go into injury time. Sensing the possibility of another battle, the man with this sign will be reluctant to end things neatly.

Where he places you

Somewhere between Elaine from *Seinfeld* and Boadicea. He'll dream about you with red hair, even if you're a blonde or brunette. If you are happy to strut around in a red Amazon leotard, like Wonder Woman, then so much the better.

 **taurus**
moon-venus

HIS IMAGE OF YOU

He has great admiration for your taste, and your bargain-hunting abilities. You're a material girl, to some extent, and he enjoys your preference for the finer things in life. The quality he sees in your wardrobe is the quality he also sees in you. Alternatively, if you channel your love of the best into cars, houses or collectables, he'll admire your discerning taste that way.

You also have a framework of other values and he has something to learn from you here. You appear to know the true price of things, and they are not always material. He both needs and enjoys a woman who thinks this way. With Venus in Taurus, he loves your taste, but he also loves your value system. With the Moon in Taurus, he needs your discerning eye, but he also needs your appreciation of the fact that there are some values in life which money can't buy.

The Taurus Moon or Venus man also appreciates dependability. He needs to know where he stands. His image of you is rather orderly, organised and trustworthy. You represent something solid in his life. You may be a creature of habit, but if he has the Moon in Taurus, he'll really need that consistency. The Venus in Taurus man craves something pragmatic in the woman he loves. If you're always there, then he's more willing to stick around, too. Billy Joel, who has Venus in Taurus, just about summed it up with this lyric: 'I like you just the way you are … I need to know that you will always be the same old someone that I knew.'

He also likes a woman who doesn't give up. Staying power is strongly associated with Taurus, and a man with the Moon or Venus in this sign really appreciates it. If you persist with the relationship, and if you are patient enough to hang in there when things are difficult, he'll respond in kind. Or at least 50% of him will — remember, what he's looking for in you consists of a combination of both Moon and Venus sign qualities. If he has one planet in Taurus, but the other in a slightly wilder sign, you may find you have to be both predictable and unpredictable by turns!

Taurus is associated with beauty and love, and an intense kind of femininity. His image of the beloved is scented, girdled and seductive — only a Moon–Venus Libra man has such a traditional view of what is erotic. (If he has either planet in that sign as well, you'd better buy some white lacy lingerie and retire.)

With the Moon in Taurus, he needs to have love as well as material security, so the more you can provide in that department, the safer he'll feel. With Venus in Taurus, he takes pleasure in a beautiful environment, as well as creature comforts. Once again, you'll either need to direct your bank balance in this direction, or (if he's wealthy) live the life of a lady of leisure. Do be aware of his tendency to believe that if something is easy on the eye, or comfortable to the touch, he must own it immediately. If you have planets in signs which resist this kind of relationship, you may find the atmosphere rather too contained.

Taurus is associated with sensuality, and all the senses in a Taurus Moon–Venus man intensify when he is in love. His sense of smell becomes attuned to your perfume, his eyes will take photos of you and his skin will respond with an extra high frequency when you touch him. Music is strongly associated with Taurus, and with the Moon or Venus in this sign, he will either be musically talented, or strongly tuned in to the musical talent of other people. Taurus Moon–Venus romances always seem to be date-stamped by particular songs — either for him, or for you.

Part of the Taurus myth involves woman as Nature Girl. So if you love the natural world as much as you love your CD player and your precious collections, you'll definitely make an impact. Wandering around the great outdoors, or packing everything up and heading for the beach, is the Taurus Moon–Venus idea of bliss.

However, it is hard for him to ignore your material side (one of Billy Joel's other hits, incidentally, was 'Uptown Girl'). The Taurus

Moon or Venus man will appreciate the way you look, love the fact that you are attuned to nature and will be able to relax when he knows he can depend on you. But no Taurus-influenced man will be able to sleep at night without being secure in the knowledge — even by looking — that you're rich enough to afford the good life. Another reason why being financially independent is a good idea? The Taurus Moon–Venus man can mistake a penniless wife for just another beautiful possession very easily. And because money and value systems always get mixed up in this man's life eventually, a separation could become problematic on a *material* or *financial* level.

Prince Charles is a good example of a Taurus Moon. He chose a beautifully dressed, independently wealthy woman as mother for his children, however despite this, when divorce came, it came at a high price. If you and your Taurus Moon or Venus man do marry or move in together, sorting out the realities of your mutual assets, resources and finances is definitely a smart move. Your value systems have to match, too. This man needs and enjoys the finer things, but he will draw the line at certain things which betray his sense of what is ethical or really worthwhile.

Where he places you

Somewhere between Christie Brinkley and Joanna Lumley. You're gorgeous, have exquisite taste, but know what a recycling bin or a blade of grass looks like.

HIS gemini moon-venus

HIS IMAGE OF YOU

He thinks you're unusually intelligent, more than a little amusing, and the best antidote to boredom he's ever taken to bed. You're always on the phone, or writing something, or reading — or so it seems to him. When people get stuck with the crossword, he passes them on to you. You're witty, which the man with Venus in Gemini finds extremely sexy. You always know what's going on, which makes the man with the Moon in Gemini feel totally comfortable.

He knows he can take you absolutely anywhere, because you'll talk to absolutely anyone. He also knows that when he takes you home, you'll spend two and half hours gossiping about what just went on, either to him, or your friends. He knows you can be *frighteningly* intelligent. But if he's been in a relationship with you for a while, he'll also believe that you've inherited some female gene for gossip.

He'll keep all your letters and cards. He'll remember the words you use, the sound of your voice and certain, selected phone calls. Some men with a Gemini Moon or Venus conduct their love lives by fax, note, card, answering machine or e-mail. They need words, or love words, and because of this, they associate a sexual relationship with the brain, first and foremost. Your vocal chords and lips come a close second. Wordplay is foreplay to this man.

He likes it if you're witty, and then he can quote you. You'll share jokes together, and if you're truly committed, create nicknames or strange abbreviations for each other. When a Gemini Moon or Venus man enters the batso stage of love, he'll even create a special language with you.

What he's looking for in his image of perfect womanhood — at least half the way along — is a kind of lightness and sparkle. Femininity, to him, is amusing, hard to pin down, quick and bubbly. Women may catch his eye, but what he really needs, or wants, is a woman who can also catch his *ear*.

Billy Connolly is a Gemini Moon. When he married fellow comedy actor and writer Pamela Stephenson, he found the lifelong supply of wit that he needed. Noel Coward created many of his sharp, cool and lightly amusing heroines by using the power of his Gemini Moon. In his fantasies, you're wearing a flapper dress and dropping bon mots over the champagne.

Of course, this Geminian angle is only half the story. Unless he is in the unusual position of having both the Moon and Venus in the same sign, 50% of his other desires or needs will be supplied by a different spin on womanhood. Nothing, though, will ever lead him to a bimbo. Half of him wants you to be a casual genius, and you can't really complain about that! If you have planets in Gemini, of course, you'll find it even easier to cope with. The writer David Williamson has a Gemini Moon. He married another writer. Jason

Alexander, who plays George on *Seinfeld*, is married to a scriptwriter. I had a male Gemini Venus client once. He had left school at sixteen, but was now dating an Honours graduate from the University of Melbourne and was madly in love.

With Venus in Gemini, you have a man who is also looking for a social companion. He'll take enormous pleasure in watching you operate on a party level. He enjoys women whom he can take out to dinner, leave switched on and come back to later. If everybody else is stunned by your scintillating conversation or jokes, then so much the better.

With Moon in Gemini, you have a man who needs a snappy, lively atmosphere at home. If you are going to marry or live together, you will have to supply a few one-liners. He needs conversation, too — on no level at all is this a grunt-and-newspaper man. On the other hand, deep and meaningful excursions into his psyche may not be the preferred option. Unless he has a planet in an emotional Water sign — Cancer, Scorpio, Pisces — he is unlikely to want to do more than chat, or kid around.

He dislikes a rut, and feels most comfortable around a woman who also has a need for continual diversions and distractions. So you're flying to Alaska tomorrow? Great. So you're entering the next bantamweight Mensa championships in Tahiti? Terrific. Just don't yawn, click into gear and hand him the same domestic, or sexual, routine. The Moon in Gemini man, in particular, just cannot live with it.

He would, in all honesty, prefer it if you were occasionally tricky and hard to catch. Part of him would rather tolerate the uncertainty of never being entirely sure of you than have you where he wants you. Of course, if his other Moon or Venus sign is in Water (again, Cancer, Scorpio, Pisces) or Earth (Taurus, Virgo, Capricorn) you are going to have to supply a weird mixture of flippancy, restlessness and something a bit more reassuringly substantial.

When he's feeling uncharitable, he'll complain that you're too gossipy, too lightweight and maybe too, too two-faced. The irony, of course, is that he is also capable of all these things, yet may find it easier to hang it on you. However, if you've been looking for a relationship which allows your brain to sprout wings and your mouth to go into overdrive, this is the one.

Where he places you

Somewhere between Mary Tyler Moore and Jane, the heroine of *Broadcast News*. If you can joke around like Pamela Stephenson and hurl one-liners as if you were in a Noel Coward play, then that is all to the good.

HIS cancer
moon-venus

HIS IMAGE OF YOU

There's something wonderfully peaceful, comfortable and secure about the woman this man chooses to be involved with. If he has the Moon or Venus in Cancer then his image of perfect womanhood is caring, home-loving and clan-conscious. If you have planets in Cancer, or a Cancer Rising sign, then you'll click particularly well with this image in his mind's eye.

Wherever your planets are, it may help to realise that his image of the feminine is home-based. He's looking for a woman who is there to give him a sense of belonging, and he'd prefer it if you have the same strong feelings for your own turf or territory that he has for his. Inevitably, when these men get serious about commitment, they do so with a home in mind. (If you're looking for Mr Mortgage, this is Him.) Often, too, a family.

If his other 'female' planet — either the Moon or Venus — is in a completely different sign, this will set up a conflict for him. You may have to be two women in one package, or he may discover that he goes for two distinct types in his life — one rather emotional, introverted and tied to the home front — and the other from another space altogether.

He views women as creatures who depend on men, if he is true to his Venus or Moon sign. He sees you as a devoted person, sold on the idea of accommodating him, and making things safe for him. Something about you has a 'holding' quality if he has the Moon or Venus in this sign. He is really looking for a safe place to hide, or a safe place to go. Inevitably, with the Moon or Venus in Cancer, that safe place will have to be you.

Children and babies will be a big issue — either way — if you become seriously involved with a Cancer-influenced man. He is partly governed by the Moon, which is an archetype and a symbol for the Great Mother. Astrology has always associated both Cancer and the Moon with family issues, and you will no doubt have to confront these more seriously and more deeply than you had expected if things become permanent between you.

He'll like the fact that you have a clan, a family or a base of your own if you get together. In fact, he may identify you so much with this blood-tie collection that it will become interwoven in your relationship in subtle ways. Dr Benjamin Spock, the child and babycare guru, has the Moon in Cancer. Family and motherhood issues are crucial to this man's views on what is female, desirable and feminine.

The Cancer-influenced man is also seeking something protective in you. In fact, it may be true to say that both your 'inner children' (if you'll allow me to be a little L.A. here for a minute) will become a factor in how things are. His own relationship with his mother, and with his family, could have an enormous bearing on the degree to which he'll activate old patterns of doting and dependency — and it could work either way.

Tom Cruise has the Moon in Cancer. Adopting children with his wife, Nicole Kidman, has been a huge part of their relationship. His own, close, relationship with his mother is well known.

Men with this Moon or Venus sign can give an awful lot of power to the women in their lives, perhaps for this reason. You become their home for a while, their foundation stone and their protector. What they are seeking from you is the reassurance and familiarity of a strong pair of arms. And the breasts, of course — with Cancer, any astrologer always has to mention the breasts!

If you're kind to animals and good at babysitting, if you'll sit down and read the local kids a storybook, or give up your time for a good cause, he'll be even more interested. Can you cook? Great. It's not crucial, but it's a factor. Are you that amazing thing, an icon of unselfish womanhood? So much the better. He's seeking something spiritual and special in your femaleness. A little of it is the archetype of the Great Mother, who shelters, saves and defends.

If you do have children together, it will be one of the biggest turning points in the relationship you could ever have imagined. Some men with this Moon or Venus sign decide to skip parenthood for a different kind of reason — they feel the 'family' unit has been sealed just by the intimacy and nesting that takes place between them and their partner. With all that, they reason, why would they be looking for a child as well?

When young, these men often look for a rescuer. They like the emotion, romance and tenderness of it all as well. The initial stages, or early years, of the man with a Cancer Moon or Venus are often marked by dreaming the impossible dream, and yeaning for She Who Will Make it All Perfect. If you have planets in Cancer, Pisces, Scorpio, Taurus or Virgo this won't seem so awful. If you have a lot of Air or Fire in your chart, though (*see* the chapter called Clicking with People, page 189, for more information), then you could start to feel like a drowning woman in search of a lifebelt.

What will really grate, perhaps, are the times when he complains that you're clinging too much, that you're too sensitive, too attached to him. This is basically all him, of course, projected onto you. Be extra specially careful here!

Where he places you

Somewhere between a saintly female relative (or long-lost teacher) and a kind of Mother Goddess. Best sexual fantasy? Him in bed with chicken soup; you in a sexy nurse outfit. How does he know when he's in love? He gets ill or feels lost, and wishes you were there.

HIS leo
moon-venus

HIS IMAGE OF YOU

Above all else, this man needs to feel proud of you. When he's talking about you to his friends, his family or his colleagues, you can expect a wonderful public relations job on your behalf. If you're already beautiful, successful, smart or amazing, he'll make you sound twice as good. Even if you secretly think you're rather ordinary, don't worry. He'll quietly hype you to other people, every time. The man with the Moon or Venus in Leo needs to feel smug about having found you. He's too dignified to admit it, but what he's seeking in you is a reason to feel smug that he's actually won, claimed and bedded you.

His image of the perfect female lover is quite powerful: she has star quality. She shines. She has class. She's an incredible woman. Special. Everyone knows her. She's important, exceptional. This can be tremendously freeing for you, as it gives you permission to shine as brightly as you want to. If you have been with other men who you sensed were quite resentful or uneasy about your social or professional success, or your stand-out qualities, then this man is going to be a revelation.

In his own right, he is also quite special. He appreciates the need for life to offer something bigger and bolder than merely 'ordinary' existence. Part of what he's seeking in you is feedback for his own amazing qualities. He'll be creative or have leadership qualities if he's truly in touch with his own Leonine side. He needs to be a King and to have you as both Queen and courtier. In this instance, both taking your place beside him — and dancing attendance.

Astrologers often use mediaeval images when talking about Leo, because this sign really is about the ancient rites of kings and queens. Update it for the late nineties, and it's partly a 'royal' or 'presidential' quality that he's looking for in you — something dignified and stately perhaps, but also something starry.

His image of the beloved is a woman who is so proud that she can occasionally be snotty — or an outrageous snob. It also includes a woman who is content to create and make her days away, or spin amazing stories for passing neighbourhood kids. He sees you as someone who is either straining to create a child, and a special childhood for them, or a one-off 'creation' of your own that is a brainchild in its own right. For deeper insights on this, you may like to turn to the Planets in Leo chapter for women (*see* page 61). Of course, if you have planets in Leo you'll not only be familiar with this, you'll also be fulfilling a large part of what he's looking for.

Leo Moon–Venus men have an infuriating habit of looking smug (or talking smugly) about their ex-lovers, or ex-wives. It's the pride thing again. He has to feel proud that he chose them, and proud that he won them. Even if it ended up with shouting matches over the washing machine, he'll still quietly give the impression that she was — well, quite an unbelievable person, actually. Dignity will not permit any more details than that, especially details which are going to humiliate or embarrass him, or make him feel downgraded.

If this relationship really works between you, it may turn into one of those 'well-known couple' phenomenons, where you both end up being identified as a unit — but quite a special unit — in your own right. You may happily show off together, on all kinds of levels. Some successful relationships involving Leo Moon–Venus men include a lot of plans and projects, usually creative. Others involve the careful building up of five-star lifestyles and houses. If you have kids, he'll want to be terrifically proud of them. This is the man who looks at a small baby dribbling something white and nasty, and says, 'Nobody else's baby knows how to do that yet, do they?'

When feelings aren't so good between you, there can be awful head-tossing and frosty, dignified silences. As he sees your pride before he sees his own, he will only register your 'arrogance' or 'big ego' or 'stupid pride' and rarely see his own. This can be a problem.

In an odd way, though, he'll feel more comfortable with the occasional head-toss or sniffy silence than with the behaviour of a woman who breaks down in tears, grovels along the floorboards and generally flings herself around as if she has no dignity left. He's frankly not into nose-blowing. Eye-dabbing, yes. Desperate, sad womanhood? Definitely not.

If you embarrass him, even slightly, in front of other people it will make him feel most uncomfortable. Of course, his definition of embarrassment is a little more extreme than other men's. After all, Leo Moon–Venus men can find normal human existence embarrassing. Still, you'll get the message. Keep it dignified. Don't be sordid. Don't mention that. Don't make me look stupid.

His tremendous enjoyment of your successes will make you try harder, which will make you more successful, which will make you love each other more. It's a wonderful upward spiral with this man, and while he often seems to be the power behind your throne, it's just as true that you're often the power behind his.

Where he places you

Somewhere between the sexier members of the European royal families, and the list in the *People Magazine Celebrity Handbook*. You're a bit Jackie O, a bit Princess Caroline. He likes the fact that you've got a few VIP or famous connections in your history, too — even that autograph from Humphrey B. Bear counts with him.

HIS virgo
moon-venus

HIS IMAGE OF YOU

Hard-working. Health-conscious. Neat and cool. He loves your mind first, then the fact that you're so tied to your job, then the way your white shirts look like they have a life of their own. He sees you with glasses on the end of your nose, even if you don't have them, checking all the details on a notepad, pen in your mouth ... the picture of something smart, sexy, demure and precise, in fact.

Kinky? Yes — absolutely. And if you work together, you can double the lust factor. But if he has the Moon or Venus in Virgo, he really needs you to have some kind of work ethic. He loves intelligent women, too. That way you can dissect the newspaper together, or run over his work politics, as well as yours. Are you Queen of Accessories? Fabulous. The man with the Moon in Virgo, in particular, likes a woman who knows how to accessorise. Are you orderly and organised, do you know your doctor's first name, and have a list for everything? Great. The man with the Moon in Virgo feels comfortable with female precision.

You have to be health-conscious, and body-conscious. He is also, for positive and negative reasons (some of them are health food shop addicts, some are perpetually seeing a doctor for help, others are just thingy about their physical shape). However, when it comes to his vision of perfect womanhood, he would really prefer to know that you and your bathroom shelf are whiter than white, and that a decent bottle of vitamins is never too far away from the bottom of your handbag.

He can be a little neurotic about his own physical wellbeing but, annoyingly, hang the same criticisms on you. The 'in sickness and in health' part of the marriage vow will really resonate in your relationship if you decide to tie the knot. The state of both your bodies, and your mutual handling of the issues, will be a cornerstone of things to come. If he has a Cancer planet as well, you may as well dress up as a nurse or patient and play fantasy hospital games for the rest of your life.

Seriously, though, when he is feeling ill, he needs you there. Part of his image of the Goddess is a helpful, disinfectant-swiping, cool and caring, nurse figure. He likes it when you point out that there are four trillion calories in the ice-cream he just looked at. It makes him feel comfortable and cared for.

Remember Jackie O's neat, precise suits and hats? The matching bag and shoes? She was a Virgo Moon or Venus man's fantasy dresser. You need to look pulled together if you are with a man who has a planet in this sign. He doesn't like tarty, he likes sleek and wholesome and clean. White, white and white again. It's no surprise to discover that both John F. Kennedy and Aristotle Onassis had the Moon in Virgo. They married a woman whose talent for keeping pale colours pale was unmatched anywhere in the world. In fact, Jackie's entry for an American *Vogue* journalism competition says it all: 'You can never slip into too dismal an abyss of untidiness if once every seven days you pull yourself up short and cope with all those ragged ends,' her winning feature began. Jackie had Mars in Virgo, by the way. No wonder she was a spotless dream come true for both men and women.

It's really important to him that you are as analytical as he is. But you may need to watch his tendency of projecting his own picky habits on to you. A casual comment, at the wrong time, on a bad day, and you can find yourself being accused of hypersensitivity, or undue fussiness. He can be terribly critical, both of himself and others. It may not be something he likes in himself, so watch his tendency to hang these qualities on you!

With the Moon in Virgo, he'll be looking for a woman who makes lists — perpetually. A list on the fridge, a list in your diary, and (if you choose to marry) an awfully long list of people to thank. If he has Venus in Virgo, he will derive erotic satisfaction from watching you shower, or catching the wonderful blast of perfume, lotion, powder and toothpaste that drifts in from the bathroom when you're going out.

Need we mention his preference for a gleaming kitchen or spotless floor? We need not. Virgo is ruled by the goddess Ceres, who preferred everything in neat little piles. With the Moon in Virgo in particular, he'll virtually need therapy if you keep a disorderly house. Most of them will do their share, too — if they don't, shred one of their endless memos to themselves. That should do it.

If you really want to click, long-term, find something you can work on together. Ideally, it should involve lots of bits of paper, or something in the garden. Set a task. Name a deadline. Push those real, or imaginary, glasses down the end of your nose again. If you can work together, you can live together.

Remember, this is only one half of what he needs, or loves, in a woman. You will need to read the missing Moon or Venus half of this section carefully to try and work out where the fine-tuning is going to come in. But he really does love a woman who can match brains with him. If you've got something to labour over, or pore over, together, you will feel the heat — guaranteed.

One Virgo Moon man I know manages to satisfy his need for a working relationship by floating in and out of short-term art projects with a series of (white T-shirt wearing) women who throw themselves into the job as much as he does. It doesn't really matter where you find the mutual project, though — just try to find one!

Where he places you

It would be great if you could jog like Madonna, take care of yourself like Princess Diana used to and look as neat and slick as Jackie O always did. Of course, if you can't do all this, just pretend to be a workaholic — and drink freshly squeezed juice a lot.

HIS libra
moon-venus

HIS IMAGE OF YOU

Charming, gentle femininity. He's looking for something easy on the eye, and ear, with a Libra Moon or Venus. So his image of the female is, for all your tougher qualities, basically quite soft. The Libra-influenced man falls in love with everything that is refined and easy about womankind.

He likes you to be romantic, too. In fact, with the Moon in Libra, he'll really need that romance. A silly gesture is never a silly gesture to this man — it's poetic, on some level. It's certainly integral to his ideas about male–female relationships. With Venus in Libra, he'll find it easier to fall in love once he's assured that you enjoy the rituals that go with the territory also. There's something faintly courtly and old-fashioned about the gentle level on which he prefers you to treat each other.

Half of his story is here. So if his Moon or Venus is in a different sign, with a different feel to it, you'll probably find that his image of you swings strangely between 'that gorgeous, sweet woman' to something with a different pitch altogether.

With Venus in Libra in particular, his sensitivity to female beauty and fashion increases. He's looking for someone who can choose between shades of blue, look wonderful just about everywhere, and draw admiring glances from those around. A man with Venus in Libra enjoys and relishes female beauty. Not surprisingly, he also cares about his own wardrobe, and should probably organise a booking roster for the bathroom. In you, he's seeking a beautiful smile, the eyes of a goddess and a body to worship.

It may be politically incorrect, but he could care less. Looks really matter. So does your lingerie, your perfume, your taste in music, and the way you nod and smile at his friends. With the Moon or Venus in Libra, he needs a divine-looking, people-pleasing partner, and he may feel that something is missing if you aren't pleasing his eyes, or ears.

In the same way that he knows how to get along with people, and charm them, he needs to know that you can also supply social graces. He moves in a world of please, and thank you, and if you don't mind ... so unless he has a planet in Aries somewhere, you may as well lose the punchy four-letter curses. Unless you do, with the Moon in Libra, he'll start to feel uncomfortable around you. With Venus in Libra, he'll start to feel turned off.

As little boys, Libran types fall in love with beautiful ladies and princesses, and the message they get from the women in their world is that civilised human beings should learn good manners. He's capable of falling in love with something soft, gentle and genteel, and one of the first things you will be screened for is your understanding of the basic niceties. When he's escorting you to a party (and he always thinks of it as 'escorting' in his imagination) he wants you to be an ever-smiling, hand-shaking, politely-laughing, gently-murmuring girl. He likes harmony (another reason for his passion for music, by the way). But that harmony definitely includes your own acceptance of his social and work circle, as well as your ability to make the relationship strike the right chord.

How much does he dislike shouting matches or slamming doors? This much — he'll just murmur something and fade away. If he has the Moon or Venus in a feistier sign, like Aries, Leo, Scorpio or Sagittarius, he can probably stand the occasional scene. But otherwise, you may prefer to find civilised ways of being angry. In truth, female directness and anger is something he has a bit of a problem with.

Does he believe in marriage? Of course. He takes it very seriously. Some Libran types avoid it for this precise reason. They know what the vows and rituals of a wedding really mean, on the most basic level, and respect them so much that they would never dream of playing with the form if they weren't serious. Those Moon or Venus in Libra men who do choose to marry fall hopelessly in love with the ceremony itself: the ideal of romantic love and the prospect of all those suits and *that* dress are enough to make most of them happily dazed for weeks.

He loves the idea of being in a partnership. Buying prints or paintings together, choosing the music you both love, flinging a few well-chosen compliments at each other occasionally, and showing off your coupledom in public. Just how well this works in practice depends on his entire chart, and if you have doubts, you may prefer to check with an astrologer.

If this man has some difficult planetary aspects affecting his Libra Moon or Venus, then his desire for this kind of relationship, and that very beautiful, peaceful kind of woman, will be sincere. However, other things may be getting in the way, and you may like to have them explained to you!

If the full birth chart shows no such problems, and you are also swayed by the gentler, more romantic side of relationships, then you will be extremely happy. The worst he could possibly say about you is that you care about appearances too much, or you're too hung up on the finer points of 'the right thing' or good manners.

Where he places you

Somewhere between Queen Guinevere and any supermodel, singer or actress you care to name. These men always have a passion for one famous beauty or another, and if they didn't believe it was unfair on you, would happily talk about their icon for hours. Ultimately? You're a lady to him. In every sense of the word.

HIS scorpio
moon-venus

HIS IMAGE OF YOU

Sexy, soulful and 1,000 kilometres deep probably sums it up. He's looking for a woman who is sexually magnetic, extremely passionate and very emotional. If you have water signs — Cancer, Scorpio, Pisces — in your chart, that shouldn't be too much to ask. If these Water signs are also your Rising sign, you may also be familiar with the kind of emotional intensity and depth he needs. If you're strictly a Fire–Air girl, though (Aries, Gemini, Leo, Libra, Sagittarius, Aquarius) you may have a few problems.

He is more vulnerable to the image of the femme fatale than most men. And he needs or enjoys women who need and enjoy sex. Sometimes, perhaps, sex for its own sake can be the drawcard. With the Moon or Venus in Scorpio, his image of the divine has a lot to do with the raging desire that exists without the niceties or formalities of romantic love. Sex that nobody's parents could possibly approve of. Occasionally, perhaps, women who are breaking some kind of code just by being with them are the kind who appeal most. It should be evident, by now, why you are going to have to have a few sympatico planets of your own. The man with the Scorpio Moon or Venus presents a fairly powerful challenge to the woman in his life. You may need a strong Earth or Water streak of your own in order to understand that raging passion.

Men who are well known for putting sex at the top of their list have planets in this sign. Rod Stewart, who based an entire song around a woman's legs, is a Scorpio Moon. And anyone out there who sat through his video for 'Tonight's the Night' (log fire, champagne glasses, innuendos and Britt Ekland) should have a fairly good idea of what this sign is all about. The British entertainer Dudley Moore is a Scorpio Moon. Henry Miller was a Scorpio Moon. Prince Andrew is a Scorpio Moon. Last, but by no means least, Warren Beatty is a Scorpio Moon.

Sex for the sake of sex. It's an interesting concept. But to this man, it is more than just a theoretical ideal. It is a basic need (if he has the Moon here) or an act of love (if he has Venus here). If there's something slightly X-rated about you, so much the better. If his family, or yours, get nervous about it, great. Most people, it must be said, can sense the sexual vibes in a Scorpio Moon or Venus man's relationship a mile off. Yes, in church, and on the Big Day, too. It's a sex thing. And you have to understand that.

Nick Cave has Venus in Scorpio. The man with planets here finds darkness sexy, and sex rather dark. I think astrologers could literally write an entire book on the things that a Scorpio Moon or Venus man finds erotic (and it would probably have to be issued in a plastic bag). This is a complicated man you've managed to nail here. Remember, Prince Andrew, a Scorpio Moon, was not only called Randy Andy, he was the only member of the Royal Family ever to date an ex-porn star. Remember Warren Beatty, a Scorpio Moon, is one of the few men to have ever taken on Madonna, the author of a soft-porn autobiography, *Sex*.

For more information on the needs and preferences of the Scorpio Moon or Venus man, you may want to see the film *Henry and June*, about the convoluted sex life of Henry Miller. Or maybe you should just listen to a 'Derek and Clive' tape, featuring the banned, banned, banned comedy of Scorpio Moon Dudley Moore, with his partner Peter Cook.

This man has a kind of lip-curling contempt for nice girls who pass the sugar and say please. He really doesn't want that. If you can out-filth him, fabulous. If not, maybe you had better lean hard on any other signs that turn up in his chart. If he has both Moon and Venus in Scorpio at the same time, you may as well give up your day job and resign yourself to a life of joyful depravity at home.

Of course, there is more than sex here. He needs, and craves, soul. He's looking for something deep and powerful. Something in the way you move, perhaps (George Harrison is a Scorpio Moon). This is an all-or-nothing sign, and unless he feels his soul burn up, and the bed rumble, and the blood rush, then he can feel desperately uncomfortable or unmoved. He's looking for something so close, so intimate, so private, that anyone knocking on the door is going to want to scream and run away. That's his image of you: a co-conspirator and fellow confidante.

He'll accuse you of jealousy, of course, when it's really his problem. With Venus in Scorpio, he'll sense something toxic and complicated in you, when it's really his own blood which just turned dark. Moon in Scorpio men can also throw blame towards the woman in their lives ('You're so suspicious, so manipulative') when they are probably guilty of much the same thing.

The price of all that passion and intensity is fairly high, and if you are going to commit to each other, it will involve resentment and jealousy. Keep it private between you, too. He needs a closed door, not a public address system. Whatever is between you, is just between you — that's all. He may not be able to give a lot away, either. The Scorpio Moon or Venus man is usually 100 complicated feelings in search of a filing cabinet. Whatever leaks through will strike you, in the most powerful and profound way. But just as he sees you as a femme fatale, all smouldering eye contact and secrets, you'll come to know his privacy, too.

Where he places you

Somewhere between an X-rated goddess, a stripper and a soulmate. Morticia Addams, Pussy Galore and the Bride of Dracula should do nicely. Just don't skip the black lingerie in favour of the sensible flannel nightie — he'll throw up.

HIS sagittarius
moon-venus

HIS IMAGE OF YOU

If you've travelled around the planet or like films with foreign subtitles, so much the better. He likes women who have a huge window on the world. Perhaps for this reason, men with a Sagittarius Moon or Venus occasionally fall in love with women who have fallen in love with other countries or cultures. He likes it if you know where Wonderland is — or at least one other galaxy. Lewis Carroll and the astronauts Neil Armstrong and Gus Grissom were all Sagittarius Moons. If this was 1967, he'd want you to be a far-out chick. In the 1990s, he just wants to know that you've seen something of the planet.

This is only 50% of his desires, of course. Unless he has both Moon and Venus in Sagittarius, he'll want another level from you as well. With a planet in Taurus, Virgo or Capricorn, for example, he'll want you to come back down to earth and unpack occasionally.

These men like it if you're funny, too. Michael Hutchence has Venus in Sagittarius. Bob Geldof has the Moon in Sagittarius. Common factor? Paula Yates, author of *Rock Stars in Their Underpants* and other over-the-top tomes. She has planets in Aries, too, which might explain the fact that she seems to have clicked spectacularly with both men. You don't have to have loads of Aries, Leo or Sagittarius in your own chart to be with this man, though. Just a huge appetite for horsing around.

These men desperately need playtime. And they are really looking for an enthusiastic partner on the Twister mat, if truth be known. Other signs in his chart might incline him to more serious pursuits, but as his image of perfect womanhood is fun, raring to go and lively, you may as well put down your copy of War and Peace and kick your shoes off instead.

You see life philosophically, in his view. You have a theory or a worldview that makes everything fit. Nothing is so tragic, or hideous, that it becomes meaningless in your universe. And it really doesn't matter who your guru is, or where your particular view of reality comes from. As long as it includes space for positive thinking, he will depend on it — and you.

He likes women who have a kind of frankness and spontaneity about them. With the Moon in Sagittarius, he needs you to be outspoken. Don't slink away behind the couch with a magazine over your head — just say it! With Venus in Sagittarius he finds it more erotic when you tell it like it is. His idea of sexy is eyes wide open, and a straight-talking mouth. He likes that bluntness. Part of him genuinely needs it, too.

His sexual fantasies range from hiking boots, tiny khaki explorer shorts, a pit helmet and a tan to . . . extreme lingerie. He likes free spirits, wild and crazy chicks, women with a sense of adventure and wanderers. If the label on your bra says 'Made on Mars' then so much the better. He yearns for that restless, searching quality in a woman.

When he's travelling and single, he's never felt more single in his life. You may like to bear that in mind. When unattached, a lot of the Sagittarius Moon or Venus man's erotic adventures occur in strange places. Out in the middle of nowhere. On the trail in Katmandu. In someone's New York loft. Exotic places are erotic to these men, and so are women with exotic accents, or at least strange cooking ingredients.

When he's feeling less than enthusiastic about the relationship, he'll resent the fact that you can be too hyped up, too unrealistic, too offhand. Of course, he can be all these things, too. When he's experiencing difficult planetary trends — hitting either the Moon or Venus in Sagittarius — then he'll start having a problem with the woman in his life. If this happens to be you, then you may feel quite unfairly treated when he sighs at your silliness, or finds you holier-than-thou when there is nothing there to justify it.

Unless he has a planet in Scorpio, or a tough Pluto in his chart, he won't be a game-player. No way. And he expects you to be just as upfront. The dreaded 'I love you' is not so dreaded with this man. It's just there. And you can be honest about it. Perhaps for this reason, he tends to cross the street if the prospect of a tangled, convoluted, awkward or manipulative relationship comes up. He likes it when you come clean. Do it dramatically, do it colourfully, but show him what you're feeling.

Several of the women in his life will be popular social animals who know what's going on, who fits in where, and why they should be there. Sagittarian types attract women who know the social score, or always seem to be at the right parties. They also find them very attractive. One of the things that will impact most on him is the fact that you're smart enough to know who you should be with, and where you should be.

With Venus in Sagittarius in particular, he needs you to be broadminded. *Sexually* broadminded. Also, perhaps, open and non-possessive about whichever popular, vivacious etc., etc. females lie in his past. When he falls in love, one of the first things he notices about himself is that he finds the relationship more genuine when he can grant you your freedom and space. The only problem is, you will need a few Air or Fire planets (Aries, Leo, Sagittarius, Gemini, Libra, Aquarius) to click with this. Be prepared for it!

Where he places you

Somewhere between Diane Fossey, Margaret Mead and an Indian love goddess. Certainly up there with Miss Universe — or maybe just Miss Universal.

capricorn
moon-venus

HIS IMAGE OF YOU

He thinks you're a remarkable woman. You're as ambitious as he is, but you're also prepared to work to get there. If he is thinking of marrying you, it will be no doubt very much with both your careers in mind. Status and achievement issues follow him around, and consequently follow your relationship around. He could take a backward step, and sleep with someone who would splash red paint on his career reputation — but it's unlikely. Whatever other sign is making up the 50% of the romantic equation, the Capricorn Moon or Venus will not let him commit to someone who doesn't make him look good.

That can sound rather cold. But it is a basic fact of life with this man. In return, he will praise your seriousness, your amazing self-discipline, your hard-working style and your solid, unshakeable class. There is something orderly and organised about you, and he finds that like a rock to rest on.

If he has the Moon in Capricorn, he is looking for someone who can help him build a solid lifestyle. He wants concrete under both your feet, and a document that says the future has been organised. With Venus in Capricorn, he wants you to give him a mature relationship. He's looking for something where mutual wisdom and experience will finally pay off.

What he needs and loves is constancy. Nothing too peculiar, unreliable or uncertain. Other parts of his chart may incline him towards rather wilder experiments, but his Capricorn Moon or Venus will never let him near a woman who isn't going to stick around.

He's looking for a good woman, something which is unfashionable, but to him, both erotic and irresistible. He's searching for someone who can love him seriously, and seriously love him. It's in your eyes, basically: solid intentions and trustworthy pupils. If you can't look at him and make him feel he can lean on you forever, then he will commit elsewhere.

Interesting things will happen if you do decide to marry, or build a home or family. It begins with the ceremony. I think 'dignified' is the word he is looking for, followed by 'practical' and 'making use of what's there' and 'traditional'. Part of him, or part of you, may also want the naked sky-diving, but Capricornian common sense usually wins out on the day. Some of them are rampant traditionalists, so be prepared. Whatever form the wedding takes, though, you can expect composure and self-control from him. It's not a denial of passion, not at all: it's the best indication you could possibly get that he's about to explode with it!

In you, he sees a practical soul, a woman who has seen enough of love and life to offer him something solid, and mature. You can leave the joke bra with the tassels behind — really. One half of him wants a woman with a traditional, or classic, wardrobe. (Yves St Laurent has the Moon in Capricorn.) His image of the feminine is tailored, timeless. He also wants you to know the social score, to know how to behave in front of his colleagues, and how to tell the builders where to move the kitchen wall.

Because his career, and his ambitions, are so important to him (he loves or needs his work) you will have to fit in around that. Napoleon Bonaparte had a Capricorn Moon. You may also hear 'Not tonight, Josephine' when duty gets in the way and he's too tired to punch a pillow — let alone engage in anything more interesting. Quite a few politicians have a Capricorn Moon or Venus.

Still, he wouldn't have fallen for you — hard — if you weren't also enamoured of the long climb to the top. He needs you to have soaring ambitions of your own, or to be so fully identified with his success that his job victories also become yours. Life becomes *our* promotion, or *our* success story. Men with a Capricorn Moon who become fathers often have to make difficult decisions about the value of their career, as well as the value of their children. His view of you, too, will have a lot to do with your decision on career versus motherhood — or career versus home. If you commit to each other, jobs will be a big deal in the relationship.

He would prefer it if you had your own brilliant career; or if he needs a career 'wife' then he will make it clear that he needs a cross between a PR person, a function organiser, a gourmet chef and a five-star hotelier. Being his wife will, in its own way, become a job. Most Capricornian types fall in love with your ambition and achievements, though, as well as your cool exterior. These men are incapable of dating just anyone. You have to have a decent title — or at least an engraved business card.

Many of these men, in love with their careers, meet their wives and lovers literally on the job. If not, when you meet up, one of the very first questions will be 'What do you do?' (although he'll express it more elegantly than that) and inevitably, too, his working life will form a sizeable part of the conversation.

The parts of himself that he cannot reconcile may be projected on to you, so be prepared. If he thinks you're too inflexible, too hard to reach, too money-minded, too work-oriented, then it won't take much imagination to see who he's really talking about. On the plus side, when he's madly in love, you couldn't hope for a more serious gaze, or a steadier commitment.

Where he places you

He sees you as a classic beauty and, above all other things, a credit to him. You're his rock — a cross between The Girl Most Likely to Succeed, and The Girl Who's Already There.

HIS IMAGE OF YOU

The man with the Moon or Venus in Aquarius craves — or adores — an unusual woman or an unconventional relationship. He needs and values everything that is cool, progressive or different in womankind. He actually prefers it if you're not like everybody else. And he loves and needs whatever you can give him in the way of space, freedom and unpredictability. A slightly mad relationship, or a female who is simply not like the rest, will feed 50 to 100% of his needs or desires. Dylan Thomas, born with the Moon in Aquarius, was once asked by journalists why he had come to America. He replied, 'In pursuit of my lifelong quest for naked women in wet mackintoshes.'

Give him love, but above all give him eccentricity and liberty. He is so popular, so friendly and so seductively unusual, that it is easy to fall in love with him. But he does not want your dependency, does not feel comfortable with being a 'rock' to any woman, and has a horror of any relationship, marriage or de-facto arrangement which he believes will tie him down.

If you are to come to a satisfactory arrangement with this man romantically or emotionally, you will have to appreciate his need for activities, work, interests or friendships which have nothing to do with you. This is not somebody who necessarily wants to clock up a lot of time with you. If he does — you will still be dealing with a noticeable kind of distance. Love does not thrive on a round-the-clock basis here. Nor does he necessarily swallow conventional society's rules for happiness. A white wedding, followed by cosy domestic routines until death parts you, is just not in it.

His image of the beloved is a woman who is non-possessive and who does not register jealousy. He is not being deliberately cruel in this regard. He honestly and quite innocently cannot fathom why any woman would be hurt, angry or upset by his interest in, or feelings for, any other woman in his life. What he wants is a progressive, free-thinking, easygoing female who takes an advanced view of human relationships.

If either Uranus, the planetary ruler of Aquarius, or the sign itself are prominent in your personal chart, you may be able to accommodate this. It is highly likely that you also find it hard to deal with a man who will not tolerate or understand your light connections to other men in your life.

In women, he loves and needs originality. There has to be something quite remarkable or different about you to attract him. He has a penchant for women who are refined and cultured, slightly bohemian or alternative, or — frankly — an odd choice for him to make. However, he also needs a female who is keen to experiment — particularly romantically or sexually — and who prefers a lot of freedom. He'll have his friends, and he wants you to have yours. There may be platonic friendships on either side of the fence for both of you. If you are independent and rather cool, you will certainly attract him. If there is something noticeably unexpected about your style, your interests, your attitudes, your lifestyle or your appearance, you will fascinate him even more. To keep things going between you, though, you will personally need to appreciate and understand his difficulty with the watery world of feelings. Part of him fears he will drown to death in them.

Women who have been through suffocating and stifling relationships with jealous men, or lovers who have been scarily intense or close, often find Moon or Venus in Aquarius men like a shot of oxygen. There is no intense, heavy breathing with this man. And he will not cling to you, or resent the time you do not spend with him. Being with him can be like a wake-up call. And it can feel tremendously exciting (he is always, reliably, exciting) and also full of possibilities for you.

This happy, unusual state of affairs can only come about if you are prepared to rethink your ideas on relationships, though. What he will probably require from you is a very unlikely set-up where closeness, emotion and true intimacy are just not possible. He may have a heavy work schedule — or a lot of outside interests — that require you to go off and do your own thing while he is doing his. He may be a radical Moon or Venus in Aquarius man, in which case he will make it very clear that he wants an open relationship, or an affair (being with you and being with his partner at the same time guarantees that he will never have to feel too close to either of you). This sign is about invention. He may make up the rules as he goes along. He'll see that side of you, too — the unafraid, experimental side.

If you are wise, you will honestly examine your own needs at the beginning of the relationship. And don't be afraid to challenge him on what he wants as well. He won't be offended. As long as your questions don't 'crowd' him (this is a favourite word with Moon or Venus in Aquarius) he will give you the truth quite openly. This is not a dishonest man, unless there are contradictory indications in his chart. He prefers complete frankness and openness and is not a game player. However, you will have to accept his terms. No matter how much compromise or middle ground you can find together — and he is always amenable to logical debate — the basic reality of Moon or Venus in Aquarius is that his need to be exactly who he is will somehow always dictate what goes on for both of you.

Where he places you

Somewhere between Yoko Ono, Soon-Yi Previn, Juliette Greco, Simone de Beauvoir and Caitlin Thomas. He finds you odd, unusual, original and very exciting. When you're not clicking, he finds you cold, weird and unemotional. His image of the beloved is totally unaffected by convention — or what other people think he 'ought' to be doing with his love life!

HIS pisces
moon-venus

HIS IMAGE OF YOU

You're some kind of mermaid in his book. Hard to pin down, mysterious and magical. You may quite literally be a fantasy woman, too — the founder of the Playboy empire, Hugh Hefner, has the Moon in Pisces. Your man's view of perfect womanhood is very gentle, always fluid and fascinating and slightly off the planet.

Be prepared. You may not always be real to him. Still, being around you will make him want to write poems or read them, and tell you the contents of all his dreams (inevitably, they'll be full of convoluted and peculiar images of you, when he's in love).

Three of the most famous men in modern music had a Pisces Moon: Prince, Michael Jackson and Elvis Presley. The common link here, apart from the fact that Lisa-Marie Presley is an odd connection between her father and ex-husband, is this: dream women. When you walk by in a raspberry beret, doves cry. This man can't help but see you in fantasy, mythical terms — especially when he's falling in love. He sees you in colours — and he's hugely romantic.

What registers with him is your mysteriously, slightly spacey aura. Your imagination is extraordinary, but your interests (yes, astrology is on the list) are even more so. You're spiritual and special. He can't see you buying toilet paper, or putting the garbage out. It's possible, but it's just not in his frame of reference.

You're a mind-reader. Your eyes are like crystals and you tune in to him, as well as the future. You're sensitive in other ways, too. Music and prose, poetry and spirituality touch you. The things that are so fascinating to you will come to fascinate him, eventually, too. But remember — unless he has the Moon and Venus both in Pisces, this is only 50% of his dream of you. The rest of him, placed firmly in another sign, will want a different spin on the mermaid.

When you're with him, you seem to understand him, quite instinctively, and there isn't always a need to talk. You relax him. You're tolerant of him, and you bend and squeeze your way around the sharp edges of your life together. When his head aches, you massage his temples, or find him the aspirin. The Moon Pisces man fantasises a home with amazing books on the shelves, extraordinary music on the CD player and you in a long dress lying on the sheets in a dream bedroom. From you, he's seeking the exotic and the romantic.

The man with Venus in Pisces is looking for a saint, a soulmate, a poet, a mediaeval queen and a friend to living things. Tall order? Absolutely not. Enjoy the fantasy — because it is a fantasy — but remember that even if all he is registering is your love of small furry things and your amazing lingerie, that's enough. For the Venus Pisces man, a sexual fantasy is, quite literally, a sexual fantasy. He believes in sexual healing, too.

You have to be kind with this man. Give him anything, but give him that. His dream of perfect womanhood is a gentle, selfless soul, who would give herself up tomorrow if it meant saving someone — or something. One of Michael Jackson's female icons is Elizabeth Taylor (a Sun Pisces, who clicks perfectly with his Moon Pisces). Now, if only that woman was several decades younger ... but still. It is her charity work, her fairytale quality and the myth of the violet-coloured eyes that must keep drawing him back.

These men are very sensitive to colour. How to tell if he's in love with you? Ask him, on the phone, what colour he thinks your eyes are. If he's there, he'll know. The impressionist painter Paul Cezanne was a Pisces Moon: he saw the world in soft colours.

If he has Venus or the Moon here, he may cling to music, or poetry, or pictures of you, to try and pin your beauty down. It can be hard for him to put his feelings into words, because his image of you is so exotic, and sometimes exists on such a peculiar plane. Part of him may be looking for something quite different, but his Piscean side has you painted in oil, sung in chords and described in verse.

If you have planets in Pisces, or the other Water signs — Scorpio and Cancer — then this feeling of dreamy, watery merging should be complete. Do be aware that sensitivity — yours and his — will be a big issue in the relationship, though. Also, classically, someone seems to be the saviour, and someone the rescuer. I have seen enough men with a Pisces Moon or Venus to know that they have to paint the relationship in mythic, romantic hues. So you become his healer, or his saving grace. Without you, he might never have made it. Until there was you, he was lost.

It works the other way, too. He sees himself as the man of peace, the man of compassion, who is there to help you, rescue you and, if necessary, bring you back to life again. This does not mean, on any level, that there is something false about these aspects of your relationship. On the contrary. There may be a genuine reason why he feels that someone has been rescued or helped by the other. A lot depends on how you feel about this in your own life, though. At its lowest pitch, a Pisces-influenced relationship or marriage can turn into a game where one of you is always playing martyr.

Where he places you
Between Marina, the aquatic heroine of *Captain Scarlet*, and the Little Mermaid. You're exotic and erotic to him — he'll think of you in terms of a favourite poem, painting or song.

YOUR FUTURE

LIFE

to **2005**

Astrology is like weather forecasting when it is used for predictive work. It's pretty general, fairly reliable and, depending on your state of mind, you'll either hang on every detail, or ignore it completely.

Astrologers look at what the planets are doing to your birthchart to decide how life will be for you. Is Saturn travelling through the career department of your horoscope? You can expect a difficult two years, with a bigger workload. Is Jupiter travelling through the friendship sector of your horoscope? You'll be introduced to some fabulous new people, and one of your old friends will have a successful and happy year.

The predictions you read in magazines are based on birthcharts which have been drawn up for the whole population, which makes them even more general. When I prepare my weekly and monthly columns, I calculate horoscopes for a fictitious Arian person, Taurean person, and so on. The results are pretty good — at least as good as a weather forecast. When I write sentences like this: 'Expect pressure on the home front,' it's pretty much like the weather forecaster telling you there's a cloudy patch on the far northern coast of Australia. Your TV set can't tell you at what precise time the clouds will appear, what shape they will be, what colour they will be and over which suburb they will have the biggest effect — at least, not on the 6 p.m. news. However, if you dropped into the Bureau of Meteorology, you could probably get further information.

Astrology is like this also. What this section of the book achieves is a bit like a trip to the Bureau of Meteorology, as opposed to a casual flick through your favourite magazine. I'm going to use your birthtime, as well as your birthday, to set up some basic predictions from now to 2005.

There just isn't the space to consider the effect of every planet — Neptune and Uranus alone require a book to themselves. If you're looking for in-depth predictions, you will almost certainly need to book in with an astrologer for a face-to-face reading, or call a reliable clairvoyant.

I'm concentrating on Sun, Pluto and Jupiter cycles in this section, as these dictate the rhythms of the year. The Sun builds your confidence, Jupiter provides opportunities, and Pluto changes your life.

There's something called a Saturn Return which may be familiar to those of you who have picked up an astrology book, or know an astrologer. This is a landmark event in women's lives, and takes place around 28–30, and again at 58–60. The Saturn Return is one of the biggest learning experiences you will ever have, and I don't think it's any accident that a lot of my first-time clients start booking appointments at about the 29th year of their lives.

Your time of birth also identifies what your Rising sign, or Ascendant, is. Once again, people who are reasonably familiar with astrology will know this one.

Many astrologers believe the Rising sign describes the journey you take over your entire lifetime. I tend to agree with this. Once you have worked out your Rising sign by using your birthtime and birthday, you can then decide if you are taking an Arian journey, a Taurean journey, a Geminian journey, and so on.

Sometimes, the particular journey you are taking will have such a huge impact on you that it will leave a kind of 'sign' impression on your personality — even on your appearance. To give you an example of this, I know an Aries Rising woman who has taken a typically Arian journey. She's become involved in lots of sports, works in a very competitive field and has a lot of friction in her personal life.

She is actually a Sun Pisces, Moon Cancer, Mercury Pisces, Venus Taurus, Mars Taurus. But after being on an Aries Rising journey for about 38 years, she has developed a kind of 'fake' Arian feel about her. Being put in competitive career situations has helped her to develop a lot of assertiveness skills that the rest of her chart doesn't show. Her sporting interests have given her a few knocks and scars on her head, which Aries rules.

Health and the body, incidentally, seem to be very affected by the Rising sign journey. If you're interested in this aspect of prediction, you may want to read up on your Rising sign later in this section. Doing this, you will be able to see the extent to which your particular life journey has given you some of the qualities or peculiarities of the sign concerned.

If your Rising sign is the same as your Sun, Moon, Mercury, Venus or Mars signs, then you will be a kind of super-representative of what that sign is all about. As an English astrologer friend of mine puts it, 'You will *reek* of the sign, darling!'

Finally, I've written about the global trends we can all expect to 2005 and beyond. Some astrologers will agree with me, some will not. What I'm using here are the slow-moving outer planets, like Uranus, Neptune and Pluto, to judge the global mood as we leave the 1990s. The things the world becomes fascinated and obsessed with in any decade are described by the signs occupied by Neptune and Pluto. The biggest areas of change in our lives are described by Uranus. Will we still be obsessed with our careers after 2000, and if not, why not? This is where I get to put on my Madame Zaza headscarf and wave my hands around!

YOUR saturn return

Between 28 and 30, and 58 and 60, you will experience your Saturn Return. Saturn, the planet known as the Great Teacher — and also the Old Devil — will swing around to exactly the same place it was in on the day you were born. This is a big deal in astrology because it is such a rare event — and an even bigger deal for *you*, the person going through it. And because this planet is associated with long loathsome learning experiences it is definitely more difficult than the others, but at times you will feel as if just about everything is being shaken, inspected and held up to the light for flaws. Any of the cornerstones of your life — relationships, health, career, home, family, money, friendships — may be seriously affected.

Typically, anything that is meant to be for the long term will be firmed up and set in concrete. You will end up committing yourself, very seriously, and in a way that makes you feel like that wonderful thing, A Mature Woman Making a Mature Decision. There may also be parts of your life that you are familiar with, or even that you want very much — but at Saturn Return time, they will go. You may cut away things that aren't right for you deliberately. Or, if you are not aware of how inappropriate things have been for you, it's likely you'll feel quite fearful or anxious about the fact that things are changing.

I have seen enough Saturn Returns in the lives of my clients to know that one piece of advice will always work: go with it. Saturn can feel quite relentless — and end up making you feel thoroughly miserable and depressed — if you hang onto the things it wants you to let go of.

Just as important at this time is the idea of making the Big Decision. Just as you will have to let some things pass, there is also every chance that you will be presented with a chance to seriously commit yourself to something that is right for you. It may well have been on your agenda for years. Saying yes to it in a serious way will make you feel terribly responsible and terribly adult. But the good, constructive things that get firmed up now will be with you for a long time to come.

People divorce and marry on their Saturn Return. They emigrate. They have children for the first time. They buy houses. They change jobs. I left a seven-year relationship at 29, and then left my job as a journalist to form an astrology company at 30. Several friends of mine married on their Saturn Returns.

Another interesting thing happens just after you're recovering from the stresses of your twenty-eighth and twenty-ninth years. As you dive into your early thirties, the planet Jupiter makes the best possible pattern in your chart. Jupiter is associated with opportunities, optimism and expansion. Characteristically, women go through a chain of events that looks like this:

1. Anxiety over elements of life that seem to be fading, or disappearing from your life. Difficult losses, and an acknowledgement that some things in your life were never going to be realities.

2. A difficult, but potentially rewarding commitment, to life changes which are going to affect you for years to come. A rather serious feeling that what you do now must take you forward into the future, too. Typically, a conviction that you are getting older and that you now have to get real about life.

3. After a couple of years of feeling terribly mature, sensible — and, let's face it — older, about things, you lighten up. Saturn's influence fades as you move between 30 and 31, and now that you know where you stand in life (you've been building the foundations, after all) you can relax and take risks again. As you move into your early thirties you will have a strong sense of 'knowing who I am' and even though the very end of your twenties may have been difficult and exhausting at times, you are now ready to do amazing things.

Real-life stories

Tina Brown, born in 1953, was 31 when she moved from London to New York to accept the huge task of becoming Editor-in-Chief of *Vanity Fair*.

Jane Campion, born in 1954, was 31 when she started making her Oscar-winning film, *The Piano*.

Coco Chanel, born in 1883, opened her first boutique in Paris in 1914, aged 31.

Agatha Christie, born in 1890, published her first book, *The Mysterious Affair at Styles*, in 1920, aged just 30.

Hillary Clinton, born in 1947, married Bill Clinton in 1975, aged 28. Their mutual career expansion took off in the years after this.

Cindy Crawford, born in 1966, ended her marriage to Richard Gere in 1995, aged 29 — right in the middle of her Saturn Return.

Marie Curie, born in 1867 co-discovered radium in 1898 — aged 31.

Princess Diana, born in 1961, separated from Prince Charles in 1992 — aged 31. The hard Saturn Return years preceded the hopeful, risk-taking time in her early thirties. Diana's choices were very common, by the way. The 28th and 29th years often see women in bad marriages facing up to difficult realities. As they move towards 30 and 31, Jupiter's fantastic optimism drives them to do something about it. Jupiter will also provide the opportunity you have been waiting for to farewell the marriage.

Daphne du Maurier, born in 1907, published her most famous novel, *Rebecca*, in 1938, just as she approached her thirty-first year.

Germaine Greer, born in 1939, published *The Female Eunuch* in 1970, aged 31. Her Saturn Return, just before this, coincided with her serious acceptance of feminism — not merely as an idea on paper, but as a principle she would have to live with on a personal level, too.

Dame Naomi James, born in 1949, was just 29 in 1978 when she broke the world solo sail record. Incidentally, many women comparing notes on their Saturn Return years say that 28–30 is just like sailing alone in a storm. Life seems hard, cold, uncomfortable and you're permanently tired while it's going on! Still, the amazing feeling of 'pulling through' is also there when it's over.

Carole King, born in 1942, released her multiple platinum album, *Tapestry*, in 1971, aged 29. Many successful musicians who spend years struggling seem to have 'overnight success' between 28 and 30.

Courtney Love, born in 1964, took on both her husband's death, her new baby, Frances Bean, and her own stardom during her Saturn Return years 28–31.

Sarah, Duchess of York, gave birth to her first child, Eugenie, at the age of 29.

Cher filed for divorce with Sonny in 1974, at age 28.

Actor Joanne Whalley-Kilmer separated from husband Val Kilmer at the age of 30, citing irreconcilable differences after seven and a half years of marriage.

Doris Lessing, born in 1919, published her first novel, *The Grass is Singing,* in 1950, aged 31.

Jean Muir, the designer, born in 1933, opened her first shop in 1961 aged 28.

Sylvia Plath, the poet and author of *The Bell Jar,* born in 1932, separated from husband Ted Hughes in 1962, aged 30.

Dame Edith Sitwell, born in 1887, published her first book of poems aged 28.

Oprah Winfrey, born in 1954, started the successful *Oprah Winfrey Show* aged 31 in 1985.

Tori Amos, born in 1964, started playing the piano at age three, and won a scholarship at age five. Her success is far from overnight, although it appeared that way, when she passed the Saturn mark after 28 and had coasted to success by 31.

Sheryl Crow, born in 1963, collected three Grammy awards in 1994, aged 31.

Writer Nora Ephron, born in 1941, wrote her first book, *Wallflower at the Orgy,* in 1970, aged 29.

Melissa Etheridge, born in 1961, won her first Grammy at 29.

Princess Stephanie married Daniel Ducruet, the father of her two children, at the age of 30.

Melanie Griffith took some of the most serious decisions of her life at age 29. She finally entered rehabilitation for addiction problems — and reunited with her divorced husband of ten years, Don Johnson.

AT AGE 58

Is it coincidence that women are bringing their retirement ages forward to 60, or is something astrological going on here? It may not be your working life that is affected at your second Saturn Return — it could also be your decision to try a new relationship, do something about your health, move house or tour the world.

Just note the sequence from your late twenties and early thirties. First, the serious challenges. Next, the inevitable learning experiences. And after that? You take what you've learned about yourself, lean all your weight on the platform you've been building up, and prepare for take-off. By 61 you should be embarking on some interesting new discoveries. The second Saturn Return experience of Elizabeth Taylor is a case in point. She married her seventh husband, Larry Fortensky, at 59, and accelerated her AIDS work, her perfume interests and her film career after that.

It doesn't matter if you're going from 28 to 31 or 58 to 61: the decisions you make just before those years are with you, for better or for worse. The best thing about the Saturn Return years? They feel authentic. You probably know yourself better in these years than at any other time in your life, even if it isn't always easy.

MERCURY madness

Mercury is the planet of communication and travel. And every now and then, it does something quite bizarre — it appears to go backwards, or get stuck. When this happens, things go wrong. How wrong? Well, this is what happened in April 1998, just as this book was going to the printer's.

World Cup soccer tickets went on sale in France — by phone. Some 20 million calls went through, the English phone lines jammed, and the Dutch system came crashing down.

Author Will Self had all copies of his new book *Tough, Tough Toys for Tough Tough Boys* taken out of the bookstores and pulped, following mistakes in computer typesetting for the book. In the same month, Antony Beevor's book *Stalingrad*, published by Viking, was pulled after software printing errors. And *The Eros Hunter*, by Russell Celyn Jones, featured a scramble of wrongly numbered pages.

I lost my passport and the disc which contained all the copy for this book, and went temporarily insane.

What happened to you between March and April 1998? The odds are high that you suffered typical Mercury glitches. I've kept notes on this stuff over the years, and inevitably everyone from my local bank tellers to my editors in magazine-land go through chaos. In other years, Mercury going backwards has also coincided with big banking errors, and computer hacker chaos. Treaties, contracts and agreements produced while Mercury is off balance tend to come undone later. Strikes affect delivery of parcels and letters. Computers play up. Car parts don't arrive. Public transport schedules go off-track. Lawyers leave their laptops in taxis. Mobile phones get swallowed by golden retrievers.

Something else happens when Mercury backtracks. Long-lost documents and objects — sometimes even long-lost people — turn up. In 1986, a previously unknown Shakespeare poem turned up in Oxford during one of these periods. And as I was writing this chapter, *The Times* ran a photograph of a statue of Mercury himself, the Messenger of the Gods, which had been stolen years before from County Hall in Northallerton and had subsequently turned up in a hole in the ground in an English country garden. You guessed it. He turned up just as Mercury was stopping its backward motion and going forwards again. In August 1998, another Mercury Retrograde — missing pages from Anne Frank's diary — turned up.

You can make your life easier by backing up documents and taking extra precautions with transportation, travel, communication and information when Mercury goes backwards. It may not be the moment to sign a contract or make a massive investment. Media enterprises which launch under mad Mercury periods tend to flop, go through staff chaos, or suffer phone problems. I signed a contract with a radio station under a Mercury Retrograde period. Three months later, the radio station pulled the show. Whoops.

Travel can be a nightmare under Mercury Retrograde. Here are some other first-hand accounts, gathered from friends and clients:

- A dog mix-up at Heathrow airport, resulting in one confused white terrier being sent back to LA, where he'd originally flown out from.
- A well-known airline decided to send its London–Sydney flight out an hour early, resulting in one missed wedding, and a whole week's worth of re-scheduling.
- A train that physically separated into two carriages at a railway line junction with — you guessed it — the unfortunate Mercury victim on the wrong half of the train, heading for parts unknown.
- A stolen bicycle in Cambridge which turned up — right on cue — just as Mercury stopped going backwards and started going forwards again.

Robert Wilkinson, whose book A *New Look At Mercury Retrograde* is rather wittily printed in backwards writing on the cover, has studied the planet in depth. He gives many more examples in his book, but admits that his own life has not been immune from Mercury madness.

'I bought a state-of-the-art answering machine just prior to a Mercury retrograde period,' he writes. 'It proceeded to malfunction three times in five weeks, each time needing repairs.'

For your information, then, here are the next periods of Mercury chaos, into the next century.

1999

11 March–3 April

13 July–7 August

6–26 November

2000

22 February–15 March (Note: This is a few weeks after the Millennium Bug is supposed to hit.)

24 June–18 July

19 October–9 November

2001

4–24 February

4–27 June

30 September–22 October

2002

18 January–7 February

14 May–7 June

13 September–5 October

2003

1–22 January

25 April–19 May

27 August–19 September

16–31 December

2004

1–5 January

5–29 April

9 August–1 September

29 November–19 December

2005

19 March–11 April

22 July–15 August

13 November–3 December

I've noticed from years of Mercury-watching that the effects also seem to kick in a week or two before the actual dates in question. Many of my friends have noticed that this is when their fax goes wrong, or their e-mail starts bouncing, or their mail gets re-directed — but doesn't arrive. It may be worth taking notes or keeping an eye on things over a 12-month period to see how it personally affects you. And keep your sense of humour about promises made or received during a Mercury madness period. It may pay to be flexible — at least until the planet has corrected itself.

One other point. It's not worth staying in bed for. When Mercury goes backwards, it's a good time to re-file, review, re-organise. Anything with a 're' in front it, basically. Use your astro commonsense. This is not the moment to take wild and crazy risks with airline tickets, train connections, the postal service or your computer. You shouldn't let it stop your life, though. As with eclipses and other strange planetary phenomena, it's just a gentle warning from the universe that you need to take more trouble with things than you normally do. If it involves communication, transportation or information, don't leave it to chance.

By the way, if you have a Mercury story for me, I'd love to hear it. You can e-mail it to jessica@zip.com.au. Just don't do it when we're in the loony cycle, though. It may end up in some other Jessica's computer.

WHOAAA

spooky!

Astrology is becoming quite a cut and dried business these days. If you type your date, time and place of birth into a computer, a 30-page document will come back, giving you information about your personality and your future. Astrologers are also becoming more scientific, and some research is now beginning to support their theories. Dr Percy Seymour's book, *The Scientific Basis of Astrology* (Quantum) is full of examples of this new, hard-nosed approach.

Funnily enough, this isn't what gets most people excited about the stars. More than anything else, it's the mystery, the meaningful coincidences, the magic and the element of 'Whoaaa, spooky!' that makes the difference.

SYNCHRONICITY

Astrology is such a symbolic system that it lends itself to what Carl Jung called synchronicity — those striking, amazing moments when the universe seems to be giving you some kind of message or reminder, usually using symbols which mean something to you. An actress friend of mine was looking for a new agent, and knew she had found the right one when she saw the stone lion's head above their office door. She had three planets in Leo and had been looking for an agent who would treat her with respect (a particularly Leonine desire). I had been discussing this with her just a few hours beforehand — her need for an agent who would help her to 'do' her Leo side. When she saw the lion, she knew she'd made the right decision (she did).

The English astrologer Maggie Hyde has written a great book called *Jung and Astrology* (Aquarian) which has many similar examples. Carl Jung himself was studying the Age of Pisces and fish symbolism when all on one day he had fish for lunch, was shown paintings of fish by a former patient, and then later on dealt with a client who had been dreaming about fish. Just as he finished noting all these synchronicities in his book, Jung went for a walk and came across . . . a dead fish.

In your own horoscope, there will be plenty of symbols and strong associations which are there thanks to your Sun, Moon, Mercury, Venus, Mars and Rising signs. If the universe seems to be sending you a particularly meaningful and strong message about your Pisces side, for example, you may well encounter plenty of fish. It happens.

When Pluto was passing through the sign of Scorpio, I had a particularly difficult landlady to deal with. In true Pluto fashion, my entire home situation was being transformed as a result. I decided to end my lease, and emptied out a cardboard box to look for the papers. A live, tiny scorpion fell out. I trapped it under a jar. Within a few days my landlady was trapped as well — by financial problems. I decided to stay. The whole episode had a particularly Scorpionic flavour, though. I was becoming quite intense about domestic trivia that shouldn't really have run quite so deep. My landlady was rather obsessive, and also quite secretive. Was she a Scorpio? I never asked. But one day I saw her with her young son. He was wearing a Walt Disney windcheater with a picture of Pluto on the front! At that point, I think I decided to tell the Universe, 'Thanks, I think I just got the message'.

D R E A M S

Dreams are particularly good examples of astrological symbols at work. And not only the signs come through — planets also have an impact. I've lost count of the number of people I know going through their Saturn Return who end up dreaming about ice, snow, fridges, and other typically chilly Saturn symbols (by the way, I knew someone who dreamed she was eating chillies, which is a convoluted way of receiving the same message). If you're going through a Neptune cycle you may dream about water a lot. If it's Jupiter, you might dream about fat people, or you may wake up laughing (or let's face it, trying to eat the pillow).

It's quite reassuring that we can subject astrology to scientific testing methods, feed it into a computer, and still find mystery in it.

HOW DIVINE

Astrology is also being used as an oracle along the lines of Tarot or I Ching these days, and the results here are also satisfyingly spooky. My friend Lynda Hill specialises in something called Sabian Symbols with her husband Richard. Sabians are symbols (with meanings attached) for each sign and degree of the zodiac. They stretch from Aries 1 to Pisces 30. You can use them with your horoscope, if you know your planet degree as well as your planet sign. Or you can shuffle the red and blue cards which come with the book, and pick a sign and number at random, to answer a question or focus your thoughts.

As I am writing this, I have decided to ask the Sabians what will be the impact of this book you're holding — The New Astrology For Women. My red card is Cancer, my blue card is 23. The symbol is: The Meeting of a Literary Society. Lynda and Richard's interpretation reads in part, 'Shared higher knowledge. Print media, libraries, written word'. It also warns against chatting instead of doing, so I'd better get on with it.

Another Sabian Symbols fan, the American astrologer Alice Kashuba, discovered that one of the Sabian Symbols for the horoscope drawn up for the last episode of Seinfeld was Aries 28 — 'A Large Disappointed Audience'. At times like this, you really do have to say 'Whoaaa, spooky!' and leave it at that. By the way, the Sabian Symbols were channelled by a clairvoyant several decades ago. Certainly long before Americans had even thought about Junior Mints, the Bubble Boy and other Seinfeld-isms. If you would like to experiment with Lynda Hill's mysterious Sabian Symbols on the internet, go to http://www.zodiacal.com/cgi-hts/htmlscript?oracle.hts.

The astrologer Liz Greene has a card and book set called Mythic Astrology (Simon & Schuster). Right now, I'm interested in hearing what the cards have to say about a new plan for astrologers to buy William Lilly's cottage in England — Lilly was the astrologer who predicted the Great Fire of London, among other things. His cottage is up for sale and there's a global effort to raise the required money to buy it for the astrological community.

I've drawn two cards, showing two signs of the zodiac — Aries and Gemini. The Aries card shows two rams locking horns in a fierce fight. I think there's going to be hot competition for this cottage. And no doubt an Aries will play a big part in the story that unfolds. And there, in the Gemini card, is a picture of an old house — white, with a brown thatched roof. I kid you not, it looks just like Lilly's centuries-old house. In the card picture, the cottage is standing at the bottom of a temple of learning. Ironically, that's why astrologers want to buy Lilly's house — they'd like to turn it into a library, or a research centre. Watch this space, I guess.

You can use *Mythic Astrology* with a real chart as well, to really dig your way quite deeply into what the planets and signs mean for you.

Then there's the American astrologer Sheryl Simon's A*S*K cards, which are once again based on ancient astrological principles. You can use A*S*K to teach yourself more about astrology, or you can close your eyes, concentrate on a question and shuffle.

I experimented with Sheryl's own deck when I was travelling through the US to launch the first edition of this book. I drew Saturn in Taurus in the Second House while she watched. As most astrologers will know, this means major tests and learning experiences in connection with money and possessions. That was the day the Australian dollar plunged, and my planned shopping expedition to Barney's in New York began to look like a non-event.

The deeper meaning of Saturn in Taurus in the Second House came out for me afterwards. I was asked to participate in an astrological business venture which basically meant selling out to a get-rich-quick scheme that I decided I didn't believe in. Mind you, it would have made the Barney's shopping expedition more than possible. A typical Taurean dilemma.

Finally, a few days later, I found myself in London at the Victoria & Albert Museum staring at a particularly hideous sculpture of a bull's head. The bull's brains were exposed in the sculpture (by the way, if you want to avoid it, don't go anywhere near the ground floor). I nearly fell over in my new Patric Cox loafers when I saw it. Just a few days before, I had used these very words to an astrologer friend:

'I could make a lot of money from this business scheme, but it's so brainless.' I'm sure this means nothing to anybody else, but seeing the horrible Taurean bull's head sculpture with the exposed 'brain' meant a lot to me — if confirmed my gut feeling, symbolically.

That's the basic law of 'Whoaaa, spooky!' astrology, by the way. The stronger the effect all these twists, turns and mysterious omens have on you personally, the less they seem to make sense to those around you. It's a personal thing. And that's why it means more and may even end up changing your life, in small or large ways.

If you're interested in pursuing this side of astrology, then here are some pointers:

Sabian Symbol International Newsletter
In USA, contact: Alice Kashuba, 10240 Dolphin Rd, Miami, Florida 33157. In Australia, contact: Lynda Hill, 20 Harley Rd, Avalon NSW 2107. These are also the best places to enquire about ordering the Sabian Symbols book and card pack. Enclose an SAE.

Jungian Synchronicity in Astrological Signs and Ages
Alice O. Howell, Quest Books

Jung and Astrology
Maggie Hyde, Aquarian

A*S*K Astro Star Kards
Internet address — www.astrodepot.com
PO Box 19055 Ft. Lauderdale
Florida USA 33319

Liz Greene's Mythic Astrology
Simon & Schuster, Australia

TRENDS to 2005

Why did *Charlie's Angels* take off in the '70s? Why were the Beatles big in the '60s? What makes kids salivate over Cabbage Patch dolls in one decade and Teletubbies in the next? Pop culture and more serious global trends — like safe sex, or political conservatism — are indicated by the particular sign of the zodiac that the big three planets — Uranus, Neptune or Pluto — happens to be passing through in any given decade.

Until very recently Pluto was in Scorpio, the sign ruling sex and death. The world got a French perfume called Poison and an English cigarette brand called Death. People were hooked on *Sex, Lies and Videotape*. Ellen de Generes became the world's first lesbian sitcom star. And on a terrifying scale, sex and death became linked for the first time as AIDS took hold. Scorpios, or people with the Moon or other planets in that sign, completely fascinated us — k.d. lang, Oprah Winfrey, Julia Roberts, Hillary Rodham Clinton, Winona Ryder, Demi Moore, Whoopi Goldberg, Prince Charles, Calvin Klein — the list goes on. Scorpio Michael Crichton wrote the book that became the all-time international box-office champ — *Jurassic Park*.

To understand how Pluto in its new sign, Sagittarius, will change the future, it may help to review the incredible impact it had on the world in the recent past, while it was in Scorpio between 1984 and 1995.

SCORPIO RULES	THE WORLD GOT
Sewers	*Teenage Mutant Ninja Turtles*
Black	*Men in Black*
Vampires	*Dracula*
Obsession	Calvin Klein's Obsession
Bats	*Batman*
Sex	*Sex* by Madonna
Revenge	*Fatal Attraction*

Prostitutes	*Pretty Woman*
Murder	*Murder, She Wrote*
Secrets	*Secrets* by Danielle Steel
Satan	*The Satanic Verses* by Salman Rushdie

In short, the mood of the times was *Melrose Place* meets Vincent Price. And now? Well if you think the world's become a little more cosmic, a little more spiritual and a little happier, you're right. Pluto is now in Sagittarius. This sign rules religious belief and philosophy. It rules the search for meaning. It rules travel. It rules comedy. In short, it's about as different from Scorpio as the new-look Madonna (flowing robes, flowing hair, less bondage, more karma) is from the old-look Madonna.

Back in the original *Astrology For Women* (the precursor to this book, written in 1996) I expressed the opinion that Pluto in Sagittarius might lead to a very different kind of comedy in the '90s and '000s. I rather optimistically wrote: 'Comedy will tackle more taboo issues and go into riskier areas, and a new breed of television or film comedy will emerge.'

Well, so far the revolution hasn't happened. Pluto has until 2008 to complete its cycle, and a lot's going to happen between now and then. Especially when I *Dream of Jeannie* is still on repeats. But the fact that Ellen Morgan, the character played by Ellen DeGeneres, came out as sitcom's first lesbian in 1997 has to be an early sign of Pluto power. What's deemed funny now is edgier than it ever was in the era of *Cheers* or *Open All Hours*. Just look at *Seinfeld* (and more on that later).

As well as comedy, travel and religion (a mixed bag, I know, but that's Sagittarius for you) the sign is also linked to size. It's interesting that the world's first truly super supermodel, Sophie Dahl — a size 14 plus — emerged right on cue as Pluto entered Sagittarius in 1995. In the first edition of this book I wrote that I thought the emphasis on size transformation might mean a revolution in the fashion industry, and even the way clothes are cut and made. I certainly thought the end of the waif supermodel was coming close. It's interesting to see the way these things work out. My friend Maggie Alderson, who is something of a global fashion journalism supremo, told me that Levi's now have US outlets where you can get jeans cut to fit you. Now that's Pluto in Sagittarius!

 predictions

In *Astrology for Women*, I also wrote that I thought the travel industry might undergo some kind of crisis, leading to a revolution in the way people organise their holidays. This stems from the ancient association of Sagittarius with travel. Pluto, the change planet is in Sagittarius — consequently we're all up for a revolution in the travel industry, right? While I was writing this chapter, I opened the *Village Voice* in New York and found a full-page ad for a new internet travel site, promoted by none other than *Star Trek*'s William Shatner. This site is turning travel agents on their heads in the US, simply by asking travellers to e-mail their preferred destination, dates — and the money they're prepared to pay for a fare. The website gets back to the airlines (you guessed it, it's all based on good old-fashioned auction methods) and with a little luck the traveller in question will receive his or her e-ticket, by e-mail, and be ready for immediate take-off. Watch this space. By the time Pluto in Sagittarius has done its work, the way you fly in 2010 will bear about as much resemblance to your '80s style of travel as Concorde does to a camel.

We're already getting a preview of the impact changes in religion, spirituality, cults and other belief systems are having. This is Sagittarian territory too. It may seem weird to think that the sign rules both travel and religion, but in the old days of astrology, the ancient seers linked both to the idea of 'seeing broadly' — so that may help to understand it. Pluto in Sagittarius is coinciding with large numbers of people obsessing over their image of God, or their ideas about What It All Means. Gurus with extreme power — lethal power — will become more prevalent. In other words, *Heaven's Gate* was our trailer advertisement for Pluto in this new sign. In that sense alone, we'd all better be careful.

Pluto is not a lightweight. Given that this planet usually delivers drastic results, at some point, the legal issues surrounding cults and similar religious, spiritual or philosophical organisations will have to be reviewed. Pluto's role, after all, is to create dramatic change in whatever it touches. The power of religions and cults — and the rights of the individual against them — may have to be re-examined in the light of the current laws. Inevitably, established religions — fundamentalist religions are an obvious example — will become more powerful, and will involve their members more intensely. Remember what a powerful hold sex had on global thinking over the last ten years? It seems likely that the same kind of international obsession will transfer to religion, philosophy, belief systems and all the rest of it. Yes, you can include astrology in that — if you wish to. Or the new sexy science — the science that seems to seamlessly blend with certain ancient spiritual and religious thinking.

And because Pluto rules recycling — it tends to destroy things, then recreate them in a new form — it's likely that certain religions will also be broken down and restructured. Pluto is the great renovator of the zodiac. For many astrologers, Catholicism seems the most likely of the old, established religions to be 'renovated' while Pluto is in Sagittarius. Scientology may get renovated. Buddhism may get renovated. This stuff — stargazing — could also be knocked down and rebuilt. Pluto's like that!

Finally, Sagittarius rules education. (What a sign — ruling comedy, size, travel and belief systems all at once.) When Pluto, the change planet, goes through Sagittarius, the education sign, you can expect huge upheavals in the way we learn, why we learn, where we learn, and how we learn. If you happen to work in the education system, or if you're a student, you may already be sensing things or sniffing them, or just beginning to think about what might change. How about this for an idea? A world classroom, bringing together kids in the Bronx, and old people in — oooh, how about Botswana? Everyone logs in on the net and learns as a group, using CU-CME (See You, See Me) technology. There are any number of possibilities. But once again, as always with Pluto, the buzzwords are transformation, renovation, reconstruction. And as always with astrology, the biggest changes are usually so big that even astrologers like me (who are paid to do this kind of thing) can't see all of it at once.

PLUTO POWER IN YOUR LIFE

Just by knowing your Sun sign (or usual star sign) you can find out a lot about Pluto's likely effects on you. Using a technique called solar chart forecasting, which is what most media astrologers use in their columns, it's possible to give you a sneak preview of the next few years — and a way of understanding what's already going on now.

WHAT PLUTO WILL DO FOR YOU BETWEEN 1995 AND 2008

ARIES

By the time Pluto has finished doing his stuff in 2008, you'll have a completely different way of looking at the world. It's possible that you'll have a period of obsession with some kind of belief system, philosophy or religion. Pluto will transform your view of the world, and your understanding of heaven and hell, life and death — and above all, why we're here and what it all means. When Pluto is working for you, rather than against you, you'll probably find that your new ideas and beliefs about things give you a greater sense of control than you've had before. Psychologically, there could be a tremendous effect on how you feel, both about yourself, and about the world. You'll receive both the positive and negative effects of Pluto over this 13 year period, though. In your search for something a bit deeper and more powerful from life, you may encounter people who are rather controlling or have an unhealthy interest in manipulating people and situations.

Any local or international travel you undertake between 1995 and 2008 is likely to have a deep and powerful effect on you. There may be one particular country, or town, which has an almost hypnotic effect. That's because Pluto never does anything by halves. You can never be a tourist when Pluto is around — you tend to get truly involved with the place and the people you are visiting. Some of you may even switch countries in the 1995–2008 cycle. The locals, the buildings, the culture and the atmosphere of the places you visit will transform the way you think about yourself, and the world. It's common for women going through this cycle to visit somewhere like India, for example, and come back with an entirely new angle on life.

TAURUS

Between 1995 and 2008, you can expect your finances and lifestyle to undergo a complete change. There will be one particular episode when it feels as if everything is breaking down. A mortgage may undergo a complete restructure, for example, or a superannuation policy you have held for years may be closed. Some of you — unfortunately — will find that you are involved in a separation or other kind of loss, involving a partner, lover, associate or relative who was bound up with your money, your house or flat, or your possessions. If this is the case, then you literally will have to start from scratch.

Pluto never leaves things the same way they were at the start. So if you backtrack to 1994, just before the planet started influencing your finances and lifestyle, you may well find that by 2008 just about every aspect of what you had has changed. You may switch banks. You may buy or sell property. You may marry, or move in with someone, bringing about a profound change in your week-to-week budgeting. The late, great astrologer Patric Walker used to say that this cycle was about 'Other people's money'. The money in question may belong to your husband or lover, or to a relative who includes you in his or her will. It may belong to your business partner or backer. Typically, it will belong to a bank.

Any new beginnings made along these lines between 1995–2008 will have quite a strong effect on your understanding of issues like money, power and control. In other words, if you sign contracts with financial institutions or partners, then you will be much more sharply aware of who is actually in pole position. This may sound cynical (and very unromantic, if we are discussing your partner or lover). However, it may help to be aware of Pluto's typical emphasis on the balance of power. This is a good time to ask yourself who stands where, and to aim for something more moderate if the piece of paper you are signing actually gives one side an unhealthy ability to call every shot. On several occasions, you will be reborn (in terms of your finances or lifestyle) thanks to the powerful input of a second person, or larger organisation, which is prepared to go in with you in some way.

This cycle also has something strong to say about sex. Don't be surprised if you find yourself becoming obsessed with some aspect of your sexuality over the next few years. Pluto tends to fixate women on the areas of the horoscope it touches. Through some fairly intense and profound experiences, you are likely to enter the next big sexual era of your life. Pluto is such an X-rated planet that I have no wish to go into all the possibilities here. However, one thing is certain. You will look more deeply into your body and its responses than you have ever done before.

Finally, death. (This cycle isn't exactly an episode of *Happy Days*, I'm telling you.) By 2008, your ideas on death and dying will have changed. This could happen for all sorts of reasons — you may attend a funeral, you may have a near-death experience yourself, you may lose someone close to you, or you may have some kind of spiritual or religious breakthrough which changes your mind on things. If you need to explore this further, there are some very good books on Pluto in connection with this — ask your local New Age bookshop.

GEMINI

The effects of this new cycle in your life will vary, depending on where you are today — single or attatched.

If you are single, expect a new relationship of the deep, meaningful, profound and compelling type. An affair with more than a hint of obsession, perhaps, or a marriage with a depth and intensity that you can honestly say you haven't yet experienced. By 2008 you may have taken on something that will change your life — or even ended up in a series of intense new relationships. A relationship or marriage which forms in this cycle is also unlikely to stay still. Something about both your personalities in combination means that things will repeatedly be restructured, reworked and reorganised.

There is no point in glossing over Pluto's negative effects, either. This planet has a reputation for creating a whole range of *Dynasty* or *Dallas*-type scenarios. Jealousy, sexual obsession, physical threats, stalking, obscene phone calls, blackmail ... you name it, astrologers have blamed it on Pluto. On a less dramatic level, Pluto can manifest as game-playing, manipulation, controlling or jealous behaviour, or big power struggles. On the positive side you get powerful, healing, transforming, deep, unforgettable, passionate, intense, sexy and erotic partnerships. It all depends on how skilled you are at sidestepping Pluto's landmines.

If you choose to remain single until 2008, then the same issues — power, control, intensity, passion — will be channelled through a Significant Other who has nothing to do with love and sex, but may be your partner in a business, work, financial or practical sense. This relationship, built for solid and rather un-emotional reasons, is likely to have the kind of depth and complexity you might expect from a sexual relationship.

Pluto rules taboos, the forbidden or unacceptable topics which are far too deep, sticky and dark for the pair of you to throw around in casual conversation. Based on research with Taureans (the last group of people to experience this cycle) I can only offer up this list to give you a general idea of what might come up:

- Abortion
- Life-threatening illness
- Legal wills
- Miscarriage
- Affairs
- Criminality
- Exes
- Euthanasia

Of course, the correct phrase should be, 'A general idea of what might *never* come up.' The taboo you have to work through in your partnership is likely to be squashed down, or deliberately covered up.

I don't want to give you the impression that every taboo topic on the list above will apply to you. It's equally likely that the taboo in your marriage or partnership will be something very personal to you. For some de facto Gemini couples, for example, the very subject of weddings or babies might in itself become a completely forbidden and dangerous topic!

The partnership itself will transform in the years to 2008. Your partner may go through the most dramatic and profound changes and experiences, which in turn alter the tone of the relationship. Or it may be you who deals with some kind of transformation, which seems to filter down into the partnership, and alter everything from the way you eat together, to the way you have sex. One thing is sure.

A partnership in these Pluto years will have to change in order to survive. If it can't transform from its very depths, it may come to a close. It's also very likely that you will reach a new, profound stage in the marriage or relationship which makes all those Plutonian phrases and songs — 'Til death do us part' and 'I would die for you' resonate with extreme meaning and power. So much for your reputation as the lightweight of the zodiac!

CANCER

Between now and 2008 Pluto will change the way you work, or do your home duties. As the majority of women are now working full-time or part-time, you're most likely to experience Pluto's effects on the job. If you have always worked a certain way, or followed your professional routines and rituals in a specific manner, you can expect that to completely transform. If you were the Queen of the Filofax before, you may find a new way to structure your days. If you've always been chaos on two legs, the introduction of new equipment, new training or other x factors is likely to force you to shape up.

It's extremely likely that your current job may end or take a new direction. There will be plenty of endings and beginnings before 2008. Some of these power-packed changes will be of your choosing, some will happen without any input from you. You will build certain work or business associations which go beyond the usual skin-deep level of these things — some may feel quite intense, or represent something quite profound to you. You are also going to have to deal with power and control issues in the workplace or business sector. Don't be surprised if you find yourself caught up in something which feels a lot more tangled, dark and difficult than the usual 'Good morning, Miss Jones' relationship.

If you work with computers, you'll get a more powerful computer. If you rely pretty much on contacts and networking to help your career, you'll get some really powerful and influential people backing you. You may join an organisation which has a lot more clout than anything you're used to. Or you may find yourself in a new work set-up where the boss, or some other co-worker, has an extraordinary amount of influence over people. That influence may not be obvious at first. Handle your relationship with them very carefully.

This cycle also rules your health and well-being. Pluto is likely to change the way you eat (or what you eat), the way you drink (or what you drink), the kind of health insurance you have, the sort of attitude you have towards fitness and exercise, and even your understanding of the way the mind influences the body. The American astrologer and psychic Gail Fairfield associates this cycle with 'Health issues involving sexuality, genitals and the elimination system' in her book, *Choice Centered Astrology* (Weiser). As the last sign to get this cycle before you was Gemini, you may want to ask your twin-sign friends or relatives about that. As a Pluto-watcher from way back, I have to say that it does seem to coincide with anything 'below the waist' if I may be so bold.

Health in general will become a bigger deal, though. You may decide to de-tox in a major way, because Pluto likes to get rid of rubbish, and the idea that you can get rid of the rubbish from your body may begin to fascinate you. Only one word of caution — Pluto can produce obsession, so if you find yourself fixating on the gym, or a particular diet, or a specific level of fitness, it may be time to pull back.

LEO

You have the weirdest, most intense relationship forecast of all the signs over the next few years. Pluto, the planet in question, is in your department of sex and babies. Then you have two more planets, Uranus and Neptune, in your department of commitment and marriage. If you want to know what's in store, ask a Cancerian. They've just spent the last ten years or so going through this. Space doesn't allow for a discussion about Uranus and Neptune, but it's certainly possible to predict what Pluto will do.

In short, expect this:

• A new quality of intensity in your sex life
• A complete transformation of the way you handle the physical side of love
• Experimentation with what other people might call sexual taboos

- Deeper and more meaningful sex
- Sexual obsession, from you or your partner.

Pluto is the x-rated planet. Consequently, unless HarperCollins decided to publish this in a plastic wrapper, it's not possible for me to go into each and every permutation of this cycle. But I hope you get the general idea. If you've never really thought about sex much before, or if you've left it to trot along by itself, then this cycle will change that. By 2008 you will have taken several giant steps towards a new, restructured kind of sexuality. It may do something basic, like change the way you express yourself in bed (or from the chandeliers, if that's your preference). It may do something unbelievably powerful and deep, like send you to a therapist if sex has been a bit of an issue for you. Check back with Cancerian friends, as they went through this before you!

This cycle also rules children, babies and pregnancy. Don't be surprised if you go through periods of mild obsession and unusually intense emotion where these issues are concerned. If you do give birth in the 1995 to 2008 cycle, it's likely to be something enormously powerful and profound for you. Some women just churn babies out and go home. With Pluto in this cycle, you can't do that. They call Pluto the 'shrink' planet in astrology, because it encourages you to look more deeply into what makes you tick, and then it tends to change you. By proceeding with a pregnancy in this cycle — or even by going through a termination or miscarriage — you are likely to experience the 'shrink' planet in an incredibly personal way.

It's common for mothers to face big issues about power and control in reference to their son or daughter in this cycle. Your child may involve you in one of those situations where you really have to decide where the boundaries are. If you're an older Leo, there may be difficult questions about grandchildren — who has the control? You, your grandchild, or your own children, who gave birth to them? There may be power questions which involve the nanny, the babysitter or teachers. As usual, Pluto will try to confront you with the most basic human issues, and control is top of the list.

Finally, this cycle has a lot do with self-expression and creativity. It is associated with having a brainchild of some kind. Whatever you produce or pour yourself into during this cycle will probably bring out the obsessive-compulsive side of you. You may also find yourself becoming a control freak over certain aspects of the end product! On the positive side, Pluto will lend real power and depth to what you are producing, no matter if you're an artist, writer, dancer, film-maker or Queen of the Weekend Hobbies. As with any Pluto cycle, if you feel yourself frothing at the mouth, tell this planet to get back in its box.

VIRGO

During this long-running cycle, the way you see certain family members or relatives is likely to change quite profoundly. The pre–1995 family situation and the post–2008 family situation will be dramatically different. Sometimes Pluto can bring a death in the family, or a divorce or separation — this is an obvious cause of the sweeping transformations which occur. As a result of this loss, the chemistry between all the members changes. There may be a domino effect — because one person passes away, or decides to leave the family circle, changes seem to flow on to everybody who is in the clan.

This is one possibility. There may also be some skeleton in the family closet which is released at this time. You don't go through the death, separation or divorce — but secrets which have been successfully buried for years may come out. Another possibility? A family member comes out of the closet in sexual terms. Then there are the families who find that one member survives a life-threatening illness, or one member goes to jail. You may find someone illegitimate in the family tree, or Great Uncle Bob may turn out to actually be Great-Aunty Betty.

All of this is not meant to alarm, by the way. Your life is not about to become a soap opera by 2008. It's just that Pluto has to be discussed in a fairly upfront, unafraid way — and these are standard, recorded examples of events which have occurred in this cycle. For you, the family chemistry change may be for more subtle reasons. One of your parents may switch jobs, or find a new role in the community, thus changing his or her attitude — the domino effect will affect the whole family eventually, as the standard parental roles alter. A family member may even win the lottery — it happens — and the money suddenly changes everything overnight, including the way certain relatives deal with each other!

Some astrologers have noted that women going through this cycle have some kind of power struggle with their parents or brothers and sisters. It may not always be an obvious thing, either. The actual dynamics of the game which is being played could be very buried, and not always conscious.

Pluto is the great revamper. It also achieves what the Americans call 'empowerment' which, although it sounds good, is a slightly confusing term. Basically, it means that if you were always low on the family power scale, you'll probably creep up. Even if you run the entire show, you may gain even more influence. None of this happens overnight, though. Pluto is a slow mover. It's possible that someone — hopefully not you — will turn into a total control freak in this cycle. These kinds of situations can be prevented in the first place if you (using your cunning astrology knowledge) can sniff the potential for a problem before it begins.

This cycle also famously affects your house or flat situation. By 2008 you will have moved, renovated or decorated. It will be an intense process. You may even uproot altogether and emigrate. At the very least, some part of your current flat or house will be replaced or added onto. The usual 'power freak' rule applies to real estate and housing issues now. In other words, if you sense that you are dealing with a builder, decorator or real estate agent who has a definite dark side, you may want to keep things *very* flexible! One other point. If you dig up your garden, make sure the man with the machine doesn't dig into the earth's crust.

LIBRA

Your last Pluto cycle involved your money, your lifestyle and your possessions. In the last few years, you've restructured your budget or your source of income. You've had crashing lows, and pretty powerful highs. Some famous Librans — like Sarah Ferguson — have been wiped out. Actually, she's quite a good example of what might have been happening to you (but without the Weight Watcher's contract). In a more moderate way, you've probably also suffered losses or big changes you could have done without, affecting your money, your business interests, your security, your lifestyle or your possessions. In typical Pluto fashion, you've since restructured things, rebuilt things, or recycled the set-up you had before so that it becomes truly viable.

At this stage in your astrological destiny, you are allowed to put your calculator down. The big, sweeping transformation is over, and the next cycle is underway. It actually kicked in during 1995. And it will be with you until 2008. It's going to change the way you communicate.

Here are some concrete examples:

- Learning HTML, the internet language
- Learning a foreign language
- Work or career changes ask you to add technical terms to your vocabulary
- If you're deaf, you may learn new signing skills
- If you're living with a disability, new technology may help you to 'speak'
- Your vocabulary or wordpower may increase — without subscribing to *Reader's Digest*
- You may discover a talent for poetry, fiction, or other forms of communication — ESP counts, too
- You may learn public speaking
- If you can't read or write, you may join a literacy programme
- New technology — e-mail, mobile phones, faxes, language scramblers — will alter the way you stay in touch
- Learning different listening skills, thanks to a new course or interest.

On an ordinary everyday level, you may just find that you become more powerful and effective when you are putting things in writing, or getting your point across. As with all Pluto cycles, the only problem is the risk that you will become too intense for people. Watch the way you come across, ask people for feedback if you need to, and re-read what you put in writing. If you're too wild-eyed and worked up about everything, then that's a sure sign that Pluto's negative effects are operating, and you may have to pull back or chill out.

SCORPIO

Pluto is going to spend several years in an area of your solar chart ruling money, possessions, income and property. Expect a transformation in stages, rather than one giant sweeping change. Typically, the second half of May and first half of June will regularly present you with familiar issues. How much control do you have over your cashflow or lifestyle? Is there a power play going on in terms of money, property or possessions, no matter how well disguised?

The second house of your chart also goes deeper than dollars and cents, pounds and pence, and all the things they can do for you. It's concerned with your value system. What you tend to personally put a cash value on, and the kinds of things which go beyond money or materialism. Pluto could change you from a communist to a capitalist, or vice versa. It may show you, in quite a profound way, what it costs to 'sell out' or sell yourself short. Ultimately this planet will pose one question to you — what do you most value?

Here are some other common manifestations of Pluto in this particular cycle:

- Obsessive spending creates a financial wipeout
- A fixation with your earning power distracts you from other things in your life which have their own (non-monetary) value.
- Through intense encounters with others, you learn that money really is power.
- Your value system, which may dictate everything from the sort of job or role you choose to the kind of lifestyle you adopt, changes forever.
- A complete restructuring of your earning power and personal budgeting.

Pluto can create a wipeout situation if you take things to extremes. However it is also the planet of rebirth and resurrection. Even if you do hit a critical point with property, money or possessions you can build everything up again, in a new form.

Pluto can actually give you control and power as a result of your assets, business position or finances too. You may come to see, in a very raw way, exactly what ownership and earning capacity can do for a person.

SAGITTARIUS

Pluto is now in your own sign, and you may have already felt its effects. A revamp of your face, hair or body is an early sign that this planet is making its presence known. In the first house of your solar chart, Pluto influences your image, your physical appearance and your persona. The woman you seemed to be before this cycle began will not be the woman people see afterwards. Plenty of Sagittarians are already deliberately changing their outer persona or fate is intervening and changing it for them.

Pluto is opposing the descendant, or partnership area of your chart at the same time. So the profound changes in your closest relationships and partnerships over these years will also alter the way you look, the way you act, the way the world sees you, and the way you see the world. If you are by yourself during this cycle, then expect some quite in-depth and transformative changes of attitude. You may transform your view of what marriage, commitment, partnership and singledom means. In the process, you will also change yourself.

The second half of May and first half of June in any year, and the second half of November and first half of December in any year, are key times for these issues. In fact, after a few years you may begin to detect a pattern.

Here are some common manifestations of this kind of Pluto cycle:

- Dramatic weight loss or cosmetic surgery
- A deliberate attempt to project a different image to the world
- A change in personal style or wardrobe
- A noticeable change in the way people regard you, thanks to changed circumstances
- Intense one-on-one situations, probably in your love life, alter you inside or out.
- Inner work — therapy, self-help, self-education — transforms you.

This Pluto cycle classically results in some kind of re-launch. Same person, different name. Same person, different clothes. And on it goes — but the outer changes are also a manifestation of deeper personality changes taking place within. After Pluto's out of Sagittarius in a few years from now, you may even have relaunched or relabelled yourself a couple of times.

CAPRICORN

This is the most complicated Pluto cycle of all. This planet is now passing through the most mysterious part of your solar chart — astrologers have all sorts of opinions on what it means. Some link it to hospitals, institutions, prisons and asylums. Eek! I don't necessarily agree, by the way. What it means more than anything else is this — time to yourself, time to think, time to reflect. You can see why this might mean a short stay with a psychiatrist, of course. But more typically, what will happen in this cycle is a profound change in your relationship with the inner you, or the hidden you. This can happen through a fascination with dreams and their meanings. It can happen because you take off to Bali for a month to gaze at your navel. It may happen through a profound spiritual experience, perhaps one where you are required to go on a retreat or spend more time praying or meditating alone. You may see a psychic or astrologer who re-introduces you to yourself.

I hope you get the drift. You can still pick up some astrology books which talk about the twelfth house of the chart (where Pluto is now) as some kind of doom and gloom place, full of people in white coats carrying clipboards. After years of looking at charts with a big twelfth house emphasis, though, I'm more inclined to say that it's about self discovery through retreat. Because Pluto is extreme, this may happen in an extreme way. But enough generalisation. Here's a list of Plutonian possibilities:

- You buy a home, time-share or holiday home where you can take regular retreats. It ends up changing your life.
- You become obsessed with a special pastime or pursuit which you must necessarily do alone, or privately. In the process you transform yourself at quite a deep level.

- Destiny will set up circumstances which take you off the merry-go-round of life if you do not consciously choose to take time out occasionally.

- Dreamwork, psychic experiences, astrology, psychology, psychiatry or other means of peering into the human psyche begin to have a strong effect on you.

- Anything locked in the basement of your mind which you haven't consciously known about or chosen to face may now reappear, so be prepared.

- Odd experiences — omens, coincidences, obvious pieces of synchronicity and spookiness — send strong messages. It's very likely that this is your unconscious trying to get through to you when nothing else is working.

People who have been through this cycle before you report getting a lot of mileage from dream journals and notebooks. This cycle is linked to the unconscious mind, so a quick flip through the works of Freud or Jung may also be useful. Art is another way of releasing Pluto's energy in this period, but don't be surprised if your abstract painting turns out to be free therapy.

AQUARIUS

Friends you've known forever will go through some incredible transformations during the few years that Pluto is in Sagittarius. One of them may go through a crisis, only to be reborn at a later date. Another may change before your very eyes, in a way which means the friendship itself has to alter if it's going to survive.

Here are some other typical manifestations of this kind of Pluto cycle:

- You become quite intensely involved with a group of people and find that you just aren't the same person after it's all over.

- Agreeing to a specific role within a group gives you more power or influence than you would ever have enjoyed alone — or even with a partner.

- A friendship changes and becomes more like a convoluted game of snakes and ladders than the sociable bond you remember. If it's going to last, then it will have to alter.

- For some reason, friends — and even casual social acquaintances — have a more profound and in-depth effect on you. It's more than coffee and conversation, these people have the potential to bring about great changes in you.
- New friends emerge in your life — passionate, complex, soulful, intense, driven people.
- Through friends or group activities, you come face to face with some of life's most taboo subjects — death, sex, the occult — anything which is normally hidden or off-limits.
- A move, relationship change or other dramatic lifestyle alteration results in you having to wave goodbye to some friendships or even start from scratch with a whole new social network.

Pluto can never leave anything the same. So when it's passing through an area of your solar chart which rules friends, your social acquaintances and your group involvements, you can expect a whole new set-up. The faces may remain, but the chemistry between you may be very different in the long run. New people will come along, and a completely different way of operating socially is the likely result.

Pluto is the planet of obsession, too. You may become completely transfixed by some kind of group, team, club, association or network. And don't be surprised if you make friends who have a strong dose of Scorpio in their personal charts, or a profession or personality which seems very typically Scorpionic or Plutonian. You will make at least one powerful friend in this cycle. Aquarians are the masters of networking, casual friendship and group chemistry but even you will learn to run things along different lines in the next few years.

PISCES

Oh, the joy of Pluto, passing over the midheaven of your solar chart. It's here to transform your goals and ambitions. Not overnight, naturally. This process will take several years. Save all your old CVs and then come back to them after this cycle is over. You will honestly have difficulty in accepting them when Pluto has finished doing his work. This planet has a habit of taking you further and further away from what you thought you were working towards.

Some of you are already experiencing Pluto's influence. You may be considering giving up what has seemed like a perfectly okay career or study path until now. You may have recently become obsessed with a brand new mission in life. Or perhaps there's just a twist in a time-honoured career path for you . . . Pluto can take the same basic goals and reinvent them.

The last group of people to go through this solar chart cycle before you were Aquarians. They spent the best part of 1984–1994 throwing in jobs, reinventing their careers, switching courses, rethinking their ambitions and transforming their roles. Here are some famous examples to ponder:

- Mia Farrow, who went from being Woody Allen's muse to playing her own parts
- Oprah Winfrey, who left radio behind for talk-show TV — in spectacular style
- John Travolta, who reinvented himself via Quentin Tarantino
- Boris Yeltsin — need I say more?

Pluto is about focus, desire and burning intensity. Don't be too surprised if you find yourself becoming deeply fixated on a particular project, job, goal or ambition. Rely on your friends and family to tap you on the shoulder if you become too fixated, though.

Pluto is also about power, control and influence. You will test the water in these areas while this cycle is operating. If you can remember the basic universal rules about not abusing this power, or manipulating people and situations, then Pluto could end up doing you some favours. Look at Oprah. Do avoid power struggles, though — no matter if they are heavily disguised and played under the surface, or right out there where everybody can see them. There can be something very compulsive about Pluto power struggles. If you feel yourself being dragged into the web, concentrate just as hard on pulling yourself out again. Otherwise you may end up losing a lot of sleep.

This Pluto cycle will put you in touch with classic issues like this one — 'Where am I going/What am I doing/What does it all mean?' This is not such a bad thing. It may occasionally take you to a critical stage, when everything has to change. Or, if you are mindlessly plodding along with a career or a life path that is utterly false, destiny may change that for you in an instant. Pluto is extreme by nature, and the process may feel unnecessarily intense.

However, many astrologers say that Pluto never changes anything without a purpose. In other words, some bits and pieces of your life were never meant to be there for the long term. So if something appears to be going, going, gone then maybe you should take a philosophical approach. Conscious transformation is probably a good idea. This cycle will confront you, in a very direct way, about who you are and what you're supposed to be doing with your life. If it's not deep, profound and wholly involving then either you — or the universe — will want to do a u-turn. For more information on what this cycle might involve, ask a friendly Aquarian (and they're usually all friendly).

TIMING issues

WHEN IS ANYBODY THE RIGHT AGE FOR ANYTHING ANY MORE?

One of the great things about astrology is that it's about timing, not age. In astrology, you can be ready for your first big career push at 35. You can find your first major dose of maturity at 14. You can fall in love for the first time at 60, or have a baby at 40 if that's what is right for you. Your chart is the key to timing, rather than the constraints placed on you by society.

When I was appearing on a radio programme called *The Spook Show* (which consisted of me, a medium, an aura reader and some tarot card experts) I used to get calls from women who believed they were past it at 40. They wanted to ask me about their love lives, but they were almost too sheepish to do so. One caller even said, 'I suppose I'm over that sort of thing by now'... Now, this is very sad. And astrologically speaking, it's just not true either.

This is not a platitude and I am not going to chirrup, 'You're as young as you feel,' because that always sounds as if you're trying to convince people when you're not even convinced yourself. However. These are the facts, as astrology sees it:

1   Life begins at . . . any age at all. Your chart holds the clues.
2   Just because someone gives you a big cardboard silver key on your 21st birthday doesn't mean you're ready to unlock anything, necessarily.
3   Your horoscope isn't ageist.

Given the way the planets move around your horoscope (rather like a gigantic clock) there will be many repeated opportunities in your life to start grand passions, travel, educate yourself ... in short, to do whatever you want to do. And, typically, there is no 'right' time for any of these things. It's personal to you. And your horoscope, of course.

When I was 18, I was legally old enough to vote, but I have to say I don't think I was really ready to make a decision on anything politically until I was at least 23 years old. Women I know have been told that they really 'should' have their careers underway by 30, but I have seen too many people in their 40s starting successful small businesses to believe that one. I once knew a famous English television scriptwriter — who shall remain nameless — who was truly, madly, deeply in love for the first time at 62 years of age. Ignore that word 'should' — it can waste an awful lot of your time, especially when it's applied to age.

If you get your chart sorted out by an astrologer, you'll be given all kinds of useful information about the various 'golden ages' ahead for you. You'll be given quite specific information which is personal to you — so keep an open mind.

I have called this section 'When Is Anybody The Right Age For Anything Any More?' because astrology has convinced me that age is awfully irrelevant to many, many things. I've met too many people who are living their lives at their own pace, happily and successfully — and seen too many people who regretted being pushed into big decisions just because a voice in their head was saying, 'Hey, you're 30, *shouldn't* you have done this by now?'

If you don't believe it, think back to people you know who have turned 18 or 21. Would you say in all cases that they were ready to drive, knowledgeable enough to vote, ready for sex, ready for their first job? People seem to tick over at their own speed, and according to astrology, it's usually when their horoscope is triggered by the slow, regular cycles of Jupiter, Saturn, Uranus, Neptune and Pluto.

In the meantime, here is a basic guide to common cycles that affect all of us. I've already covered the Saturn Return, but here's what you can expect from the other planets.

JUPITER return

AGE 23 TO 25

This is a big opportunity to exploit a big opportunity. It may be a makeover, a pay rise, your first car, a mortgage, a baby, a new job, a marriage, an inheritance, a trip, an award, a new social life or a spiritual awakening. It depends on your own chart, really. When Jupiter travels around the sky to come back to the very same place it was in at the moment of your birth, stuff happens. Doors swing open. All you have to do is push yourself through.

How to spot it

A general feeling that life is flowing your way, that thinking big is a good idea, and that being positive can take you places.

And don't forget

Jupiter keeps on coming back. The expansion, optimism, luck and 'open doors' feeling will be with you approximately every 12 years, on a regular basis. It shouldn't be too hard to pinpoint the months that you really feel Jupiter operating between 23 and 25.

Once you've done that, count forward roughly 12 years. So, if you got some kind of career breakthrough (for example) at the age of 23 and 8 months, then at around 35 and 8 months, a similar leap forward will appear.

Then count forward again — at approximately 47 and 8 months, 59 and 8 months, 71 and 8 months, 83 and 8 months . . . well. You get the general idea. Basically with Jupiter, your luck never runs out, and you never stop growing.

URANUS opposition

AGE 38 TO 42

Please, do me a favour and pronounce this Ur-arn-us. This planet is about radical change, freedom and breaking away. When people describe a mid-life crisis, it's usually about this — Uranus, the planet of liberation, doing all sorts of bizarre things to your chart as it travels through the zodiac.

In his classic book *Planets In Transit* (Whitford Press) the revered astrologer Robert Hand says, 'This is the crisis of middle age when you have to come to terms with a number of realisations that may not all be pleasant.'

It's amazing how many men respond to this by buying little red sports cars and running off with their secretaries. But this is a big, dumb waste of what Uranus is really all about. So let's take a closer look . . .

How to spot it

Uranus may feel like an itch you have to scratch. You may feel wired, practically buzzing as you lie in bed at night, unable to stand the compromises you have made or unwilling to go on in the same old ways. At this point, women classically do something that leaves those around them reeling. In the 70s, a lot of them 'got' women's liberation. Basically, Uranus is a massive lie detector. If some part of your life entails you faking it — for whatever reason — then Uranus will shake everything up.

Your mantra at this time will be 'Freedom, freedom, freedom.' As a general rule, the more free and honest your life has been to date, the less dramatic this period will feel. But if you've managed to lock yourself in a box, or if you're off on a life path which isn't really authentic or 'alive', then expect electrifying changes.

This cycle reminds me a bit of the giant foot in Monty Python. You'll be minding your own business, trundling along the street one day, and — BAM! Suddenly you're stopped in your tracks. Uranus really is the giant foot of the zodiac.

There are many more astrological possibilities for your life than this, and I don't want to bore you with astro-lingo, but what about the amazing things that will happen if transiting Uranus trines your natal midheaven?

Then there's that powerful, amazing period when Pluto trines your natal Sun (actresses Sandra Bullock and Lisa Kudrow are both recent candidates).

So basically, the message is this. If someone tells you at age 13 that you are too young to have your nose in a chemistry set, if they tell you at 38 that you're too old to join a band, if they tell you at 70 that you're too old to take a second honeymoon . . . well, just tell them one word. Uranus.

THIS is the dawning

The Age of Aquarius will not be about full-frontal nudity and dancing around with a bad haircut. Sorry about that. It's more likely to be about internet language scramblers, new custom-made laptops (choose your own shape and colour — how about white, or purple?) and communal living. On the morning I wrote this, I opened up the *New York Times* and read this headline — 'A Leading Futurist Risks His Reputation With Ideas on Growth and High Technology'.

Peter Schwartz, chairman of the Global Business Network, based in California, predicts high-speed net access for everyone by 2005. By 2015 he sees simultaneous language translation, made possibly by computer chips 100 times more powerful than today's. As an astrologer, I think Peter is on the ball. Stay tuned — this man predicted the collapse of oil prices, and Shell took his advice, to their advantage. I can't think of anything more Age of Aquarius than language translators on the internet — it's high technology linking the world, breaking down the global barriers. Aquarius is about hi-tech stuff, one world thinking and true progress. Peter's prediction has a ring of 'rightness' about it for an astrologer. Put it this way. I know I'll be talking to my stockbroker about the first sign of any such invention!

Astrologers argue all the time about when the Age of Aquarius actually starts. Me, I think it began to creep in when Uranus, the planet which rules Aquarius, first dropped into that sign in 1995. What fixed it for me was the birth of the internet — or rather, the birth of the Worldwide Web, the user-friendly face of the internet. If you have ever used the net and typed in a website address, you've probably tapped in these letters: www.

~~~

It spells W, W, W — Worldwide Web. But it's also the Aquarius logo. By cosmic accident, of course. And when you look at the list of things which Aquarius rules, the birth of the internet makes perfect sense.

THE AQUARIAN TOP FIVE

- Technology
- Freedom
- New Age
- Friends
- Groups

Technology

Computers and Aquarius go together like Bill Gates and nerd jokes. In 1997 Garry Kasparov lost a six-game chess rematch with IBM's Deep Blue supercomputer. Blue also happens to be the Aquarian colour — for many astrologers around the globe, that was a defining moment. If we'd missed it to date, we couldn't miss it any longer. The Age of Aquarius was well on the way.

Freedom

One of the sure signs you're actually 'in' an Age is when pop culture starts churning out films, TV shows, songs and celebrities which have a theme or feeling strongly linked to the particular sign ruling that Age. Freedom is a major issue with Aquarius. Its ruling planet, Uranus, was discovered in 1781 when people power was in full swing and the French Revolution was under way. Aquarius is big in the charts of famous feminists for the same reason — after all, women's liberation is just another way of saying women's freedom.

The internet itself is also becoming a battleground for freedom issues — at the time of writing, Microsoft is in court facing US Federal and State lawyers on the little issue of control and monopoly. Both sides are talking about 'freedom' in their own defence. And if you've been on the net for a while now, you'll probably be familiar with the Freedom of Speech online lobby group. It started up almost as soon as the Worldwide Web did.

New Age

Aquarius also rules astrology, along with other unusual, alternative and 'out there' parts of life, like aliens and science fiction. It made the cover of *Life* magazine last year, and the last *USA Today* survey showed that the number of people who state that they believe in astrology has risen by 37% since 1976. And no, I'm not just saying that.

From March to July 1997, the movie and TV show internet sites most requested by users of the Lycos search engine were *Star Wars* and *Star Trek*. Followed by *The X-Files*. And in fourth place? *The Simpsons*. Look at the way the hair is drawn on Bart Simpson — WWW — there's that Aquarian logo again. Bart is a typical Age of Aquarius icon, too. He's a rebel. He's from the most eccentric family in Springfield. He was also created by Matt Groening, who has the Sun in Aquarius.

Right now, the world is experiencing two changes in mood. The first comes from Pluto in Sagittarius, which is why we're all forming stronger opinions on religion and spirituality, and why all we want to do is travel. The second is coming directly from the effects of Neptune and Uranus in their radical new sign, Aquarius.

Friends

A TV show called *Friends* is winning top ratings worldwide. That's Aquarius. Calvin Klein's new perfume campaigns revolve around models posing as groups of friends, rather than alone or in couples.

Calvin's always been on the money, astrologically speaking. In fact, I'm sure the guy must have his own personal astrologer. All those intense, sexy ads in the late '80s and early '90s — and the launch of a perfume called Obsession — tied in perfectly with the Pluto in Scorpio zeitgeist.

Groups

Now we're in the Age of Aquarius and the vibe is about loose, casual friendship. Men and women spending time together without having to have sexual undercurrents getting in the way. Mixed-race friendships. Old/young friendships. There is a perception that this is a young people's thing. It's not. People who are 50 plus are getting into the friends/groups mood as well. There's a huge, booming 'grey power' company in the UK called Saga, which organises everything from computer classes to Greek cruises for older people, and it's changing the face of the travel and leisure industry.

Forget package tours à la *Australian Women's Weekly* World Discovery Tours. Saga is Age of Aquarius thinking applied to an old idea.

Finally, if you're thinking about an image for the Age of Aquarius, think of Benetton ads. I suspect they hire an astrologer there as well. It's uncanny how those group shots of black, white and Asian faces, represented as groups of friends, sum up the Age of Aquarius.

Aquarian signals

More on the computer front — Apple Macintosh has come up with a Think Different campaign (very Aquarian). And icons who have emerged in pop culture in recent times — *Seinfeld*'s Kramer, *Shine*'s David Helfgott, the weird and wonderful Tori Amos — undeniably fit the Aquarian archetype of the brilliant eccentric. Watch this space. By the time Neptune leaves Aquarius in 2012, an entire passing parade of oddballs, geniuses and oddities will have collected Oscars, Emmys, Grammys, Baftas and Logies. When Neptune, the planet of fascination, is in Aquarius, the sign of the extreme individual, the world is destined to fall in love with men and women who stand out in a crowd.

I've recently been noticing something else about the Age of Aquarius. Computers are rebelling, too (that's a double Aquarius statement, as the sign rules both rebellion and technology). Maybe the machines want to be liberated from us? I don't know. But you've probably experienced predictable unpredictability with your own computers. Weird electronic breakdowns and crazy information meltdowns seem to be part of the deal with this technology.

As I write this it's something the world is just starting to gnaw on — we're all waiting for the Millennium Bug (or Year 2000 Bug, as it's also known) to create chaos in our phone systems, supermarkets and banks on 1st January 2000 — mainly thanks to our computers. Until the year 2004, when Uranus finally quits Aquarius, there is likely to be more techno-anarchy, from satellites which don't bounce to massive global communications systems which crash. The great American pager disaster of May 1998 — when satellite problems dragged all pager communications in America to a screeching halt — could easily turn out to be an appetiser.

Remember, the expression 'Crazy Technology' is a double Aquarian statement (two sign key words in one phrase). When that happens, *stuff* happens.

If we peer further into the future we may see another double Aquarian phrase — Technology Rebellion — coming to pass. Unlike the Luddites, we can't throw our clogs into the machinery, but astrologically speaking, some kind of radical backlash against computers, microchips and all the rest of it (even digital alarm clocks) looks pretty likely. An anti-internet movement may well gather speed. Not just for the obvious reasons, like objections to online porn and weird online cult membership, but against the way the internet takes the warmth and intimacy from the kind of connections we make with each other. Eventually people will want real smiles, not emoticons — I wonder what name the new anti-tech movement will give itself?

The hippies in the stage musical *Hair* saw the Age of Aquarius as some kind of nudie paradise, where both the brotherhood and the sisterhood would be provided for. Er, not quite. While the internet has certainly created amazing global communities, it has also shown its other Aquarian face — a distinct coolness. A certain detachment. I mean ... really. How can you do a hairy group hug when you're communicating with someone whose modem happens to be in Moscow? Yes, the Age of Aquarius is bringing people together in a common spirit of sharing. But it doesn't get much closer than e-mail. Aquarius isn't about intimacy or emotion, it's about a certain distance — friendly distance, but distance nonetheless. The very nature of the internet makes that sort of connection inevitable.

And for you ...?

If you have planets in Aquarius, you'll feel completely at home in the Age of Aquarius — in other words, right now. Some of the things which were vitally important and close to your heart ten, 20 — even 30 — years ago are now becoming part of everyone's lives. No wonder you finally feel as if you're in tune, somehow — and that feeling will only increase as Uranus and Neptune proceed, slowly, through the wavy, weirdo sign. Guess what? The world is finally catching up with you.

If your package of Sun, Moon, Mercury, Venus and Mars signs shows no Aquarius, and if it's heavy on signs like Leo, Taurus and Scorpio, then you may have a few problems. You may hate the computers, the radical weirdo freaks who keep confronting you on the TV news, and the mass trend towards groups of friends, rather than intimate one-on-one relationships. Most of all, you'll probably be infuriated by Tamagotchi, the ultimate Age of Aquarius toy (you too can give birth to an electronic chicken).

age of aquarius

Pagan Kennedy is an American writer and guru whom *Mademoiselle* magazine described this way:

'That nutty, fun-loving, friendly, bicycle-riding, committed-to-recycling, pop culture-crazed creature we thought the media had invented so it could use the label 'Generation X' — only she really exists.'

She's also produced a book called Pagan Kennedy's Living — The Handbook for Maturing Hipsters (St. Martin's Griffin, New York) which is so Aquarian my jaw dropped.

I don't know her chart, but I suspect Aquarius/Uranus (Uranus is the ruler of the sign) is all over it. Here's what Pagan thinks about:

SOCIETY

'A lot of people are quietly pioneering a different kind of life for themselves. They're patching together bizarre families, inventing new types of romantic relationships to suit their needs, finding low-budget and creative ways to raise their kids, tuning out the mainstream media, doing what they love, and trusting that the money will follow.' '

LOVE ON THE INTERNET

'Cyber-dating is great. It's the StairMaster of love — you use it to keep in shape, not to climb to where you want to be.'

Pagan also has opinions on smoking, telephone etiquette, sex, the media, therapy, travel, babies and more (if you're into this Age of Aquarius stuff, or if you are reading this and feeling the call of kinship with Pagan, I suggest you find a copy of the book, or check out her website at:

http://www. birdhouse. org/words/pagan/

Finally, here she is on friends — *the* big Age of Aquarius issue.

FRIENDS AND FAMILY

'In this rootless age — when people so often move away or grow away from their relatives — a family is no longer something we're born into. We have to make it ourselves.'

Well, that's Pagan, but I thought so, too, a couple of years ago, when Australian *Vogue* asked me to write a story on what I thought was starting to move and shake in society. I was noticing that share accommodation (group living, very Aquarian) was reinventing itself — no longer a tragic case of *Young Ones*-styled chaos and mess, with optional second-hand couches, but a new and groovy alternative for the divorced, the single, and the free-spirited. I was also noticing how friends were becoming substitute family. In just about every big city in the world you'll see it happening. Nothing can replace parents or families, of course, but at the end of the day it's your friends who will nurse you through hospital, lend you money, give you somewhere to live and cook for you.

In some way these changes are being forced upon us, and we're not choosing them. Marriages are breaking up at such a huge rate that the old 1950s dream of a perfect, unchanging suburban family unit has gone. Then there's the rapid changes in employment. Often, to get work these days, you have to move. All of this, plus a bit of Uranus in Aquarius mystery, seems to be pushing us into a brave new world where friends are becoming the new family. It's going to make a big difference to older people, as well. Forget nursing homes. What about communal accommodation centres, like the Findhorn project? Just think of it. Like the apartments in *Melrose Place*, but without all the sniping, sex and craziness. (The Age of Aquarius, for all its benefits, just won't ever get that emotional or personal.)

Because all those planets — Pluto, Uranus, Neptune — tend to work off each other, we may find that our new obsession with having some kind of spiritual belief, philosophy or search for meaning dovetails with the net, and that most of us end up using computers to network with our fellow believers — maybe in the same way that the Victorians used to turn up to church on Sundays. Certainly you can see why computers may change the travel industry forever. And perhaps the new Aquarian 'cool' ethos — friendly, group-oriented, but never too close — will sow the seeds for the kind of new comedy that's on the way. In this respect, *Seinfeld* may well have been the forerunner of something which will become quite established by the next century.

And with that, onto the next section, where I'll get into *Seinfeld* a little more. All in the name of serious astrology, you understand . . .

READING A FULL HOROSCOPE

A horoscope chart can be a frightening thing. It basically looks like a frisbee with squiggles all over it. Below is the horoscope for the very last episode of *Seinfeld*, which went to air in America as I was writing the new edition of this book.

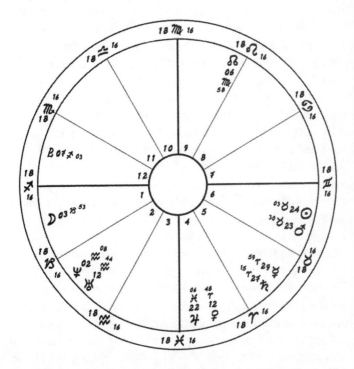

Some things look obvious on the frisbee — the Moon looks like the Moon, on the far left of the wheel. And you can probably spot the wavy, wiggly Aquarian symbols, also on the far left of the wheel. Unless you're an astrologer, though, you'll be clueless about the rest of it. I won't confuse you further with talk of yods and T-squares and progressions. For now, just think of this horoscope as a drawing of a moment — in this case, the moment that the last *Seinfeld* appeared on TV in New York.

It may seem bizarre that you can work out a horoscope for a moment in time as well as for a human being. The strange thing is, however, this picture of time (the frisbee-shaped wheel you see) will actually describe the subject of the show, the mood of the programme, and even what Kramer is likely to get up to. The horoscope can — in all seriousness — also point to the things critics and the public will pick up on.

Like most astrologers, I've done charts for the birth of business ventures. I did one for a magazine which started up when Mercury, the planet ruling the media, was going backwards. Two months later, the magazine failed and went back to the drawing board. Whoops. With astrology, it's possible to draw up a horoscope for virtually anything — the birth of a baby, the birth of a golden retriever, or the birth of a haircut. I'm serious. They have conferences in Switzerland devoted to these things!

The 'last *Seinfeld*' horoscope shows Sagittarius, the comedy sign, is its Rising sign. So this episode is on a Sagittarius journey. (BBC TV in England — renowned for its comedy since the days of *Monty Python* — also has a lot of Sagittarius in its 'birth' horoscope.) If you had to pick one sign which might have turned up in the *Seinfeld* chart, it would probably be Sagittarius — only Gemini comes close in terms of laughs.

Look around the wheel. Each slice represents a department of life — astrologers call them houses, and there are twelve of them. Some have planets in them, some don't. The slices with planets in them are always more significant — a big deal. In this instance they'll tell you what the episode is going to be about.

If you've seen it or read about it, you'll know the plotline of the final episode. The four friends — Jerry, George, Elaine and Kramer — hear that Seinfeld's idea for a new show, *Jerry*, has finally been accepted. They're given a private plane by the TV station but come close to crashing in it. Saved from that fate, they then find themselves witnessing a fat man being mugged. Instead of helping him, they video the whole thing. They are arrested as a result, and in the court case which follows, character witnesses shoot them down in flames so successfully that all four of them are jailed.

The slice of the wheel which rules jails is in the 9 p.m. position, and you can see it on the wheel. Pluto, the planet of obsession, crisis and change, is contained in that slice. No wonder this episode was going to put them behind bars. The slice of the wheel which rules aeroplane flights is close to the 12 p.m. position. The squiggle in there is the symbol for what they call the Moon's node. This represents the destiny, or fate, of the person (or the TV show). It's in a difficult placement because it's clashing with Pluto. No wonder Kramer nearly causes an air disaster.

You can work out the character, or personality, of the show by using the same method you've used in this book to work out your own profile. What we have here is as follows:

- Sun in Taurus
- Moon in Capricorn
- Mercury in Aries
- Venus in Aries
- Mars in Taurus

The show was a Taurus–Capricorn–Aries type. Thanks to the Taurus influence, it was hung up on money (true: the cost of commercials for this final episode slot — and the actors' salaries — set new records). The Capricorn dose made it rather ambitious (too ambitious, some critics said). The Aries part of its overall 'feel' was reflected in the furious fighting and brawling in the courtroom scene. Funnily enough, Jerry Seinfeld is a Taurean and Julia Louis-Dreyfus is a Capricorn. Part of the plotline involved them nearly-but-not-quite admitting undying love for each other. Cosmic.

Alice Kashuba, who is an American astrologer specialising in Sabian Symbols (360 channelled images representing each degree of each sign of the zodiac) looked up the symbol for Saturn, its sign and its degree in the *Seinfeld* horoscope. Saturn rules the tough news in the chart, the learning experience or the difficult obstacle. In *The*

Sabian Symbols Oracle, by Lynda and Richard Hill, which Alice uses, the *Seinfeld* horoscope translates as 'a large disappointed audience'. The day after the show aired, critics and fans did indeed round on the show, complaining that it was below Seinfeld's usual high standard. In true, spooky Sabian Symbol fashion, though, there were also diehard fans who were obviously just disappointed that their favourite programme was off the air. (If you're interested in hearing more about the mysterious Sabians, by the way, go to the Whooaa! Spooky! chapter, page 322.)

With Sagittarius Rising, this last episode was always destined to travel, too. Ten years from now, it will probably be on syndication in the Congo, dubbed into a dialect Jerry Seinfeld never dreamed of.

Now, to the horoscope of someone who used astrology quite a bit . . .

THE BIRTH CHART FOR DIANA, PRINCESS OF WALES

At an astrology conference I attended recently, one of the lecturers said that if anybody else mentioned Diana or her birth horoscope, he was going to walk out. She has become the most scrutinised woman in 20th-century history anyway, never mind astrology.

Ever since her marriage to Prince Charles in that amazingly puffy and desirable dress, she was destined to have her birth details punched into computers about a zillion times by astrologers all over the world. Not just because we wanted to know more about her (everyone wanted to know more about her) but also because she was the perfect astrological subject.

She had confirmed birth details — time, date and place — which isn't always easy to get with famous people, as so many of them lie about their age. She was also a big fan of astrology, and had at least three astrologers of her own (Debbie Frank, Penny Thornton and Felix Lyle) so we didn't feel so bad about looking at her chart. Finally, she had such a public life that you could literally track everything that happened to her — the wedding, the birth of her sons, the separation, the *Panorama* interview, the AIDS and landmines work — and watch it coming to life in her horoscope.

When she died, I got the cheque I'd just received for writing a story about her and Dodi and re-directed it to the Victor Chang Foundation in Sydney — one of Diana's favourite charities. In common with many media people, and especially media astrologers, I felt like a vulture after her death. I never met her, but I wrote about her — all the time. If you were anywhere near a women's magazine in the '80s and early '90s, it was unavoidable.

When I left flowers for her on the steps of the Sydney Opera House, which was one of many tribute sites around the world, I attached a card with her sign, Cancer, engraved on the front. And I vowed that I would never write about her again.

And here we are, a few years later, and I've changed my mind. Why? Because she remains the best subject in astrology, and there's no getting away from it. Her life is also a lesson in how to take on astrological advice and use it well.

English astrologer Frank Clifford, in *Data Plus* UK, says she often:

'used electional astrology in an attempt to secure a favourable public reaction — most notably the Panorama interview decision . . . Advice and friendship garnered from astrologer Debbie Frank, for example, did much to ease Diana through her personal transitions and painful separations.'

My friend Robert Currey, from The Astrology Shop in Convent Garden, also reckons that Penny Thornton's advice to Diana might have helped her more than most people realise.

Could any astrologer have foreseen her death? Some people will always be able to foresee just about anything. But for me, horoscopes have never been about that. They're really about life, first and foremost. It's true that at the time of the crash, a pattern involving Mars, the planet of speed and violence, and Pluto, the planet of (among other things) death — was triggered in her chart. And it all happened in the slice of the horoscope which falls at the 12 p.m. position — ruling foreign travel. (It's the slice which features in the last 'plane crash' episode of *Seinfeld*, too.)

What's happier to dwell on is the simple fact that at the time of the accident, Cancerians were having some blissfully happy, romantic astro-patterns. At the end of August 1997, Venus the planet of love was very much on her side.

But enough about the future — or as it stands now, the past. Diana's whole life was her future, as personality is so often destiny. Here, then, is the full birth chart interpretation for Diana, Princess of Wales. If it opens new doors into astrology for you then you may like to get your own chart read. Much as I'd like to give you the whole enchilada in the book you are holding now, there is no substitute for a full horoscope reading or written, personal chart.

A FAMILY WOMAN WITH A FREE SPIRIT

This looks exactly like another frisbee with graffiti all over it, I'm afraid. Unless you have the basics of astrology under your belt, it's probably going to look like squiggles and nothing more.

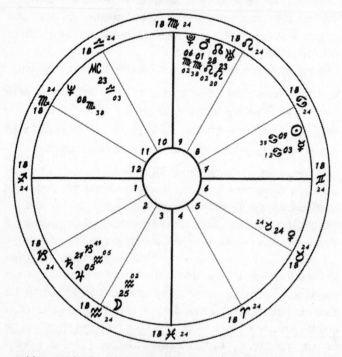

Hidden inside the squiggles, though, is a snapshot in time. This wheel shows an astrologer exactly what the planets were doing at the minute that the baby Diana was born, at 7.45 p.m. on 1st July 1961 in Sandringham, England. Her mother gave astrologers the time so we know it's accurate.

The new astrology for women

The first thing to look for is the Sun, because it describes what's going to be important to you, and what you're proud of, and how you feel about yourself. It's in Cancer, the sign of families, homes and mothers. Diana also had Mercury in that sign, so she had a double dose.

Would she be a typical double-Cancerian type, though? The rest of the chart will show this, and you start by looking at the Moon, which rules Cancer — just to see what sort of shape it's in.

In a nutshell, it's not in good shape at all. It's clashing with mad, unpredictable Uranus. From this, it's possible to predict that in childhood, Diana would have one major episode involving her mother, and her home, and her family, which would seriously rattle her cage. Consequently, all her natural instincts as a double Cancerian would be thrown off centre. Yes, there could be no doubting the importance of her mother — but it was not going to be an easy relationship. Yes, home mattered — but it would not always be a safe or secure place to be. There are even indications in the chart of domestic chaos in later life, just because it would feel familiar — according to her chart, it's one of the first things she would ever experience.

Psychologists know, and commonsense dictates, that childhood is where most people's character-forming experiences take place. So an awful lot of who Diana was, and what she was about, hinges on this childhood episode involving her security and stability with her mother. Looking at the chart, and using a technique called Moon progressions, an astrologer might estimate that the full impact of it would have been felt well before her teens — and all this without necessarily having to ask for details.

Typically, an astrologer might explain that in turn, when the time came for her to consider motherhood as an adult, similar issues would most likely have come up. All that Cancerian/Moon stuff about being needed, and feeling needy — and wanting to protect, and not feeling safe yourself — would crop up in her life. The Moon also rules food. Many astrologers might have asked a simple question about how she — Diana, the client — felt about her appetite and diet at that stage of the reading. The Moon has such crazy patterns going around it in her horoscope that it's highly likely she couldn't just 'eat' food — she probably had quite a complex view of it.

The slices of Diana's horoscope rule life departments, just as they did in the *Seinfeld* example. The first slice with planets in it is the department of money and possessions. Saturn and Jupiter, two major planets are here. Are we looking at a future stockbroker, an antiques collector, a business whizz or a bank teller?

This is where the get-real side of astrology comes in. Contrary to popular opinion, astrologers are not there to perform party tricks and give their clients information out of a hat. Common sense comes into it, and an astrologer doing your chart will ask you questions. Are you working-class or middle-class or born into the aristocracy? Are you living in the town or the country? It's not cheating — it just brings the symbols in the horoscope down to earth.

Diana, born into the Spencer family, was unlikely to become a bank teller — unless her chart shows some extreme sign of rebellion, which it doesn't. Given her tiaras-and-ponies background then, the main thing you could say about that department of money and possessions is that she was probably going to be a collector, she was likely to end up being fabulously wealthy, and retail therapy would be something she would take seriously.

This is backed up by her Taurus side, too — she had Venus in Taurus. But as always, when Taurus is involved things go way beyond big bank accounts and fabulous handbags. There are issues here about values, and ethics, and morals, in relation to money.

The next slice of the wheel which counts rules brothers, sisters, short trips and the media. This appeared to be a complicated, emotional area in her life. In fact, putting the information together like a detective, it might be possible to say that what happened in Diana's childhood involving her mother would also have intricately involved her siblings. And the relationships with her siblings in adulthood were always going to be at the heart of what made her tick — for better or worse. This, of course, came uncannily true at her funeral, when her brother Earl Spencer changed the world with one speech.

Now, not every ordinary person is going to have a relationship with the media written into their future, although Diana obviously did. Planets there in the third house of media might mean a special interest in newspapers, TV, radio or magazines for a regular human being. An astrologer might joke, 'You're not going to be able to live without them.' More seriously, though, if Diana had ended up in a calling where reporters and photographers counted, then an astrologer might have spent a long time going over it with her. Her chart shows that the media would have filled a need in her — both to communicate, and to be heard. However, there's too much painful sensitivity there, too. Reading the press or watching TV programmes about herself wouldn't have been something she could have just brushed off.

At this stage it's also possible to see that her Moon sign was Aquarius, which is all about eccentricity, freedom, independence, computers, astrology and feminism. How on earth was she going to work all that into her life? The mystery of astrology is that people nearly always do. Apart from the computer side of things, Diana managed to 'do' her Aquarian side to its full extent. She saw a feminist counsellor, Susie Orbach, about her eating disorder. She indulged her eccentric side by finding weird and wonderful alternative health treatments. She hired at least three astrologers and regularly saw a celebrated medium, Rita Rogers. And Diana also made freedom and independence her defining life statement in relation to her marriage and the Royal Family — she couldn't have 'done' her Aquarius side more expertly if she'd tried.

The next slice of the wheel with a planet is the one ruling work, routine and health and wellbeing. Venus, the planet of enjoyment, flirtation and pleasure is there. Looking after her body would never be a chore or a bore for Diana. According to her chart, she would see it as a luxury she could afford. Similarly, everyday routines and duties which might get other people down would have provided an excuse to flirt. Venus means you flirt with men, women, old ladies, dogs and children — pretty much the way Diana did, on her endless rounds of hospitals and schools. I think she genuinely loved her daily routines and rituals. And the chart said the word 'duty' was synonymous with love for her.

It's not surprising that the slice of the wheel ruling love and marriage also has a couple of planets wedged in there. The Sun and

Mercury are doing a kind of double act. One represents partners who are important, well-known and confident. The other represents quick wit, intelligence and education. Together they describe Diana's version of a soulmate. Everyone knows who that was to be — and she would admire his brains. The only problem was, the more she put her man on a pedestal, or built him up as her intellectual superior, the more she would deny her own importance, her own brain and her own ability to shine.

The slice of the wheel with the most planets wedged inside it rules foreign people, overseas travel, higher education and self-education. It's amazing that Diana didn't make university. Had she lived, perhaps she might have taken it on. She certainly fulfilled the promise of travel and foreign friendships shown by the planets here, though. However, these aren't particularly easy or peaceful planets. Uranus, Mars and Pluto never are — especially when they're all jammed together. Travel — as shown by this chart — was never going to be an easy or fun experience for her. In actual fact, it may have provided intense, deep and transforming experiences. Diana fulfilled all this in her lifetime by touring the world on behalf of the Red Cross and other humanitarian organisations.

There is another important point in the horoscope to consider after this. The MC, or Midheaven, which describes your career or calling in life, is in the sign of Libra. This is all about looking good, being charming, playing the diplomat, showing style or taste and being in touch with the creative or enjoyable side of human existence. Diana might well have been a diplomat, although she was certainly the archetypal trophy wife as well. In fact, the only thing standing in the way of a diplomatic role for anyone with a chart like this is all those intense, powerful messages about foreign people and foreign travel. Part of her would have been extremely good at the smiling and nodding that goes with diplomacy, but part of her would have invited some odd and dramatic incidents as a result of some of her overseas contacts. Libra also rules flowers. Had she not been from the English aristocracy, she might have become a florist! As it was, flowers became her global signature at her death.

The last slice of the wheel to contain a planet rules friendship, social life and membership of groups, organisations, clubs and teams. Traditionally this has a lot to do with the sign of Aquarius, and because Diana's Moon sign is also Aquarius, this was going to be a major part of her life. Neptune is the planet in question. Wherever it falls in a chart, you find a bit of magic, a bit of fascination and a way to escape the boring realities of life. An astrologer looking at Diana's chart might have explained it this way: 'Your friends and your social life will be your escape path.' Being some kind of 'joiner' — of a rock band, netball team or a specific cause (like Greenpeace or Amnesty International) might also have been recommended. Once again, though, the chart has to be related to the human being in question. As a Royal, Diana could hardly form the Windsors' version of Spice Girls, but she could — and did — become involved in a whole range of charitable and humanitarian organisations. For her, it was probably where the magic was.

Membership of group organisations, and good friends, may have been easier for her than certain family relationships, according to this horoscope. Given this kind of chart, an astrologer might gently have pointed her in this direction. A lot of astrology is about this kind of encouragement — but the funny thing is, nine times out of ten, the people you are reading for usually know exactly what you are talking about, and all you are doing is confirming thoughts they've had for a long time.

This has been a whistle-stop tour through a standard chart reading — although for a decidedly non-standard woman. And by the way, if you do happen to be an astrologer, I've used the Equal House system only because it's my own preference — you might like to use Placidus for Diana, which many astrologers have.

If you pay to have your own chart written up and sent to you by an astrologer, you will find several dozen pages to wade through, and a lot more in-depth detail than I've used here. A personal consultation is even more fascinating, because you are giving the astrologer something she can work with, and by working together you can really dig quite deeply into your horoscope and your life. You may find you spend an hour or two, and come away with a full cassette tape. Or you may even book in for regular readings, which is something Diana obviously found useful.

The birth chart can work as a tool for understanding yourself and your past, and as a predictive tool for the future. It really depends what you're looking for at the time. Do you have a serious question about your career, your marriage or your money for the next six months? Or do you just need to sort yourself out? Either way, as a friend of mine once said, the best thing about having your horoscope done is that it gives you a valid excuse to sit down and talk about yourself for a few hours! If you'd like more information, please go to the Ten Questions section at the back of this book.

FIND your rising sign

Your Rising sign (also known as your Ascendant) tells you about the way you see the world. Fate plays a part in this. If you have Cancer Rising, destiny says that you will keep on experiencing family issues, and particularly key situations involving your mother, and subsequently your outlook will become quite clan or mother-oriented.

If there are also important, emotional episodes for you which touch on topics such as fertility, near pregnancy, miscarriage, adoption, actual pregnancy or abortion, then equally you can see how someone might end up with a Cancer-styled perspective on life — no matter what their Sun, Moon, Mercury, Venus and Mars signs happen to be. This is the way fate contributes to the life path of someone born with Cancer Rising.

To continue with this example, if you have Aries Rising, destiny might throw you into a chain of situations where it always seems that you have to compete, to fight, to win. No wonder you end up looking at life in an Aries way. And no wonder some people might mistake you for an Aries, even though you're actually a Taurus–Virgo–Libra type underneath.

Your Rising sign is not the real you (unless it's the same as your Sun, Moon, Mercury, Venus or Mars sign.) In actual fact, it's a very good mask. It's your outer style — the bit of you that people see at parties, at job interviews and in any first-impression situation. It describes all the different scenarios and situations which you meet in your life, again and again, until you're practically 'trained' by destiny to function like your Rising sign in public. Fate sent Margaret Thatcher into politics, where she had to be secretive, and intense and powerful. She has Scorpio Rising. It also made her the only woman prime minister in the history of England. Every time she stood up in a dress and heels, people were reminded of her sexuality and so was she. That's Scorpio Rising, too.

How do you go about working out your Rising sign? My first recommendation is to use the internet (*see* Ten Questions, page 519) to get a free chart, which will tell you what you need to know with complete accuracy. My second recommendation is to order a cheap chart — also known as a basic chart — from any of the sources in Ten Questions.

By the way, it's crucial to have your accurate time of birth. The most common problem I see as an astrologer is the client who can't remember exactly, or whose mother has got it wrong. Most people are only an hour or two out though. So if the Rising sign you sort out for yourself doesn't make sense, look at the one before, and the one after it. If one of these fits like a glove, that's probably it and you're anything from half an hour to an hour out. You wouldn't believe how many mothers out there get their kids' birthtimes wrong — especially if they've had more than one. So — scrutinise your Rising sign carefully.

For people who can't be bothered using the internet or paying for a cheapie chart, I do have a faster option for you. It's called the 30-Second Check.

THE 30-SECOND CHECK

Find your Sun sign (regular star sign) in the left-hand column then look along the top to find your birth time bracket. If you were born during daylight saving or other artificial time changes, you'll need to adjust for that first. In other words, if you were born in Sydney in summer 1973, take off an hour from the time you were told you were born. If you were born in London in summer 1943 you'll need to take off two hours.

The simple 30 Second Check is going to work for most of you, but it's not perfect. If you have any doubts, look at the sign just before,

YOU WERE BORN BETWEEN

your SUN is in	Mid-2am	2-4am	4-6am	6-8am	8-10am	10-12pm	12-2pm	2-4pm	4-6pm	6-8pm	8-10pm	10-mid
ARI	CAP	AQU	PIS	ARI	TAU	GEM	CAN	LEO	VIR	LIB	SCO	SAG
TAU	AQU	PIS	ARI	TAU	GEM	CAN	LEO	VIR	LIB	SCO	SAG	CAP
GEM	PIS	ARI	TAU	GEM	CAN	LEO	VIR	LIB	SCO	SAG	CAP	AQU
CAN	ARI	TAU	GEM	CAN	LEO	VIR	LIB	SCO	SAG	CAP	AQU	PIS
LEO	TAU	GEM	CAN	LEO	VIR	LIB	SCO	SAG	CAP	AQU	PIS	ARI
VIR	GEM	CAN	LEO	VIR	LIB	SCO	SAG	CAP	AQU	PIS	ARI	TAU
LIB	CAN	LEO	VIR	LIB	SCO	SAG	CAP	AQU	PIS	ARI	TAU	GEM
SCO	LEO	VIR	LIB	SCO	SAG	CAP	AQU	PIS	ARI	TAU	GEM	CAN
SAG	VIR	LIB	SCO	SAG	CAP	AQU	PIS	ARI	TAU	GEM	CAN	LEO
CAP	LIB	SCO	SAG	CAP	AQU	PIS	ARI	TAU	GEM	CAN	LEO	VIR
AQU	SCO	SAG	CAP	AQU	PIS	ARI	TAU	GEM	CAN	LEO	VIR	LIB
PIS	SAG	CAP	AQU	PIS	ARI	TAU	GEM	CAN	LEO	VIR	LIB	SCO

Your Rising sign is: _____

and just after, the one you've found for yourself. By using the Rising Sign Test on these pages, and by a careful flick through the longer sections on the Rising Sign journeys in this part of the book, you should be able to confirm it.

Examples

Simone de Beauvoir
3.51 am 9 January 1908 (Capricorn)
Scorpio Rising

Princess Caroline of Monaco
9.27 am 23 January 1957 (Aquarius)
Pisces Rising

Coco Chanel
4.00 pm 19 August 1883 (Leo)
Sagittarius Rising

I wish that Rising signs weren't so curly to calculate, but when something is based on the precise minute and geographical latitude and longitude of a baby's birth, you can't ever get it 100% right unless you've got a computer doing it for you. Still, have a go — most of you will get it right first time unless you were born in a ladies' toilet in darkest Peru during quadruple daylight saving time.

If you're really in agonies, please go to an internet cafe armed with the net addresses you'll find in Ten Questions (*see* page 519) — for the price of a coffee plus a few dollars or pounds more, you can have the last word on your Rising sign (and everything else) in ten minutes flat. Finally if you've already had your chart done and it says you're Virgo Rising and you use this table and it says Leo Rising, go with the chart. (It's that old one before, one after rule again — and yes, you were probably the baby in the Peru ladies' loo.)

Here's the running order of the signs in case you need to know the Rising sign just before and just after the one you've found.

Aries Taurus Gemini Cancer Leo Virgo Libra Scorpio Sagittarius Capricorn Aquarius Pisces Aries Taurus . . . and so on.

And now it's time for . . .

THE RISING SIGN TEST

You know you've got Aries Rising if ...

You see the world as a competitive place, and you believe you have to be faster or tougher than other people to hold your own. You like clothes, accessories or cars that let people know how energetic and 'out there' you are. If people want to get to know the real you, you're well aware that they must first get past the act you sometimes put on — that of the bold, fearless, go-getter action woman. Your first approach to people is usually fast, gutsy.

You know you've got Taurus Rising if ...

You see the world as place where money rules pretty much everything. To feel at home in this world, you either have to have a strong set of values that goes beyond money and materialism, or you have to have a very good accountant and investment portfolio! You like clothes, accessories or cars that let people know you value the good things in life. If people want to get to know the real you, they have to get past your down-to-earth, practical act.

You know you've got Gemini Rising if ...

You see the world as a place to make connections in, a place to make contact, swap gossip, exchange information and news and then be on your way. To feel at home in this world you have to have good communication skills — written or verbal. You like clothes, accessories or cars that let people know that you're just a little more intelligent or well-informed than the average person. School or the education process was a big deal for you.

You know you've got Cancer Rising if ...

You see the world as a place where everything leads back to the family and childhood — you can't help this psychological view of the world. To feel at home out there, you feel you have to have some kind of place to call your own — a particular region, homeland or a treasured house or flat. You like clothes, accessories or cars that protect you. If people want to get to know the real you, they have to get past that caring, sensitive persona first.

You know you've got Leo Rising if ...

You see the world as a place where you have to be confident about what you do, and who you are — or nothing works. To feel as if you belong out there, you automatically look for a career or calling (which may have nothing to do with your job) where you can take a respected, leading role. Finding an outlet for creative self-expression is also vital, in your opinion. To get to know the real you, people have to get past the impressive exterior first.

You know you've got Virgo Rising if ...

You see the world as a place where a job worth doing is worth doing well. Your approach to life is basically about fulfilling the high expectations you set yourself, and if that occasionally makes you look like a workaholic to other people, you'll put up with it. You like to present an exterior which is as good as you can get it, so the details of your body, hair, face and wardrobe count for a lot. To feel at home in the world you pursue perfection.

You know you've got Libra Rising if ...

You see the world as a place where people stand or fall by their charm, their outer image, and their ability to glide smoothly and easily through life. To feel as if you belong in this world, you develop a popular persona — lots of smiles, and good manners. To get past this to the real you, people must look beyond the glossy surface, and you probably know that by now. Looking presentable, or even well-designed and put together, is part of the deal.

You know you've got Scorpio Rising if ...

You see the world as a place where a certain amount of secrecy, discretion and confidentiality is the key to staying in control. You're so aware of the sexual vibes that flow between people that you either deliberately dress to play it all down, or you go the other way and crank it up. To get past the image to the real you, people must first deal with your intensity, which is quite noticeable on a first meeting. You may even use it on purpose.

You know you've got Sagittarius Rising if ...

You see the world as place to explore, take adventures in, and find meaning in. To feel at home in this world, you believe it's important to travel, either in and around your own area, or venturing overseas. To get past the outer you to the real person underneath, people have to look beyond the sense of humour, and the positive persona you project. You like clothes, accessories or cars which say you're a world citizen, or you've explored life a bit.

You know you've got Capricorn Rising if ...

You feel that the world is quite a structured place, and you're fairly shrewd about the way the whole thing works. You certainly understand the part that hierarchy plays, no matter if you're talking about the world of work, or the world of status and social standing. To get to know the real you, people have to get past the ambitious, feet-on-the-ground persona you send out. You prefer a wardrobe which allows people to take you seriously.

You know you've got Aquarius Rising if ...

You see the world as an interesting, challenging place — but the main challenge is being true to yourself when all around would like you to conform or compromise — in other words, to fit in. To make things work for you in this world, you've come to accept that you have to do your own thing, in your own way. To get to know what you're really like underneath people have to get past the odd bit of weirdness or eccentricity. You're your own person.

You know you've got Pisces Rising if ...

You see the world as a mysterious, fascinating place where there is more to practically everything than meets the eye. If an impressionist painting doesn't convince you of that, then a psychic reading or a scuba-diving session will. To get to know what you're really like, people must first see past the sensitivity, the emotion and the occasional vagueness or elusiveness. You prefer a look which says you're imaginative rather than boringly practical.

aries

If you were born when the sign of Aries was rising on the horizon, you came into the world at a time when this kind of journey was being mapped out for you — fast, full of challenges and a real competition to be number one. Your Sun, Moon, Mercury, Venus and Mars signs will describe the resources you have to deal with this kind of life journey!

LEARNING TO WIN

Because life will often put you in situations which feel like a contest or a battle, you will discover that there is a part of you that won't accept coming second. Competitive sport is one department of life that seems to have an interesting effect on Aries Rising types, as it is here that you play out some of the tensions, and pleasures, of this sign. Feeling that life is a race, or a contest, is something that will become more familiar to you as time goes by. You will also have something to learn about winning and losing, too.

Part of you may intensely dislike lagging behind, or being left at the start. So one of the challenges with this Rising sign is to reward yourself for the victories, but also to understand that being a poor loser, or a 'difficult' finisher, is not going to help you in the next race you face. Arguing with the opposition, or arguing with the umpire (whoever is playing that role) will not do you any favours either. The first taste of success, or the greatest victory, is something that will stay in your memory for a long time. There will be quite a few of these events in your lifetime, but it may be the memory of the last one along that gives you the inspiration to keep going for the next time.

YOUR ENERGY LEVELS

On a physical level, this Rising sign has something to say about your energy levels. One of the reasons patience may not be part of your journey is that patience taxes your muscles, stops the adrenalin and seems quite alien to what you are all about. Leading a stopwatch existence suits you rather better. Perhaps because it senses that you will be up for a few races and battles in your lifetime, your body will also complain if you leave it lying dormant for too long. Many women with Aries Rising learn to head for a high-energy diet, or stick to regular fitness or sport routines once they discover just how much their body influences everything else that is going on in their lives.

You may find that if you don't create a physical outlet for the energy that is zipping around your system, you become twitchy, or restless. As a child, you may have been one of those girls who were always running around, falling off things, and you may carry some bumps, bruises or scars as a result. This is one of the reasons traditional astrology books will tell you that Aries Rising women tend to have old 'battle' wounds on their skin. It's not inevitable, but it does happen sometimes. More obvious, perhaps, is the fact that you may have one of those bodies which looks as if it's ready for action, or ready to stand its ground!

THE NEED FOR ACTION

Destiny says you will often be thrown into situations where there is only one answer: action, and lots of it. This immediacy and straightforward, direct approach, is part of the Aries Rising package. There will be times when to wait, or debate the issue, will seriously work against you. So, after repeated experiences, you learn that action can solve quite a few things.

Very few Aries Rising women like waiting around. This is partly because, after a certain age, the fates will have accustomed you to getting out there, and getting what you need. You learn to push, push, push your way through life. This may occasionally earn you a reputation for being aggressive or self-interested. But to drag your feet, or lie in bed, would be unthinkable. Destiny says you always have to get out there, and keep moving. Psychologically, too, a strong sense of enthusiasm is one of your characteristics.

GOOD TIMING

You will have to develop a sense of timing that works for you, but is also practical for those around you. This may have been evident at the moment of your birth (your Rising sign often describes the conditions at the time you were born). With this fast and frank sign on the ascendant, you will often be placed in a position where others are making you wait — which you will find impossible — or where you are leaving people behind, and consequently losing support. Neither situation is particularly useful, and one of the things about your journey that will teach you the most is the situation where a) You do it quickly, but not too quickly, and b) You finally find people who can snap into things as speedily as you.

With this Rising sign, it is inevitable that you will always leave someone, somewhere, behind. But even though this has the flattering effect of making you a leader, or an Amazon type, you need to watch out for the patches when you leap ahead so quickly that you end up clumsily falling over, and having to start again.

For more information and a stronger Arian 'feel' you may want to scan the chapter on Planets in Aries (*see* pages 6–19). Some of the words, images and symbols listed at the end of the section may turn up in your life's journey in synchronous ways. It is also common for Aries Rising women to encounter Arian types along the way. These people are usually guide figures, who have specific lessons to teach you about the right way to do the Arian thing, and the wrong way!

taurus

If you were born when the sign of Taurus was on the ascendant you will spend your life looking for stability, as well as a financial security that will allow you to spend on the pleasures that are so important to you. Learning about financial values, as well as the other kind, will be a major part of what lies ahead. Your Sun, Moon, Mercury, Venus and Mars signs will describe the resources you have to deal with this kind of life journey.

MATERIAL GIRL
You will often be put in financial high and low situations where you must work out a different sense of values each time. Eventually,

the Material Girl days will be balanced by a concern for the things that money cannot purchase. Your deep enjoyment of that elusive thing, Quality of Life, may swing between having the right kind of CDs in your collection, having all that is sensual, creative and artistic around you, and ... just having a good life! You will be put in many professional or personal situations where the dilemma is being rich in material things, but poor in other areas. In this way, you learn to find your limits. You will go through your madly hedonistic periods, and you will also spend a great deal more than you have to. Equally, you will have to become used to the idea that someone is always going to see you as a provider — the woman who brings the money home for others. There will be moments when it feels rather like meeting a quota.

YOUR VALUE SYSTEM

Because you like natural things — and Taurus is, after all, an Earth sign — you will ultimately have to decide how much it costs to be able to stop and smell the roses occasionally. Some women with Taurus Rising have also become involved with the conservation movement for this reason, but there are an equal number who just enjoy being where the trees are. Still, one cannot enjoy the natural world if there is money to be made, or shopping to be done, and at some stage in your life you are going to have to choose. Equally, perhaps, there will come a point when you realise that some aspects of your lifestyle are just not compatible with the earth's welfare — or the ocean's.

The singular, instructive experience in your life will be the prospect of Selling Out. Some of you will, and some of you won't, but it will remain a crucial stage in your journey. Often, you face this decision on a professional level. Going where the money is, you find yourself compromising other values. You price yourself into one market, but price yourself out of another market, which does not rest on money for its values, but on the things which are beyond price.

If this does not occur on a professional level, it may do so in your private life. Your partner's financial status, and the question of your mutual lifestyle, or income, will be a big one. The Taurus Rising journey is full of these kinds of decisions. One client of mine from years ago was in the odd position of enjoying a huge annual salary in a corporate position she loathed and wanting to give everything up to work for an overseas charity. Your journey is about being an accountant or stockbroker, on a symbolic level. You will be doing a lot of adding up or subtracting, but what you are dealing with is not shares in an oil company, but shares in your own life. Only you can decide which shares are worth what!

EYES AND EARS

The sensual world is going to be very important on your journey. I have called this section 'Eyes and ears' because your sense of visual and musical appreciation is so important to your enjoyment of the path ahead. Many of you seem to be born to an artistic, creative or musical life, and it doesn't seem to matter what your day job is. Others are fortunate enough to follow their 'sensual world' on a professional level.

With Taurus Rising, you have a strong feeling for design, form, line, colour and shape. And this applies as much to your own wardrobe as it does to the world outside you, or the objects in your house. Music, too, is strongly associated with this Rising sign. You may identify your life as one big soundtrack — in fact, songs will jog memories, and songs or soundtracks will create the hour and set the time. The records, tapes or CDs in your collection are real reflectors of your life, led over a period of time. Because sensuality, and the aesthetic, are so vital to you, you may find that nature has kindly given you an attractive exterior, or the skills and time to develop one! Astrologers throughout the years have come to associate Taurus Rising with a good-looking, or easy-on-the-eye appeal. For you, appearances do matter.

YOUR OWN PACE

You prefer to go out into the world rather slowly, in your own time, with the calm and steady movements that this Rising sign is famous for. You just won't be pushed!

For more information and a stronger Taurean 'feel' you may want to scan the chapter on Planets in Taurus (*see* pages 20–32). Some of the words, images and symbols listed at the end of the section may turn up in your life's journey in synchronous ways. It is also common for Taurus Rising women to encounter Taurean types along the way. These people are usually guide figures, who have specific lessons to teach you about the right way to do the Taurean thing, and the wrong way!

gemini RISING

If you were born when the sign of Gemini was on the ascendant you will spend your life in the world of words, before anything else .Your enjoyment of good books and good conversation will be a big part of the journey. You'll be on the move a lot, too, and will become one of life's jugglers. Your Sun, Moon, Mercury, Venus and Mars signs will describe the resources you have to deal with this kind of life journey.

WITTY AND VERBAL

The pen is mightier than the sword. Wit is a weapon. Because life will often be tough, you develop a sharp, amusing response to it. It's more than a way of seeing the world, it's also a particular talent for expressing your view of it. The typical Gemini Rising woman is witty, an entertaining correspondent or phone companion and full of quotable quotes. The writer Virginia Woolf had Gemini Rising. This sign can be sarcastic and acidic, too. If anybody underestimates your intelligence, they are likely to find themselves on the receiving end of another quotable quote from you. Virginia Woolf was known for her novels and literary criticism and for being co-founder and co-publisher of the Hogarth Press, but it is her gossipy diaries, letters and journals which stand out today.

THE LIFE OF THE MIND

Educating yourself, or being formally educated, becomes very important with this life journey. You were born at a time when Gemini, the sign of all mental activity, stamped itself quite clearly on your path ahead. You will find that your early school days are a big make-or-break period in your life. They matter for everyone, of course, but because the life of the mind is so important to Gemini Rising, teachers and the education process will become pivotal in terms of the rest of your life.

Some Geminian women develop minds like filing cabinets, and this may occur because of the profession you find yourself in, or because of a particular sense of vocation, or calling. Because people will often be seeking the facts from you, you will go to some lengths to make sure you are well-informed. Because you discover, when young, how good it feels to know the answer, you will get into the habit of always needing to know. Anyway, information and loose news always seems to follow you around. It can operate on any level, too, as gossip or hard news. A mine of information, or a formal piece of instruction. Your life's journey will strongly involve the life of the mind, which is one reason why astrologers often associate this path with care of the mind, too. Like any other part of you, it needs to be nurtured. The mental processes with Gemini Rising are always emphasised: anything from memory, to peace of mind, to concentration. On the outside, you may have that rather quick, lively aura that comes with this sign. On the inside, an astrologer can only have three words to say to you: brain, brain, brain.

SIBLING FIGURES OR TWINS

You will pick up a big sibling or 'twin' issue with this Rising sign. Gemini is the sign of the twins, and if you had this sign rising at the moment you were born, destiny says a brother or sister will be a Very Big Deal. Some of you find a cousin takes on that role, too. Or you acquire a 'brother' or 'sister' figure in your life who seems to perform the twin function. In the original myths surrounding Gemini, there is rivalry between the twins, but also a special bond. Virginia Woolf's relationship with her sister, Vanessa Bell, was crucial to her. Michael Jackson has this Rising sign, too (I'm sorry, but someone had to tell you). His relationship with all of his brothers and sisters in turn has been colourful, complex and occasionally creative. For some of you with this Rising sign, the big issue may have been the brother or sister you didn't get. But in the end, you find a twin figure anyway — a substitute sibling, who presents you with all the issues of competition, attachment and complexity that go with the territory. For more information on the myth of Castor and Pollux, by the way, you may want to read the chapter on Planets in Gemini (*see* pages 33 and 36).

HAVE SHOES, WILL TRAVEL

Your journey is going to be full of short hops, regular zipping around the local scene, and plenty of changes of pace. Gemini is associated with the connection of individuals, ideas and places. This is the country–city Rising sign, but also the Sydney–Melbourne and the London–Dover and the New York–Los Angeles. Destiny says you will often be put on the move, without even trying. But there will also be times when you realise that there is nothing worse than feeling tied down or rotting in a rut. Consequently, you deliberately seek out a lifestyle where you are always moving around. It really is a case of 'Have shoes, will travel' with Gemini Rising, but planes, trains and automobiles are as strongly connected to your journey as anything else. A mobile phone wouldn't go astray either.

For more information and a stronger Geminian 'feel' you may want to scan the chapter on Planets in Gemini (*see* page 33). Some of the words, images and symbols listed at the end of the section may turn up in your life's journey in synchronous ways. It is also common for Gemini Rising women to encounter Geminian types along the way. These people are usually guide figures, who have specific lessons to teach you about the right way to do the Geminian thing, and the wrong way!

cancer RISING

How did you learn to be so protective? Probably by having a series of lame ducks, needy people and lost sheep wandering across your path. The Cancer Rising journey is a little like this. It is, however, also about becoming a great cook and moving an awful lot of furniture around.

CREATING A HOME

At various times in your life, you will be living in spaces which just yelp for a decorator, a renovator or an interior designer. That person is going to be you. The Cancer Rising journey is about turning houses and flats into homes.

Some of you may become involved with property, housing, environment or accommodation issues along the way. Others will be content to take the Cancerian journey by hanging around hardware stores and guiding removal trucks into the driveway.

A SENSE OF PLACE

Your Cancer Rising journey also involves finding a sense of place on a national level — culturally or geographically — and working out what it means to be patriotic, or identified with your country of choice. The word *homeland* strongly applies to the Cancer Rising life path. You may occasionally feel as if you are playing hostess to all of life's travellers, wanderers and tourists. Life will hand you several chances to define your own sense of home and country to yourself and welcoming others — comparing notes on a variety of homelands — is one way of achieving this. The Cancer Rising journey always seems to include several dramatic homecomings, too. By travelling away, you better understand what it is to be *home*.

The Cancer Rising journey also involves a lot of feeding. The Moon, your ruler, is associated with food, and this may have a special meaning on many different levels for you. On a more basic note, your life will involve more stirring, serving and washing up than most. The feeding that you do will also be emotional. Because you will be intimately involved with the kind of lame ducks and lost sheep mentioned at the beginning, you will develop a shoulder to lean on, a supportive listening style, the strong arms of a nurse, and the good timing of a natural cook.

THE MATERNAL ROLE

Playing Mother, or being Mother, is natural on a Cancer Rising journey. The 'feeding' theme may be quite literal, too. Not every woman with Cancer Rising finds herself on the path to motherhood, but you are there to nourish people — and even the occasional animal — as part of the journey. Because nobody else cares, you will have to. Because people are hungry, you will have to provide. Because waifs and strays need adopting, destiny asks you to do it. Somehow, the Cancer Rising journey always seems to ask for a combination of psychologist, cook, cleaner and nurse from you. If you do have a child, it will probably be the biggest journey of your life. If you do not, you will gather other kinds of dependents and 'offspring' around you.

FAMILY AND CLAN

Dynasties are important in the Cancer Rising journey. For one reason or another, family members will exercise a great deal of influence over what you do with your life, and the choices you make. Your relationship with your mother, and all other 'mother' figures within the clan will be particularly vital, and could have a lot to say about the various turning points you reach in childhood, adolescence and adulthood.

The link with the Mother comes from the planet which rules Cancer, the Moon. The Moon is also connected with the female menstrual cycle and female fertility, reproduction and mothering. You can read more on these themes in the Planets in Cancer chapter (*see* page 47). Suffice to say, your life path will have quite a lot to do with your own perception of motherhood.

MONEY AND POSSESSIONS

A great deal of astrology really does come from primitive roots. The ancient, tribal association of Cancer with families usually involved some mention of money and possessions. Dowries and family jewels, inheritance and family domains, houses and ownership, dynasty 'sharing' and the passing on of property. Your journey in life will ask you to preserve what has been passed on to you by others, no matter how small, and also to 'build' for your own future, so that whichever clan you have chosen to surround you can also benefit. Because something must be secured and kept safe, you learn to be careful with the resources you have. Because Cancer is interested in providing, you learn to stockpile provisions. This is a shrewd, economical and far-sighted journey you have chosen. Let's hope your Sun, Moon, Mercury, Venus and Mars signs aren't too extravagant, or the journey will always seem like a struggle for you!

For more information and a stronger Cancerian 'feel' you may want to scan the chapter on Planets in Cancer (*see* page 47). Some of the words, images and symbols listed at the end of the section may turn up in your life's journey in synchronous ways. It is also common for Cancer Rising women to encounter Cancerian types along the way. These people are usually guide figures, who have specific lessons to teach you about the right way to do the Cancerian thing, and the wrong way!

leo

Destiny says that Leo Rising women have a journey that puts them on display a lot of the time. Your Sun, Moon, Mercury, Venus and Mars signs will explain how comfortable you feel about that! This is what the Leo Rising journey involves:

WINNING RESPECT

Life can be pretty low, and people can be pretty undignified, and this will often strike you as you live your life. Dealing with the distasteful people or situations in life in a gracious way will be part of your journey. You can expect to encounter several challenges, either in your career, or in your personal life, where you must exhibit grace under pressure. The situation may be disguised in different ways each time, but the issue is the same: human nature can be low — keep your standards high. Your Leo Rising journey is designed to teach you that you can win respect, recognition and appreciation by holding your head high. Also, perhaps, keeping a stiff upper lip. Spinal complaints are associated with a Leo Rising journey, and I think it may be because women born to this life path strain so much to keep this posture, and maintain their grace. There will be a few times when you lower yourself to the level of other people, or dip your standards, and you will feel that you have paid a very high price for doing so. Perhaps because of this, the Leo Rising journey is ultimately about handling life in an elegant and graceful way after the occasional mistake. In this way, you win permanent respect.

ENCOURAGING OTHERS

From school to career, the Leo Rising journey is about encouraging others. Because you will be confronted by people who seem to be looking to you for advice, or silently hoping for an example, you will have to respond properly. You will also meet this difficult situation once or twice: someone who you honestly tried to guide or encourage withdraws, leaving you with the impression that you have been 'too much' or too dominating. Destiny says that many of the people who wander in and out of your professional or personal life will be less ambitious than you, followers rather than leaders, and perhaps less capable or motivated than you. The Leo Rising journey is about recognising that you must take command because nobody else can, will or is able to. However, it has to be done in a way that also uplifts and encourages other people. You will also find this phenomenon: you will have quite a few guides. These people will convince you that you are right to be ambitious, that your enthusiasm and spirit of enterprise is a wonderful thing, and that you have what it takes to become a guide or leader figure for others. This is definitely one of the enjoyable parts of the Leo Rising journey.

SELF-EXPRESSION

Because others will ask to be entertained or diverted, you will find you have to oblige. The Leo Rising journey is very much about self-expression, and it arises partly because you have no choice to accept that there is a crowd, or an audience, out there — and partly because of this phenomenon: the blank canvas. This may be a blank canvas quite literally, and you may dabble in painting or make it your life's pursuit. The 'blank' can also be found on a sheet of paper, a film negative, an empty stage or in a deserted sports arena.

Several times in your life, you will get this message very strongly: people are looking for drama, style and diversion. Awkward experiences where you *know* you have turned in a less than fabulous performance will occur repeatedly until you do the proper Leonine thing and decide that you can dramatise the ordinary and elevate the mundane. This is partly what you are here for. The way in which you do this will be described by your Sun, Moon, Mercury, Venus or Mars signs. These planets may point to particular talents or abilities, and it is up to destiny to provide the setting for them — which it often will. This 'chance' side of the Leo Rising journey may feel rather like a series of signposts. It 'just happens' that fate will repeatedly hand you opportunities and chances to express yourself.

DEVELOPING LOYALTY

Your loyalty to some of the most important people in your life will be seriously tested with Leo Rising. Destiny has a way of putting obstacles in your path. You may be betrayed. You may be tempted to change sides. You may have *unbelievably* good reasons for deserting people, or turning against them.

Whenever you do this, Fate steps in, and things may go wrong. In this way, perhaps, you learn a fierce loyalty, both to people in your life, and perhaps institutions and ideals. Sometimes you are not even given the option of desertion. For a number of reasons, you simply have to hang in there, stand by people, stick to what you have and remain unmoved in the face of difficult circumstances. The other hallmark of a Leo Rising journey is the occasional attacks or criticisms that are made: people or things that you are very much a part of become held up for condemnation or scrutiny. In this way, too, you learn to develop a fierce kind of loyalty — one of the most admirable things about your life journey is your refusal to desert or bolt.

For more information and a stronger Leonine 'feel' you may want to scan the chapter on Planets in Leo (*see* page 61). Some of the words, images and symbols listed at the end of the section may turn up in your life's journey in synchronous ways. It is also common for Leo Rising women to encounter Leonine types along the way. These people are usually guide figures, who have specific lessons to teach you about the right way to do the Leonine thing, and the wrong way!

virgo RISING

If you were born with Virgo Rising, then your journey will be about working hard, using your brain, communicating and being healthy. Virgo rules House Six of the horoscope, which is where bodies are perfected, healed and repaired, and work gets done. Your Sun, Moon, Mercury, Venus and Mars signs will describe the resources you have to deal with this kind of life journey.

ATTENTION TO DETAIL

As a great deal of your journey will be spent locked in your own head, you may decide to get things right from day one, and become a natural researcher or analyst. Because you will often need to get things absolutely right in your working life, you will find that life asks you to apply your mind as often as possible. In this way, you develop an orderly thinking style. Lists will probably be a big part of your life, too. The kind of career you end up choosing — or having chosen for you — will demand an early start, or a late finish. An enormous amount of detailed work will be involved, and you may also find that your quest for perfection keeps you there much longer, perhaps, than others are prepared to tolerate.

There is a difference between approaching life in an intellectual, cerebral way and merely ending up in brain-knots. One of your challenges along the way will be feeling your way through life a little more instinctively. Otherwise, you can end up rationalising and sorting everything so much that your peace of mind, or concentration skills, are affected.

BROTHERS AND SISTERS

Because Mercury is the ruler of Virgo, this god (and symbol) has a huge say over your journey. The myth explains that Mercury stole from his brother, Apollo, but then charmed his way back into his affections again. If you have a brother or sister in your life, there may be some tough issues here, as well as an unusually special bond. There are two famous Virgo Rising women in the files of most astrologers: Madonna, who has had a strong, if complex, relationship with her brother all her life, and Abigail van Buren, the advice columnist. Her twin, Ann Landers, became her partner in gossip columns and they even married in a double ceremony. If you have Virgo Rising and destiny passed on a brother or sister for you, you may develop a complex, platonic relationship with a man over the course of your life (literally like a brother) or a 'sisterly' bond with another woman.

BODY-CONSCIOUSNESS

Having mentioned Madonna as an example of Virgo Rising, the idea of body-consciousness begins to make a lot more sense. Things seem to work in two directions here: either you have an uncanny ability to understand skin, bone, iron count and muscle resistance from the start, or you end up dragging your body into such unhealthy territory that you have to virtually become your own doctor or dietitian. It's an interesting mixture with Virgo Rising. Some of you even end up in the caring or health professions as a result of it. While an astrologer can accurately say that body-consciousness will be a big part of your life, it is not always on the terms you might imagine!

Destiny says you will be put in touch with your body by whatever means possible. This may happen because you enter a career, or an interest area, where bodies are the centre of all known existence. It may also happen when you survive time out in hospital, or at home: the repair and restoration process has something to say about how you will regard your body in future. Ultimately, you will go out into the world looking for a kind of purity — in your diet, in the air, in the sea, in your blood — that you feel is essential for you. The natural world, and the natural equilibrium of the body, will become important to you for this reason.

ORDER AND ORGANISATION

Because the other link with Virgo is Ceres, the goddess of order and organisation, your journey will also be about sifting, sorting and finding purity in the middle of chaos. Because you will often be thrown random piles of madness in your life (or so it will seem to you, anyway) you will have to learn how to create order. Because you find your irritation or anxiety levels will increase with these kinds of sloppy or slippery situations, you may develop standby methods and tricks to help you cope. The result is an existence that could easily end up becoming a masterpiece of ruthless organisation, if you give in to yourself.

LOOKING FOR PERFECTION

In your teens and twenties, there will be quite a few episodes where you feel you have personally fallen down, or others have missed the mark. These stick in your consciousness more strongly than others might expect, and may be a turning point in the way you manage your life and times after that. Your Virgo-influenced journey is really about looking for the ultimate, for the best, for the most precise and orderly result. In a way, you're on the path of the perfectionist.

For more information and a stronger Virgoan 'feel' you may want to scan the chapter on Planets in Virgo (*see* page 75). Some of the words, images and symbols listed at the end of the section may turn up in your life's journey in synchronous ways. It is also common for Virgo Rising women to encounter Virgoan types along the way. These people are usually guide figures, who have specific lessons to teach you about the right way to do the Virgoan thing, and the wrong way!

libra RISING

If you were born when the sign of Libra was on the ascendant, having a husband, soulmate or business partner (or maybe all three) will be a big part of your journey. Your taste, and sense of aesthetics, will also be important. Your Sun, Moon, Mercury, Venus and Mars signs will describe the ways in which you will make the most of this kind of life journey, but here's what's in store:

BALANCING PARTNERSHIPS

I don't know if you've ever heard the music written for *Romeo and Juliet*, but it was the work of a Libra Rising composer, Sergei Prokofiev (who had a Libra Moon, too, so he was especially romantic). With this Rising sign, you're always looking for the harmony between people. In your own life, you can expect a cradle-to-grave quest for your missing half, or opposite number. Prokofiev's other great composition was based on *War and Peace*, which also pinpoints what lies ahead. Because you will often be put in situations where balance, peace or harmony is threatened, you will learn some remarkable diplomacy skills. Because it's the threat of discord that affects you most strongly, you learn to take the soft handle with people — especially that person you consider to be your mate.

Libra Rising is something of a destiny pointer, as it will throw you certain people who naturally end up on the other end of the see-saw with you. Many women with this Rising sign spend their life in units, doubles and couples. For more information on this tendency to double up, you may want to scan the section on Planets in Libra. If you also have the Sun, Moon, Mercury, Venus or Mars in this sign, then one particular marriage, relationship or balancing act will be the big defining statement of your life. The dance teacher Kathryn Murray had this Rising sign. She was married to her husband, Arthur, for 35 years, and was also his partner in the American Murray Dance Studios — that is just one example of a Libra Rising journey.

RELATING SKILLS

Because you go out into the world wanting people to accompany you, and travel with you, it's crucial that you have some handbook of relating skills. The etiquette expert Emily Post had Libra Rising. But you may not have a notebook at all — just a mental list of what passes for gentleness and charm in this world of car alarms and single-digit gestures. Libra Rising women I have known are natural Public Relations experts. With this sign Rising, you know how to establish social harmony, and how to smooth things over between people. There will be some definite low points which precede this process. Ugly atmospheres, violent feelings or cloddish, philistine behaviour affect you most. So, when you see any of these around you, you never forget them, and develop an extraordinary tact, charm and calm as a result. Because you cannot tolerate those snarling or snappy silences between people, you learn how to soften things up.

You may find that it is your job which is the focus point of these Libra Rising experiences, or your family, friendships or personal life. It's rather like discovering that you're a swan in a pond of angry ducks. But as you move through life with more experience, you will find yourself swimming away from the baser kinds of human experience, and happily gliding through beautiful surroundings, in the best kind of company. It's peace you crave, above all other things Alfred Nobel, who left $9 million to fund, among other things, the Nobel Peace Prize, had Libra Rising. Your ideal is harmony and understanding. And there is just one thing that will get in the way of that. Ready?

DEALING WITH INJUSTICES

The Libra Rising journey involves righting wrongs. Destiny says you'll see some blatantly unfair things in your life, and perhaps the occasional serious miscarriage of justice. Because of this, you develop a passion for balancing the scales, and the only time you will break your famous rule of 'smoothing, smiling and nodding' is when you realise you have to declare war to get peace. It rankles when you believe that you or others have been unfairly accused. Or if one group, or species, is suffering at the hands of another's prejudice and bias. The Libra Rising journey dictates this fact: you will encounter conflict or injustice along the way. Striving for a more civilised, or fairer state of affairs, will be a real mission for you. To get there, you will use your Sun, Moon, Mercury, Venus or Mars sign, and often with amazing results. Alfred Nobel made his millions partly by inventing dynamite. He never got over the guilt — creating the Nobel Peace Prize for humanity was his way of taking the journey.

SOUND AND VISION

Along with the other Venus-ruled Rising sign, Taurus, you are more affected by aesthetics and music than anything else. Your feeling for colours, textures, sounds and forms, will be an integral part of what you do with your life. There are art collectors with this Rising sign, but also musicians, and women who are passionate about music. You may find your career sidetracks you into all that is easy on the eye or ear, or it may be your life outside work which provides the backdrop. Beauty counts!

For more information and a stronger Libran 'feel' you may want to scan the chapter on Planets in Libra in the first section of the book (*see* page 89). Some of the words, images and symbols listed at the end of the section may turn up in your life's journey in synchronous ways. It is also common for Libra Rising women to encounter Libran types along the way. These people are usually guide figures, who have specific lessons to teach you about the right way to do the Libran thing, and the wrong way!

scorpio RISING

Fate says that part of your journey is going to be quite intense. Scorpio is closely tied to the story of the phoenix, which rose from its own ashes. Surviving crises, and becoming a new woman as a result of them, is part of your life story, too. Inevitably, the complicated world of sexuality and erotic feeling is also part of your journey.

HUMAN SEXUALITY

Scorpionic sexuality tends to be taboo, for one reason or another. Because what is taboo in our society is pretty much decided by the Church and the State, it would not be surprising if you encountered lessons and learning experiences related to these areas: gay men, gay women, adultery, nudity, sexual assault, group sex, erotica, pornography, prostitution — or any of the aspects of life which polite society would prefer to censor or ignore. Obviously, some aspects of human sexuality and desire will be more palatable for you than others. Your Scorpio Rising journey will tend to involve you quite intensely in your own physical wants and needs. You may also find that you become an experienced expert on the drives and desires of other people, which often seem to fall into a file labelled 'Off Limits' as far as the rest of the world is concerned.

KEEPING SECRETS

Your path is also about keeping secrets. The original Pluto myth, linked to Scorpio, was about dark places and the world of night. There isn't a lot of space for light in many corners of a Scorpio Rising life — the stakes are often just too high. Because you will be confronted with the most sensitive and delicate issues, you will learn how to keep confidences. Because you will be dealing with taboo subjects or hidden areas of life, you will find that it is necessary to be inscrutable. Sometimes women with this Rising sign find so many repeated secrets and confidences occur that they develop the classic 'inscrutable' Scorpio Rising expression. Put dark glasses on it and you're absolutely impenetrable!

RISING FROM THE ASHES

The Scorpio Rising journey is inevitably associated with death, and some women who have this life path may have to deal with the reality of the death of someone close or they may themselves survive a brush with death or a life-threatening illness. The deeper meaning of the Scorpio Rising journey, though, is actually death and resurrection.

The kind of crises you encounter are transformative by nature. Scorpio Rising women will commonly describe life-changing events as times of real pain and darkness, but something quite extraordinary happens after the long trawl through the depths: they become new versions of their old selves. I think the Scorpio Rising journey is about *survival*, above all other things. The survival of the spirit after a literal or symbolic death experience is something you may end up appreciating in quite an intense way. For your own part, this tendency to 'die' and be reborn may result in quite a lot of physical changes in your lifetime. Scorpio Rising women honour and recognise the times they rise from the ashes by changing their bodies, faces, clothes or hair.

One thing you may prefer to avoid altogether is the low-level expression of Scorpio: self-destructive choices, which precede periodic 'cleansing' for you. Your fantastic ability to remake and regenerate yourself is not really served by any artificial crisis–cleanse–heal process. Keep an eye on any tendencies to self-sabotage. You rise from the ashes every time, but there is no reason for you to build the fire that has to take you down!

A WOMAN OF PASSION

Your life journey is associated with incredible passions and desires — not always physical, often professional or vocational. Astrologers associate Scorpio with passion because Pluto, your ruler, was always a slave to desire. Apart from the obvious working-out of the sign — the incredible romantic obsessions and longings — you also have the capacity for *total involvement* in your goals. Because you cannot deliver half-measures, you have to give everything. 'Better than sex' is how one Scorpio Rising woman described her obsession with her business to me. Your journey will throw you into situations, time and time again, where you know your success or failure depends on complete dedication.

The fates will send you a memo that says, 'This goal requires everything you have. If you cannot take it with you to breakfast, lunch, dinner and bed — don't bother.' Not surprisingly, Scorpio Rising women end up doing amazing things with their lives because of this quality. You will need to fine-tune your life, though. You are vulnerable to fanaticism. You can also punish yourself for not trying hard enough. Somewhere in between manic obsession and scratching the surface, you will find just the right amount of intensity. That is what destiny will ask you to give to your life. No wonder the Scorpio Rising journey so frequently shows you what real influence and power is.

For more information and a stronger Scorpionic 'feel' you may want to scan the chapter on Planets in Scorpio (*see* page 102). Some of the words, images and symbols listed at the end of the section may turn up in your life's journey in synchronous ways. It is also common for Scorpio Rising women to encounter Scorpionic types along the way. These people are usually guide figures, who have specific lessons to teach you about the right way to do the Scorpionic thing, and the wrong way!

sagittarius  RISING

If you were born when the sign of Sagittarius was rising (or on the ascendant) then your life journey will involve an awful lot of space and freedom. There will be plenty of journeys within the journey, too, as Sagittarius Rising points to travel. Your Sun, Moon, Mercury, Venus and Mars signs will describe the ways in which you will make the most of these experiences.

AWFULLY BIG ADVENTURES

You go out into the world wanting to take more of it in — it's as simple as that. So you wander as far as you can, save up for overseas treks or find a career which takes in all of the world, not just the end of the street. Destiny may intervene and send you off on cross-cultural adventures anyway. Some of you end up near the Taj Mahal, others disappear in the depths of Darwin. A Sagittarius Rising sign is a passport to other passports, though, and well worth taking advantage of. It describes a life journey where space and freedom are the most basic guides, and although the times when you are tied down can seem unbearable, it is these experiences which will teach you the most.

Because life will often throw you in a box, you will spend a great deal of your time trying to get out of it. Not only physically, or geographically, but also mentally. This Rising sign describes broad horizons for the brain, as well as the suitcase in your hand. For every piece of domestic restraint or boring deadlock, there will be a time when you vow never to put up with it again.

Destiny says you'll sometimes be stuck with detail freaks and clingers and controllers. From them, you learn how not to behave. However, you also develop a better sense of your own need for exploration and adventure. Being around narrow-minded or shut-in people reminds you that there is an urgent need for you to look further afield. Somewhere out there, or up there, is your answer, even though it may take a lifetime of exploration to find it.

GIVING TIME AND ENERGY

Princess Diana had this Rising sign. Her journey was about other countries, but also about giving time and energy. Sagittarius Rising women find themselves surrounded by people who have very high hopes, or very big needs, of them. The fates will conspire to throw you into situations where everybody is hanging on a promise from you. Because you are sensitive to the fact that nobody else is going to be the provider, you end up generously supplying what is required.

Because you will also be thrown into situations where people are looking for a cheerleader, or hoping for a pep talk, you will find that you develop a kind of enthusiasm, good humour and optimism that acts as a protective coating. You find yourself playing the role of a warm-up person, a coach or an enthusiastic supporter. One of the most important points in your journey will be this one: you find yourself going over the top, promising things that you cannot possibly deliver, or applying too much of yourself to a situation that, frankly, didn't need it.

From here, you learn to fine-tune your ability to take over, or lead the way. You also learn to be more discriminating about the people who are destined to benefit from your wide smile, endless supply of jokes and lust for life. Some people, by the time you hit your forties or fifties, will consider that you were born lucky. This may, or may not, strike a chord with you. But if Sagittarius Rising women seem to have bigger breaks than the rest of humanity, it probably has something to do with the payback principle. From an early age, you do people favours, put in time and energy, and learn how to give. Some ancient natural law decrees that you will be repaid in kind in your lifetime, so you walk happily into breaks, lucky escapes or amazing chances.

A SENSE OF MEANING

Finding something, or someone, to believe in, will be a key part of your journey. Jupiter, the ruler of Sagittarius, was connected to ancient laws — not only legal, in the strict sense, but moral and ethical. Bordering on religious or political, too, in some cases. Because you will be turned off by some of the superficial or pointless theories and beliefs you hear along the way, you will become fascinated by what is really meaningful in this life. And because you will find yourself in occasionally chaotic situations with no rhyme or reason to them, you will develop a sound ideological, spiritual or intellectual framework in which to explain things to yourself — or others.

An awful lot will depend on your judgement in this lifetime. Consequently, you will become aware, on more than one occasion, that you must develop some kind of moral or ethical code which is far-sighted and all-encompassing. It's important to you to know where the black, white and grey exists in this world — and perhaps beyond it. Certainly, you are more interested in a framework of meaning, or belief, which applies to the planet as a whole. You like to take the long view.

For more information and a stronger Sagittarian 'feel' you may want to scan the chapter on Planets in Sagittarius (*see* page 117). Some of the words, images and symbols listed at the end of the section may turn up in your life's journey in synchronous ways. It is also common for Sagittarius Rising women to encounter Sagittarian types along the way. These people are usually guide figures, who have specific lessons to teach you about the right way to do the Sagittarian thing, and the wrong way!

capricorn  RISING

If you were born when the sign of Capricorn was rising (or on the ascendant) then your life journey involves a quest for solid foundations. Faced with disorder, you will have to create order. Soaring ambition, and a sense of responsibility, are things you will develop in your career or vocation. Your Sun, Moon, Mercury, Venus and Mars signs will describe the ways in which you will make the most of all these experiences.

STRUCTURING YOUR WORLD

Because there will be times when you feel unable to help, or do very much, you will learn from the experience and develop a sense of structure which grounds you. Destiny says the biggest turning points will be the times that you take over the reins. Once you know where you're going and what you should be doing, it all becomes much more manageable.

The times that you overstep the mark and float off into territory that you are convinced does not belong to you, are just as important. This applies as much on a personal level as it does on an academic or professional one. You quickly discover that you need rules, or traditions: a prescribed way of doing things. From here, you can structure your world, and pursue the ambitions which appear — and they usually do so quite rapidly with Capricorn Rising women.

You need to know where you stand, and you need to know what has worked before, so you can repeat the process and actually end up getting somewhere. Because the memories of floundering in risky or experimental disasters seem so difficult by the age of 35, you may spend a great deal of your time after that trying to nail everything down where you can deal with it. The Capricorn Rising journey is about establishing and securing — not really about leaping off into the dark.

The signs of your personal planets — the Sun, Moon, Mercury, Venus and Mars — will describe what you have to give to this process, and what you will be drawn towards. Fate, however, will always steer you in the same direction — towards ambitions which are high, yet achievable, and towards a professional or personal challenge which cries out for organisation.

PAST INFLUENCES PRESENT

The times that you risk your energy and time on untried, or unproven, areas can be quite difficult for you. It is when you see the beauty or order in the established or traditional, though, that you finally feel at home. In some parts of the world, you can still hear the old-fashioned phrase, 'If it ain't broke, don't fix it'. This strongly applies to your life. Your journey will be about settling into established and proven ways of living or working, and if that makes you a traditionalist in some respects, then you won't have a problem with it. From the past comes a foundation you can build on for the future. That will become increasingly clear to you as your life goes on. There is a kind of safety, and wealth of common sense, in following what has gone before, and worked before.

THE WAITING GAME

Destiny also says that you will be asked to find reserves of patience, often at the really crucial points of your life, because so much of what you encounter will ask for a steady, thorough kind of understanding. The waiting games will repeat throughout your life and times, and the word *time* itself may have a special meaning for you. The idea of age, and experience, is something else that seems to resonate with Capricorn Rising women. Something about your life will repeatedly tell you to slow down, think, hesitate and, above all, wait. Waiting games are sometimes the real cornerstones of a Capricornian woman's life and times, but this may not make complete sense to you until you have counted a few decades of your life in.

PRACTICAL AND MATERIAL

Your journey will involve you in key questions about who fits in where and how the hierarchy is hanging together. This applies in your career, but also perhaps, in your personal life, too. You cannot avoid being practical about these matters, because the fates say you will be put on an intensely practical path. Seeing life as it really is — and it is not always a film by Walt Disney — you learn how to work out where you stand in the scheme of things, how to move up and how to maintain position.

Materially, too, your Rising sign has a lot to say about the issues you will face. When you are faced with financial lows and crises, you will develop amazing abilities to use what you have, and make more of the resources that are around you. When you have financial highs, you will still find shrewd ways of handling the options. A certain amount of anxiety always seems to accompany the really serious financial, assets or property questions for Capricorn Rising. Destiny says you'll become astute as a result.

For more information and a stronger Capricornian 'feel' you may want to scan the chapter on Planets in Capricorn (*see* page 132). Some of the words, images and symbols listed at the end of the section may turn up in your life's journey in synchronous ways. It is also common for Capricorn Rising women to encounter Capricornian types along the way. These people are usually guide figures, who have specific lessons to teach you about the right way to do the Capricornian thing, and the wrong way!

aquarius

If you were born when the sign of Aquarius was rising (or on the ascendant) then your life journey will involve both your friends and fellow travellers, but also your own solo space. Playing the rebel will involve you part of the way, too, and it goes without saying that your life will be an utterly original expression of yourself. Your Sun, Moon, Mercury, Venus and Mars signs will describe the ways in which you will make the most of all these experiences.

FITTING IN WITH FRIENDS

Finding the right company will be an interesting exercise. It's the times you spend alone — or lonely — that you remember best. But at the same time, because you will encounter a few people who are too ordinary for you (or too fond of imitating a code, or a norm) you will need to choose very carefully. You will also find yourself surrounded by literally hordes of congenial people along the way — which means you must find a way to touch base and remain friends with everyone, without seeming too cool with each of them.

You will be handed some amazing company by the fates, and there will be platonic friendships with the opposite sex, as well as a sense of real equality and genuine fellowship with the women in your life. Some of the turning points for you will involve the occasions when potential friends, or allies, are too clearly turned off by your ideas or ideals — your originality or your desire for change. This can be an uncomfortable situation for you, because as much as you loathe being left utterly alone, you are still destined to move only in friendships which will allow you to be exactly who you are. You will fine-tune your basic rebelliousness and 'differentness' to accommodate some of these people, yet the irony for you is this: you cannot be a friend to everyone, nor have everyone as a friend, no matter how wonderful this would be. Something inside you will not let yourself compromise or fake it, so certain people will always be beyond your reach.

CHANGE AND REFORM

Faced with too many constraints, or too many (bad) old ideas, you will have almost no option but to pursue changes in your life. Because you will continually be surrounded by the mundane, the everyday and the mass-produced (and this applies to social norms, as well as to what is popular) you will have to kick out. Aquarius Rising women are often associated with unusual taste, or an unusual appearance. This is sometimes the case, though not always. For every one of you who expresses her need for change and new ideas through her hair or clothes, there is one of you who looks like a classic dresser par excellence, but is a closet anarchist or radical. It's an interesting effect of this Rising sign. Some of you are literally born different, though, and this should probably be pointed out. I have known Aquarius Rising women who were born very tall, or rather larger than the norm. Equally, there have been some real beauties among you, and you have felt awkward of different because of that.

For those of you who basically look like everyone else, there is no question of you feeling like everyone else. You tend to react to what is around you in a fairly anti kind of way. The more obsolete or dead on its feet it seems, the more you crave some kind of change. New ways of doing old things and devising a blueprint for tomorrow, are very much part of it. The Aquarius Rising journey always seems to involve you with necessities, so that you are better placed to be the Mother of Invention. Your journey involves reform and change, in all kinds of ways. It can be as exciting for you as it is occasionally alarming to more conservative or cautious souls around you.

THE HUMAN FAMILY

There has to be a better way in human terms, too. Faced with what to you are insurmountable, broad problems — how can we all go on like this? Where is the world going to end up? — you come up with solutions. Some of you follow theories, others will invent them. Germaine Greer, an Aquarius Rising student, came up with Women's Liberation.

Because you will occasionally feel stifled, trapped or unfairly pigeonholed — or have strong, direct experience of others who are in this predicament — you learn to see the big picture. The big turning points in an Aquarius Rising life are those which steer you in the direction of humanitarian ideals. The other, crucial, change is when you see just how much a theory or an idea can lose sight of its original purpose.

You respect the right of others — and this often includes animals — to be as free as you want to feel. Destiny says you'll be locked in a box so many times in your life that it will become natural for you to pursue freedoms. From here comes a life which is essentially democratic.

For further information and a stronger Aquarian 'feel' you may want to scan the chapter on Planets in Aquarius (*see* page 146). Some of the words, images and symbols listed at the end of the section may turn up in your life's journey in synchronous ways. It is also common for Aquarius Rising women to encounter Aquarian types along the way. These people are usually guide figures, who have specific lessons to teach you about the right way to do the Aquarian thing, and the wrong way!

pisces

If you were born when the sign of Pisces was rising (or on the ascendant) then your life journey will involve some wonderful dreams and escapes, as you slip in and out of the real world in a way that only Pisces Rising can. There'll be real compassion for others, too, as destiny says this is a healing journey. Your Sun, Moon, Mercury, Venus and Mars signs will describe the ways in which you will make the most of all these experiences.

DREAMS AND FANTASIES

As your life journey will involve some criticism from others (and the occasional encounter with someone who believes they can define *everything*) it's not surprising that you will find all kinds of dreams, fantasies and escapes to slide into.

You're really entitled to run away from the boring basics and create something more for yourself, for everything that is spiritual, special, elevated and ideal is Piscean territory. Because you can only take so much of other people's reality in this lifetime, you will come up with wonderful ways of escaping by yourself. Some women with this Rising sign become habitual dreamers or daydreamers. Others find fantasy in their reality by pursuing dream jobs, or by aiming straight for weekend escapes.

The big turning points in your life come when you are listening, for the hundredth time, to someone pointing out the bleeding obvious — suddenly, something happens and you are off on a different course entirely, sailing for waters which only mermaids, poets, goddesses and spirits inhabit. You develop imagination in response to an unimaginative world, and destiny says you will have had more than enough of it by your late twenties!

Because life is full of signposts, maps and instructions, you will enjoy getting lost. There are any number of ways to do this. Some Pisces Rising women have followed drink, or strange substances, to leave it all behind. Some of you have dived into the creative or imaginative arts. There is frequently something dreamy, ethereal or hard-to-catch about women with this Rising sign, and I guess it comes from a lifetime of conscious escape. Pisces Rising eyes, in particular, are either slightly unfocussed, full of inner life, or just about ready to close! If the eyes are the windows of the soul, then yours are like a light show.

Born into a family of pig breeders? Become an air hostess and spend your weekends in Morocco. Fed up with people telling you to get a proper job in your teens? Become a modern-day saint and work in an understaffed hospital. One thing is sure — when you meet bores and critics, your instinct is to turn, and turn again.

BLURRED BOUNDARIES

You will occasionally become involved with people, professionally or in your personal life, who don't seem to have any boundaries. Their mental fence, and yours, get built over each other. You'll find yourself feeling and suffering along with them, and thinking of ways to help them. This applies to animals, too, in some cases (your sensitivity to the pain of all living things is increased on this journey).

Sacrifices will be made on the pathway. That is very clear with Pisces Rising types. Giving up or giving in seems to come with the territory. Putting yourself last in the name of kindness is one way to see it, but it may also be a function of those blurred boundaries: it can be so hard to detach yourself from the other, that the other becomes you, and you act in both your interests.

You will reach a crossroads when you see that you have become a martyr to the cause or a needless sacrifice. This will happen only occasionally, but it is an important part of the Pisces Rising journey. Finding the clear definition of your own ego, quite apart from the egos of everyone else involved, will be vital as you go through life. It is the times when reality hits you over the head, and you trade in your doormat, that you will learn the most. You are here to give, and feel for, others — but you will have to choose wisely, and having done that, work out when enough is enough.

WORKING WITH WATER

Water images are very appropriate for Pisces Rising women, and seem to make a lot of sense to those who have this sign. When you feel as if you are drowning, or all at sea, you'll need to find a lighthouse, or a rock. Just remember that it is not the rock or lighthouse doing the saving — it is you, making the choice to lift yourself up, and out, and remembering to breathe afterwards. Diving in is another appropriate metaphor for Pisces Rising. When life looks too dry, just do it. As long as you are diving into something which is clean, clear and still, you can find enormous relief there. Whenever you dream of watery images, remember them: they tend to contain important messages and images for Pisces Rising types. Swim around in them for a while!

For further information and a stronger Piscean 'feel' you may want to scan the chapter on Planets in Pisces (*see* page 161). Some of the words, images and symbols listed at the end of the section may turn up in your life's journey in synchronous ways. It is also common for Pisces Rising women to encounter Piscean types along the way. These people are usually guide figures, who have specific lessons to teach you about the right way to do the Piscean thing, and the wrong way!

TIMING your cycles to 2005

To time your Sun and Jupiter cycles, you will need to work out your Rising sign, using the Tables section. Your Rising sign information will let you know at what time of year you can expect a Sun cycle and in what years you can expect a Jupiter cycle.

If you have your Rising sign calculated by an astrologer, she will do it to the *degree*. This accuracy makes it possible for her to give you an actual start date and finish date for the cycle. The method used in this book is more general than that, but still quite useful. Although it will not pinpoint cycles quite so sharply, you should still get a good general idea of what issues will be important when.

Taking Princess Diana as an example, it's possible to see that as a Sagittarius Rising woman, she always had a Sun Cycle Seven in May–June of any year. Partnership and marriage start to become more important at these times. This makes sense in terms of her life — she married and divorced around her Sun Cycle Seven. However, her personal horoscope, which also shows the *degree* — or specific timing influence — of her Sagittarius Rising sign, actually reveals the end point of the cycle is July, so even though things start moving in May, they are still very much around a month later.

Bear that in mind when you read the Sun cycles (which stay the same every year, so will become familiar to you). After a while, you may even be able to guess the day or week in which any of your Sun cycles begins.

Jupiter cycles will be different for you every year, and a full list of the 1998–2005 cycles is included here. Once again, bear in mind that the time-frame you are given is approximate. For a reasonable slice of the time-frame you are given, you will most definitely experience that particular Jupiter cycle. Remember, though, that it could start early, midway, or even rather late in the years mentioned. If your Rising sign degree is rather early — say, 1 or 2 degrees — then you'll begin your Jupiter cycle earlier. With a 29 or 30 degree Rising sign, you won't start the Jupiter cycle mentioned until towards the very end of the time-span.

If you have a need to know exact start and end points for the days, months and years of each cycle, you will have to consult an astrologer. For further information, look up the chapter headed Ten Questions (*see* page 519).

aries

Sun Cycle One — begins March-April
Sun Cycle Two — begins April-May
Sun Cycle Three — begins May-June
Sun Cycle Four — begins June-July
Sun Cycle Five — begins July-August
Sun Cycle Six — begins August-September
Sun Cycle Seven — begins September-October
Sun Cycle Eight — begins October-November
Sun Cycle Nine — begins November-December
Sun Cycle Ten — begins December-January
Sun Cycle Eleven — begins January-February
Sun Cycle Twelve — begins February-March

1998 The majority of Aries Rising women enter Jupiter Cycle Twelve this year. For most of you, it will begin at any time between February and December, and, once again, the later your Rising sign degree, the later the start. The last batch of you will begin this new cycle in February 1999. For the majority, the story this year is definitely about looking inward.

1999 Jupiter Cycle One starts for most of you this year. You'll feel it at any time after February, with the middle group starting around April, and the later group closer to the second half of the year. The last batch of you will still be experiencing the early stages of the cycle around February 2000!

2000 Jupiter Cycle Two takes place now. For a reasonable chunk of this year, you'll be concerned with money, possessions and values above all other things. By June 2000, absolutely all of you will have begun this new cycle. There is a Saturn Cycle Two going on at the same time, too (an astrologer can explain this), which means the last year of the century really is going to be crucial for your financial position as you go into 2001.

2001 Jupiter Cycle Three will affect most of you this year, so expect expansion in your communications with people — you might get new technology in your life, like answering machines, faxes, mobile phones, pagers or e-mail which lets you do this. You may learn a language, or increase your vocabulary à la *Reader's Digest*! Some of you will be in Cycle Two this year, though — so it looks as if a bit of financial increase or spending power is coming.

2002 Most of you are in Jupiter Cycle Four this year, so go for the mortgage, the home improvements, the family plans or the garden expansion — within reason, the opportunities will be there. A small number of you may also start Jupiter Cycle Five now — you'll know it when your personal or creative life offers more. Finally, there's a small group still going through Cycle Three, so please read the above. (Jupiter's eccentric movements this year are to blame.)

2003 This is going to be a Cycle Five or Cycle Six year, depending on the degree of your Rising Sign. Cycle Five means chances to bring children or babies into your life, open doors on creative projects or hobbies, and a bigger range of sexual options. Cycle Six is all about work and lifestyle improvements, and that includes your health — meaningful advice is around you.

2004 You will either be finishing Jupiter Cycle Six this year, or starting it. This is your chance to fix a long-standing body problem. You'll also get benefits in lifestyle terms, thanks to developments involving your job, your studies or your daily routine. Cycle Six rules small animals, too, and it's amazing how people's pets suddenly jump into the foreground now.

2005 Jupiter Cycle Seven is around you, as this planet goes through the sign of Libra, ruling partnerships and double-acts of all kinds — past, present, future, romantic or strictly business. This is a problem-busting year for you. And if you're single, you'll get the chance to move things right along in your love life. Marriages and divorces are both common in this cycle, as one way or another Jupiter wants you to have a meaningful personal life — and you know what that means!

taurus

Sun Cycle One — begins April-May
Sun Cycle Two — begins May-June
Sun Cycle Three — begins June-July
Sun Cycle Four — begins July-August
Sun Cycle Five — begins August-September
Sun Cycle Six — begins September-October
Sun Cycle Seven — begins October-November
Sun Cycle Eight — begins November-December
Sun Cycle Nine — begins December-January
Sun Cycle Ten — begins January-February
Sun Cycle Eleven — begins February-March
Sun Cycle Twelve — begins March-April

1998 Most Taurus Rising women enter Jupiter Cycle Eleven this year. For the majority, it will begin at any time between February and December, and, once again, the later your Rising sign degree, the later the start. The last of you who are affected will begin this new cycle in February 1999. For most of you, the idea this year is to pursue your social life and friendships.

1999 Jupiter Cycle Twelve starts for almost everyone this year. You'll feel it at any time after February, with the middle group starting around April, and the later group closer to the second half of the year. The last numbers of you trickling through will still be experiencing the early stages of the cycle around February 2000!

2000 Jupiter Cycle One takes place now. For most of this year you'll be surrounded by opportunities that make sense on the most personal level. By June 2000, absolutely all of you will have begun this new cycle. There is a Saturn Cycle One going on at the same time, too, so the last year of the century is vital for forming your self-image as you go into 2001.

2001 Jupiter begins Cycle Two this year, as it zips through the sign of Gemini. Some of you may spend longer in this cycle than others, but it amounts to the same — a new expansion of your value system, chances to make more money, lucky breaks involving earning power, property or possessions, and a bit of problem-solving on the bank account or business level of your life.

2002 One way or another you're going to get a lot — or a little — of Jupiter Cycle Three in 2002. You'll do more with your mind, your written skills, your communication abilities, your office (or home office) set-up, your study (or your studies) and ... a brother, sister or cousin will be woven into some kind of breakthrough or improvement in your life. Short trips are on offer now, too.

2003 Depending on your own chart, you'll either be caught in Jupiter Cycle Four or Five for most of this year. Four means a move of house or flat, a chance to buy, sell or lease, decorate, renovate or ... see family improvements and expansion. Five will be equally obvious. Kids may come into your life, or a child currently with you will represent some kind of opportunity. A brainchild could take off. So could aspects of your romantic or sexual life, so be on the lookout.

2004 Cycle Five and Cycle Six will catch you this year, depending on your time of birth (if you want to really check this out, see your local astrologer). If it's Five, see above — that personal or creative optimism will be quite obvious. If it's Cycle Six that is starting for you, you'll get good health or fitness advice, a chance to eat, sleep or exercise better, and overall improvements in your daily routine. For many of you that will mean your job. Work offers bonuses, perks, lurks and all sorts of possibilities. If you're in Cycle Six you may get promoted or find a new position.

2005 Cycle Six or Cycle Seven begin this year, depending on your own chart. If it's Six, you'll notice the above effects starting. If it's Seven, then any marriage or relationship hassles could be resolved by counselling or agreement. Singles will have a chance to form new love, or revive old love. If it's financial, property or business partnerships you're interested in, that's where you'll see the improvements. A double-act of any kind will be awfully lucky and more than once.

gemini

Sun Cycle One — begins May-June
Sun Cycle Two — begins June-July
Sun Cycle Three — begins July-August
Sun Cycle Four — begins August-September
Sun Cycle Five — begins September-October
Sun Cycle Six — begins October-November
Sun Cycle Seven — begins November-December
Sun Cycle Eight — begins December-January
Sun Cycle Nine — begins January-February
Sun Cycle Ten — begins February-March
Sun Cycle Eleven — begins March-April
Sun Cycle Twelve — begins April-May

1998 Most Gemini Rising women enter Jupiter Cycle Ten this year. For most of you, it will begin at any time between February and December, and, once again, the later your Rising sign degree, the later the start. The last batch of you will begin this new cycle in February 1999. It's a career year for most of you, though.

1999 Jupiter Cycle Eleven starts for most of you this year. You'll feel it at any time after February, with the middle group starting around April, and the later group closer to the second half of the year. The last batch of you will still be experiencing the early stages of the cycle around February 2000!

2000 Jupiter Cycle Twelve takes place now. For most of you, this is the year you start looking inward. By June 2000, absolutely all of you will have begun this new cycle. There is a Saturn Cycle Twelve going on at the same time, too (an astrologer can give you more information on this), which means the last year of the century is an inner sorting-out time as you go into 2001.

2001 Jupiter is in Gemini this year, and at some stage all of you are going to begin Jupiter Cycle One. Makeover time! You'll do more with your image or appearance. You'll be 'out there' a lot more, being seen and being appreciated. It's a good year to work on the inside as well. Do you feel the urge to self-improve? It's not unusual in Cycle One. And there'll be opportunities to do it

2002 At some stage this year you're going to experience Jupiter Cycle Two (some of you have it for a few months, others all year long). Chances to make more of your money, property or possessions are here. A bonus or raise, or better-paid position, is not out of the question. Lucky deals, big bargains — all you have to do is look. But don't overdo it or Jupiter will get you.

2003 Jupiter hops into Leo for all of you sooner or later, thus starting you up in Cycle Three. This has special impact for you, as Jupiter is in an area of your chart which Gemini actually rules. Your love of words, reading, talking, communicating, trading, gossiping, swapping, selling — all forms of Gemini energy, in fact — takes off now. Brothers or sisters may take on an expanded role in your life. If you wish you could see more of your own country, you'll get a chance to do so.

2004 Once again, either for part or all of this year, you have a new Jupiter cycle to yourself. (Depending on your birth time you may even get two Jupiter Cycles in this year.) Let's focus on Jupiter Cycle Four, though. It matters from a family perspective, because this is where big family plans take off, or family wounds get healed. On the home front, it would be no surprise at all if by the end of 2004 you hadn't decorated, renovated, bought, sold, moved or expanded.

2005 Jupiter Cycle Five will once again impact you for quite a large chunk of 2005, or just a month or two — depending on your time of birth. In any case, it's good news. That novel, tapestry, play, painting, sculpture, film or creative cake-decorating course will take off. You may have a child, adopt a child, or find a child seems to 'adopt' you. The sexual world opens up now, too.

cancer

Sun Cycle One — begins June-July
Sun Cycle Two — begins July-August
Sun Cycle Three — begins August-September
Sun Cycle Four — begins September-October
Sun Cycle Five — begins October-November
Sun Cycle Six — begins November-December

Sun Cycle Seven — begins December-January
Sun Cycle Eight — begins January-February
Sun Cycle Nine — begins February-March
Sun Cycle Ten — begins March-April
Sun Cycle Eleven — begins April-May
Sun Cycle Twelve — begins May-June

1998 The majority of Cancer Rising women enter Jupiter Cycle Nine this year. For most of you, it will begin at any time between February and December, and, once again, the later your Rising sign degree, the later the start. The last of you will begin this new cycle in February 1999. For most, this year brings far-flung people or places into focus.

1999 Jupiter Cycle Ten starts for most of you this year. You'll feel it at any time after February, with the middle group starting around April, and the later group closer to the second half of the year. The last batch of you will still be experiencing the early stages of the cycle around February 2000.

2000 Jupiter Cycle Eleven takes place now. For an important part of this year, you'll be concerned with friendships, group involvements and networks. By June 2000, all of you will have begun this new cycle. There is a Saturn Cycle Eleven going on at the same time — as your personal chart will reveal — so the last year of the century really is a sorting out time for your social life.

2001 This begins Jupiter Cycle Twelve, when all good Cancer Rising people should keep a dream diary. Why? Because this cycle is all about the unconscious, and what you dream will hold many golden keys to unlocked doors in your psyche — treasure may be piled up behind. But hey, that's Cycle Twelve for you — spooky, mysterious, symbolic. Your best bet this year is a conscious period of hibernation. Take time out to navel gaze, you won't regret it.

2002 By August at the latest all of you will have started your journey through Jupiter Cycle One. This one is about your personality, self-image, reputation, appearance, body, hair, face, smile ... and name. You'll improve on things, or make more of what you've got — or you could choose not to, but still — Jupiter will throw you the opportunity so why waste it?

2003 Once again, by August at the latest Jupiter will have begun Cycle Two, so financial expansion or more 'stuff' will form part, or all, of your experience in 2003. If money, property or possessions have no place in your life then it's your personal values which will be lucky and prosper. Classically, women get more of what they ask for, or they get better returns than they expected. They earn more, or bargain more fortunately, or experience the odd windfall.

2004 By September all of you will be starting this new Jupiter Three cycle. You'll get it at different parts of 2004, depending on your individual birth time. Neighbours, cousins, brothers, sisters could all bring about improvements in your life, or your relationship with them will improve. Want to increase your vocabulary, see yourself in print, learn to debate or chair meetings, learn a language, or improve your work skills? Luck (and Jupiter) will provide.

2005 Some of you will begin Jupiter Cycle Four as late as October, others will begin much earlier in the year. Watch real estate advertisements, read home and lifestyle magazines, think about what you could be doing in terms of your current lease or mortgage. Jupiter will throw quite a few breaks your way. Want to see some kind of expansion or improvement through the family? Jupiter will provide. A special plan or family development could grow like Topsy.

leo RISING

Sun Cycle One — begins July-August
Sun Cycle Two — begins August-September
Sun Cycle Three — begins September-October
Sun Cycle Four — begins October-November
Sun Cycle Five — begins November-December
Sun Cycle Six — begins December-January
Sun Cycle Seven — begins January-February
Sun Cycle Eight — begins February-March
Sun Cycle Nine — begins March-April
Sun Cycle Ten — begins April-May
Sun Cycle Eleven — begins May-June
Sun Cycle Twelve — begins June-July

1998 The majority of Leo Rising women enter Jupiter Cycle Eight this year. For most of you, it will begin at any time between February and December, and, once again, the later your Rising sign degree, the later the start. The last batch of you will begin this new cycle in February 1999. For the majority, the story this year is definitely about financial expansion.

1999 Jupiter Cycle Nine starts for most of you this year. You'll feel it at any time after February, with the middle group starting around April, and the later group closer to the second half of the year. The last batch of you will still be experiencing the early stages of the cycle around February 2000!

2000 Jupiter Cycle Ten takes place now. For a reasonable chunk of this year, you'll be concerned with ambitions, career and goals above all other things. By June 2000, absolutely all of you will have begun this new cycle. There is a Saturn Cycle Two going on at the same time, too (an astrologer can explain this), which means the last year of the century really is going to be crucial for your ultimate career status as you go into 2001.

2001 You will all begin Jupiter Cycle Eleven this year. A new friend, group involvement or social acquaintance will open up your life and make at least one of your life departments much, much better. You'll make more friends, and may decide to join a club, team, association, committee or other network — it will do more for you than you probably thought possible.

2002 By July at the latest you will have started Jupiter Cycle Twelve. Creeping through watery, private Cancer, Jupiter will do nothing loud or obvious. However, any psychological hang-ups can be cleared up under this influence. Dreams and psychic experiences will have extraordinary and positive results. Time alone is time very well spent, so don't be afraid to drop out for a while

2003 By August Jupiter Cycle One will have begun, and that can only be a good thing for your outer self. Of course, you know it's what matters on the inside that counts ... but hey, who's going to complain if you end up with a heaven-sent haircut, better skin, or just a better self-image? This is a very good year for opportunities linked to image and appearance. If there's something about your outer self in personality terms you think you could improve on, that's possible, too.

2004 By September, Jupiter Cycle Two will have started for everyone with Leo Rising. You may spend all, or part, of this new year seizing all sorts of financial opportunities. Good deals, from the most trivial sales bargains to the biggest investments, are now possible — but for really nail-biting decisions, you might like to see your own personal astrologer for more details.

2005 Some of you will start Jupiter Cycle Three as late as October, while others will be finishing then. But this year, whatever your personal chart story, you will have the opportunity to play the Gemini role — which means messenger girl, with a vengeance. Lots of networking, communicating, writing, talking, listening, learning and zipping around is in store. A good year to consider how you're getting through to people, and how you might improve upon it, too.

virgo RISING

Sun Cycle One — begins August-September
Sun Cycle Two — begins September-October
Sun Cycle Three — begins October-November
Sun Cycle Four — begins November-December
Sun Cycle Five — begins December-January
Sun Cycle Six — begins January-February
Sun Cycle Seven — begins February-March
Sun Cycle Eight — begins March-April
Sun Cycle Nine — begins April-May
Sun Cycle Ten — begins May-June
Sun Cycle Eleven — begins June-July
Sun Cycle Twelve — begins July-August

1998 The majority of Virgo Rising women enter Jupiter Cycle Seven this year. For most, it will begin at any time between February and December, and, once again, the later your Rising sign degree, the later the start. The last batch of you will begin this new cycle in February 1999. For the majority, the story this year is definitely about romantic relationships or work-based partnerships.

1999 Jupiter Cycle Eight starts for most of you this year. You'll feel it after February, with the middle group starting around April and the later group closer to the second half of the year. The last numbers of you affected will still be enjoying the early stages of the cycle around February 2000.

2000 Jupiter Cycle Nine takes place now. You'll be concerned with travel, foreign contacts, relocation or higher education soon. By June 2000, absolutely all of you will have begun this new cycle. There is a Saturn Cycle Two going on, too (an astrologer can explain this), so along with the opportunities will come learning experiences.

2001 Career opportunities, professional growth or study satisfaction are now on offer. By the end of the year, all of you will have begun Jupiter Cycle Ten, and that could bring you anything from a promotion to a new small business, or a new qualification. Jupiter is now at the midheaven (or top) of your horoscope, where it will open doors and provide signposts if you're willing to look.

2002 By August everyone with Virgo Rising will have started Jupiter Cycle Eleven and some of you may be halfway through it, depending on your birth time. The year 2002 is about friendship and social life expansion. It's about joining groups and networks, for fun or for practical reasons. Friends are lucky for you now. An old friend may go through a cycle of amazing opportunities, too.

2003 This year is all about hibernating and retreating. The biggest luck comes from what you do in your own time, or what you see in your own navel. Meditation, dream work, yoga, psychic exploration, therapy, counselling, diary or journal keeping and inner transformation all suit Jupiter Cycle Twelve perfectly. By August at the very latest you will have begun this new cycle.

2004 By October some of you will be starting Jupiter Cycle One, and some of you will just be finishing — it depends on your birth time. Either way, 2004 is amazing for those of you who are seeking a better or bigger image, a self-makeover, improvements to your wardrobe, face, hair or body — or just a better public profile. You can make much more of yourself now.

2005 Jupiter Cycle Two is all about earning more money, or just making it — on whatever level you're ready for. Your personal value system will also grow this year, and you'll come up with a more meaningful, personalised idea of what money, possessions and property really count for. By October, every woman with Virgo Rising will have started this new cycle.

libra  RISING

Sun Cycle One — begins September-October
Sun Cycle Two — begins October-November
Sun Cycle Three — begins November-December
Sun Cycle Four — begins December-January
Sun Cycle Five — begins January-February
Sun Cycle Six — begins February-March
Sun Cycle Seven — begins March-April
Sun Cycle Eight — begins April-May
Sun Cycle Nine — begins May-June
Sun Cycle Ten — begins June-July
Sun Cycle Eleven — begins July-August
Sun Cycle Twelve — begins August-September

1998 The majority of Libra Rising women enter Jupiter Cycle Six this year. For most of you, it will begin at any time between February and December, and, once again, the later your Rising sign degree, the later the start. The last numbers of you will begin this new work-oriented cycle in February 1999. For the majority, the story this year is definitely about job or health pluses.

1999 Jupiter Cycle Seven starts for most of you this year. It will begin at any time after February, with the middle group of you feeling it around April, and the later group closer to the second half of the year. The last batch of you will still be experiencing the early stages of the cycle around February 2000! It's worth waiting for, as Jupiter will remove any love life problems and provide opportunities for singles.

2000 Jupiter Cycle Eight takes place now. For a reasonable chunk of this year, you'll be concerned with big financial decisions. By June 2000, absolutely all of you will have begun this new cycle. There is a Saturn Cycle Eight around, too, so use 2000 to lay financial foundations for the future.

2001 If you want to travel more around your own country, or even span the globe, this year is perfect because more lucky breaks, options and opportunities are around you. Depending on your birthtime, you will begin this 'Explorer' cycle early, midway or late in

2001 but do be open to journeys, as Jupiter will offer them. Publishing and study are other growth areas.

2002 Follow every lead, every offer and every expression of interest. Your success depends on it, as Jupiter only triggers your achievement department every twelve years or so. At some stage in 2002 you will be starting Jupiter Cycle Ten, or find yourself midway through it. People or large organisations will be all smiles, so when you get the signal, take the green light.

2003 Jupiter is in Cycle Eleven now, in an area of your chart ruling old and new friends, social contacts, groups you are a part of, and special invitations you'd like to accept. This is going to be a boom period for your social life, and someone will turn out to be a true friend, for more personal or meaningful reasons. By August everybody will have at least started this cycle, so do get stuck in.

2004 By October some of you will be finishing Jupiter Cycle Twelve, some of you will just be starting it. You'll know which group you're in because part of you will be crying out for an escape hatch or a retreat of some kind. Health farm, hideaway, holiday or (as Virginia Woolf said) A Room Of One's Own? It doesn't matter, but by taking time out by yourself you'll grow.

2005 Jupiter is in Libra this year, and you get to experience Jupiter Cycle One, which will really crank up the Libran face you present to yourself (for more information on this, refer back to the Libra section at the front of the book). You will be 'out there' a lot more than usual, and lucky breaks will enable you to improve anything connected with image or appearance.

scorpio RISING

Sun Cycle One — begins October-November
Sun Cycle Two — begins November-December
Sun Cycle Three — begins December-January
Sun Cycle Four — begins January-February
Sun Cycle Five — begins February-March
Sun Cycle Six — begins March-April
Sun Cycle Seven — begins April-May

Sun Cycle Eight — begins May-June
Sun Cycle Nine — begins June-July
Sun Cycle Ten — begins July-August
Sun Cycle Eleven — begins August-September
Sun Cycle Twelve — begins September-October

1998 Most Scorpio Rising women enter Jupiter Cycle Five this year. For the majority, it will begin at any time between February and December, and, once again, the later your Rising sign degree, the later the start. The last batch of you will begin this new cycle in February 1999. For the majority, the story this year is sex, parenthood or bright ideas.

1999 Jupiter Cycle Six starts for most of you this year. You'll feel it at any time after February, with the middle group starting around April, and the later group closer to the second half of the year. A minority will be entering this cycle as late as February 2000.

2000 Jupiter Cycle Seven takes place now. This year is about solving marital or de facto problems, finding someone new, or going on to greater heights together. By June 2000, absolutely all of you will have begun this new cycle. There is a Saturn Cycle Seven going on at the same time, too (an astrologer can explain this), so along with the opportunities will come serious questions.

2001 Jupiter Cycle Eight will help you with a home mortgage, a bank loan, a credit card, investments, or partnership finance. This year you will make more of other people's money, possessions or property. Your individual birth time will dictate which month in 2001 precisely begins this cycle for you, but if you're really curious your local astrologer will be able to help.

2002 You can get a bigger window on the world this year — but only if you're willing to travel, either geographically or in the mind. Anything from an overseas trek, to emigration, to an internet subscription could eventuate. A course of study or a mind-blowing evening course may also be on offer. It depends what you're open to, and in Jupiter Cycle Nine, be open to all of it!

2003 By August everybody with Scorpio Rising will have kicked off Jupiter Cycle Ten, and this really is the big one if you want to impress your boss, get a better job, outscore your rivals academically, go into business for the first time, expand your current profession, win an award, or get recognition. Is that enough? Just one warning though. Don't go over the top.

2004 This year takes you into Jupiter Cycle Eleven, which is fun in terms of your social life. More people will come into your life, and if you find yourself feeling unusually popular on two or three memorable occasions, don't be surprised. Joining a team, band, club, association, network or other organisation is a good idea, generally speaking. Jupiter will bring you bonuses here.

2005 By October at the very latest you will have started Jupiter Cycle Twelve, so you won't need any excuses to withdraw and recharge your batteries. Amazing benefits will come from looking more deeply into yourself, your past, and the workings of your psyche. As a Scorpio Rising person you are probably drawn to this soul-searching anyway, but this year it's especially fortunate.

sagittarius

Sun Cycle One — begins November-December
Sun Cycle Two — begins December-January
Sun Cycle Three — begins January-February
Sun Cycle Four — begins February-March
Sun Cycle Five — begins March-April
Sun Cycle Six — begins April-May
Sun Cycle Seven — begins May-June
Sun Cycle Eight — begins June-July
Sun Cycle Nine — begins July-August
Sun Cycle Ten — begins August-September
Sun Cycle Eleven — begins September-October
Sun Cycle Twelve — begins October-November

1998 The majority of Sagittarius Rising women enter Jupiter Cycle Four this year. For most of you, it will begin at any time between February and December, and, once again, the later your Rising sign degree, the later the start. The last of you will begin this new cycle in February 1999. For the majority, the story this year is definitely about house, flat or family bonuses.

1999 Jupiter Cycle Five starts for most of you this year. You'll feel it at any time after February, with the middle group starting around

April, and the later group closer to the second half of the year. The last batch of you will still be experiencing the early stages of the cycle around February 2000 but it is worth looking out for, as Jupiter will boost life for you as a parent or lover.

2000 Jupiter Cycle Six takes place now. For a reasonable chunk of this year, you'll be concerned with work and health. By June 2000, absolutely all of you will have begun this new cycle. There is a Saturn Cycle Six going on, too (an astrologer can explain this), which means the last year of the century really is going to be crucial for your working life as you go into 2001.

2001 At some stage this year you begin Jupiter Cycle Seven (your individual birth time will tell you the month, but an astrologer can work it out for you). In any case, 2001 is about expansion through your partner — romantic, financial, business. If you don't have a 'balancer' person in your life, you will be given an opportunity to find him or her. Old relationship wounds heal now, too.

2002 This year is going to pay financial or practical dividends. Jupiter Cycle Eight is now officially underway, yet the benefits don't really come from your own earning or spending power — it's what you do in connection with other people — bank, family, partners, organisations — that opens the doors. Others' good feelings towards you could offer big rewards.

2003 Jupiter Cycle Nine is going to take you into new territories, mentally or globally. This is the big break-out year you might have been waiting for. With Sagittarius Rising, Jupiter Cycle Nine is going to have special and personal meaning for you, because 2003 is all about learning, travelling, expanding, understanding and growing. This is the year you were made for, you know!

2004 Jupiter now passes through Virgo, and travels through Jupiter Cycle Ten, so you now have three or four chances to become a bigger deal, professionally or academically speaking. When Jupiter jumps the right way, the universe gives you a nod and a wink, and you're pretty much on the road to success — if you want it. Think big, keep your feet on the ground and go for it.

2005 Jupiter Cycle Eleven is always a buzz in social terms, because it introduces you to new people who have only their friendship, time, energy and luck factor to offer — and it's unconditional. Old friends will also be very good for you, and if you've ever wondered what it would be like to join a group, team, class, band, club or association maybe this is the year to experiment.

capricorn

Sun Cycle One — begins December-January
Sun Cycle Two — begins January-February
Sun Cycle Three — begins February-March
Sun Cycle Four — begins March-April
Sun Cycle Five — begins April-May
Sun Cycle Six — begins May-June
Sun Cycle Seven — begins June-July
Sun Cycle Eight — begins July-August
Sun Cycle Nine — begins August-September
Sun Cycle Ten — begins September-October
Sun Cycle Eleven — begins October-November
Sun Cycle Twelve — begins November-December

1998 The majority of Capricorn Rising women enter Jupiter Cycle Three this year. For most of you, it will begin at any time between February and December, and, once again, the later your Rising sign degree, the later the start. The last batch of you will begin this new cycle in February 1999. For the majority, this year is about short trips away, self-education and job skills.

1999 Jupiter Cycle Four starts for most of you this year. You'll feel it at any time after February, with the middle group starting around April, and the later group closer to the second half of the year. The early stages of the cycle will be felt by a minority of you as late as February 2000.

2000 Jupiter Cycle Five takes place now. For a reasonable chunk of this year, you'll be concerned with a chance to make more of your sex life, children or creative talents. By June, all of you will have begun this new cycle. There is a Saturn Cycle Five going on at the same time, too (ask your astrologer), which means there are also brick walls to go around in these areas.

2001 It's all about lifestyle this year. Jupiter Cycle Six can open your life up, by making the tiny details of your everyday existence more satisfying for you. Small things like sleep, nutrition, exercise and relaxation levels — and bigger issues like work, home duties or study — come up now. There are endless possibilities to improve things and step up your quality of life.

2002 By August all of you will have started Jupiter Cycle Seven, which is when a new romantic partnership could form, a new financial or business double-act could begin, and an existing partnership could take off. Truly serious love-life problems will be fixed up one way or another, with less pain than you might expect. Opportunities to form meaningful relationships will arrive.

2003 Once again, August is the latest month in 2003 when your new Jupiter Cycle will begin — most of you will be in the thick of it by the middle of the year. This one is all about doing more with what other people have to lend, share or give — it has obvious financial, property or practical rewards. This is Jupiter Cycle Eight, and some of you will still be experiencing it by 2004.

2004 Jupiter Cycle Nine starts for everyone by October this year, and you are going to be offered several different chances to expand your horizons. Staying with the same angle on life is probably a waste, as this year is all about learning, reading, listening, travelling, netsurfing, exploring, wandering and taking life in. People from foreign backgrounds are lucky signposts for you.

2005 Jupiter Cycle Ten is an appropriate cycle to go out on. This year you will be given a chance to increase your career chances and improve your reputation. You can think small if you like, but it would be a waste. Individuals or larger companies are willing to let you prove yourself, and this is quite a good time to think positively about where you'd like to be in twelve years.

aquarius RISING

Sun Cycle One — begins January-February
Sun Cycle Two — begins February-March
Sun Cycle Three — begins March-April
Sun Cycle Four — begins April-May
Sun Cycle Five — begins May-June

Sun Cycle Six — begins June-July
Sun Cycle Seven — begins July-August
Sun Cycle Eight — begins August-September
Sun Cycle Nine — begins September-October
Sun Cycle Ten — begins October-November
Sun Cycle Eleven — begins November-December
Sun Cycle Twelve — begins December-January

1998 Most Aquarius Rising women enter Jupiter Cycle Two this year. The majority will begin at any time between February and December, and, once again, the later your Rising sign degree, the later the start. The last of you affected will begin this money-boosting new cycle in February 1999.

1999 Jupiter Cycle Three starts for most of you this year. Some of you leap in after February, with the middle group starting around April, and the later group closer to the second half of the year. The last batch of you will still be experiencing the early stages of the cycle around February 2000 — this one is about opportunities to improve your verbal and written skills.

2000 Jupiter Cycle Four rolls in now. You'll be concerned with chances to improve the home front shortly. By June 2000, absolutely all of you will have begun this new cycle. There is a Saturn Cycle Four going on at the same time, too — so house, flat or family issues are rather serious. For more advice, see your local astrologer!

2001 This is Jupiter Cycle Five — the year you've been waiting for in terms of creative satisfaction, fulfilment through children or meaningful sexual discovery tours (please tick one, although Jupiter has been known to deliver all three at once). In 2001 you could land a child, a brainchild or a sexual leap forwards. Positive thinking and the conscious snapping up of opportunities will bring results.

2002 Jupiter Cycle Six will have kicked off by August at the very latest, and if you've been dying to switch jobs, enjoy your course more or do something more meaningful with your life at home, this is your year. You could be promoted, get better equipment or end up with nicer colleagues in your current job. There may be perks and lurks, or a whole new slant on your lifestyle.

2003 Jupiter Cycle Seven is the Mr Fix-It cycle in terms of relationships and love. If you need to get over your ex husband, find someone new, learn to flirt again, turn a de facto arrangement into a marriage, turn a wedding into a two-week extravaganza — or just get a pain-free divorce — this is a good bet. Jupiter is the Mr Smiley of astrology. Good humour will open many doors.

2004 Jupiter is now in Virgo, in Cycle Eight. With Aquarius Rising, freedom is always your big priority, but even you need security and material comfort, so this is what you'll lean towards this year. Your lover, husband or partner may decide to merge his possessions, property or money more meaningfully with yours. The bank may help you. There could be a business pay-off, or a family inheritance.

2005 Jupiter Cycle Nine will give you the thumbs-up for interstate, regional or overseas travel if you are prepared to learn as much as you can about the world. This is not a tourist cycle, it is a traveller cycle. Travellers and people who have lived, loved and worked overseas will play a huge role in your existence. If you want to study, write or learn this is also a hot cycle.

pisces RISING

Sun Cycle One — begins February-March
Sun Cycle Two — begins March-April
Sun Cycle Three — begins April-May
Sun Cycle Four — begins May-June
Sun Cycle Five — begins June-July
Sun Cycle Six — begins July-August
Sun Cycle Seven — begins August-September
Sun Cycle Eight — begins September-October
Sun Cycle Nine — begins October-November
Sun Cycle Ten — begins November-December
Sun Cycle Eleven — begins December-January
Sun Cycle Twelve — begins January-February

1998 The majority of Pisces Rising women enter Jupiter Cycle One this year. For most of you, it will begin at any time between February and December, and, once again, the later your Rising sign degree, the later the start. The very last batch of you will begin this new cycle in February 1999. Cycle One is fabulous for organising your own makeovers — or personal luck.

1999 Jupiter Cycle Two starts for most of you this year. You'll feel it at any time after February, with the middle group starting around April, and the later group closer to the second half of the year. Some of you will be experiencing the early stages of the cycle around February 2000, as financial opportunities creep in.

2000 Jupiter Cycle Three starts this year, and mind-expansion and skill-boosting is the key. By June, all of you will have begun this new cycle. There is a Saturn Cycle Three at the same time so that projects, plans or mental challenges will only bring reward after effort.

2001 Jupiter Cycle Four kicks off now, so this is your cue to move houses or apartments, sell your current property, add or extend, decorate or renovate. If you wish to get a stronger sense of place — by getting citizenship, tracing your family tree, visiting your roots — this is also the year when Jupiter will pass you the opportunity to do so. Family and relatives hold lots of keys, too.

2002 Jupiter Cycle Five will have started by August at the latest, and you will find benefits and advantages in one of the following areas: a creative or self-expressive project, your relationship with a child or baby, your own sexual growth and learning. Cycle Five is also about old-fashioned fun and games, so no matter if it's music, sport, art, films or ping-pong, you'll get more of it than you counted on.

2003 Jupiter Cycle Six is an important one, because you will have a chance to improve your health and build up your wellbeing. The right people at the right time will come your way. Work or study will also benefit. You may switch to new people, equipment, places or opportunities or find that some golden chances to upgrade your current situation land in front of you.

2004 Jupiter in Virgo will travel around your chart until it kicks off Jupiter Cycle Seven, and this twelve-month period will see the start of relationship and partnership trends you haven't seen for around twelve years. If you have love-life problems, it will be easier than you think to sort things out. If you're looking for someone new, Jupiter will provide you with an opportunity. Happy? Another big step awaits you.

2005 Jupiter Cycle Eight makes perfect sense for those of you who met the right partner or became engaged in 2004, because this year is all about mutal financial or lifestyle expansion. Didn't get quite so lucky? The finances, possessions or property pay-offs will come from other areas — strictly-business partners, the bank, or family members. Watch your lifestyle grow ... and grow.

jupiter

BODY OPTIMISM

For around twelve months, you'll be in the perfect frame of mind to do something about your skin tone, shape and health. Actually, this cycle is less about the inside of the body than the outside. What you eat and drink will only become an issue in relation to the outer package. Still, Jupiter will send a guru or true believer your way, and this person's influence will be a big factor. It may be on the printed page, or in a face-to-face session, but you'll find the experience gives you inspiration. It's a good cycle for a makeover — conducted by you or a professional. The results in the mirror should be good.

PERSONAL BELIEFS

Your own personal philosophy or code will be given a workout in this cycle. Your beliefs may be put on the line by events around you, or you will be in touch with issues which make you realise how you *really* feel — politically, spiritually or philosophically. Some people will clearly be with you, but it's just as likely that others will be against you, or just naturally working from a completely different viewpoint. It's possible that this may be quite removed from you. If someone close is involved, expect a larger-than-life episode.

THE WORLD OPENS UP

Bags get packed in Jupiter Cycle One. If the money and time are available, you'll take some important journeys in this twelve-month period for this is the cycle of the big overseas trek, the long interstate haul and — in some cases — a completely new way of life. If money and time aren't there, you'll stay where you are, but find a huge amount of far-flung stimulation in people with strange accents who can speak knowledgeably about multicoloured bits of the globe, books, courses and programmes which remind you that there are places where people still sleep for most of the day, or weave jumpers out of goat's hair. If you do travel in this cycle, it will be a 'What the hell' trip, you'll expect it to be wonderful and so it will prove to be. Maximise the fun if you're marooned somewhere by learning a language.

TAKING GAMBLES

Jupiter will tempt you to take more deliberate gambles in this cycle. Your calculated risks may be romantic, professional or purely for fun. It's important to size up the odds, though. Some of the things you chase now could be completely inappropriate — or the odds may be rather long — yet nothing will make sense until later. It is notoriously difficult to know when you are being *over the top* when Jupiter is around. Those who aren't so closely involved with your madly optimistic gambles may have their own, private doubts. As long as you do not place too much faith and hope in the outcomes (not all of them are going to work out) this should be a harmless time when you discover what it's really like to coast along on pure positive thinking.

jupiter  **CYCLE 2**

MORE MONEY

You will have more money to spend or save in this cycle, and the only mystery is how it gets there from here. Some women have received credit card approvals in this cycle, others have received a bonus, pay rise or payout. A very few win enormous amounts through gambling, but they are the exception, not the rule. You'll handle notes of bigger denominations, make bigger transactions, borrow or lend larger sums or accumulate more than you've seen for some time. If you're in your thirties or over, count back around twelve years. What was going on then, financially? This will provide clues.

HEY, BIG SPENDER!

The only problem with the extra cash is the lure of big spending sessions, or one blow-out on a larger-than-life purchase. Jupiter in Cycle Two loves the good life, loves flinging money around, and, above all, in this particular cycle, loves lingerie and perfume. The window shopping theory works well here. Give Jupiter his day by speculating on female feel-good purchases, or sensual, natural delights. Two weeks in Bali? Janet Reger underwear? Well, fine, but window shop first. Then compare prizes. Then repeat the Jupiter mantra, 'I feel lucky,' and see what happens. This planet has a remarkably good track record with genuinely lucky deals and bargains. But try a little restraint or you could end up broke.

YOUR BELIEFS AND VALUE SYSTEMS

This will all sound terribly straight after talk of Bali and Janet Reger underwear, but in this cycle you will have to confront your basic beliefs and values — especially as they relate to money and materialism. Some women probably join the Socialist Worker's Party in Jupiter Cycle Two (and win the raffle). Most of you will be put in situations in your love lives, family lives or working lives where you have to ask yourself the question: 'Am I selling out?' You may also find these clichés become a living, breathing part of your life: the best things in life are free, money talks, money can't buy you love, everyone has their price ... Jupiter describes what you believe in and what is morally or ethically correct for you. Cycle Two is about what you truly value in this life. Be prepared!

BEAUTY COSTS

Women find beauty in different things. Some of you find it in paintings and collector's items. Some of you find it in gardens and rainforests. Some of you find it in clothes, skincare, make-up and hair. Cycle Two belongs to Venus as much as to Jupiter, and you will spend on her desire for beauty at this time. Venus actually had two lives. When she was feeling invulnerable, she spent her time threading her hair with jewellery, spending on roses, trying on exotic new girdles and dreaming of gold and silver. When she was feeling vulnerable, she ran wild and dumped the material in favour of natural beauty. In this cycle, you'll find yourself outlaying for either the beauty you can keep and admire, or the beauty which is wild or natural.

jupiter

EDUCATING YOURSELF

Cycle Three is about mind expansion, and improved written and verbal skills. You may attend important courses or seminars in connection with your job, or, if already studying, may find yourself with one of those teachers or lecturers who has a huge capacity for their field. You may also choose to educate yourself in a less formal capacity. It's common for women in Jupiter Cycle Three to do more reading than usual, to take home heavier piles of books from the library, or to launch a one-woman assault on the local bookshop. A computer, or any other means of communication — typewriter, mobile phone, fax — may become a bigger part of your life in this cycle. You will also come into contact with people who have something to teach you, once again, probably on an informal level. If you do happen to be enrolled in study full-time, the subjects you are committed to will do more for you than you expected — and your chances of successful results will be better and bigger than usual.

PEOPLE AROUND YOU

Cycle Three describes your neighbours, people in the local community and your brothers, sisters or cousins. You will encounter Jupiter's beneficial effects through or around these people. The generous attitude of a sibling, cousin or neighbour could make a huge difference to things. Or you may find that luck — that random force — enters your world through these people, who may be agents for Jupiter's positive influences. Some astrologers have noticed financial benefits coming through brothers, sisters and cousins — or your parent's brothers and sisters. Working with clients in Jupiter Cycle Three, I have also seen women start romances with neighbours, and also pick up real estate bargains after a quick phone call from a cousin! One woman combined several of the effects of Jupiter Cycle Three simultaneously when she bought a computer from her brother, and enrolled in a creative writing course.

MAKING CONNECTIONS

Jupiter is now influenced by Mercury, the Messenger of the Gods, who spent most of his time rushing around in winged sandals. This cycle is associated with a lot of short journeys, or an increase in the amount of running around you are doing locally. It's also associated with planes, trains and automobiles, as for around twelve months or so, you will be making more connections than usual. Jupiter's beneficial influence may be channelled through a new car, the trip of a lifetime, or even something as small, but important, as a change in a bus route which directly benefits you! As long as you do not go over the top, which is always a concern with this planet, you could reasonably target anything connected to communication, transport or travel with great success. Incidentally, if you happen to be involved with Mercury-ruled areas anyway, or have planets in Gemini, you'll just find that this part of your life becomes a very big deal indeed — and full of promise. If you have a Geminian side, it may expand wildly now!

jupiter CYCLE 4

MORE ROOM TO MOVE

You'll have an opportunity to create more space in your house or flat around this time. You may move to a property which has a more expansive feeling of light and space, or find a way to make more of what is already there. Renovation and decoration are quite common in a Jupiter Cycle Four. You may find yourself more concerned with storage space in this cycle, but also with the atmosphere of your home: if it doesn't seem bright or uplifting enough, Jupiter will throw you a few chances to make some changes. If you have a garden you'll extend that, too, or perhaps open up various parts of it.

FAMILY ATTITUDES

If there have been any stumbling blocks between family members, Jupiter will encourage a wiser and more philosophical attitude. Humour will be an important part of the bridging process. If the family ties in your life are basically healthy and happy, then Jupiter will simply increase the generosity between you — you'll do more for each other. There may also be family expansion, as in some cases new babies are born, children are adopted, or marriages introduce a whole new set of in-laws to the family network. This cycle will help you to take a broad view of your family ties, and get the big picture. It's useful for those of you who need to get family issues in their correct perspective.

A BIGGER SENSE OF PLACE

Cycle Four also describes your roots, heritage and sense of place. It points to a stronger connection with your homeland, rather than just your home. If you were born in Australia, you may explore your own country more widely, and develop a bigger sense of the big country. If you were born elsewhere, you may have an opportunity to travel back to your roots, or destiny may put you in touch with your homeland in another way. Events going on around you will encourage a more philosophical attitude towards issues like patriotism. Some women have become Australian citizens in Jupiter Cycle Four, while others have been caught up in events going on in their original homelands. A bigger sense of belonging is often the result of this cycle, and it's quite enjoyable.

PEOPLE AROUND THE HOME

If you are married, in a de facto relationship or are married with children, this is an important time. Jupiter will present you with quite a few opportunities to make more of what you have, and to be philosophical about the things you cannot change. If you have flatmates, a more generous attitude between you — or just more jokes — will be in evidence. If you have new flatmates in this cycle, they may be Jupiter types — generally happy, a bit larger-than-life, and much-travelled. If you live alone, you may have more guests than usual, or find yourself playing the generous hostess. If real estate contacts are important in this cycle, you'll notice that they fit the Jupiter description as well. Those you live with or share with could get lucky this year, too.

jupiter

EXPRESS YOURSELF

You will express yourself in much more creative ways in this cycle. If you have talents in this area to begin with, you will be more prolific now, and you'll find the flow of inspiration is accompanied by opportunities to make more of your abilities. Some women enter art competitions in Jupiter Cycle Five, while others write books. One client of mine embarked on a huge quilt in connection with the AIDS Quilt Project. Cycle Five is about you, your mode of self-expression and your need to produce something in the world. You may receive generous approval from others now, as your abilities will find a bigger audience. If you're involved in sport, you'll put in a 'personality' performance. There may also be more money, bonuses, awards or other 'pure luck' events around if you are involved in creative pursuits on a professional level. You may find your creative voice for the first time, or do something on a personal level for *you*.

BABIES AND CHILDREN

If you have children, the parent–child relationship will benefit from Jupiter Cycle Five. If things have been tough, or continue to be challenging, you may also have other cycles going on (your astrologer can explain this). Jupiter, however, will wave things aside, create opportunities and open the doors. Your belief system, or your personal philosophy, will be strongly influenced by your role as a mother. Not surprisingly, many women report pregnancies or births in this cycle. If your children are older, they may become a bigger and more enjoyable part of your life, or they may be agents for the famous Jupiterian luck factor. If you have no kids at all in your life, be aware that on a sexual level, you may be more fertile than usual. Kids may enter your life in other, happy, ways at this time as well.

YOUR SEX LIFE

If single, you will have at least one opportunity for a largely sex-based relationship now, and maybe more than one! Your partner is likely to be very tolerant, generous and open-minded about you, which means you can relax in bed, and obviously out of it, too. If you are already in a relationship, your sexual horizons may broaden through all kinds of different or exotic ways. If sex has been a problem — probably due to other planets making waves — Jupiter will open some doors and give you a chance to fix things up. Some women report meeting Jupiter in human form in Cycle Five. They end up with men who are larger-than-life, funny, with a different background and with a lust for travel. (If you want to test this theory for yourself, read the chapter on Men with Planets in Sagittarius on page 266). Whatever their sign, Cycle Five men may express Sagittarian characteristics. Your horizons will expand through the lover you select in this cycle. Of course, the choice is yours. If you are looking for something which is more than just a lust option, you may keep your legs firmly crossed, and your phone off the hook. But with Jupiter's propensity to send opportunities, you can still count on options which are glaringly obvious.

jupiter CYCLE 6

HEALTH AND WELLBEING

You will be given opportunities to improve your health and wellbeing now. If you really are a confirmed couch potato and doughnut addict, not much will change. However, Jupiter will knock several times over the next twelve months or so, and if you are willing to answer, you could end up with a better body, more energy and a fuller sense of wellbeing. Cycle Six is about cures, healing, diet, massage, order and routine. Some of the women I have seen in Cycle Six become heavily involved in yoga or start experimenting with a meat-free diet. If you have serious health problems, it is more than likely that other planets — Saturn, Uranus, Neptune or Pluto — are also influencing you. Jupiter, however, will even out the picture. It will offer you the chance for genuine improvements and before this cycle is through, grounds for real optimism as well.

THE WORK ETHIC

If you are looking for a job in this period, you will find at least one lucky opportunity, and possibly more — Jupiter tends to supply things in excess sometimes! If you are currently working, you will meet Jupiter's benefits through the people you work with or for, or through the work environment itself. Better conditions, happier company, more support, or more perks and lurks are common outcomes of this cycle. Because Jupiter is associated with travel, some women have found enjoyable trips away come with the job package at this time. Perhaps more importantly than any of this is the idea that your job will give you a sense of meaning now. If you are studying full-time, the work ethic will be rather different, but the same trends apply. Expect more room to move, more options, a better academic set-up, and the odd lucky break, too.

MEETING JUPITER IN PERSON

This planet has an odd habit of manifesting in human form. In Jupiter Cycle Six, you may meet someone through the areas of work or health who seems rather Jupiterian or — because Jupiter is the ruler of Sagittarius — Sagittarian to you. This person may be noticeably optimistic, rather generous, a firm believer in positive thinking, and either physically larger than life, or psychologically a bit over the top. Sometimes people will appear who act as Jupiter's carrier pigeons. If you become more closely involved with them, you may meet both the wonderful and not-so-wonderful qualities of the planet. The general optimism and positive spin on life co-exist with a kind of recklessness and carelessness. Generosity exists side by side with a tendency to be *too much*. A nurse going through Jupiter Cycle Six, for example, may find herself with one of those ever-smiling patients who are admitted with a weight problem and still smuggle chocolate in under the sheets. Another example: the student who takes a part-time job in a café, working for an over-the-top chef who lets her eat all she wants, but cooks things which are too over the top for most of the clients. You can find Jupiter anywhere in life now!

jupiter

MARRIAGE AND COMMITMENT

Yes, it's true — an awful lot of women find opportunities to marry, or move in with, their chosen partner in this cycle. But I have also seen just as many happy separations and joyful divorces. The most accurate way to sum up Jupiter Cycle Seven is this: through the area of partnership, marriage or de facto relationships, you will meet a big opportunity. Now, that may be an opportunity to get in, or an opportunity to get out. But as with all Jupiter cycles, the motivation and initiative must come from you. If you're ultimately not interested, or if other planetary cycles are getting in the way (an astrologer can explain this) then the door may swing open, but you'll have no interest in going through it. Here's an example: a single woman moved to a new city, New York, in Jupiter Cycle Seven. By an amazing stroke of coincidence, her ex was there, too. She knew he was interested — and they could have moved in together — but in the end she chose to stay solo.

THE PARTNERSHIP PRINCIPLE

If you are already in a good relationship or marriage, Jupiter will provide even more expansion, opportunities and benefits that have special meaning for you as a couple. This planet also affects the partnership principle as a whole, though. On a work or business level, it is common to find all kinds of double-acts and partnerships forming, and, once again, you can expect a generous or tolerant atmosphere between you. The dominant feeling with Jupiter Cycle Seven is that you can do more together than you ever could alone. I have seen a film produced under this cycle — one of the creative women involved in starting it up found funding through a partner during her Jupiter Cycle Seven. Equally, I know one woman who was in a lopsided business partnership where she felt she was not receiving her fair share of the profits. It wound up, in a satisfactory way, during her Jupiter Cycle Seven.

THE POWER OF TWO

Because Jupiter tends to supply an excess of what you need, you may find lots of double-acts forming over this twelve-month period. You just seem to fall into a unit of two with people, and this may happen at home, or through work or study, as well as in your personal life. Once again, it's possible to meet Jupiter in human form this way — so you team up with a happy, optimistic person who is also a little over the top. The give-and-take principle, which is what Cycle Seven is all about, is strongly related to Libra. If you have planets in Libra, you may experience this cycle in a very powerful way, and may want to re-read the chapter on this sign in the 'You' section. For those of you who really are with the right person, Jupiter Cycle Seven will bring a big wedding, with plenty of far-flung guests, and a special interest in the philosophy or beliefs that go with commitment. In other words, Jupiter's concerns will blend with the meaning of Cycle Seven in a very obvious way. Singles should keep an eye out for a lucky chance — but it's up to you to take it. It's a good cycle for patching things up with exes, too.

jupiter CYCLE 8

OTHER PEOPLE'S MONEY

You will gain from the support or backing of other people in this cycle, which will benefit you financially, in property terms or through other kinds of resources, possessions or assets. One or more opportunities will appear which allow you to take advantage of something passed on by a partner, a family member or even the bank. The source may change, but the message is the same: Jupiter, the Great Benefactor, will give you a broad set of opportunities which emphasises just how generous someone else is being with you. One client of mine — a broke student — got to travel in her new boyfriend's Mercedes and sleep in his four-poster. Princess Diana received her divorce settlement around the time of her Jupiter Cycle Eight.

This cycle also asks you to re-assess your values and beliefs in line with money. Jupiter describes your philosophy of life, and what you have faith in. Other people's money, resources, property or assets will connect you with your own ethics, values or beliefs. If finance is a huge problem (other planets may be interrupting this cycle) then Jupiter will serve to protect, or provide an opportunity for damage control.

TABOO SUBJECTS

Cycle Eight belongs to Scorpio, which astrologers associate with taboo subjects. Sexuality is the most obvious of these, and you may learn more and accomplish more through your sexuality in this cycle. Benefits may come to you through those areas of human sexuality which are off-limits or hard to discuss for some reason. You may undergo some kind of healing process if sex has been a problem, or, if you enjoy your sex life, will find ways to improve and expand your erotic repertoire. Apart from sex, society's other big taboo area is the occult. You may meet a guide figure through this area now, or expand your knowledge of occult philosophies.

Finally, and perhaps most difficult to discuss on one page, Cycle Eight is about death and dying. An assortment of experiences will deepen your knowledge and understanding of this most off-limits area of life. I know of a woman who had a near-death experience in Cycle Eight. Another managed the family's affairs when her uncle died. A third client found a sense of meaning by exploring Buddhism, which helped her to develop a philosophy about her own mother's death five years before. This cycle works in a variety of ways. But it will help you to work out what you believe.

TEACHER FIGURES

Jupiter is very likely to manifest as a specific person in your life in this twelve-month period. Watch for a person who is a teacher, or guide figure. He or she may show you the way in any of the areas commonly associated with Cycle Eight. The most obvious one is money and resources, but you may also learn about your sexuality, your beliefs, your attitude to death and dying, through a special teacher figure in disguise.

jupiter CYCLE 9

TRAVEL AND TRAVELLERS

You will have the opportunity to travel in Cycle Nine. Depending on your circumstances, this may either be an overseas haul, an interstate trek, or trips to the countryside or ocean. The location is not as important as the process that will accompany it, which is basically eye-opening and mind-expanding! As with all Jupiter cycles, the choice is yours. I knew a woman who was offered a three-year student exchange to Berlin in Jupiter Cycle Nine, but turned it down. She now admits it probably would have changed her life. As well as travel, you can expect well-travelled or foreign people to play a special part in your life now. Through one of these people, you will also be thrown opportunities and possibilities, options and chances. They may turn out to be lucky in some way. You will cover more ground, or more territory, in Jupiter Cycle Nine. Some women just find themselves zipping around between town and country, and experiencing life from a bigger perspective. Others develop a passion for somewhere exotic and they take off and live there.

BROADER HORIZONS

You may be just a girl from Little Rock when this cycle begins, but it will bring you a window on the world. If you're already an experienced traveller, you may take off for a location which turns all your ideas on their head. You may also find amazing experiences — usually instructive ones — which let you see more possibilities in life than you had ever considered. Some women study the most enormous subjects in Cycle Nine. Most of these areas will lead straight back to the Jupiterian themes of belief systems, faiths, ideas, philosophies and worldviews. Even if you're not in formal study, you may come across books or films which have an amazing effect on your perspective. You will be around people who are agents for these changes, too — intriguing, vastly different types, often from foreign backgrounds, who show you there's more going on out there than you'd ever thought about.

CYCLE NINE AND SAGITTARIUS

If you have planets in Sagittarius, then the issues associated with that sign will be very strong now. You may want to re-read the chapter in the 'You' section to understand and appreciate this side of yourself again. Most of you will experience the Sagittarius theme in other ways: by becoming more involved with people who are classic Sagittarian 'types' or those who have their Rising sign or planets placed here. Many of the images, symbols and themes listed at the end of the Planets in Sagittarius chapter (pages 117–131) will shortly enter your life, sometimes in a major way. Publishing, for example, is associated with this sign, and some of you may go into print now, on a large or small scale. Legal matters are also described by Sagittarius, and some of you will meet Jupiter in this area. Your generosity, or that of another party, will be a key factor in the way things develop for you. Above all, Sagittarius is linked with the big picture. Finding out as much as you can about the world, knowing and experiencing more, are what this cycle is all about.

jupiter

CAREER OPPORTUNITIES

If you are looking for a job in this cycle, you will find one opportunity, or possibly more, and will have quite an important choice to make. If you are satisfied with your current position, you will experience Jupiter's abundance and benefits through a promotion, special recognition, perks and lurks, or a change in the work environment which makes everything seem bigger and better. If you are in business for yourself, you will expand under this cycle, and as long as you do not go over the top, should benefit from doing so. The general idea with Jupiter is to create opportunities for other people, double the luck or chances for everyone, and generally let positive thinking feed off itself. If you take even a tentative step in this direction in Cycle Ten, you will see Jupiter working for you in spectacular ways. It happens like this: you take advantage of a work-related opportunity to do something useful or generous for others, and the ripples just spread out.

BIG AMBITIONS

You can do a lot in this cycle, if only because you are more prepared to think big than at other times. As long as your ambitions are fairly evenly matched to what you are capable of, some incredible things may be possible. A student I saw in Cycle Ten had her eyes on the Law prize in her faculty. She was already doing quite well, and it seemed a reasonable thing to aim for. Not only did she collect that prize, but about three others she had not even considered!

Jupiter can sometimes be quite excessively lucky if the energy is clicking your way. If you are having enormous job or study problems in Jupiter Cycle Ten, you are probably having a difficult time with another outer planet (an astrologer can pinpoint this for you). Jupiter will help to cushion your situation, provide an exit for you and even throw in a lucky break to get you out of the tightest spot.

MEETING JUPITER THROUGH WORK

If you have read this far, you may have become aware that Jupiter symbolises certain kinds of people (optimistic, open-handed, a bit over the top) and certain kinds of themes — expansion, travel, foreign people, travellers, the Law, publishing, education. Through your job or study in this cycle, you may meet Jupiter in a very direct way, as these loose ideas and themes seem to manifest in your career or course. Turning to my client list again, I can see a woman who found a terrific new job in Cycle Ten — working for a Greek businessman who threw in lots of business trips with her package. She was working while finishing a business studies course, which means she was basically experiencing about four or five Jupiter themes simultaneously. Sometimes Jupiter is like that — if you can sense this planet around you, chase the possibilities. A great deal will now be possible for you.

jupiter

A BIGGER SOCIAL CIRCLE

In Cycle Eleven, Jupiter brings opportunities to expand your friendships, and make your usual circle of friends wider. If you are determined to be a hermit for the twelve months or so that this planet is around, then you can try. But people will still be ringing you up or knocking on your door.

The idea with this cycle is to repair, renew and rejuvenate any friendships which need patching up. Also, perhaps, to make more of the friendships which are really worthwhile and enjoyable. If you are experiencing another planet in this cycle at the same time, you could find yourself in a social whirl that becomes more important than your love life and your career combined! Your address book will fill up with more names and numbers this year. Leave space.

FRIENDS IN YOUR LIFE

Jupiter will affect the friends you already have — one or two of them will have a good year, be in 'expand, expand!' mode, and extend their time, energy, money or other forms of generosity to you. Put simply, one of your friends may just get very lucky.

You will also form a closer friendship with someone who is Jupiter made flesh. They may have the sign Sagittarius, which Jupiter rules, dominant in their horoscope. They may have a Jupiter or Sagittarius-styled life. (*See* the chapter on Planets in Sagittarius on pages 117–131 for more information.) The good thing about Jupiter Cycle Eleven is that any difficulties or problems with friends can be patched up or healed through the generous attitude of either person. If you're already on the right track with friends, they may open up your world for you in a terrific way.

GROUP ENERGY

Cycle Eleven is really an Aquarian cycle. If you have planets here, a lot of your Aquarian qualities will be brought out very strongly, too. Part of what this sign is all about is group energy. In this cycle, you may have a chance to become involved in a big group project, or just a big group or network of people. Yes, running the local Brownie pack does come under this category! Some musically-minded women I know have spent their time in Cycle Eleven in rock *bands* and virtually any term that describes a group — a pack, a club, a team, a collective, an organisation, a network, an association — may now become important. Being part of the wider group will also help you to increase your knowledge, experience and sophistication (yes, even the Brownies can do this for you!). Some women in Cycle Eleven get together with friends to form businesses. The possibilities are endless for you now.

AQUARIAN THEMES

If any of the life areas described at the end of the Planets in Aquarius chapter (pages 146–160) turn up at this time, pursue them. They are being lobbed into your life by Jupiter, which is now giving you a chance to explore the Aquarian side of existence more fully. Astrology comes under this category, which may explain why some of you are now starting to read this book!

jupiter CYCLE 12

BIG SPIRIT

Cycle Twelve is the cycle of Big Spirit, and it will put you in touch with spiritual, special and rare sides of existence. Some of you will certainly get religion at this time, or read a book which inspires you on a spiritual level. Sometimes it takes a very small experience to prompt a very big Jupiter experience. *The Getting of Wisdom* is not just a good book, it's also a good phrase to borrow for this cycle. This cycle is not so much about the car, the cash, the career or the Casanovas. It's about that part of you which is involved in something bigger and more mysterious. Some of you will get heavily into meditation at this time. I personally know one woman who saw her first ghost in Jupiter Cycle Twelve, which gave her a radically different view of reality and What It All Means!

GIVING IT UP FOR OTHERS

A tremendous need to put your self-interest aside and do things for others is part of this cycle. Yes, there will be a big sacrifice. No, it will not hurt. Instead, it will connect you to something more special and mysterious in life. In fact, after Cycle Twelve is over, very few things will look the same. You get to see a different kind of reality in this cycle, and it is not necessarily something you can put into words. You can't price or describe what it feels like to put yourself last in favour of a principle, a person, a life or a project. It's still going to be a remarkable source of inspiration for you, though, and it will have a staggering effect on your particular philosophy or beliefs. I realise this doesn't sound very exciting when compared to a Cycle Two or a Cycle Five but some of my clients have described this one as more powerful than all the rest!

NEPTUNE'S DREAM DOMAIN

Neptune — which rules Cycle Twelve — also rules dreams, and you will have some huge dream experiences in Cycle Twelve. There will be the opportunity to decode other areas of your life — and increase your self-knowledge — by doing all your travelling in your head. Conscious daydreaming, or positive visualisation, is a technique that seems to work particularly well in Cycle Twelve. The meaning of the two planets together — Jupiter (Positive) and Neptune (Visualisation) certainly seems to blend pretty well. Some of the clients I have seen over the years not only have extraordinary experiences with dreams and positive visualisation, but also with recreational drugs. Cycle Twelve is very personal, though. Although the basic theme (other realities) is true for all, it's up to you to find your version of it.

PISCEAN THEMES

Because Neptune rules Pisces, you may find the chapter on Planets in Pisces (pages 161–174) a useful guide to some of the experiences you are now going to encounter. If you have planets in Pisces, then Jupiter Cycle Twelve will increase your awareness of this imaginative side of your personality, in ways that will be quite beneficial. And after this cycle? It all begins again ...

sun **CYCLE 1**

PEOPLE IN FOCUS

People whose professional concern is image, body or appearance.

You may be more involved with hair, beauty, fashion, health, fitness or diet professionals. Or you may be caught up with people who are in the business of holding up a mirror to others: photographers, psychologists, counsellors or camera operators. The most important figures in this cycle will be those whose authority you respect when it comes to the way you look, or the sort of qualities you project. An astrologer may also fall into this category.

People who are trained or qualified in areas which are extremely *personal* will play an important role in this cycle. You may also have the distinct impression that you are being assessed or judged from the outside now — someone you know, or even someone you have never met — may play the role. Self-help and self-improvement gurus may have a part to play now, too.

ISSUES IN FOCUS

This is quite a self-absorbed time, when you will spend more energy on The Wonderful World of You. This may occur because fate puts you in touch with people or possibilities that encourage you to dwell on yourself and your image. Alternatively, this cycle may coincide with a spontaneous decision to do something about your face, hair, body, voice or 'outer shell'. Self-improvement and self-development — along with a reasonable amount of vanity and introspection — are quite permissible.

This is the time of the year when you test how confident you feel about your outer self. You know what's going on inside and that is another issue entirely. But what seems to count more is the way acquaintances or even total outsiders rate you. You'll be more interested in books and magazine articles which talk about highly personal, individual issues.

IMPORTANT PRIORITIES

When this Sun cycle is hassle-free, your main priority will be basking in good feedback, or ego-boosting images of yourself. It will take little effort to feel good about yourself when a Sun cycle flows for you. There will be some years when other planetary patterns mean this Sun cycle could be challenging. When this happens, your confidence about your body, face or overall image may be dented. This will serve an important purpose. The idea here is to take a closer look at why you might feel 'dented' and what you can do about it. The Sun will enlighten you, quite literally. And it is at this precise point of understanding — the 'Oh, I see' factor — that you will begin to rebuild your confidence step by step. Some women make major decisions about their presentation skills, health or appearance at this time. Destiny says you will be on display in a more obvious way now. People will be looking your way, or talking about you more. All this means that you will be assessing just how confident you feel about yourself.

sun

PEOPLE IN FOCUS

Accountants ★ Financial advisers ★ Stockbrokers ★ Employers ★ Bank tellers ★ Bank managers ★ Insurance salespeople ★ Sales staff ★ Merchants ★ Traders ★ Businesspeople.

This is the cycle when you contact people whose authority you respect and acknowledge in the financial area. It may also be the cycle when you just have to step back and acknowledge others' authority, even though you may have mixed feelings about it! For obvious reasons, money and possessions become more important during Sun Cycle Two, and a few destiny figures will float past as these issues are hammered home. This is one of several cycles in the year when you could seriously gain by learning from an enlightened source so it's not a bad idea to pick up a book by a financial or business expert you trust or have recommended to you. If you share your finances with your partner, there may be discussions about you–me–us decisions.

ISSUES IN FOCUS

Along with the obvious emphasis on your income, budget, and financial stability, you will also be considering your values. Money and lifestyle are part of it, of course, but you will find that circumstances make you think more deeply about what you really value in life. If this Sun Cycle Two occurs at a time when other planets are involved — and this may happen in any year — then the questions may be quite serious. Your private life, career or business interests may be the areas in which these ethical points are considered. If nothing so dramatic is going on, this will just be a time of working out what you want, and what you need — what counts, and what doesn't. Is money the issue, are valuable possessions and indulgences the issue, or are other things pushing your buttons?

IMPORTANT PRIORITIES

Financial management has to be at the top of your list. If this cycle coincides with a 'gain' cycle — which will happen in some years, when Jupiter is making favourable patterns — then you may need to see an accountant or financial adviser to work out gain strategies. At least one amount of money is going to become a huge priority, and this may either be money owed to you, or money owed by you. The financial in and out trays look fairly active in Sun Cycle Two, and if you have planets in Taurus, you may find this time of year puts you in touch with your Taurus side. No matter what kinds of signs you have in your chart, you may 'make like a Taurus' in this cycle. This means building your wealth and making canny purchasing or sales decisions. It also means confronting the age-old Taurean issues about selling out, or pricing the things that money can't buy. Should you also be experiencing an outer planet involving itself in this same cycle (an astrologer can tell you more about this) expect major financial drama.

sun **CYCLE 3**

PEOPLE IN FOCUS

Brothers ★ Sisters ★ Cousins ★ Uncles and aunts ★ Neighbours ★ Couriers ★ Messengers ★ Traders ★ Students ★ Teachers ★ Writers ★ Telephone company staff ★ Computer people ★ Editors ★ Journalists ★ The mass media ★ Local councillors ★ Lecturers ★ Debaters ★ Public speakers ★ Agents ★ Car salespeople ★ Bike and car mechanics ★ Taxi drivers ★ Publishers ★ Stationery staff ★ Printers ★ Booksellers ★ Post office staff ★ Thieves ★ Travel agents ★ Gossips.

The people who come centre stage in Sun Cycle Three point to any sibling relationships within your immediate or wider family. You will also be in touch with people who are the agents of communication, and bridges for your own communication skills. People in the local environment become more important in Sun Cycle Three — neighbours are a classic example. The Third House sometimes points to petty thieving, so be more watchful than usual. If another planet happens to be making waves here at the same time you may be more vulnerable to this than usual. (An astrologer can tell you more about this.)

ISSUES IN FOCUS

The trivia of everyday communication from faxes to answering machines, to telephones and the postbox, will matter more in this cycle. You may find that one letter, or one message, or one call, even ends up being the focus of your entire existence for a few days! Your confidence in your own written and verbal abilities may go backwards and forwards by turns, but the Sun will help you to develop your self-image in connection with your communication skills. If you are going to pick up recognition or good feedback for your written or verbal skills, now is the time when it may happen. Along with all the emphasis on communication also comes an emphasis on how well you learn and listen, and how highly you rate yourself in terms of your concentration, memory and knowledge. Cycle Three also rules siblings, cousins and neighbours, so this four-week period of your life will focus you on the quality of these relationships.

IMPORTANT PRIORITIES

Feeling confident about expressing your opinions may — or may not — come easily to you. One way or another, though, this cycle will make it very clear that you will have to put your views on the line. Developing a stronger sense of self-esteem through improving your powers of communication is a key message of this cycle. Hit the books now, or do your 'homework' in whatever context that makes sense to you. This is an important part of the year for shaping up your skills and getting your particular message across. It's also essential to get relationships with brothers, sisters, cousins, aunts or uncles into good shape now. This is one of those rare times of the year when you can shed light on anything that might be getting in the way of this — or, if things are basically happy, to focus on a plan or idea which will make things even better. Neighbours? The same story.

sun

PEOPLE IN FOCUS

Parents ★ Real estate agents ★ Builders ★ Decorators ★ Plumbers ★ Painters ★ Immediate family ★ Extended family ★ Furniture sellers ★ Auctioneers ★ Flatmates ★ Removalists ★ Upholsterers ★ Home entertainment sales staff ★ Children ★ Cleaners ★ Housesitters ★ Storage staff ★ Delivery drivers ★ Cooks ★ Babysitters ★ Caterers ★ Gardeners ★ Home insurance staff ★ Tenants ★ House guests.

Cycle Four is very obviously about the environment you live in, your roots and your sense of family. People who are connected to your house or flat situation, and your immediate or extended family, will show up strongly in your life during this cycle. A great deal will hinge on the kinds of relationships you have with people who define how confident you feel about home. Home means your own personal living space, but also 'home' in a wider context — your sense of roots and belonging, defined by a bigger sense of family or place. Cycle Four also touches off the career, status and achievement area of your horoscope. Around this time you may also be focussing on bosses, headhunters or similar figures.

ISSUES IN FOCUS

This is one time of the year when you should aim to build your confidence and satisfaction with your living environment. It's a good time to work out what is really important to you, and this not only applies to practical home and domestic issues, but also emotional ones. Right now, you'll be sorting things out with your parents or other family members so that you are clear on your relationship with them. Feeling good about yourself in terms of your role as daughter, wife, mother, sister, niece or granddaughter to people matters. This may be a good time to jot down ideas about the kind of house or flat set-up, or the sort of domestic situation, you'd prefer for the future. If other planets are supporting you in this cycle, and this will happen periodically, it will be a plus or bonus time for real estate or the family. If other planets are out of synch, challenges in the 'home' area of your life will spur you on to cope, and resist. (An astrologer can tell you more about this.)

IMPORTANT PRIORITIES

Your aims, goals and ambitions will strike a big note in this cycle, along with all the emphasis on the home front. The Sun will pick up the achievement-oriented area of your chart around this time — if not in Cycle Four, then just before or after it. Consequently, your ego will be a lot more involved with what happens in terms of your job, or your success rating. This cycle is really about getting things secure and settled for the future. You will need to have a strong sense of home — or place — to return to after Sun Cycle Four, or it may be harder to find it at other times. Re-establishing and improving what is already in place, or searching for something new, are typical outcomes of this cycle. If you have a Jupiter Cycle Four going on at the same time (or a Saturn, Uranus, Neptune or Pluto cycle) you will move house, uproot from your state or country or face enormous changes between family members during this cycle.

sun

PEOPLE IN FOCUS

Babies ★ Children ★ Family planning staff ★ Sex therapists ★ Lingerie sales staff ★ Men or women seeking an affair ★ Potential sexual partners ★ Creative advisers ★ Gifted teachers ★ Entertainers ★ Musicians ★ Artists ★ Actors ★ Writers ★ Dancers ★ Condom manufacturers ★ Childcare experts ★ Nannies ★ Babysitters ★ Teachers ★ Adult erotica suppliers ★ Romance novelists.

For singles, the most obvious and important person in this cycle will be the Definite Possibility who floats past. The meaning of this cycle is sexual and erotic above all other things, though, so it may be helpful not to confuse serious relationships with other factors. It may be the beginning of something big, but it depends on other key cycles (your local astrologer can give you information). If you are in a relationship, you will be more than usually concerned with your partner, and the balance between you. Parents will be sharply aware of child/baby issues.

ISSUES IN FOCUS

Cycle Five can be summed up in three ways — sex, kids and creativity. If you come up for your annual Cycle Five and another planet is also involved, you may find a lover, become pregnant and star in a ballet all in the same week. You have been warned! It's common for women to find themselves painting, playing, singing, scribbling or otherwise pouring themselves into self-expression in Sun Cycle Five. This is also — very simply — the House of Fun, so you'll be going out more to be entertained by other people's creative talents. If you're involved in sport during this cycle, you'll get to show off more. Sex is a big part of this cycle. This is the time of the year that you will be building your confidence up in this area, and getting to know yourself better through the physical side of relationships. Parents will find their children or babies become much bigger priorities now, and you'll be concerned with parental pride issues.

IMPORTANT PRIORITIES

The idea of Sun Cycle Five is primarily to feel better about yourself sexually. The Sun will shed light on what is going right, as well as what might be going wrong. You will spend time building your confidence about either your powers of attraction, or your enjoyment of sex, and in some years this will be handed to you on a plate. At other times, there may be challenges, which nudge you to do something about your self-image and self-esteem in connection with your sexuality. Many women read widely about erotica and relationships in a Cycle Five or have more sexual dreams. You will find that your child becomes a centrepoint of your life and times, and, once again, you will have some years when you have good reason to feel very proud of them, and others years when your confidence as a parent is tested, so you have to work harder. Creatively, this is an important time in your life, and if you're having a Jupiter Cycle Five, too, significant opportunities could be in the air at this time.

SUN CYCLE 6

PEOPLE IN FOCUS

Employers ★ Colleagues ★ Staff ★ Clients ★ Supervisors ★ Job Centre staff ★ Doctors ★ Nurses ★ Health insurers ★ Gym instructors ★ Masseurs ★ Osteopaths ★ Naturopaths ★ Chiropractors ★ Dietitians ★ Health gurus ★ Pharmacists ★ Fitness trainers ★ Sports store staff ★ Healthfood shop staff ★ Teachers ★ Superiors ★ Careers officers ★ Headhunters ★ Relief staff ★ Employment agencies ★ Homeopaths ★ Yoga teachers ★ Health writers.

From this selection, you should get the general idea that Cycle Six is about both the body and the mind. Your working life, job situation and general feelings about duty and service come into view. People who hire you, fire you or work for you (or with you) are a priority. So, too, are the legions of people around who can help you to feel more confident about your health, fitness and wellbeing. This is the time of the year that you measure the people around in a work or health capacity, and they'll no doubt measure you on some level, too.

ISSUES IN FOCUS

If you happen to be looking for work in this cycle, you'll find your confidence, self-esteem and sense of self-value are the really big issues. If you are already in a job, but less than satisfied, you will spend around four weeks sorting out what the priorities really are. You may be surprised to find out just how trivial some of your all-encompassing concerns turn out to be. How you feel about your colleagues, employers or clients will depend a great deal on how well you manage to support each other's egos at this time. Good working relationships should be the ultimate aim of this cycle. Your relationship to your body may surface this way: illness forces time off work, which forces you to think hard about your job. More commonly, this is simply a time when circumstances or 'chance' happenings ask you to add up how you really feel about your health.

IMPORTANT PRIORITIES

Having confidence in the way you perform on the job is the thing to aim for now. In some years this will be easier than others. If you are seeking new work, you'll need to sort out the difference between your good self-opinion, and the opinion potential employers have of you. Finding a way to detach your ego from the word 'job' may be hard work. This period should be used to review your current and future employment situation from all angles, and seek advice, if necessary, from people who are authorised to comment. Your diet, sleep, fitness, rituals and routines are also extremely important now, and if all is not what it could be, then you should really be using this period to shape up. Even if you are not consciously seeking out the opinions of people who deal with the human body, you may come across conversations, books or articles which influence your thinking. If you hit a Jupiter Cycle Six now, strong new health or work directions result.

sun

PEOPLE IN FOCUS

Husbands ★ Fiancés ★ De facto partners ★ Serious lovers ★ Business partners ★ Marriage counsellors ★ Wedding celebrants ★ Lawyers ★ Judges ★ Potential lovers ★ Enemies ★ Civil celebrants ★ Ex-partners ★ Ombudsmen ★ Mediators.

This is one of the most important times of the year for building your confidence in partnerships. For many women, this means your feelings about your husband — or even your ex-husband. Single women will focus on a prospective partner now, and spend more time coming to terms with previous relationships. Some women get married around Cycle Seven, and some split up. If the Sun is picking up another planet in this same cycle, you may well be dealing with legal eagles or church people for these reasons. (An astrologer can you give you more information about this.) Cycle Seven rules enemies, too: another reason why peacekeepers may be around. A relationship guru or self-help author may play a part.

ISSUES IN FOCUS

Cycle Seven is always about marriage and — more importantly — how confident both partners feel about each other. All other aspects of the mating game also come into sharper focus in Cycle Seven, and I have known women to dash off to introduction agencies at these times — or fight things out with ex-husbands! You may need to talk to, or get advice from, people who are authorities on marriage and serious commitment now. Even long-married (or much-married) friends fall into this category. Someone who has the authority to speak about your ex-partner or ex-lover may also provide a new angle. This cycle is about relating, above all other things. It may seem strange that it points to lovers, as well as obvious enemies, but the message about co-operation, compromise and 50–50 arrangements is the same. Singles may have the interesting experience of adding up exactly which qualities they are seeking in a serious partner or potential husband.

IMPORTANT PRIORITIES

You may find yourself identifying with your partner — or your enemy — more strongly. This place-swapping can be useful and instructive, but this cycle is also about defining your own importance or role. This is as true for a happy partnership or relationship as it is for an open state of war. In both situations, you may have to work out your particular part in the scheme of things. This is a strongly Libra cycle, and it is about the need to co-operate and merge, yet the Libran sensitivity to unfairness is more pronounced now. If you do become involved in feuds or arguments, make sure the principle is worth it. Many of you will register the importance of marriage as an institution now. Those of you in partnerships which exist for financial or work reasons may have to take a closer look at the structure of these alliances, and work out where the priority is — in the partnership, or in your own desires.

sun CYCLE 8

PEOPLE IN FOCUS

Many of the people who are important in Sun Cycle Two may also emerge now. They include:

Accountants ★ The Tax Office ★ Investment advisers ★ Property consultants ★ Lawyers ★ Bank managers ★ Loan agents ★ Government agencies ★ Other people connected with your money and security.

Cycle Eight also concerns taboo issues — death, sex and the mysteries of life rank pretty highly on the list. You may come into contact with people in the spiritual, religious or caring professions for this reason. Sexual gurus and sexual helper figures may also turn up at this time. Taboo is a personal thing — it means different things to different women. Whatever is an off-limits, sensitive or obviously 'difficult' subject for you may become the centre point for a while. Some of you may consult psychics now — or deal in forbidden topics.

ISSUES IN FOCUS

Cycle Eight is really about other people's money, resources and property. This may be your current partner's, or even the bank's. How confident you feel about these you–me–it situations will be a key point of this cycle. You may have to answer difficult questions about who really has the authority, or who counts more, in agreements which tie in your own finances and security.

This is also an important time of year for going more deeply into the hidden aspects of life. The Sun sheds light on whatever it touches, so some fairly secret or sensitive matters may be dragged out from the Underworld into the light of day now. When you are not addressing serious money issues, you may well be confronting your strengths and weaknesses in taboo areas. Sexuality — in all its forms — and death and dying issues come up for some women. (One of my clients became involved in a seance in Sun Cycle Eight.) There are many taboos around death as well, and in some years this cycle will have special meaning for you as the Sun spotlights the really important issues.

IMPORTANT PRIORITIES

You'll make progress if you treat this part of the year as a confidence-building time for your finances. So much of it will be deeply connected to other people, or other institutions, that you may not be able to make entirely independent decisions. But you could end up being your own best accountant if you are determined to focus on your own security.

The aspects of life which you, or other people, find awkward, dark or even unmentionable, will come into view now. If you feel insecure or unsure of yourself in these taboo areas, then now is the time to seek out people who have the authority to help you.

Serious money issues may also have this slightly 'touchy' feeling now, and there may be an edge to all your feelings about finances.

In some years, you'll find Sun Cycle Eight brings windfalls and bonuses — in others, it's really just a financial lesson.

sun CYCLE 9

PEOPLE IN FOCUS

Travel agents ★ Teachers ★ Students ★ Lecturers ★ Barristers ★ Judges ★ Solicitors ★ Publishers ★ Mass media types ★ Foreign filmmakers ★ Migrants ★ Travellers ★ Guests ★ Course instructors ★ Airline employees ★ Travel professionals ★ Foreign hosts ★ Global thinkers ★ Spiritual leaders ★ Religious people ★ Jet setters.

Cycle Nine is about expanding your horizons. People who are strongly connected to other states, territories or countries may become important in obvious ways. You may also broaden your worldview by becoming absorbed in a particular class, course or learning experience now, so a teacher figure may come through in a major way. People with different accents or over-stamped passports may come centre-stage. This cycle is also connected to belief systems and moral and ethical codes, which is why religious or legal figures may turn up. The 'broad' feel of knowledge in this cycle also means it has a connection with publishing and media.

ISSUES IN FOCUS

The world gets bigger during a Sun Cycle Nine. Some of you may even have your first brush with the Internet now, which literally brings people from other countries to your computer. Holidays and changes of scenery are particularly common during Cycle Nine, and just being in a different place will give you a totally different perspective on life at home. If this cycle coincides with a Cycle Nine involving another planet (your astrologer can explain this) then major journeys, or major involvements with foreign-born people, will begin. If Jupiter Cycle Nine is around at the same time, it may turn out that your contact with other faces and other places is a life-changing experience. Cycle Nine has a lot to do with the word 'mass' — mass media, mass knowledge, mass morality. It's where you get to sort out what you really know, and also what you believe is right and wrong.

IMPORTANT PRIORITIES

You will identify more strongly with your beliefs in this cycle, and work out what is really important to you ethically, spiritually, politically or morally. This is why legal issues so often criss-cross at these times. This will not occur every time, though, and sometimes the belief-sorting you are doing is personal to you and just reflects your own particular view of the world. Feeling confident about your ability to bridge the gap with people from other countries is a major part of this cycle. In some years, this may be a challenge. At other times, these out-of-town or long-distance friend-ships and connections will be purely pleasurable. This is your time to leap out of a rut, if you believe you are in one, and definitely a cycle to use in a big way. The more you deliberately reach out for foreign, or vastly different, experience — the more you will grow in self-understanding. This cycle is about self-education.

sun CYCLE 10

PEOPLE IN FOCUS

Employers ★ Bosses ★ Principals ★ Authorities ★ Colleagues ★ Job contacts ★ Employment agents ★ Headhunters ★ Clients ★ Professional rivals ★ Professional admirers ★ Staff ★ Judging panels ★ Superiors.

Because this cycle connects you with your biggest aims, goals and ambitions — and future trends for your career — the people who come centre-stage now will be a comment on your progress. If you are seeking work in this cycle, authority figures really will be quite influential or awe-inspiring in their own right. Depending on other cycles around this time, you will either be around people who build you up in terms of your status and success, or dent your ego. Both are valuable, as they will put you in touch with what is really important to you. Sometimes status and success can be misleading when viewed in terms of career and professional kudos. This cycle is all about dealing with people who can show you the difference between the shades of grey that define 'success'. For most of you, a boss figure will be a huge focus now.

ISSUES IN FOCUS

The thinking behind Sun Cycle Ten is simple: you need to gain a stronger sense of self-esteem and a certain amount of pride from the way you are achieving your ambitions. Finding the balance between putting your ego 'out there' and, alternatively, feeling like a sat-upon mousegirl, may be a challenge.

In some years it will be easier than others, and these are the times that you may land fabulous jobs, scoop up much sought-after contracts, or find some kind of glory. In other years, Sun Cycle Ten will coincide with an especially difficult time for career or achievement, and you will learn the most important lesson of this cycle: to find a sense of pride in who you are, through what you do. This may involve some difficult decisions in some years. Mostly, though, this will be a time to shine more brightly, even when clouds are around, and to make sure others notice.

IMPORTANT PRIORITIES

For most of you, the big priority will be establishing a strong relationship with your boss or employer — or, in other cases, a VIP client. Mutual confidence needs to be built up. Finding a niche for your abilities and talents is also important at this time, and a sense of display will go with the territory.

In certain cycles, your confidence may be dented, even though you have put on a 1,000-watt performance. In the long term, this will not be a problem: even the dents will put you more strongly in touch with what is really important to you in life. Many of you will change jobs or follow new vocational goals in this cycle. Others will find their social status shifts somewhat.

Cycle Ten is all about your outer face, and role away from home. At the same time, it will pick up on the 'home and family' angle of your chart, so there may be key issues to deal with there as well now.

sun

PEOPLE IN FOCUS

Old friends ★ New friends ★ Clubs ★ Teams ★ Organisations ★ Networks ★ Collectives ★ Groups ★ Bands ★ Packs ★ Leagues ★ Idealists and radicals ★ Companies ★ Ensembles ★ Boards.

This cycle is about the wider groups that you belong to, and the most important people for four weeks or so will be *friends*. Some of your most vital plans and goals will involve them, and one friend in particular may be a big focus. You may encounter people who are ahead of their time, radical or visionary in some way — Cycle Eleven is linked to Aquarius, and these archetypal Aquarian characters may turn up. Your attention will also switch to larger groups of people who exist for a common goal or purpose. Sports teams are an everyday example of this, but so are groups and organisations of all kinds. Cycle Eleven is often when women feel the urge to join a class or club and make new *friends*.

ISSUES IN FOCUS

If you do happen to be part of a club, team or other kind of collective group, your own role within that network of people will be a big deal. Your self-interest and personal concerns may need to be weighed up against the wider concerns of the group. Sometimes this will click very easily — but there may be years when this cycle coincides with problems. Your ego, and the egos of everyone else concerned, need to be working together for you to get the most out of this cycle. You'll think more carefully and deeply about your friends now, sorting out the elements of the friendship which make you feel connected to each other. You'll also make new friends or acquaintances. One of these people will be rather confident, fairly important or impressive for some reason, and well known. This cycle also stirs up your own ideals and thoughts about the future. If you have Aquarius planets, or are naturally this way inclined, then it may be a key time for these issues, too.

IMPORTANT PRIORITIES

Working out which friendships are important may take up a lot of time now. The energy will be worth it, as this is one of the rare times in any year that you will be able to understand which friendships work for you, and why. It's also a good time to build confidence in your social skills, and you can do this at any speed you like. There may be a fair amount of tiptoeing-around-egos between friends and social ties now, but it will be a useful experience. If you are involved in some kind of group situation, Sun Cycle Eleven will enable you to sort out which matters most to you — your own self-interest, the self-interest of others or the general goals and aims of the group. You'll learn a lot about the part that egos can play in group dynamics, but in some years, this cycle will coincide with amazing highlights for, and through, your friends.

sun

PEOPLE IN FOCUS

Confidantes ★ Counsellors ★ Therapists ★ Health professionals ★ Hypnotists ★ Meditation gurus ★ Yoga experts ★ Self-help writers ★ Creative people — artists, photographers, musicians, writers ★ Drug users ★ Alcoholics ★ Dream therapists ★ Spiritualists ★ Mediums ★ Psychics.

Cycle Twelve people are an assorted bunch! Some of them are there to help you work through the most private and sensitive issues, usually in seclusion — and these may affect your emotional, physical or psychological health. Others are truly Piscean types (Cycle Twelve is linked to Pisces) and they may seem to have a unique grasp of reality — fuelled by creative visions, in some instances, and in other cases by drugs or alcohol or even contact with unseen worlds. The scenario will change from year to year, but the effect will be the same — you end up delving into mysteries.

ISSUES IN FOCUS

Cycle Twelve rules the unconscious mind and at this time of year you will discover just how much your unconscious runs the show. Illness, accidents or other strange events that just 'happen' to you should be carefully screened for their after-effects and results. Sometimes you get what you unconsciously want or need in Cycle Twelve. It may appear to be entirely beyond your choice or control, but check again. Maybe it would not have taken place without these 'outside forces'.

Your dreams and night-time experiences will become far more important to you in Cycle Twelve, and some of the big key messages about your life and times will come via some potent dream symbols. If you have any psychic ability or connection to the spiritual world, it will become a bigger issue than usual. Every few years, Sun Cycle Twelve will catch you in a hibernation phase. Work demands, or other unusual circumstances, will require you to lock yourself away from the outside world and exist in isolation for a while.

IMPORTANT PRIORITIES

Matters which are secret and confidential could easily zip to the top of your list now. There is something rather sensitive and deeply personal about the issues around you in Cycle Twelve and it will help to have someone to confide in — or perhaps a diary to write in. Through the association with Pisces, you may find that typically Piscean themes — sacrifice is a big one — enter your life. Cycle Twelve can be rather mysterious and variable, so it may help to read the chapter on Planets in Pisces (pages 161–174) to understand some of the factors, and some of the people, you can expect to play a part. Things you keep to yourself, or activities which lock you away from the passing parade, may be crucial. If you hit Cycle Twelve when another planet is also passing through, this may be a life-changing time, when you come into contact with qualities in yourself that have previously gone unnoticed or unrecognised by you.

WORKING IT ALL

OUT

USING the tables

For most of you, this chapter is simple. To find out your Sun, Mercury, Venus and Mars signs, just find your birthday in the tables that follow, looking up the year, then the day. The Moon has a special section of its own, but it shouldn't take you more than five minutes to use the Moon Wheel (*see* inside back cover) and work out what your Moon sign really is. After that, please fill in your Sun, Moon, Mercury, Venus and Mars signs in the space on page 5 at the front of this book. There's space for your Rising sign, too, which you will already have worked out in the previous chapter.

I've deliberately simplified this chapter since publication of the first edition of this book. Too many people were going cross-eyed trying to do all the calculations, which I'd originally based on time, longitude and latitude of birth.

So — you wanted it, and here it is. The fast and easy version. But to cut time, I've also had to round a few corners off. Consequently, I have to add a few cautions:

WERE YOU BORN ON A SIGN-CHANGE DAY?

On 11th January 1981, for example, Venus changed signs from Sagittarius to Capricorn. On 10th February 1959 Mars changed signs from Taurus to Gemini. If the tables show you were born on a sign-change day, there's a slight chance that your Sun, Mercury, Venus or Mars sign is the one just after, or just before, the sign you've got written down. Born on 10th February 1959, for example, there's a chance your Mars sign might be Taurus, not Gemini. Why? Time zones, birth times, longitude and latitude. But you don't need to know about that. You can fix it — in five seconds.

GETTING YOUR CHART DONE

If you're on the net, it won't cost you anything to use one of the many horoscope calculation sites now available. For information on this, go to Ten Questions (*see* page 519). If you're not on the net, you can pay around $10 for the same kind of service — once again, go to Ten Questions. These wheel diagrams of your chart, based on your birth place, time and date will settle any confusion if you were born on a sign-change day.

THE ROUGH CHECK

Alternatively, if your Mars sign — for example — doesn't feel right, and you're sure you're not just blocking it out, then do check the one before or after. Chances are, one will be noticeably spot-on. Here's a rough checking mechanism.

Caught between a planet in Aries and Taurus?

Aries speeds you up, makes you more competitive, gives you more energy. Taurus calms you down, makes money more important, makes beauty a priority in your life.

Caught between a planet in Taurus and Gemini?

If you've got a planet in Gemini you'll be a natural phone addict or letter writer, fond of magazines and gossip. If it's Taurus, you'll be less verbal or wordy, and more down to earth.

Caught between a planet in Gemini and Cancer?

Your Cancerian side will make your mother a strong issue in your life, for better or worse. With Gemini, it's more likely to be a brother, sister or cousin.

Caught between a planet in Cancer and Leo?

This isn't hard to pick. If you have a dose of Leo, you'll be interested in the creative, arty or entertainment-oriented side of life. If it's Cancer, the family is more important than other things.

Caught between a planet in Leo and Virgo?

People who are more Virgoan tend to be into their bodies or their health — because they choose it, or because they have no choice! Leo influences make you more creative, more self-expressive.

Caught between a planet in Virgo and Libra?

Your Libran side will be design, colour or texture-conscious, noticeably in your wardrobe or home. With Virgo, you're going to be more practical, more detail-conscious, harder-working!

Caught between a planet in Libra and Scorpio?

This is easy to spot. If you have a dose of Scorpio you'll give very little away, you'll be drawn to books, films or music with an intense, dark edge. Libran planets? You're into flirtation and fun.

Caught between a planet in Scorpio and Sagittarius?

Your lust for travel or the great outdoors, or just foreign exotica, will have shown itself by now with planets in Sagittarius. With Scorpio planets, you're more secretive, and more complicated.

Caught between a planet in Sagittarius and Capricorn?

Capricorn planets make you climb, climb, climb — especially in terms of social status or career success. Sagittarius planets result in a more obvious sense of humour, and a less ambitious streak.

Caught between a planet in Capricorn and Aquarius?

Your Aquarian side will be offbeat, off the air occasionally, a bit alternative, a bit 'out there'. Your Capricorn side — if it comes down to a contest — makes you more practical, mature, steady.

Caught between a planet in Aquarius and Pisces?

If it's Pisces, then you'll be more emotional, less cool and detatched about things. If it's Aquarius, you'll be less vague, more head-oriented, and a real individual in the crowd.

Caught between a planet in Pisces and Aries?

If it's Aries, you'll be less patient, more energetic, more fired up, more enthusiastic. If it's Pisces, you'd rather wander off among the daffodils, listen to music, or have an aromatherapy massage.

AND DON'T FORGET

Your Moon sign, which you can work out by following the instructions and using the wheel given on the inside back cover of this book, has also been averaged out for convenience. I can't promise 100% accuracy to each and every woman using the wheel. If you are in any doubt at all, then the particular birth time and place you are working with could very well be influencing the result. Once again, read up on the sign just before, or just after, the one you have calculated. To really put your mind at rest, though, use the internet or a cheap 'quickie' chart from your local astrologer to confirm things.

1920

SUN			MERCURY			VENUS			MARS		
mth	dy	sign	mth	dy	sign	mth	dy	sign	mth	dy	sign
JAN	1	Cap	JAN	1	Sag	JAN	1	Sco	JAN	1	Lib
JAN	21	Aqu	JAN	8	Cap	JAN	4	Sag	JAN	31	Sco
FEB	19	Pis	JAN	27	Aqu	JAN	29	Cap	APR	23	Lib
MAR	20	Ari	FEB	13	Pis	FEB	23	Aqu	JUL	10	Sco
APR	20	Tau	MAR	2	Ari	MAR	18	Pis	SEP	4	Sag
MAY	21	Gem	MAR	19	Pis	APR	12	Ari	OCT	18	Cap
JUN	21	Can	APR	17	Ari	MAY	6	Tau	NOV	27	Aqu
JUL	23	Leo	MAY	8	Tau	MAY	31	Gem			
AUG	23	Vir	MAY	24	Gem	JUN	24	Can			
SEP	23	Lib	JUN	7	Can	JUL	18	Leo			
OCT	23	Sco	JUN	26	Leo	AUG	12	Vir			
NOV	22	Sag	AUG	2	Can	SEP	5	Lib			
DEC	22	Cap	AUG	10	Leo	SEP	29	Sco			
			AUG	31	Vir	OCT	24	Sag			
			SEP	16	Lib	NOV	17	Cap			
			OCT	5	Sco	DEC	12	Aqu			
			OCT	30	Sag						
			NOV	10	Sco						
			DEC	11	Sag						
			DEC	31	Cap						

1921

SUN			MERCURY			VENUS			MARS		
mth	dy	sign	mth	dy	sign	mth	dy	sign	mth	dy	sign
JAN	1	Cap	JAN	1	Cap	JAN	1	Aqu	JAN	1	Aqu
JAN	20	Aqu	JAN	19	Aqu	JAN	6	Pis	JAN	5	Pis
FEB	19	Pis	FEB	5	Pis	FEB	2	Ari	FEB	13	Ari
MAR	21	Ari	APR	14	Ari	MAR	7	Tau	MAR	25	Tau
APR	20	Tau	MAY	1	Tau	APR	25	Ari	MAY	6	Gem
MAY	21	Gem	MAY	15	Gem	JUN	2	Tau	JUN	18	Can
JUN	21	Can	MAY	31	Can	JUL	8	Gem	AUG	3	Leo
JUL	23	Leo	AUG	8	Leo	AUG	5	Can	SEP	19	Vir
AUG	23	Vir	AUG	23	Vir	AUG	31	Leo	NOV	6	Lib
SEP	23	Lib	SEP	9	Lib	SEP	26	Vir	DEC	26	Sco
OCT	23	Sco	SEP	29	Sco	OCT	20	Lib			
NOV	22	Sag	DEC	5	Sag	NOV	13	Sco			
DEC	22	Cap	DEC	24	Cap	DEC	7	Sag			
						DEC	31	Cap			

1922

SUN			MERCURY			VENUS			MARS		
mth	dy	sign	mth	dy	sign	mth	dy	sign	mth	dy	sign
JAN	1	Cap	JAN	1	Cap	JAN	1	Cap	JAN	1	Sco
JAN	20	Aqu	JAN	11	Aqu	JAN	24	Aqu	FEB	18	Sag
FEB	19	Pis	FEB	1	Pis	FEB	17	Pis	SEP	13	Cap
MAR	21	Ari	FEB	9	Aqu	MAR	13	Ari	OCT	30	Aqu
APR	20	Tau	MAR	18	Pis	APR	6	Tau	DEC	11	Pis
MAY	21	Gem	APR	7	Ari	MAY	1	Gem			
JUN	22	Can	APR	22	Tau	MAY	25	Can			
JUL	23	Leo	MAY	7	Gem	JUN	19	Leo			
AUG	23	Vir	JUN	1	Can	JUL	15	Vir			
SEP	23	Lib	JUN	10	Gem	AUG	10	Lib			
OCT	24	Sco	JUL	13	Can	SEP	7	Sco			
NOV	23	Sag	JUL	31	Leo	OCT	10	Sag			
DEC	22	Cap	AUG	15	Vir	NOV	28	Sco			
			SEP	2	Lib						
			OCT	1	Sco						
			OCT	5	Lib						
			NOV	8	Sco						
			NOV	27	Sag						
			DEC	17	Cap						

1923

SUN			MERCURY			VENUS			MARS		
mth	dy	sign	mth	dy	sign	mth	dy	sign	mth	dy	sign
JAN	1	Cap	JAN	1	Cap	JAN	1	Sco	JAN	1	Pis
JAN	21	Aqu	JAN	4	Aqu	JAN	2	Sag	JAN	21	Ari
FEB	19	Pis	FEB	6	Cap	FEB	6	Cap	MAR	4	Tau
MAR	21	Ari	FEB	13	Aqu	MAR	6	Aqu	APR	16	Gem
APR	21	Tau	MAR	13	Pis	APR	1	Pis	MAY	30	Can
MAY	22	Gem	MAR	30	Ari	APR	26	Ari	JUL	16	Leo
JUN	22	Can	APR	14	Tau	MAY	21	Tau	SEP	1	Vir
JUL	23	Leo	MAY	1	Gem	JUN	15	Gem	OCT	18	Lib
AUG	24	Vir	JUL	8	Can	JUL	10	Can	DEC	4	Sco
SEP	24	Lib	JUL	23	Leo	AUG	3	Leo			
OCT	24	Sco	AUG	7	Vir	AUG	27	Vir			
NOV	23	Sag	AUG	27	Lib	SEP	21	Lib			
DEC	22	Cap	OCT	4	Vir	OCT	15	Sco			
			OCT	11	Lib	NOV	8	Sag			
			NOV	2	Sco	DEC	2	Cap			
			NOV	20	Sag	DEC	26	Aqu			
			DEC	10	Cap						

1924

SUN			MERCURY			VENUS			MARS		
mth	dy	sign	mth	dy	sign	mth	dy	sign	mth	dy	sign
JAN	1	Cap	JAN	1	Cap	JAN	1	Aqu	JAN	1	Sco
JAN	21	Aqu	FEB	14	Aqu	JAN	19	Pis	JAN	19	Sag
FEB	19	Pis	MAR	5	Pis	FEB	13	Ari	MAR	6	Cap
MAR	20	Ari	MAR	21	Ari	MAR	9	Tau	APR	24	Aqu
APR	20	Tau	APR	5	Tau	APR	5	Gem	JUN	24	Pis
MAY	21	Gem	JUN	13	Gem	MAY	6	Can	AUG	24	Aqu
JUN	21	Can	JUN	29	Can	SEP	8	Leo	OCT	19	Pis
JUL	23	Leo	JUL	13	Leo	OCT	7	Vir	DEC	19	Ari
AUG	23	Vir	JUL	30	Vir	NOV	2	Lib			
SEP	23	Lib	OCT	7	Lib	NOV	27	Sco			
OCT	23	Sco	OCT	24	Sco	DEC	21	Sag			
NOV	22	Sag	NOV	12	Sag						
DEC	22	Cap	DEC	2	Cap						
			DEC	31	Sag						

1925

SUN			MERCURY			VENUS			MARS		
mth	dy	sign	mth	dy	sign	mth	dy	sign	mth	dy	sign
JAN	1	Cap	JAN	1	Sag	JAN	1	Sag	JAN	1	Ari
JAN	20	Aqu	JAN	14	Cap	JAN	14	Cap	FEB	5	Tau
FEB	19	Pis	FEB	7	Aqu	FEB	7	Aqu	MAR	24	Gem
MAR	21	Ari	FEB	25	Pis	MAR	4	Pis	MAY	9	Can
APR	20	Tau	MAR	13	Ari	MAR	28	Ari	JUN	26	Leo
MAY	21	Gem	APR	1	Tau	APR	21	Tau	AUG	12	Vir
JUN	21	Can	APR	15	Ari	MAY	15	Gem	SEP	28	Lib
JUL	23	Leo	MAY	17	Tau	JUN	9	Can	NOV	13	Sco
AUG	23	Vir	JUN	6	Gem	JUL	3	Leo	DEC	28	Sag
SEP	23	Lib	JUN	20	Can	JUL	28	Vir			
OCT	23	Sco	JUL	5	Leo	AUG	22	Lib			
NOV	22	Sag	JUL	26	Vir	SEP	16	Sco			
DEC	22	Cap	AUG	27	Leo	OCT	11	Sag			
			SEP	11	Vir	NOV	6	Cap			
			SEP	29	Lib	DEC	5	Aqu			
			OCT	17	Sco						
			NOV	5	Sag						

1926

SUN			MERCURY			VENUS			MARS		
mth	dy	sign	mth	dy	sign	mth	dy	sign	mth	dy	sign
JAN	1	Cap	JAN	1	Sag	JAN	1	Aqu	JAN	1	Sag
JAN	20	Aqu	JAN	11	Cap	APR	6	Pis	FEB	9	Cap
FEB	19	Pis	JAN	31	Aqu	MAY	6	Ari	MAR	23	Aqu
MAR	21	Ari	FEB	17	Pis	JUN	2	Tau	MAY	3	Pis
APR	20	Tau	MAR	6	Ari	JUN	28	Gem	JUN	15	Ari
MAY	21	Gem	MAY	13	Tau	JUL	24	Can	AUG	1	Tau
JUN	22	Can	MAY	29	Gem	AUG	18	Leo			
JUL	23	Leo	JUN	12	Can	SEP	11	Vir			
AUG	23	Vir	JUN	29	Leo	OCT	5	Lib			
SEP	23	Lib	SEP	5	Vir	OCT	29	Sco			
OCT	24	Sco	SEP	21	Lib	NOV	22	Sag			
NOV	23	Sag	OCT	9	Sco	DEC	16	Cap			
DEC	22	Cap	OCT	31	Sag						
			NOV	28	Sco						
			DEC	13	Sag						

1927

SUN			MERCURY			VENUS			MARS		
mth	dy	sign	mth	dy	sign	mth	dy	sign	mth	dy	sign
JAN	1	Cap	JAN	1	Sag	JAN	1	Cap	JAN	1	Tau
JAN	21	Aqu	JAN	5	Cap	JAN	9	Aqu	FEB	22	Gem
FEB	19	Pis	JAN	24	Aqu	FEB	2	Pis	APR	17	Can
MAR	21	Ari	FEB	10	Pis	FEB	26	Ari	JUN	6	Leo
APR	21	Tau	APR	17	Ari	MAR	22	Tau	JUL	25	Vir
MAY	22	Gem	MAY	6	Tau	APR	16	Gem	SEP	10	Lib
JUN	22	Can	MAY	21	Gem	MAY	12	Can	OCT	26	Sco
JUL	23	Leo	JUN	4	Can	JUN	8	Leo	DEC	8	Sag
AUG	24	Vir	JUN	28	Leo	JUL	7	Vir			
SEP	24	Lib	JUL	14	Can	NOV	9	Lib			
OCT	24	Sco	AUG	12	Leo	DEC	8	Sco			
NOV	23	Sag	AUG	28	Vir						
DEC	22	Cap	SEP	14	Lib						
			OCT	3	Sco						
			DEC	9	Sag						
			DEC	29	Cap						

1928

SUN			MERCURY			VENUS			MARS		
mth	dy	sign	mth	dy	sign	mth	dy	sign	mth	dy	sign
JAN	1	Cap	JAN	1	Cap	JAN	1	Sco	JAN	1	Sag
JAN	21	Aqu	JAN	16	Aqu	JAN	4	Sag	JAN	19	Cap
FEB	19	Pis	FEB	3	Pis	JAN	29	Cap	FEB	28	Aqu
MAR	20	Ari	FEB	29	Aqu	FEB	22	Aqu	APR	7	Pis
APR	20	Tau	MAR	18	Pis	MAR	18	Pis	MAY	16	Ari
MAY	21	Gem	APR	11	Ari	APR	11	Ari	JUN	26	Tau
JUN	21	Can	APR	27	Tau	MAY	6	Tau	AUG	9	Gem
JUL	23	Leo	MAY	11	Gem	MAY	30	Gem	OCT	3	Can
AUG	23	Vir	MAY	28	Can	JUN	23	Can	DEC	20	Gem
SEP	23	Lib	AUG	4	Leo	JUL	18	Leo			
OCT	23	Sco	AUG	19	Vir	AUG	11	Vir			
NOV	22	Sag	SEP	5	Lib	SEP	4	Lib			
DEC	22	Cap	SEP	27	Sco	SEP	29	Sco			
			OCT	24	Lib	OCT	23	Sag			
			NOV	11	Sco	NOV	17	Cap			
			DEC	1	Sag	DEC	12	Aqu			
			DEC	20	Cap						

1929

SUN			MERCURY			VENUS			MARS		
mth	dy	sign	mth	dy	sign	mth	dy	sign	mth	dy	sign
JAN	1	Cap	JAN	1	Cap	JAN	1	Aqu	JAN	1	Gem
JAN	20	Aqu	JAN	8	Aqu	JAN	6	Pis	MAR	10	Can
FEB	19	Pis	MAR	16	Pis	FEB	2	Ari	MAY	13	Leo
MAR	21	Ari	APR	3	Ari	MAR	8	Tau	JUL	4	Vir
APR	20	Tau	APR	19	Tau	APR	20	Ari	AUG	21	Lib
MAY	21	Gem	MAY	3	Gem	JUN	3	Tau	OCT	6	Sco
JUN	21	Can	JUL	11	Can	JUL	8	Gem	NOV	18	Sag
JUL	23	Leo	JUL	27	Leo	AUG	5	Can	DEC	29	Cap
AUG	23	Vir	AUG	11	Vir	AUG	31	Leo			
SEP	23	Lib	AUG	30	Lib	SEP	25	Vir			
OCT	23	Sco	NOV	5	Sco	OCT	20	Lib			
NOV	22	Sag	NOV	24	Sag	NOV	13	Sco			
DEC	22	Cap	DEC	13	Cap	DEC	7	Sag			
						DEC	31	Cap			

1930

SUN			MERCURY			VENUS			MARS		
mth	dy	sign	mth	dy	sign	mth	dy	sign	mth	dy	sign
JAN	1	Cap	JAN	1	Cap	JAN	1	Cap	JAN	1	Cap
JAN	20	Aqu	JAN	2	Aqu	JAN	24	Aqu	FEB	6	Aqu
FEB	19	Pis	JAN	23	Cap	FEB	16	Pis	MAR	17	Pis
MAR	21	Ari	FEB	15	Aqu	MAR	12	Ari	APR	24	Ari
APR	20	Tau	MAR	9	Pis	APR	6	Tau	JUN	3	Tau
MAY	21	Gem	MAR	26	Ari	APR	30	Gem	JUL	14	Gem
JUN	22	Can	APR	10	Tau	MAY	25	Can	AUG	28	Can
JUL	23	Leo	MAY	1	Gem	JUN	19	Leo	OCT	20	Leo
AUG	23	Vir	MAY	17	Tau	JUL	14	Vir			
SEP	23	Lib	JUN	14	Gem	AUG	10	Lib			
OCT	24	Sco	JUL	4	Can	SEP	7	Sco			
NOV	23	Sag	JUL	19	Leo	OCT	12	Sag			
DEC	22	Cap	AUG	4	Vir	NOV	22	Sco			
			AUG	26	Lib						
			SEP	20	Vir						
			OCT	11	Lib						
			OCT	29	Sco						
			NOV	17	Sag						
			DEC	6	Cap						

1931

SUN			MERCURY			VENUS			MARS		
mth	dy	sign	mth	dy	sign	mth	dy	sign	mth	dy	sign
JAN	1	Cap	JAN	1	Cap	JAN	1	Sco	JAN	1	Leo
JAN	21	Aqu	FEB	11	Aqu	JAN	3	Sag	FEB	16	Can
FEB	19	Pis	MAR	2	Pis	FEB	6	Cap	MAR	30	Leo
MAR	21	Ari	MAR	18	Ari	MAR	5	Aqu	JUN	10	Vir
APR	21	Tau	APR	3	Tau	MAR	31	Pis	AUG	1	Lib
MAY	22	Gem	JUN	11	Gem	APR	26	Ari	SEP	17	Sco
JUN	22	Can	JUN	26	Can	MAY	21	Tau	OCT	30	Sag
JUL	23	Leo	JUL	10	Leo	JUN	14	Gem	DEC	10	Cap
AUG	24	Vir	JUL	28	Vir	JUL	9	Can			
SEP	24	Lib	OCT	4	Lib	AUG	3	Leo			
OCT	24	Sco	OCT	22	Sco	AUG	27	Vir			
NOV	23	Sag	NOV	10	Sag	SEP	20	Lib			
DEC	22	Cap	DEC	2	Cap	OCT	14	Sco			
			DEC	20	Sag	NOV	7	Sag			
			DEC	20	Sag	DEC	1	Cap			
						DEC	25	Aqu			

1932

SUN			MERCURY			VENUS			MARS		
mth	dy	sign	mth	dy	sign	mth	dy	sign	mth	dy	sign
JAN	1	Cap	JAN	1	Sag	JAN	1	Aqu	JAN	1	Cap
JAN	21	Aqu	JAN	14	Cap	JAN	19	Pis	JAN	18	Aqu
FEB	19	Pis	FEB	5	Aqu	FEB	12	Ari	FEB	25	Pis
MAR	20	Ari	FEB	23	Pis	MAR	9	Tau	APR	3	Ari
APR	20	Tau	MAR	9	Ari	APR	5	Gem	MAY	12	Tau
MAY	21	Gem	MAY	15	Tau	MAY	6	Can	JUN	22	Gem
JUN	21	Can	JUN	2	Gem	JUL	13	Gem	AUG	4	Can
JUL	23	Leo	JUN	16	Can	JUL	28	Can	SEP	20	Leo
AUG	23	Vir	JUL	2	Leo	SEP	8	Leo	NOV	13	Vir
SEP	23	Lib	JUL	27	Vir	OCT	7	Vir			
OCT	23	Sco	AUG	10	Leo	NOV	2	Lib			
NOV	22	Sag	SEP	9	Vir	NOV	27	Sco			
DEC	22	Cap	SEP	26	Lib	DEC	21	Sag			
			OCT	13	Sco						
			NOV	2	Sag						

1933

SUN			MERCURY			VENUS			MARS		
mth	dy	sign	mth	dy	sign	mth	dy	sign	mth	dy	sign
JAN	1	Cap	JAN	1	Sag	JAN	1	Sag	JAN	1	Vir
JAN	20	Aqu	JAN	8	Cap	JAN	14	Cap	JUL	6	Lib
FEB	19	Pis	JAN	27	Aqu	FEB	7	Aqu	AUG	26	Sco
MAR	21	Ari	FEB	14	Pis	MAR	3	Pis	OCT	9	Sag
APR	20	Tau	MAR	3	Ari	MAR	27	Ari	NOV	19	Cap
MAY	21	Gem	MAR	25	Pis	APR	20	Tau	DEC	28	Aqu
JUN	21	Can	APR	17	Ari	MAY	15	Gem			
JUL	23	Leo	MAY	10	Tau	JUN	8	Can			
AUG	23	Vir	MAY	25	Gem	JUL	3	Leo			
SEP	23	Lib	JUN	8	Can	JUL	27	Vir			
OCT	23	Sco	JUN	27	Leo	AUG	21	Lib			
NOV	22	Sag	SEP	2	Vir	SEP	15	Sco			
DEC	22	Cap	SEP	18	Lib	OCT	11	Sag			
			OCT	6	Sco	NOV	6	Cap			
			OCT	30	Sag	DEC	5	Aqu			
			NOV	16	Sco						
			DEC	12	Sag						

1934

	SUN			MERCURY			VENUS			MARS	
mth	dy	sign	mth	dy	sign	mth	dy	sign	mth	dy	sign
JAN	1	Cap	JAN	1	Cap	JAN	1	Aqu	JAN	1	Aqu
JAN	20	Aqu	JAN	20	Aqu	APR	6	Pis	FEB	4	Pis
FEB	19	Pis	FEB	6	Pis	MAY	6	Ari	MAR	14	Ari
MAR	21	Ari	APR	15	Ari	JUN	2	Tau	APR	22	Tau
APR	20	Tau	MAY	2	Tau	JUN	28	Gem	JUN	2	Gem
MAY	21	Gem	MAY	16	Gem	JUL	23	Can	JUL	15	Can
JUN	22	Can	JUN	1	Can	AUG	17	Leo	AUG	30	Leo
JUL	23	Leo	AUG	9	Leo	SEP	11	Vir	OCT	18	Vir
AUG	23	Vir	AUG	25	Vir	OCT	5	Lib	DEC	11	Lib
SEP	23	Lib	SEP	10	Lib	OCT	29	Sco			
OCT	24	Sco	SEP	30	Sco	NOV	22	Sag			
NOV	22	Sag	DEC	6	Sag	DEC	16	Cap			
DEC	22	Cap	DEC	25	Cap						

1935

	SUN			MERCURY			VENUS			MARS	
mth	dy	sign	mth	dy	sign	mth	dy	sign	mth	dy	sign
JAN	1	Cap	JAN	1	Cap	JAN	1	Cap	JAN	1	Lib
JAN	20	Aqu	JAN	13	Aqu	JAN	8	Aqu	JUL	29	Sco
FEB	19	Pis	FEB	1	Pis	FEB	1	Pis	SEP	16	Sag
MAR	21	Ari	FEB	15	Aqu	FEB	26	Ari	OCT	28	Cap
APR	21	Tau	MAR	18	Pis	MAR	22	Tau	DEC	7	Aqu
MAY	22	Gem	APR	8	Ari	APR	16	Gem			
JUN	22	Can	APR	24	Tau	MAY	11	Can			
JUL	23	Leo	MAY	8	Gem	JUN	7	Leo			
AUG	24	Vir	MAY	29	Can	JUL	7	Vir			
SEP	23	Lib	JUN	20	Gem	NOV	9	Lib			
OCT	24	Sco	JUL	13	Can	DEC	8	Sco			
NOV	23	Sag	AUG	2	Leo						
DEC	22	Cap	AUG	16	Vir						
			SEP	3	Lib						
			SEP	28	Sco						
			OCT	12	Lib						
			NOV	10	Sco						
			NOV	29	Sag						
			DEC	18	Cap						

1936

SUN			MERCURY			VENUS			MARS		
mth	dy	sign	mth	dy	sign	mth	dy	sign	mth	dy	sign
JAN	1	Cap	JAN	1	Cap	JAN	1	Sco	JAN	1	Aqu
JAN	21	Aqu	JAN	6	Aqu	JAN	3	Sag	JAN	14	Pis
FEB	19	Pis	MAR	13	Pis	JAN	28	Cap	FEB	22	Ari
MAR	20	Ari	MAR	31	Ari	FEB	22	Aqu	APR	1	Tau
APR	20	Tau	APR	15	Tau	MAR	17	Pis	MAY	13	Gem
MAY	21	Gem	MAY	1	Gem	APR	11	Ari	JUN	25	Can
JUN	21	Can	JUL	8	Can	MAY	5	Tau	AUG	10	Leo
JUL	23	Leo	JUL	23	Leo	MAY	29	Gem	SEP	26	Vir
AUG	23	Vir	AUG	7	Vir	JUN	23	Can	NOV	14	Lib
SEP	23	Lib	AUG	27	Lib	JUL	17	Leo			
OCT	23	Sco	NOV	2	Sco	AUG	11	Vir			
NOV	22	Sag	NOV	21	Sag	SEP	4	Lib			
DEC	22	Cap	DEC	10	Cap	SEP	28	Sco			
						OCT	23	Sag			
						NOV	16	Cap			
						DEC	11	Aqu			

1937

SUN			MERCURY			VENUS			MARS		
mth	dy	sign	mth	dy	sign	mth	dy	sign	mth	dy	sign
JAN	1	Cap	JAN	1	Aqu	JAN	1	Aqu	JAN	1	Lib
JAN	20	Aqu	JAN	9	Cap	JAN	6	Pis	JAN	5	Sco
FEB	19	Pis	FEB	14	Aqu	FEB	2	Ari	MAR	13	Sag
MAR	21	Ari	MAR	6	Pis	MAR	9	Tau	MAY	14	Sco
APR	20	Tau	MAR	23	Ari	APR	14	Ari	AUG	8	Sag
MAY	21	Gem	APR	7	Tau	JUN	4	Tau	SEP	30	Cap
JUN	21	Can	JUN	13	Gem	JUL	7	Gem	NOV	11	Aqu
JUL	23	Leo	JUL	1	Can	AUG	4	Can	DEC	21	Pis
AUG	23	Vir	JUL	15	Leo	AUG	31	Leo			
SEP	23	Lib	JUL	31	Vir	SEP	25	Vir			
OCT	23	Sco	OCT	8	Lib	OCT	19	Lib			
NOV	22	Sag	OCT	26	Sco	NOV	12	Sco			
DEC	22	Cap	NOV	13	Sag	DEC	6	Sag			
			DEC	3	Cap	DEC	30	Cap			

1938

	SUN			MERCURY			VENUS			MARS	
mth	dy	sign	mth	dy	sign	mth	dy	sign	mth	dy	sign
JAN	1	Cap	JAN	1	Cap	JAN	1	Cap	JAN	1	Pis
JAN	20	Aqu	JAN	6	Sag	JAN	23	Aqu	JAN	30	Ari
FEB	19	Pis	JAN	12	Cap	FEB	16	Pis	MAR	12	Tau
MAR	21	Ari	FEB	8	Aqu	MAR	12	Ari	APR	23	Gem
APR	20	Tau	FEB	27	Pis	APR	5	Tau	JUN	7	Can
MAY	21	Gem	MAR	15	Ari	APR	29	Gem	JUL	22	Leo
JUN	22	Can	APR	1	Tau	MAY	24	Can	SEP	7	Vir
JUL	23	Leo	APR	23	Ari	JUN	18	Leo	OCT	25	Lib
AUG	23	Vir	MAY	16	Tau	JUL	14	Vir	DEC	11	Sco
SEP	23	Lib	JUN	8	Gem	AUG	9	Lib			
OCT	24	Sco	JUN	22	Can	SEP	7	Sco			
NOV	22	Sag	JUL	7	Leo	OCT	13	Sag			
DEC	22	Cap	JUL	26	Vir	NOV	15	Sco			
			SEP	3	Leo						
			SEP	10	Vir						
			OCT	1	Lib						
			OCT	18	Sco	·					
			NOV	6	Sag						

1939

	SUN			MERCURY			VENUS			MARS	
mth	dy	sign	mth	dy	sign	mth	dy	sign	mth	dy	sign
JAN	1	Cap	JAN	1	Sag	JAN	1	Sco	JAN	1	Sco
JAN	20	Aqu	JAN	12	Cap	JAN	4	Sag	JAN	29	Sag
FEB	19	Pis	FEB	1	Aqu	FEB	6	Cap	MAR	21	Cap
MAR	21	Ari	FEB	19	Pis	MAR	5	Aqu	MAY	25	Aqu
APR	20	Tau	MAR	7	Ari	MAR	31	Pis	JUL	21	Cap
MAY	21	Gem	MAY	14	Tau	APR	25	Ari	SEP	24	Aqu
JUN	22	Can	MAY	31	Gem	MAY	20	Tau	NOV	19	Pis
JUL	23	Leo	JUN	13	Can	JUN	14	Gem			
AUG	24	Vir	JUN	30	Leo	JUL	9	Can			
SEP	23	Lib	SEP	7	Vir	AUG	2	Leo			
OCT	24	Sco	SEP	23	Lib	AUG	26	Vir			
NOV	23	Sag	OCT	11	Sco	SEP	20	Lib			
DEC	22	Cap	NOV	1	Sag	OCT	14	Sco			
			DEC	3	Sco	NOV	7	Sag			
			DEC	13	Sag	DEC	1	Cap			
						DEC	25	Aqu			

1940

	SUN			MERCURY			VENUS			MARS	
mth	**dy**	**sign**	**mth**	**dy**	**sign**	**mth**	**dy**	**sign**	**mth**	**dy**	**sign**
JAN	1	Cap	JAN	1	Sag	JAN	1	Aqu	JAN	1	Pis
JAN	21	Aqu	JAN	6	Cap	JAN	18	Pis	JAN	4	Ari
FEB	19	Pis	JAN	25	Aqu	FEB	12	Ari	FEB	17	Tau
MAR	20	Ari	FEB	11	Pis	MAR	8	Tau	APR	1	Gem
APR	20	Tau	MAR	4	Ari	APR	4	Gem	MAY	17	Can
MAY	21	Gem	MAR	8	Pis	MAY	6	Can	JUL	3	Leo
JUN	21	Can	APR	17	Ari	JUL	5	Gem	AUG	19	Vir
JUL	23	Leo	MAY	6	Tau	AUG	1	Can	OCT	5	Lib
AUG	23	Vir	MAY	21	Gem	SEP	8	Leo	NOV	20	Sco
SEP	23	Lib	JUN	4	Can	OCT	6	Vir			
OCT	23	Sco	JUN	26	Leo	NOV	1	Lib			
NOV	22	Sag	JUL	21	Can	NOV	26	Sco			
DEC	21	Cap	AUG	11	Leo	DEC	20	Sag			
			AUG	29	Vir						
			SEP	14	Lib						
			OCT	3	Sco						
			DEC	9	Sag						
			DEC	29	Cap						

1941

	SUN			MERCURY			VENUS			MARS	
mth	**dy**	**sign**	**mth**	**dy**	**sign**	**mth**	**dy**	**sign**	**mth**	**dy**	**sign**
JAN	1	Cap	JAN	1	Cap	JAN	1	Sag	JAN	1	Sco
JAN	20	Aqu	JAN	16	Aqu	JAN	13	Cap	JAN	4	Sag
FEB	19	Pis	FEB	3	Pis	FEB	6	Aqu	FEB	17	Cap
MAR	21	Ari	MAR	7	Aqu	MAR	2	Pis	APR	2	Aqu
APR	20	Tau	MAR	16	Pis	MAR	27	Ari	MAY	16	Pis
MAY	21	Gem	APR	12	Ari	APR	20	Tau	JUL	2	Ari
JUN	21	Can	APR	28	Tau	MAY	14	Gem			
JUL	23	Leo	MAY	13	Gem	JUN	7	Can			
AUG	23	Vir	MAY	29	Can	JUL	2	Leo			
SEP	23	Lib	AUG	6	Leo	JUL	27	Vir			
OCT	23	Sco	AUG	21	Vir	AUG	21	Lib			
NOV	22	Sag	SEP	6	Lib	SEP	15	Sco			
DEC	22	Cap	SEP	28	Sco	OCT	10	Sag			
			OCT	29	Lib	NOV	6	Cap			
			NOV	11	Sco	DEC	5	Aqu			
			DEC	3	Sag						
			DEC	22	Cap						

1942

SUN			MERCURY			VENUS			MARS		
mth	dy	sign	mth	dy	sign	mth	dy	sign	mth	dy	sign
JAN	1	Cap	JAN	1	Cap	JAN	1	Aqu	JAN	1	Ari
JAN	20	Aqu	JAN	9	Aqu	APR	6	Pis	JAN	11	Tau
FEB	19	Pis	MAR	17	Pis	MAY	6	Ari	MAR	7	Gem
MAR	21	Ari	APR	5	Ari	JUN	2	Tau	APR	26	Can
APR	20	Tau	APR	20	Tau	JUN	27	Gem	JUN	14	Leo
MAY	21	Gem	MAY	5	Gem	JUL	23	Can	AUG	1	Vir
JUN	22	Can	JUL	12	Can	AUG	17	Leo	SEP	17	Lib
JUL	23	Leo	JUL	29	Leo	SEP	10	Vir	NOV	1	Sco
AUG	23	Vir	AUG	13	Vir	OCT	4	Lib	DEC	15	Sag
SEP	23	Lib	AUG	31	Lib	OCT	28	Sco			
OCT	24	Sco	NOV	7	Sco	NOV	21	Sag			
NOV	22	Sag	NOV	25	Sag	DEC	15	Cap			
DEC	22	Cap	DEC	14	Cap						

1943

SUN			MERCURY			VENUS			MARS		
mth	dy	sign	mth	dy	sign	mth	dy	sign	mth	dy	sign
JAN	1	Cap	JAN	1	Cap	JAN	1	Cap	JAN	1	Sag
JAN	20	Aqu	JAN	3	Aqu	JAN	8	Aqu	JAN	26	Cap
FEB	19	Pis	JAN	27	Cap	FEB	1	Pis	MAR	8	Aqu
MAR	21	Ari	FEB	15	Aqu	FEB	25	Ari	APR	17	Pis
APR	20	Tau	MAR	11	Pis	MAR	21	Tau	MAY	27	Ari
MAY	21	Gem	MAR	28	Ari	APR	15	Gem	JUL	7	Tau
JUN	22	Can	APR	12	Tau	MAY	11	Can	AUG	23	Gem
JUL	23	Leo	APR	30	Gem	JUN	7	Leo			
AUG	24	Vir	MAY	26	Tau	JUL	7	Vir			
SEP	23	Lib	JUN	14	Gem	NOV	9	Lib			
OCT	24	Sco	JUL	6	Can	DEC	8	Sco			
NOV	23	Sag	JUL	20	Leo						
DEC	22	Cap	AUG	5	Vir						
			AUG	27	Lib						
			SEP	25	Vir						
			OCT	11	Lib						
			OCT	30	Sco						
			NOV	18	Sag						
			DEC	8	Cap						

1944

SUN			MERCURY			VENUS			MARS		
mth	**dy**	**sign**	**mth**	**dy**	**sign**	**mth**	**dy**	**sign**	**mth**	**dy**	**sign**
JAN	1	Cap	JAN	1	Cap	JAN	1	Sco	JAN	1	Gem
JAN	21	Aqu	FEB	12	Aqu	JAN	3	Sag	MAR	28	Can
FEB	19	Pis	MAR	3	Pis	JAN	28	Cap	MAY	22	Leo
MAR	20	Ari	MAR	19	Ari	FEB	21	Aqu	JUL	12	Vir
APR	20	Tau	APR	3	Tau	MAR	17	Pis	AUG	29	Lib
MAY	21	Gem	JUN	11	Gem	APR	10	Ari	OCT	13	Sco
JUN	21	Can	JUN	27	Can	MAY	4	Tau	NOV	25	Sag
JUL	22	Leo	JUL	11	Leo	MAY	29	Gem			
AUG	23	Vir	JUL	28	Vir	JUN	22	Can			
SEP	23	Lib	OCT	5	Lib	JUL	17	Leo			
OCT	23	Sco	OCT	22	Sco	AUG	10	Vir			
NOV	22	Sag	NOV	10	Sag	SEP	3	Lib			
DEC	21	Cap	DEC	1	Cap	SEP	28	Sco			
			DEC	23	Sag	OCT	22	Sag			
						NOV	16	Cap			
						DEC	11	Aqu			

1945

SUN			MERCURY			VENUS			MARS		
mth	**dy**	**sign**	**mth**	**dy**	**sign**	**mth**	**dy**	**sign**	**mth**	**dy**	**sign**
JAN	1	Cap	JAN	1	Sag	JAN	1	Aqu	JAN	1	Sag
JAN	20	Aqu	JAN	14	Cap	JAN	5	Pis	JAN	5	Cap
FEB	19	Pis	FEB	5	Aqu	FEB	2	Ari	FEB	14	Aqu
MAR	20	Ari	FEB	23	Pis	MAR	11	Tau	MAR	25	Pis
APR	20	Tau	MAR	11	Ari	APR	7	Ari	MAY	2	Ari
MAY	21	Gem	MAY	16	Tau	JUN	4	Tau	JUN	11	Tau
JUN	21	Can	JUN	4	Gem	JUL	7	Gem	JUL	23	Gem
JUL	23	Leo	JUN	18	Can	AUG	4	Can	SEP	7	Can
AUG	23	Vir	JUL	3	Leo	AUG	30	Leo	NOV	11	Leo
SEP	23	Lib	JUL	26	Vir	SEP	24	Vir	DEC	26	Can
OCT	23	Sco	AUG	17	Leo	OCT	19	Lib			
NOV	22	Sag	SEP	10	Vir	NOV	12	Sco			
DEC	22	Cap	SEP	27	Lib	DEC	6	Sag			
			OCT	15	Sco	DEC	30	Cap			
			NOV	3	Sag						

1946

SUN			MERCURY			VENUS			MARS		
mth	dy	sign	mth	dy	sign	mth	dy	sign	mth	dy	sign
JAN	1	Cap	JAN	1	Sag	JAN	1	Cap	JAN	1	Can
JAN	20	Aqu	JAN	9	Cap	JAN	22	Aqu	APR	22	Leo
FEB	19	Pis	JAN	29	Aqu	FEB	15	Pis	JUN	20	Vir
MAR	21	Ari	FEB	15	Pis	MAR	11	Ari	AUG	9	Lib
APR	20	Tau	MAR	4	Ari	APR	5	Tau	SEP	24	Sco
MAY	21	Gem	APR	1	Pis	APR	29	Gem	NOV	6	Sag
JUN	22	Can	APR	16	Ari	MAY	24	Can	DEC	17	Cap
JUL	23	Leo	MAY	11	Tau	JUN	18	Leo			
AUG	23	Vir	MAY	27	Gem	JUL	13	Vir			
SEP	23	Lib	JUN	10	Can	AUG	9	Lib			
OCT	24	Sco	JUN	27	Leo	SEP	7	Sco			
NOV	22	Sag	SEP	3	Vir	OCT	16	Sag			
DEC	22	Cap	SEP	19	Lib	NOV	8	Sco			
			OCT	7	Sco						
			OCT	30	Sag						
			NOV	20	Sco						
			DEC	13	Sag						

1947

SUN			MERCURY			VENUS			MARS		
mth	dy	sign	mth	dy	sign	mth	dy	sign	mth	dy	sign
JAN	1	Cap	JAN	1	Sag	JAN	1	Sco	JAN	1	Cap
JAN	20	Aqu	JAN	3	Cap	JAN	5	Sag	JAN	25	Aqu
FEB	19	Pis	JAN	21	Aqu	FEB	6	Cap	MAR	4	Pis
MAR	21	Ari	FEB	8	Pis	MAR	5	Aqu	APR	11	Ari
APR	20	Tau	APR	16	Ari	MAR	30	Pis	MAY	21	Tau
MAY	21	Gem	MAY	4	Tau	APR	25	Ari	JUL	1	Gem
JUN	22	Can	MAY	18	Gem	MAY	20	Tau	AUG	13	Can
JUL	23	Leo	JUN	2	Can	JUN	13	Gem	OCT	1	Leo
AUG	24	Vir	AUG	10	Leo	JUL	8	Can	DEC	1	Vir
SEP	23	Lib	AUG	26	Vir	AUG	2	Leo			
OCT	24	Sco	SEP	11	Lib	AUG	26	Vir			
NOV	23	Sag	OCT	1	Sco	SEP	19	Lib			
DEC	22	Cap	DEC	7	Sag	OCT	13	Sco			
			DEC	26	Cap	NOV	6	Sag			
						NOV	30	Cap			
						DEC	24	Aqu			

1948

SUN			MERCURY			VENUS			MARS		
mth	dy	sign	mth	dy	sign	mth	dy	sign	mth	dy	sign
JAN	1	Cap	JAN	1	Cap	JAN	1	Aqu	JAN	1	Vir
JAN	21	Aqu	JAN	14	Aqu	JAN	18	Pis	FEB	12	Leo
FEB	19	Pis	FEB	2	Pis	FEB	11	Ari	MAY	18	Vir
MAR	20	Ari	FEB	20	Aqu	MAR	8	Tau	JUL	17	Lib
APR	20	Tau	MAR	18	Pis	APR	4	Gem	SEP	3	Sco
MAY	21	Gem	APR	9	Ari	MAY	7	Can	OCT	17	Sag
JUN	21	Can	APR	25	Tau	JUN	29	Gem	NOV	26	Cap
JUL	22	Leo	MAY	9	Gem	AUG	3	Can			
AUG	23	Vir	MAY	28	Can	SEP	8	Leo			
SEP	23	Lib	JUN	28	Gem	OCT	6	Vir			
OCT	23	Sco	JUL	11	Can	NOV	1	Lib			
NOV	22	Sag	AUG	2	Leo	NOV	26	Sco			
DEC	21	Cap	AUG	17	Vir	DEC	20	Sag			
			SEP	3	Lib						
			SEP	27	Sco						
			OCT	17	Lib						
			NOV	10	Sco						
			NOV	29	Sag						
			DEC	18	Cap						

1949

SUN			MERCURY			VENUS			MARS		
mth	dy	sign	mth	dy	sign	mth	dy	sign	mth	dy	sign
JAN	1	Cap	JAN	1	Cap	JAN	1	Sag	JAN	1	Cap
JAN	20	Aqu	JAN	6	Aqu	JAN	13	Cap	JAN	4	Aqu
FEB	18	Pis	MAR	14	Pis	FEB	6	Aqu	FEB	11	Pis
MAR	20	Ari	APR	1	Ari	MAR	2	Pis	MAR	21	Ari
APR	20	Tau	APR	16	Tau	MAR	26	Ari	APR	30	Tau
MAY	21	Gem	MAY	2	Gem	APR	19	Tau	JUN	10	Gem
JUN	21	Can	JUL	10	Can	MAY	14	Gem	JUL	23	Can
JUL	23	Leo	JUL	25	Leo	JUN	7	Can	SEP	7	Leo
AUG	23	Vir	AUG	9	Vir	JUL	1	Leo	OCT	27	Vir
SEP	23	Lib	AUG	28	Lib	JUL	26	Vir	DEC	26	Lib
OCT	23	Sco	NOV	3	Sco	AUG	20	Lib			
NOV	22	Sag	NOV	22	Sag	SEP	14	Sco			
DEC	22	Cap	DEC	11	Cap	OCT	10	Sag			
						NOV	6	Cap			
						DEC	6	Aqu			

1950

SUN			MERCURY			VENUS			MARS		
mth	dy	sign	mth	dy	sign	mth	dy	sign	mth	dy	sign
JAN	1	Cap	JAN	1	Aqu	JAN	1	Aqu	JAN	1	Lib
JAN	20	Aqu	JAN	15	Cap	APR	6	Pis	MAR	28	Vir
FEB	19	Pis	FEB	14	Aqu	MAY	5	Ari	JUN	11	Lib
MAR	21	Ari	MAR	7	Pis	JUN	1	Tau	AUG	10	Sco
APR	20	Tau	MAR	24	Ari	JUN	27	Gem	SEP	25	Sag
MAY	21	Gem	APR	8	Tau	JUL	22	Can	NOV	6	Cap
JUN	21	Can	JUN	14	Gem	AUG	16	Leo	DEC	15	Aqu
JUL	23	Leo	JUL	2	Can	SEP	10	Vir			
AUG	23	Vir	JUL	16	Leo	OCT	4	Lib			
SEP	23	Lib	AUG	2	Vir	OCT	28	Sco			
OCT	23	Sco	AUG	27	Lib	NOV	21	Sag			
NOV	22	Sag	SEP	10	Vir	DEC	14	Cap			
DEC	22	Cap	OCT	9	Lib						
			OCT	27	Sco						
			NOV	15	Sag						
			DEC	5	Cap						

1951

SUN			MERCURY			VENUS			MARS		
mth	dy	sign	mth	dy	sign	mth	dy	sign	mth	dy	sign
JAN	1	Cap	JAN	1	Cap	JAN	1	Cap	JAN	1	Aqu
JAN	20	Aqu	FEB	9	Aqu	JAN	7	Aqu	JAN	22	Pis
FEB	19	Pis	FEB	28	Pis	JAN	31	Pis	MAR	1	Ari
MAR	21	Ari	MAR	16	Ari	FEB	24	Ari	APR	10	Tau
APR	20	Tau	APR	2	Tau	MAR	21	Tau	MAY	21	Gem
MAY	21	Gem	MAY	1	Ari	APR	15	Gem	JUL	3	Can
JUN	22	Can	MAY	15	Tau	MAY	11	Can	AUG	18	Leo
JUL	23	Leo	JUN	9	Gem	JUN	7	Leo	OCT	5	Vir
AUG	23	Vir	JUN	24	Can	JUL	8	Vir	NOV	24	Lib
SEP	23	Lib	JUL	8	Leo	NOV	9	Lib			
OCT	24	Sco	JUL	27	Vir	DEC	8	Sco			
NOV	23	Sag	OCT	2	Lib						
DEC	22	Cap	OCT	19	Sco						
			NOV	8	Sag						
			DEC	1	Cap						
			DEC	12	Sag						

1952

SUN			MERCURY			VENUS			MARS		
mth	dy	sign	mth	dy	sign	mth	dy	sign	mth	dy	sign
JAN	1	Cap	JAN	1	Sag	JAN	1	Sco	JAN	1	Lib
JAN	21	Aqu	JAN	13	Cap	JAN	2	Sag	JAN	20	Sco
FEB	19	Pis	FEB	3	Aqu	JAN	27	Cap	AUG	27	Sag
MAR	20	Ari	FEB	20	Pis	FEB	21	Aqu	OCT	12	Cap
APR	20	Tau	MAR	7	Ari	MAR	16	Pis	NOV	21	Aqu
MAY	21	Gem	MAY	14	Tau	APR	9	Ari	DEC	30	Pis
JUN	21	Can	MAY	31	Gem	MAY	4	Tau			
JUL	22	Leo	JUN	14	Can	MAY	28	Gem			
AUG	23	Vir	JUN	30	Leo	JUN	22	Can			
SEP	23	Lib	SEP	7	Vir	JUL	16	Leo			
OCT	23	Sco	SEP	23	Lib	AUG	9	Vir			
NOV	22	Sag	OCT	11	Sco	SEP	3	Lib			
DEC	21	Cap	NOV	1	Sag	SEP	27	Sco			
						OCT	22	Sag			
						NOV	15	Cap			
						DEC	10	Aqu			

1953

SUN			MERCURY			VENUS			MARS		
mth	dy	sign	mth	dy	sign	mth	dy	sign	mth	dy	sign
JAN	1	Cap	JAN	1	Sag	JAN	1	Aqu	JAN	1	Pis
JAN	20	Aqu	JAN	6	Cap	JAN	5	Pis	FEB	8	Ari
FEB	18	Pis	JAN	25	Aqu	FEB	2	Ari	MAR	20	Tau
MAR	20	Ari	FEB	11	Pis	MAR	14	Tau	MAY	1	Gem
APR	20	Tau	MAR	2	Ari	MAR	31	Ari	JUN	14	Can
MAY	21	Gem	MAR	15	Pis	JUN	5	Tau	JUL	29	Leo
JUN	21	Can	APR	17	Ari	JUL	7	Gem	SEP	14	Vir
JUL	23	Leo	MAY	8	Tau	AUG	4	Can	NOV	1	Lib
AUG	23	Vir	MAY	23	Gem	AUG	30	Leo	DEC	20	Sco
SEP	23	Lib	JUN	6	Can	SEP	24	Vir			
OCT	23	Sco	JUN	26	Leo	OCT	18	Lib			
NOV	22	Sag	JUL	28	Can	NOV	11	Sco			
DEC	22	Cap	AUG	11	Leo	DEC	5	Sag			
			AUG	30	Vir	DEC	29	Cap			
			SEP	15	Lib						
			OCT	4	Sco						
			OCT	31	Sag						
			NOV	6	Sco						
			DEC	10	Sag						
			DEC	30	Cap						

1954

SUN			MERCURY			VENUS			MARS		
mth	dy	sign	mth	dy	sign	mth	dy	sign	mth	dy	sign
JAN	1	Cap	JAN	1	Cap	JAN	1	Cap	JAN	1	Sco
JAN	20	Aqu	JAN	18	Aqu	JAN	22	Aqu	FEB	9	Sag
FEB	19	Pis	FEB	4	Pis	FEB	15	Pis	APR	12	Cap
MAR	21	Ari	APR	13	Ari	MAR	11	Ari	JUL	3	Sag
APR	20	Tau	APR	30	Tau	APR	4	Tau	AUG	24	Cap
MAY	21	Gem	MAY	14	Gem	APR	28	Gem	OCT	21	Aqu
JUN	21	Can	MAY	30	Can	MAY	23	Can	DEC	4	Pis
JUL	23	Leo	AUG	7	Leo	JUN	17	Leo			
AUG	23	Vir	AUG	22	Vir	JUL	13	Vir			
SEP	23	Lib	SEP	8	Lib	AUG	9	Lib			
OCT	23	Sco	SEP	29	Sco	SEP	6	Sco			
NOV	22	Sag	NOV	4	Lib	OCT	23	Sag			
DEC	22	Cap	NOV	11	Sco	OCT	27	Sco			
			DEC	4	Sag						
			DEC	23	Cap						

1955

SUN			MERCURY			VENUS			MARS		
mth	dy	sign	mth	dy	sign	mth	dy	sign	mth	dy	sign
JAN	1	Cap	JAN	1	Cap	JAN	1	Sco	JAN	1	Pis
JAN	20	Aqu	JAN	10	Aqu	JAN	6	Sag	JAN	15	Ari
FEB	19	Pis	MAR	17	Pis	FEB	6	Cap	FEB	26	Tau
MAR	21	Ari	APR	6	Ari	MAR	4	Aqu	APR	10	Gem
APR	20	Tau	APR	22	Tau	MAR	30	Pis	MAY	26	Can
MAY	21	Gem	MAY	6	Gem	APR	24	Ari	JUL	11	Leo
JUN	22	Can	JUL	13	Can	MAY	19	Tau	AUG	27	Vir
JUL	23	Leo	JUL	30	Leo	JUN	13	Gem	OCT	13	Lib
AUG	23	Vir	AUG	14	Vir	JUL	8	Can	NOV	29	Sco
SEP	23	Lib	SEP	1	Lib	AUG	1	Leo			
OCT	24	Sco	NOV	8	Sco	AUG	25	Vir			
NOV	23	Sag	NOV	27	Sag	SEP	18	Lib			
DEC	22	Cap	DEC	16	Cap	OCT	13	Sco			
						NOV	6	Sag			
						NOV	30	Cap			
						DEC	24	Aqu			

1956

SUN			MERCURY			VENUS			MARS		
mth	dy	sign	mth	dy	sign	mth	dy	sign	mth	dy	sign
JAN	1	Cap	JAN	1	Cap	JAN	1	Aqu	JAN	1	Sco
JAN	21	Aqu	JAN	4	Aqu	JAN	17	Pis	JAN	14	Sag
FEB	19	Pis	FEB	2	Cap	FEB	11	Ari	FEB	28	Cap
MAR	20	Ari	FEB	15	Aqu	MAR	7	Tau	APR	14	Aqu
APR	20	Tau	MAR	11	Pis	APR	4	Gem	JUN	3	Pis
MAY	21	Gem	MAR	28	Ari	MAY	8	Can	DEC	6	Ari
JUN	21	Can	APR	12	Tau	JUN	23	Gem			
JUL	22	Leo	APR	29	Gem	AUG	4	Can			
AUG	23	Vir	JUL	6	Can	SEP	8	Leo			
SEP	23	Lib	JUL	21	Leo	OCT	6	Vir			
OCT	23	Sco	AUG	5	Vir	OCT	31	Lib			
NOV	22	Sag	AUG	26	Lib	NOV	25	Sco			
DEC	21	Cap	SEP	29	Vir	DEC	19	Sag			
			OCT	11	Lib						
			OCT	31	Sco						
			NOV	18	Sag						
			DEC	8	Cap						

1957

SUN			MERCURY			VENUS			MARS		
mth	dy	sign	mth	dy	sign	mth	dy	sign	mth	dy	sign
JAN	1	Cap	JAN	1	Cap	JAN	1	Sag	JAN	1	Ari
JAN	20	Aqu	FEB	12	Aqu	JAN	12	Cap	JAN	28	Tau
FEB	18	Pis	MAR	4	Pis	FEB	5	Aqu	MAR	17	Gem
MAR	20	Ari	MAR	20	Ari	MAR	1	Pis	MAY	4	Can
APR	20	Tau	APR	4	Tau	MAR	25	Ari	JUN	21	Leo
MAY	21	Gem	JUN	12	Gem	APR	19	Tau	AUG	8	Vir
JUN	21	Can	JUN	28	Can	MAY	13	Gem	SEP	24	Lib
JUL	23	Leo	JUL	12	Leo	JUN	6	Can	NOV	8	Sco
AUG	23	Vir	JUL	30	Vir	JUL	1	Leo	DEC	23	Sag
SEP	23	Lib	OCT	6	Lib	JUL	26	Vir			
OCT	23	Sco	OCT	23	Sco	AUG	20	Lib			
NOV	22	Sag	NOV	11	Sag	SEP	14	Sco			
DEC	22	Cap	DEC	2	Cap	OCT	10	Sag			
			DEC	28	Sag	NOV	5	Cap			
						DEC	6	Aqu			

1958

	SUN			MERCURY			VENUS			MARS	
mth	dy	sign	mth	dy	sign	mth	dy	sign	mth	dy	sign
JAN	1	Cap	JAN	1	Sag	JAN	1	Aqu	JAN	1	Sag
JAN	20	Aqu	JAN	14	Cap	APR	6	Pis	FEB	3	Cap
FEB	19	Pis	FEB	6	Aqu	MAY	5	Ari	MAR	17	Aqu
MAR	21	Ari	FEB	24	Pis	JUN	1	Tau	APR	27	Pis
APR	20	Tau	MAR	12	Ari	JUN	26	Gem	JUN	7	Ari
MAY	21	Gem	APR	2	Tau	JUL	22	Can	JUL	21	Tau
JUN	21	Can	APR	10	Ari	AUG	16	Leo	SEP	21	Gem
JUL	23	Leo	MAY	17	Tau	SEP	9	Vir	OCT	29	Tau
AUG	23	Vir	JUN	5	Gem	OCT	3	Lib			
SEP	23	Lib	JUN	20	Can	OCT	27	Sco			
OCT	23	Sco	JUL	4	Leo	NOV	20	Sag			
NOV	22	Sag	JUL	26	Vir	DEC	14	Cap			
DEC	22	Cap	AUG	23	Leo						
			SEP	11	Vir						
			SEP	28	Lib						
			OCT	16	Sco						
			NOV	5	Sag						

1959

	SUN			MERCURY			VENUS			MARS	
mth	dy	sign	mth	dy	sign	mth	dy	sign	mth	dy	sign
JAN	1	Cap	JAN	1	Sag	JAN	1	Cap	JAN	1	Tau
JAN	20	Aqu	JAN	10	Cap	JAN	7	Aqu	FEB	10	Gem
FEB	19	Pis	JAN	30	Aqu	JAN	31	Pis	APR	10	Can
MAR	21	Ari	FEB	17	Pis	FEB	24	Ari	JUN	1	Leo
APR	20	Tau	MAR	5	Ari	MAR	20	Tau	JUL	20	Vir
MAY	21	Gem	MAY	12	Tau	APR	14	Gem	SEP	5	Lib
JUN	22	Can	MAY	28	Gem	MAY	10	Can	OCT	21	Sco
JUL	23	Leo	JUN	11	Can	JUN	6	Leo	DEC	3	Sag
AUG	23	Vir	JUN	28	Leo	JUL	8	Vir			
SEP	23	Lib	SEP	5	Vir	SEP	20	Leo			
OCT	24	Sco	OCT	9	Sco	SEP	25	Vir			
NOV	23	Sag	OCT	21	Lib	NOV	9	Lib			
DEC	22	Cap	OCT	31	Sag	DEC	7	Sco			
			NOV	25	Sco						
			DEC	13	Sag						

1960

SUN			MERCURY			VENUS			MARS		
mth	dy	sign	mth	dy	sign	mth	dy	sign	mth	dy	sign
JAN	1	Cap	JAN	1	Sag	JAN	1	Sco	JAN	1	Sag
JAN	21	Aqu	JAN	4	Cap	JAN	2	Sag	JAN	14	Cap
FEB	19	Pis	JAN	23	Aqu	JAN	27	Cap	FEB	23	Aqu
MAR	20	Ari	FEB	9	Pis	FEB	20	Aqu	APR	2	Pis
APR	20	Tau	APR	16	Ari	MAR	16	Pis	MAY	11	Ari
MAY	21	Gem	MAY	4	Tau	APR	9	Ari	JUN	20	Tau
JUN	21	Can	MAY	19	Gem	MAY	3	Tau	AUG	2	Gem
JUL	22	Leo	JUN	2	Can	MAY	28	Gem	SEP	21	Can
AUG	23	Vir	JUL	1	Leo	JUN	21	Can			
SEP	23	Lib	JUL	6	Can	JUL	16	Leo			
OCT	23	Sco	AUG	10	Leo	AUG	9	Vir			
NOV	22	Sag	AUG	27	Vir	SEP	2	Lib			
DEC	21	Cap	SEP	12	Lib	SEP	27	Sco			
			OCT	1	Sco	OCT	21	Sag			
			DEC	7	Sag	NOV	15	Cap			
			DEC	27	Cap	DEC	10	Aqu			

1961

SUN			MERCURY			VENUS			MARS		
mth	dy	sign	mth	dy	sign	mth	dy	sign	mth	dy	sign
JAN	1	Cap	JAN	1	Cap	JAN	1	Aqu	JAN	1	Can
JAN	20	Aqu	JAN	14	Aqu	JAN	5	Pis	FEB	5	Gem
FEB	18	Pis	FEB	1	Pis	FEB	2	Ari	FEB	7	Can
MAR	20	Ari	FEB	24	Aqu	JUN	5	Tau	MAY	6	Leo
APR	20	Tau	MAR	18	Pis	JUL	7	Gem	JUN	28	Vir
MAY	21	Gem	APR	10	Ari	AUG	3	Can	AUG	17	Lib
JUN	21	Can	APR	26	Tau	AUG	29	Leo	OCT	1	Sco
JUL	23	Leo	MAY	10	Gem	SEP	23	Vir	NOV	13	Sag
AUG	23	Vir	MAY	28	Can	OCT	18	Lib	DEC	24	Cap
SEP	23	Lib	AUG	4	Leo	NOV	11	Sco			
OCT	23	Sco	AUG	18	Vir	DEC	5	Sag			
NOV	22	Sag	SEP	4	Lib	DEC	29	Cap			
DEC	22	Cap	SEP	27	Sco						
			OCT	22	Lib						
			NOV	10	Sco						
			NOV	30	Sag						
			DEC	20	Cap						

1962

SUN			MERCURY			VENUS			MARS		
mth	dy	sign	mth	dy	sign	mth	dy	sign	mth	dy	sign
JAN	1	Cap	JAN	1	Cap	JAN	1	Cap	JAN	1	Cap
JAN	20	Aqu	JAN	7	Aqu	JAN	21	Aqu	FEB	1	Aqu
FEB	19	Pis	MAR	15	Pis	FEB	14	Pis	MAR	12	Pis
MAR	21	Ari	APR	3	Ari	MAR	10	Ari	APR	19	Ari
APR	20	Tau	APR	18	Tau	APR	3	Tau	MAY	28	Tau
MAY	21	Gem	MAY	3	Gem	APR	28	Gem	JUL	9	·Gem
JUN	21	Can	JUL	11	Can	MAY	23	Can	AUG	22	Can
JUL	23	Leo	JUL	26	Leo	JUN	17	Leo	OCT	11	Leo
AUG	23	Vir	AUG	10	Vir	JUL	12	Vir			
SEP	23	Lib	AUG	29	Lib	AUG	8	Lib			
OCT	23	Sco	NOV	5	Sco	SEP	7	Sco			
NOV	22	Sag	NOV	23	Sag						
DEC	22	Cap	DEC	12	Cap						

1963

SUN			MERCURY			VENUS			MARS		
mth	dy	sign	mth	dy	sign	mth	dy	sign	mth	dy	sign
JAN	1	Cap	JAN	1	Cap	JAN	1	Sco	JAN	1	Leo
JAN	20	Aqu	JAN	2	Aqu	JAN	6	Sag	JUN	3	Vir
FEB	19	Pis	JAN	20	Cap	FEB	5	Cap	JUL	27	Lib
MAR	21	Ari	FEB	15	Aqu	MAR	4	Aqu	SEP	12	Sco
APR	20	Tau	MAR	9	Pis	MAR	30	Pis	OCT	25	Sag
MAY	21	Gem	MAR	26	Ari	APR	24	Ari	DEC	5	Cap
JUN	22	Can	APR	9	Tau	MAY	19	Tau			
JUL	23	Leo	MAY	3	Gem	JUN	12	Gem			
AUG	23	Vir	MAY	10	Tau	JUL	7	Can			
SEP	23	Lib	JUN	14	Gem	JUL	31	Leo			
OCT	24	Sco	JUL	4	Can	AUG	25	Vir			
NOV	23	Sag	JUL	18	Leo	SEP	18	Lib			
DEC	22	Cap	AUG	3	Vir	OCT	12	Sco			
			AUG	26	Lib	NOV	5	Sag			
			SEP	16	Vir	NOV	29	Cap			
			OCT	10	Lib	DEC	23	Aqu			
			OCT	28	Sco						
			NOV	16	Sag						
			DEC	6	Cap						

1964

SUN			MERCURY			VENUS			MARS		
mth	dy	sign	mth	dy	sign	mth	dy	sign	mth	dy	sign
JAN	1	Cap	JAN	1	Cap	JAN	1	Aqu	JAN	1	Cap
JAN	21	Aqu	FEB	10	Aqu	JAN	17	Pis	JAN	13	Aqu
FEB	19	Pis	FEB	29	Pis	FEB	10	Ari	FEB	20	Pis
MAR	20	Ari	MAR	16	Ari	MAR	7	Tau	MAR	29	Ari
APR	20	Tau	APR	2	Tau	APR	4	Gem	MAY	7	Tau
MAY	21	Gem	JUN	9	Gem	MAY	9	Can	JUN	17	Gem
JUN	21	Can	JUN	24	Can	JUN	17	Gem	JUL	30	Can
JUL	22	Leo	JUL	9	Leo	AUG	5	Can	SEP	15	Leo
AUG	23	Vir	JUL	27	Vir	SEP	8	Leo	NOV	6	Vir
SEP	23	Lib	OCT	3	Lib	OCT	5	Vir			
OCT	23	Sco	OCT	20	Sco	OCT	31	Lib			
NOV	22	Sag	NOV	8	Sag	NOV	25	Sco			
DEC	21	Cap	NOV	30	Cap	DEC	19	Sag			
			DEC	16	Sag						

1965

SUN			MERCURY			VENUS			MARS		
mth	dy	sign	mth	dy	sign	mth	dy	sign	mth	dy	sign
JAN	1	Cap	JAN	1	Sag	JAN	1	Sag	JAN	1	Vir
JAN	20	Aqu	JAN	13	Cap	JAN	12	Cap	JUN	29	Lib
FEB	18	Pis	FEB	3	Aqu	FEB	5	Aqu	AUG	20	Sco
MAR	20	Ari	FEB	21	Pis	MAR	1	Pis	OCT	4	Sag
APR	20	Tau	MAR	9	Ari	MAR	25	Ari	NOV	14	Cap
MAY	21	Gem	MAY	15	Tau	APR	18	Tau	DEC	23	Aqu
JUN	21	Can	JUN	2	Gem	MAY	12	Gem			
JUL	23	Leo	JUN	16	Can	JUN	6	Can			
AUG	23	Vir	JUL	1	Leo	JUN	30	Leo			
SEP	23	Lib	JUL	31	Vir	JUL	25	Vir			
OCT	23	Sco	AUG	3	Leo	AUG	19	Lib			
NOV	22	Sag	SEP	8	Vir	SEP	13	Sco			
DEC	22	Cap	SEP	25	Lib	OCT	9	Sag			
			OCT	12	Sco	NOV	5	Cap			
			NOV	2	Sag	DEC	7	Aqu			

1966

SUN			MERCURY			VENUS			MARS		
mth	dy	sign	mth	dy	sign	mth	dy	sign	mth	dy	sign
JAN	1	Cap	JAN	1	Sag	JAN	1	Aqu	JAN	1	Aqu
JAN	20	Aqu	JAN	7	Cap	FEB	6	Cap	JAN	30	Pis
FEB	19	Pis	JAN	27	Aqu	FEB	25	Aqu	MAR	9	Ari
MAR	21	Ari	FEB	13	Pis	APR	6	Pis	APR	17	Tau
APR	20	Tau	MAR	3	Ari	MAY	5	Ari	MAY	28	Gem
MAY	21	Gem	MAR	22	Pis	MAY	31	Tau	JUL	11	Can
JUN	21	Can	APR	17	Ari	JUN	26	Gem	AUG	25	Leo
JUL	23	Leo	MAY	9	Tau	JUL	21	Can	OCT	12	Vir
AUG	23	Vir	MAY	24	Gem	AUG	15	Leo	DEC	4	Lib
SEP	23	Lib	JUN	7	Can	SEP	8	Vir			
OCT	23	Sco	JUN	26	Leo	OCT	3	Lib			
NOV	22	Sag	SEP	1	Vir	OCT	27	Sco			
DEC	22	Cap	SEP	17	Lib	NOV	20	Sag			
			OCT	5	Sco	DEC	13	Cap			
			OCT	30	Sag						
			NOV	13	Sco						
			DEC	11	Sag						

1967

SUN			MERCURY			VENUS			MARS		
mth	dy	sign	mth	dy	sign	mth	dy	sign	mth	dy	sign
JAN	1	Cap	JAN	1	Cap	JAN	1	Cap	JAN	1	Lib
JAN	20	Aqu	JAN	19	Aqu	JAN	6	Aqu	FEB	12	Sco
FEB	19	Pis	FEB	6	Pis	JAN	30	Pis	MAR	31	Lib
MAR	21	Ari	APR	14	Ari	FEB	23	Ari	JUL	19	Sco
APR	20	Tau	MAY	1	Tau	MAR	20	Tau	SEP	10	Sag
MAY	21	Gem	MAY	16	Gem	APR	14	Gem	OCT	23	Cap
JUN	22	Can	MAY	31	Can	MAY	10	Can	DEC	1	Aqu
JUL	23	Leo	AUG	8	Leo	JUN	6	Leo			
AUG	23	Vir	AUG	24	Vir	JUL	8	Vir			
SEP	23	Lib	SEP	9	Lib	SEP	9	Leo			
OCT	24	Sco	SEP	30	Sco	OCT	1	Vir			
NOV	23	Sag	DEC	5	Sag	NOV	9	Lib			
DEC	22	Cap	DEC	24	Cap	DEC	7	Sco			

1968

SUN			MERCURY			VENUS			MARS		
mth	dy	sign	mth	dy	sign	mth	dy	sign	mth	dy	sign
JAN	1	Cap	JAN	1	Cap	JAN	1	Sag	JAN	1	Aqu
JAN	20	Aqu	JAN	12	Aqu	JAN	26	Cap	JAN	9	Pis
FEB	19	Pis	FEB	1	Pis	FEB	20	Aqu	FEB	17	Ari
MAR	20	Ari	FEB	11	Aqu	MAR	15	Pis	MAR	27	Tau
APR	20	Tau	MAR	17	Pis	APR	8	Ari	MAY	8	Gem
MAY	21	Gem	APR	7	Ari	MAY	3	Tau	JUN	21	Can
JUN	21	Can	APR	22	Tau	MAY	27	Gem	AUG	5	Leo
JUL	22	Leo	MAY	6	Gem	JUN	21	Can	SEP	21	Vir
AUG	23	Vir	MAY	29	Can	JUL	15	Leo	NOV	9	Lib
SEP	22	Lib	JUN	13	Gem	AUG	8	Vir	DEC	29	Sco
OCT	23	Sco	JUL	13	Can	SEP	2	Lib			
NOV	22	Sag	JUL	31	Leo	SEP	26	Sco			
DEC	21	Cap	AUG	15	Vir	OCT	21	Sag			
			SEP	1	Lib	NOV	14	Cap			
			SEP	28	Sco	DEC	9	Aqu			
			OCT	7	Lib						
			NOV	8	Sco						
			NOV	27	Sag						
			DEC	16	Cap						

1969

SUN			MERCURY			VENUS			MARS		
mth	dy	sign	mth	dy	sign	mth	dy	sign	mth	dy	sign
JAN	1	Cap	JAN	1	Cap	JAN	1	Aqu	JAN	1	Sco
JAN	20	Aqu	JAN	4	Aqu	JAN	4	Pis	FEB	25	Sag
FEB	18	Pis	MAR	12	Pis	FEB	2	Ari	SEP	21	Cap
MAR	20	Ari	MAR	30	Ari	JUN	6	Tau	NOV	4	Aqu
APR	20	Tau	APR	14	Tau	JUL	6	Gem	DEC	15	Pis
MAY	21	Gem	APR	30	Gem	AUG	3	Can			
JUN	21	Can	JUL	8	Can	AUG	29	Leo			
JUL	23	Leo	JUL	22	Leo	SEP	23	Vir			
AUG	23	Vir	AUG	7	Vir	OCT	17	Lib			
SEP	23	Lib	AUG	27	Lib	NOV	10	Sco			
OCT	23	Sco	OCT	7	Vir	DEC	4	Sag			
NOV	22	Sag	OCT	9	Lib	DEC	28	Cap			
DEC	22	Cap	NOV	1	Sco						
			NOV	20	Sag						
			DEC	9	Cap						

1970

SUN			MERCURY			VENUS			MARS		
mth	dy	sign	mth	dy	sign	mth	dy	sign	mth	dy	sign
JAN	1	Cap	JAN	1	Cap	JAN	1	Cap	JAN	1	Pis
JAN	20	Aqu	JAN	4	Aqu	JAN	21	Aqu	JAN	24	Ari
FEB	19	Pis	JAN	4	Cap	FEB	14	Pis	MAR	7	Tau
MAR	21	Ari	FEB	13	Aqu	MAR	10	Ari	APR	18	Gem
APR	20	Tau	MAR	5	Pis	APR	3	Tau	JUN	2	Can
MAY	21	Gem	MAR	22	Ari	APR	27	Gem	JUL	18	Leo
JUN	21	Can	APR	6	Tau	MAY	22	Can	SEP	3	Vir
JUL	23	Leo	JUN	13	Gem	JUN	16	Leo	OCT	20	Lib
AUG	23	Vir	JUN	30	Can	JUL	12	Vir	DEC	6	Sco
SEP	23	Lib	JUL	14	Leo	AUG	8	Lib			
OCT	23	Sco	JUL	31	Vir	SEP	7	Sco			
NOV	22	Sag	OCT	7	Lib						
DEC	22	Cap	OCT	25	Sco						
			NOV	13	Sag						
			DEC	3	Cap						

1971

SUN			MERCURY			VENUS			MARS		
mth	dy	sign	mth	dy	sign	mth	dy	sign	mth	dy	sign
JAN	1	Cap	JAN	1	Cap	JAN	1	Sco	JAN	1	Sco
JAN	20	Aqu	JAN	2	Sag	JAN	7	Sag	JAN	23	Sag
FEB	19	Pis	JAN	14	Cap	FEB	5	Cap	MAR	12	Cap
MAR	21	Ari	FEB	7	Aqu	MAR	4	Aqu	MAY	3	Aqu
APR	20	Tau	FEB	26	Pis	MAR	29	Pis	NOV	6	Pis
MAY	21	Gem	MAR	14	Ari	APR	23	Ari	DEC	26	Ari
JUN	22	Can	APR	1	Tau	MAY	18	Tau			
JUL	23	Leo	APR	18	Ari	JUN	12	Gem			
AUG	23	Vir	MAY	17	Tau	JUL	6	Can			
SEP	23	Lib	JUN	7	Gem	JUL	31	Leo			
OCT	24	Sco	JUN	21	Can	AUG	24	Vir			
NOV	22	Sag	JUL	6	Leo	SEP	17	Lib			
DEC	22	Cap	JUL	26	Vir	OCT	11	Sco			
			AUG	29	Leo	NOV	5	Sag			
			SEP	11	Vir	NOV	29	Cap			
			SEP	30	Lib	DEC	23	Aqu			
			OCT	17	Sco						
			NOV	6	Sag						

1972

SUN			MERCURY			VENUS			MARS		
mth	**dy**	**sign**	**mth**	**dy**	**sign**	**mth**	**dy**	**sign**	**mth**	**dy**	**sign**
JAN	1	Cap	JAN	1	Sag	JAN	1	Aqu	JAN	1	Ari
JAN	20	Aqu	JAN	11	Cap	JAN	16	Pis	FEB	10	Tau
FEB	19	Pis	JAN	31	Aqu	FEB	10	Ari	MAR	27	Gem
MAR	20	Ari	FEB	18	Pis	MAR	7	Tau	MAY	12	Can
APR	19	Tau	MAR	5	Ari	APR	3	Gem	JUN	28	Leo
MAY	20	Gem	MAY	12	Tau	MAY	10	Can	AUG	15	Vir
JUN	21	Can	MAY	29	Gem	JUN	11	Gem	SEP	30	Lib
JUL	22	Leo	JUN	12	Can	AUG	6	Can	NOV	15	Sco
AUG	23	Vir	JUN	28	Leo	SEP	7	Leo	DEC	30	Sag
SEP	22	Lib	SEP	5	Vir	OCT	5	Vir			
OCT	23	Sco	SEP	21	Lib	OCT	30	Lib			
NOV	22	Sag	OCT	9	Sco	NOV	24	Sco			
DEC	21	Cap	OCT	30	Sag	DEC	18	Sag			
			NOV	29	Sco						
			DEC	12	Sag						

1973

SUN			MERCURY			VENUS			MARS		
mth	**dy**	**sign**	**mth**	**dy**	**sign**	**mth**	**dy**	**sign**	**mth**	**dy**	**sign**
JAN	1	Cap	JAN	1	Sag	JAN	1	Sag	JAN	1	Sag
JAN	20	Aqu	JAN	4	Cap	JAN	11	Cap	FEB	12	Cap
FEB	18	Pis	JAN	23	Aqu	FEB	4	Aqu	MAR	26	Aqu
MAR	20	Ari	FEB	9	Pis	FEB	28	Pis	MAY	8	Pis
APR	20	Tau	APR	16	Ari	MAR	24	Ari	JUN	20	Ari
MAY	21	Gem	MAY	6	Tau	APR	18	Tau	AUG	12	Tau
JUN	21	Can	MAY	20	Gem	MAY	12	Gem	OCT	29	Ari
JUL	22	Leo	JUN	4	Can	JUN	5	Can	DEC	24	Tau
AUG	23	Vir	JUN	27	Leo	JUN	30	Leo			
SEP	23	Lib	JUL	16	Can	JUL	25	Vir			
OCT	23	Sco	AUG	11	Leo	AUG	19	Lib			
NOV	22	Sag	AUG	28	Vir	SEP	13	Sco			
DEC	22	Cap	SEP	13	Lib	OCT	9	Sag			
			OCT	2	Sco	NOV	5	Cap			
			DEC	8	Sag	DEC	7	Aqu			
			DEC	28	Cap						

1974

	SUN			MERCURY			VENUS			MARS	
mth	dy	sign	mth	dy	sign	mth	dy	sign	mth	dy	sign
JAN	1	Cap	JAN	1	Cap	JAN	1	Aqu	JAN	1	Tau
JAN	20	Aqu	JAN	16	Aqu	JAN	29	Cap	FEB	27	Gem
FEB	19	Pis	FEB	2	Pis	FEB	28	Aqu	APR	20	Can
MAR	21	Ari	MAR	2	Aqu	APR	6	Pis	JUN	9	Leo
APR	20	Tau	MAR	17	Pis	MAY	4	Ari	JUL	27	Vir
MAY	21	Gem	APR	11	Ari	MAY	31	Tau	SEP	12	Lib
JUN	21	Can	APR	28	Tau	JUN	25	Gem	OCT	28	Sco
JUL	23	Leo	MAY	12	Gem	JUL	21	Can	DEC	10	Sag
AUG	23	Vir	MAY	29	Can	AUG	14	Leo			
SEP	23	Lib	AUG	5	Leo	SEP	8	Vir			
OCT	23	Sco	AUG	20	Vir	OCT	2	Lib			
NOV	22	Sag	SEP	6	Lib	OCT	26	Sco			
DEC	22	Cap	SEP	28	Sco	NOV	19	Sag			
			OCT	26	Lib	DEC	13	Cap			
			NOV	11	Sco						
			DEC	2	Sag						
			DEC	21	Cap						

1975

	SUN			MERCURY			VENUS			MARS	
mth	dy	sign	mth	dy	sign	mth	dy	sign	mth	dy	sign
JAN	1	Cap	JAN	1	Cap	JAN	1	Cap	JAN	1	Sag
JAN	20	Aqu	JAN	8	Aqu	JAN	6	Aqu	JAN	21	Cap
FEB	19	Pis	MAR	16	Pis	JAN	30	Pis	MAR	3	Aqu
MAR	21	Ari	APR	4	Ari	FEB	23	Ari	APR	11	Pis
APR	20	Tau	APR	19	Tau	MAR	19	Tau	MAY	21	Ari
MAY	21	Gem	MAY	4	Gem	APR	13	Gem	JUL	1	Tau
JUN	22	Can	JUL	12	Can	MAY	9	Can	AUG	14	Gem
JUL	23	Leo	JUL	28	Leo	JUN	6	Leo	OCT	17	Can
AUG	23	Vir	AUG	12	Vir	JUL	9	Vir	NOV	25	Gem
SEP	23	Lib	AUG	30	Lib	SEP	2	Leo			
OCT	24	Sco	NOV	6	Sco	OCT	4	Vir			
NOV	22	Sag	NOV	25	Sag	NOV	9	Lib			
DEC	22	Cap	DEC	14	Cap	DEC	7	Sco			

1976

SUN			MERCURY			VENUS			MARS		
mth	dy	sign	mth	dy	sign	mth	dy	sign	mth	dy	sign
JAN	1	Cap	JAN	1	Cap	JAN	1	Sag	JAN	1	Gem
JAN	20	Aqu	JAN	2	Aqu	JAN	26	Cap	MAR	18	Can
FEB	19	Pis	JAN	25	Cap	FEB	19	Aqu	MAY	16	Leo
MAR	20	Ari	FEB	15	Aqu	MAR	15	Pis	JUL	6	Vir
APR	19	Tau	MAR	9	Pis	APR	8	Ari	AUG	24	Lib
MAY	20	Gem	MAR	26	Ari	MAY	2	Tau	OCT	8	Sco
JUN	21	Can	APR	10	Tau	MAY	27	Gem	NOV	20	Sag
JUL	22	Leo	APR	29	Gem	JUN	20	Can			
AUG	23	Vir	MAY	19	Tau	JUL	14	Leo			
SEP	22	Lib	JUN	13	Gem	AUG	8	Vir			
OCT	23	Sco	JUL	4	Can	SEP	1	Lib			
NOV	22	Sag	JUL	18	Leo	SEP	26	Sco			
DEC	21	Cap	AUG	3	Vir	OCT	20	Sag			
			AUG	25	Lib	NOV	14	Cap			
			SEP	21	Vir	DEC	9	Aqu			
			OCT	10	Lib						
			OCT	29	Sco						
			NOV	16	Sag						
			DEC	6	Cap						

1977

SUN			MERCURY			VENUS			MARS		
mth	dy	sign	mth	dy	sign	mth	dy	sign	mth	dy	sign
JAN	1	Cap	JAN	1	Cap	JAN	1	Aqu	JAN	1	Cap
JAN	20	Aqu	FEB	10	Aqu	JAN	4	Pis	FEB	9	Aqu
FEB	18	Pis	MAR	2	Pis	FEB	2	Ari	MAR	20	Pis
MAR	20	Ari	MAR	18	Ari	JUN	6	Tau	APR	27	Ari
APR	20	Tau	APR	3	Tau	JUL	6	Gem	JUN	6	Tau
MAY	21	Gem	JUN	10	Gem	AUG	2	Can	JUL	17	Gem
JUN	21	Can	JUN	26	Can	AUG	28	Leo	SEP	1	Can
JUL	22	Leo	JUL	10	Leo	SEP	22	Vir	OCT	26	Leo
AUG	23	Vir	JUL	28	Vir	OCT	17	Lib			
SEP	23	Lib	OCT	4	Lib	NOV	10	Sco			
OCT	23	Sco	OCT	21	Sco	DEC	4	Sag			
NOV	22	Sag	NOV	9	Sag	DEC	27	Cap			
DEC	21	Cap	DEC	1	Cap						
			DEC	21	Sag						

1978

SUN			MERCURY			VENUS			MARS		
mth	dy	sign	mth	dy	sign	mth	dy	sign	mth	dy	sign
JAN	1	Cap	JAN	1	Sag	JAN	1	Cap	JAN	1	Leo
JAN	20	Aqu	JAN	13	Cap	JAN	20	Aqu	JAN	26	Can
FEB	19	Pis	FEB	4	Aqu	FEB	13	Pis	APR	10	Leo
MAR	20	Ari	FEB	22	Pis	MAR	9	Ari	JUN	14	Vir
APR	20	Tau	MAR	10	Ari	APR	2	Tau	AUG	4	Lib
MAY	21	Gem	MAY	16	Tau	APR	27	Gem	SEP	19	Sco
JUN	21	Can	JUN	3	Gem	MAY	22	Can	NOV	2	Sag
JUL	23	Leo	JUN	17	Can	JUN	16	Leo	DEC	12	Cap
AUG	23	Vir	JUL	2	Leo	JUL	12	Vir			
SEP	23	Lib	JUL	27	Vir	AUG	8	Lib			
OCT	23	Sco	AUG	13	Leo	SEP	7	Sco			
NOV	22	Sag	SEP	9	Vir						
DEC	22	Cap	SEP	26	Lib						
			OCT	14	Sco						
			NOV	3	Sag						

1979

SUN			MERCURY			VENUS			MARS		
mth	dy	sign	mth	dy	sign	mth	dy	sign	mth	dy	sign
JAN	1	Cap	JAN	1	Sag	JAN	1	Sco	JAN	1	Cap
JAN	20	Aqu	JAN	8	Cap	JAN	7	Sag	JAN	20	Aqu
FEB	19	Pis	JAN	28	Aqu	FEB	5	Cap	FEB	27	Pis
MAR	21	Ari	FEB	14	Pis	MAR	3	Aqu	APR	7	Ari
APR	20	Tau	MAR	3	Ari	MAR	29	Pis	MAY	16	Tau
MAY	21	Gem	MAR	28	Pis	APR	23	Ari	JUN	26	Gem
JUN	21	Can	APR	17	Ari	MAY	18	Tau	AUG	8	Can
JUL	23	Leo	MAY	10	Tau	JUN	11	Gem	SEP	24	Leo
AUG	23	Vir	MAY	26	Gem	JUL	6	Can	NOV	19	Vir
SEP	23	Lib	JUN	9	Can	JUL	30	Leo			
OCT	24	Sco	JUN	27	Leo	AUG	24	Vir			
NOV	22	Sag	SEP	2	Vir	SEP	17	Lib			
DEC	22	Cap	SEP	18	Lib	OCT	11	Sco			
			OCT	7	Sco	NOV	4	Sag			
			OCT	30	Sag	NOV	28	Cap			
			NOV	18	Sco	DEC	22	Aqu			
			DEC	12	Sag						

1980

SUN			MERCURY			VENUS			MARS		
mth	dy	sign	mth	dy	sign	mth	dy	sign	mth	dy	sign
JAN	1	Cap	JAN	1	Sag	JAN	1	Aqu	JAN	1	Vir
JAN	20	Aqu	JAN	2	Cap	JAN	16	Pis	MAR	11	Leo
FEB	19	Pis	JAN	21	Aqu	FEB	9	Ari	MAY	4	Vir
MAR	20	Ari	FEB	7	Pis	MAR	6	Tau	JUL	10	Lib
APR	19	Tau	APR	14	Ari	APR	3	Gem	AUG	29	Sco
MAY	20	Gem	MAY	2	Tau	MAY	12	Can	OCT	12	Sag
JUN	21	Can	MAY	16	Gem	JUN	5	Gem	NOV	22	Cap
JUL	22	Leo	MAY	31	Can	AUG	6	Can	DEC	30	Aqu
AUG	22	Vir	AUG	9	Leo	SEP	7	Leo			
SEP	22	Lib	AUG	24	Vir	OCT	4	Vir			
OCT	23	Sco	SEP	10	Lib	OCT	30	Lib			
NOV	22	Sag	SEP	30	Sco	NOV	24	Sco			
DEC	21	Cap	DEC	5	Sag	DEC	18	Sag			
			DEC	25	Cap						

1981

SUN			MERCURY			VENUS			MARS		
mth	dy	sign	mth	dy	sign	mth	dy	sign	mth	dy	sign
JAN	1	Cap	JAN	1	Cap	JAN	1	Sag	JAN	1	Aqu
JAN	20	Aqu	JAN	12	Aqu	JAN	11	Cap	FEB	6	Pis
FEB	18	Pis	JAN	31	Pis	FEB	4	Aqu	MAR	17	Ari
MAR	20	Ari	FEB	16	Aqu	FEB	28	Pis	APR	25	Tau
APR	20	Tau	MAR	18	Pis	MAR	24	Ari	JUN	5	Gem
MAY	21	Gem	APR	8	Ari	APR	17	Tau	JUL	18	Can
JUN	21	Can	APR	24	Tau	MAY	11	Gem	SEP	2	Leo
JUL	22	Leo	MAY	8	Gem	JUN	5	Can	OCT	21	Vir
AUG	23	Vir	MAY	28	Can	JUN	29	Leo	DEC	16	Lib
SEP	23	Lib	JUN	22	Gem	JUL	24	Vir			
OCT	23	Sco	JUL	12	Can	AUG	18	Lib			
NOV	22	Sag	AUG	1	Leo	SEP	12	Sco			
DEC	21	Cap	AUG	16	Vir	OCT	9	Sag			
			SEP	2	Lib	NOV	5	Cap			
			SEP	27	Sco	DEC	8	Aqu			
			OCT	14	Lib						
			NOV	9	Sco						
			NOV	28	Sag						
			DEC	17	Cap						

1982

SUN			MERCURY			VENUS			MARS		
mth	dy	sign	mth	dy	sign	mth	dy	sign	mth	dy	sign
JAN	1	Cap	JAN	1	Cap	JAN	1	Aqu	JAN	1	Lib
JAN	20	Aqu	JAN	5	Aqu	JAN	23	Cap	AUG	3	Sco
FEB	18	Pis	MAR	13	Pis	MAR	2	Aqu	SEP	20	Sag
MAR	20	Ari	MAR	31	Ari	APR	6	Pis	OCT	31	Cap
APR	20	Tau	APR	15	Tau	MAY	4	Ari	DEC	10	Aqu
MAY	21	Gem	MAY	1	Gem	MAY	30	Tau			
JUN	21	Can	JUL	9	Can	JUN	25	Gem			
JUL	23	Leo	JUL	24	Leo	JUL	20	Can			
AUG	23	Vir	AUG	8	Vir	AUG	14	Leo			
SEP	23	Lib	AUG	28	Lib	SEP	7	Vir			
OCT	23	Sco	NOV	3	Sco	OCT	2	Lib			
NOV	22	Sag	NOV	21	Sag	OCT	26	Sco			
DEC	22	Cap	DEC	10	Cap	NOV	18	Sag			
						DEC	12	Cap			

1983

SUN			MERCURY			VENUS			MARS		
mth	dy	sign	mth	dy	sign	mth	dy	sign	mth	dy	sign
JAN	1	Cap	JAN	1	Aqu	JAN	1	Cap	JAN	1	Aqu
JAN	20	Aqu	JAN	12	Cap	JAN	5	Aqu	JAN	17	Pis
FEB	19	Pis	FEB	14	Aqu	JAN	29	Pis	FEB	25	Ari
MAR	21	Ari	MAR	7	Pis	FEB	22	Ari	APR	5	Tau
APR	20	Tau	MAR	23	Ari	MAR	19	Tau	MAY	16	Gem
MAY	21	Gem	APR	7	Tau	APR	13	Gem	JUN	29	Can
JUN	21	Can	JUN	14	Gem	MAY	9	Can	AUG	13	Leo
JUL	23	Leo	JUL	1	Can	JUN	6	Leo	SEP	30	Vir
AUG	23	Vir	JUL	15	Leo	JUL	10	Vir	NOV	18	Lib
SEP	23	Lib	AUG	1	Vir	AUG	27	Leo			
OCT	23	Sco	AUG	29	Lib	OCT	5	Vir			
NOV	22	Sag	SEP	6	Vir	NOV	9	Lib			
DEC	22	Cap	OCT	8	Lib	DEC	6	Sco			
			OCT	26	Sco						
			NOV	14	Sag						
			DEC	4	Cap						

1984

SUN			MERCURY			VENUS			MARS		
mth	dy	sign	mth	dy	sign	mth	dy	sign	mth	dy	sign
JAN	1	Cap	JAN	1	Cap	JAN	1	Sag	JAN	1	Lib
JAN	20	Aqu	FEB	9	Aqu	JAN	25	Cap	JAN	11	Sco
FEB	19	Pis	FEB	27	Pis	FEB	19	Aqu	AUG	17	Sag
MAR	20	Ari	MAR	14	Ari	MAR	14	Pis	OCT	5	Cap
APR	19	Tau	MAR	31	Tau	APR	7	Ari	NOV	15	Aqu
MAY	20	Gem	APR	25	Ari	MAY	2	Tau	DEC	25	Pis
JUN	21	Can	MAY	15	Tau	MAY	26	Gem			
JUL	22	Leo	JUN	7	Gem	JUN	20	Can			
AUG	22	Vir	JUN	22	Can	JUL	14	Leo			
SEP	22	Lib	JUL	6	Leo	AUG	7	Vir			
OCT	23	Sco	JUL	26	Vir	SEP	1	Lib			
NOV	22	Sag	SEP	30	Lib	SEP	25	Sco			
DEC	21	Cap	OCT	18	Sco	OCT	20	Sag			
			NOV	6	Sag	NOV	13	Cap			
			DEC	1	Cap	DEC	9	Aqu			
			DEC	7	Sag						

1985

SUN			MERCURY			VENUS			MARS		
mth	dy	sign	mth	dy	sign	mth	dy	sign	mth	dy	sign
JAN	1	Cap	JAN	1	Sag	JAN	1	Aqu	JAN	1	Pis
JAN	20	Aqu	JAN	11	Cap	JAN	4	Pis	FEB	2	Ari
FEB	18	Pis	FEB	1	Aqu	FEB	2	Ari	MAR	15	Tau
MAR	20	Ari	FEB	18	Pis	JUN	6	Tau	APR	26	Gem
APR	20	Tau	MAR	7	Ari	JUL	6	Gem	JUN	9	Can
MAY	21	Gem	MAY	14	Tau	AUG	2	Can	JUL	25	Leo
JUN	21	Can	MAY	30	Gem	AUG	28	Leo	SEP	10	Vir
JUL	22	Leo	JUN	13	Can	SEP	22	Vir	OCT	27	Lib
AUG	23	Vir	JUN	29	Leo	OCT	16	Lib	DEC	14	Sco
SEP	23	Lib	SEP	6	Vir	NOV	9	Sco			
OCT	23	Sco	SEP	22	Lib	DEC	3	Sag			
NOV	22	Sag	OCT	10	Sco	DEC	27	Cap			
DEC	21	Cap	OCT	31	Sag						
			DEC	4	Sco						
			DEC	12	Sag						

1986

SUN			MERCURY			VENUS			MARS		
mth	**dy**	**sign**	**mth**	**dy**	**sign**	**mth**	**dy**	**sign**	**mth**	**dy**	**sign**
JAN	1	Cap	JAN	1	Sag	JAN	1	Cap	JAN	1	Sco
JAN	20	Aqu	JAN	5	Cap	JAN	20	Aqu	FEB	2	Sag
FEB	18	Pis	JAN	25	Aqu	FEB	13	Pis	MAR	28	Cap
MAR	20	Ari	FEB	11	Pis	MAR	9	Ari	OCT	9	Aqu
APR	20	Tau	MAR	3	Ari	APR	2	Tau	NOV	26	Pis
MAY	21	Gem	MAR	11	Pis	APR	26	Gem			
JUN	21	Can	APR	17	Ari	MAY	21	Can			
JUL	23	Leo	MAY	7	Tau	JUN	15	Leo			
AUG	23	Vir	MAY	22	Gem	JUL	11	Vir			
SEP	23	Lib	JUN	5	Can	AUG	7	Lib			
OCT	23	Sco	JUN	26	Leo	SEP	7	Sco			
NOV	22	Sag	JUL	23	Can						
DEC	22	Cap	AUG	11	Leo						
			AUG	30	Vir						
			SEP	15	Lib						
			OCT	4	Sco						
			DEC	10	Sag						
			DEC	29	Cap						

1987

SUN			MERCURY			VENUS			MARS		
mth	**dy**	**sign**	**mth**	**dy**	**sign**	**mth**	**dy**	**sign**	**mth**	**dy**	**sign**
JAN	1	Cap	JAN	1	Cap	JAN	1	Sco	JAN	1	Pis
JAN	20	Aqu	JAN	17	Aqu	JAN	7	Sag	JAN	8	Ari
FEB	19	Pis	FEB	4	Pis	FEB	5	Cap	FEB	20	Tau
MAR	21	Ari	MAR	11	Aqu	MAR	3	Aqu	APR	5	Gem
APR	20	Tau	MAR	13	Pis	MAR	28	Pis	MAY	21	Can
MAY	21	Gem	APR	12	Ari	APR	22	Ari	JUL	6	Leo
JUN	21	Can	APR	29	Tau	MAY	17	Tau	AUG	22	Vir
JUL	23	Leo	MAY	13	Gem	JUN	11	Gem	OCT	8	Lib
AUG	23	Vir	MAY	30	Can	JUL	5	Can	NOV	24	Sco
SEP	23	Lib	AUG	6	Leo	JUL	30	Leo			
OCT	23	Sco	AUG	21	Vir	AUG	23	Vir			
NOV	22	Sag	SEP	7	Lib	SEP	16	Lib			
DEC	22	Cap	SEP	28	Sco	OCT	10	Sco			
			NOV	1	Lib	NOV	3	Sag			
			NOV	11	Sco	NOV	28	Cap			
			DEC	3	Sag	DEC	22	Aqu			
			DEC	22	Cap						

1988

SUN			MERCURY			VENUS			MARS		
mth	dy	sign	mth	dy	sign	mth	dy	sign	mth	dy	sign
JAN	1	Cap	JAN	1	Cap	JAN	1	Aqu	JAN	1	Sco
JAN	20	Aqu	JAN	10	Aqu	JAN	15	Pis	JAN	8	Sag
FEB	19	Pis	MAR	16	Pis	FEB	9	Ari	FEB	22	Cap
MAR	20	Ari	APR	4	Ari	MAR	6	Tau	APR	6	Aqu
APR	19	Tau	APR	20	Tau	APR	3	Gem	MAY	22	Pis
MAY	20	Gem	MAY	4	Gem	MAY	17	Can	JUL	13	Ari
JUN	21	Can	JUL	12	Can	MAY	27	Gem	OCT	23	Pis
JUL	22	Leo	JUL	28	Leo	AUG	6	Can	NOV	1	Ari
AUG	22	Vir	AUG	12	Vir	SEP	7	Leo			
SEP	22	Lib	AUG	30	Lib	OCT	4	Vir			
OCT	23	Sco	NOV	6	Sco	OCT	29	Lib			
NOV	22	Sag	NOV	25	Sag	NOV	23	Sco			
DEC	21	Cap	DEC	14	Cap	DEC	17	Sag			

1989

SUN			MERCURY			VENUS			MARS		
mth	dy	sign	mth	dy	sign	mth	dy	sign	mth	dy	sign
JAN	1	Cap	JAN	1	Cap	JAN	1	Sag	JAN	1	Ari
JAN	20	Aqu	JAN	2	Aqu	JAN	10	Cap	JAN	19	Tau
FEB	18	Pis	JAN	29	Cap	FEB	3	Aqu	MAR	11	Gem
MAR	20	Ari	FEB	14	Aqu	FEB	27	Pis	APR	29	Can
APR	20	Tau	MAR	10	Pis	MAR	23	Ari	JUN	16	Leo
MAY	21	Gem	MAR	28	Ari	APR	16	Tau	AUG	3	Vir
JUN	21	Can	APR	11	Tau	MAY	11	Gem	SEP	19	Lib
JUL	22	Leo	APR	29	Gem	JUN	4	Can	NOV	4	Sco
AUG	23	Vir	MAY	28	Tau	JUN	29	Leo	DEC	18	Sag
SEP	23	Lib	JUN	12	Gem	JUL	24	Vir			
OCT	23	Sco	JUL	6	Can	AUG	18	Lib			
NOV	22	Sag	JUL	20	Leo	SEP	12	Sco			
DEC	21	Cap	AUG	5	Vir	OCT	8	Sag			
			AUG	26	Lib	NOV	5	Cap			
			SEP	26	Vir	DEC	10	Aqu			
			OCT	11	Lib						
			OCT	30	Sco						
			NOV	18	Sag						
			DEC	7	Cap						

1990

SUN			MERCURY			VENUS			MARS		
mth	dy	sign	mth	dy	sign	mth	dy	sign	mth	dy	sign
JAN	1	Cap	JAN	1	Cap	JAN	1	Aqu	JAN	1	Sag
JAN	20	Aqu	FEB	12	Aqu	JAN	16	Cap	JAN	29	Cap
FEB	18	Pis	MAR	3	Pis	MAR	3	Aqu	MAR	11	Aqu
MAR	20	Ari	MAR	20	Ari	APR	6	Pis	APR	20	Pis
APR	20	Tau	APR	4	Tau	MAY	4	Ari	MAY	31	Ari
MAY	21	Gem	JUN	12	Gem	MAY	30	Tau	JUL	12	Tau
JUN	21	Can	JUN	27	Can	JUN	25	Gem	AUG	31	Gem
JUL	23	Leo	JUL	11	Leo	JUL	20	Can	DEC	14	Tau
AUG	23	Vir	JUL	29	Vir	AUG	13	Leo			
SEP	23	Lib	OCT	5	Lib	SEP	7	Vir			
OCT	23	Sco	OCT	23	Sco	OCT	1	Lib			
NOV	22	Sag	NOV	11	Sag	OCT	25	Sco			
DEC	22	Cap	DEC	2	Cap	NOV	18	Sag			
			DEC	25	Sag	DEC	12	Cap			

1991

SUN			MERCURY			VENUS			MARS		
mth	dy	sign	mth	dy	sign	mth	dy	sign	mth	dy	sign
JAN	1	Cap	JAN	1	Sag	JAN	1	Cap	JAN	1	Tau
JAN	20	Aqu	JAN	14	Cap	JAN	5	Aqu	JAN	21	Gem
FEB	19	Pis	FEB	5	Aqu	JAN	29	Pis	APR	3	Can
MAR	21	Ari	FEB	24	Pis	FEB	22	Ari	MAY	26	Leo
APR	20	Tau	MAR	11	Ari	MAR	18	Tau	JUL	15	Vir
MAY	21	Gem	MAY	16	Tau	APR	13	Gem	SEP	1	Lib
JUN	21	Can	JUN	5	Gem	MAY	9	Can	OCT	16	Sco
JUL	23	Leo	JUN	19	Can	JUN	6	Leo	NOV	29	Sag
AUG	23	Vir	JUL	4	Leo	JUL	11	Vir			
SEP	23	Lib	JUL	26	Vir	AUG	21	Leo			
OCT	23	Sco	AUG	19	Leo	OCT	6	Vir			
NOV	22	Sag	SEP	10	Vir	NOV	9	Lib			
DEC	22	Cap	SEP	28	Lib	DEC	6	Sco			
			OCT	15	Sco	DEC	31	Sag			
			NOV	4	Sag						

1992

mth	dy	sign	mth	dy	sign	mth	dy	sign	mth	dy	sign
SUN			**MERCURY**			**VENUS**			**MARS**		
JAN	1	Cap	JAN	1	Sag	JAN	1	Sag	JAN	1	Sag
JAN	20	Aqu	JAN	10	Cap	JAN	25	Cap	JAN	9	Cap
FEB	19	Pis	JAN	29	Aqu	FEB	18	Aqu	FEB	18	Aqu
MAR	20	Ari	FEB	16	Pis	MAR	13	Pis	MAR	28	Pis
APR	19	Tau	MAR	3	Ari	APR	7	Ari	MAY	5	Ari
MAY	20	Gem	APR	3	Pis	MAY	1	Tau	JUN	14	Tau
JUN	21	Can	APR	14	Ari	MAY	26	Gem	JUL	26	Gem
JUL	22	Leo	MAY	11	Tau	JUN	19	Can	SEP	12	Can
AUG	22	Vir	MAY	26	Gem	JUL	13	Leo			
SEP	22	Lib	JUN	9	Can	AUG	7	Vir			
OCT	23	Sco	JUN	27	Leo	AUG	31	Lib			
NOV	22	Sag	SEP	3	Vir	SEP	25	Sco			
DEC	21	Cap	SEP	19	Lib	OCT	19	Sag			
			OCT	7	Sco	NOV	13	Cap			
			OCT	29	Sag	DEC	8	Aqu			
			NOV	21	Sco						
			DEC	12	Sag						

1993

mth	dy	sign	mth	dy	sign	mth	dy	sign	mth	dy	sign
SUN			**MERCURY**			**VENUS**			**MARS**		
JAN	1	Cap	JAN	1	Sag	JAN	1	Aqu	JAN	1	Can
JAN	20	Aqu	JAN	2	Cap	JAN	3	Pis	APR	27	Leo
FEB	18	Pis	JAN	21	Aqu	FEB	2	Ari	JUN	23	Vir
MAR	20	Ari	FEB	7	Pis	JUN	6	Tau	AUG	12	Lib
APR	20	Tau	APR	15	Ari	JUL	6	Gem	SEP	27	Sco
MAY	21	Gem	MAY	3	Tau	AUG	1	Can	NOV	9	Sag
JUN	21	Can	MAY	18	Gem	AUG	27	Leo	DEC	20	Cap
JUL	22	Leo	JUN	2	Can	SEP	21	Vir			
AUG	23	Vir	AUG	10	Leo	OCT	16	Lib			
SEP	23	Lib	AUG	26	Vir	NOV	9	Sco			
OCT	23	Sco	SEP	11	Lib	DEC	2	Sag			
NOV	22	Sag	OCT	1	Sco	DEC	26	Cap			
DEC	21	Cap	DEC	7	Sag						
			DEC	26	Cap						

1994

	SUN			MERCURY			VENUS			MARS	
mth	dy	sign	mth	dy	sign	mth	dy	sign	mth	dy	sign
JAN	1	Cap	JAN	1	Cap	JAN	1	Cap	JAN	1	Cap
JAN	20	Aqu	JAN	14	Aqu	JAN	19	Aqu	JAN	28	Aqu
FEB	18	Pis	FEB	1	Pis	FEB	12	Pis	MAR	7	Pis
MAR	20	Ari	FEB	21	Aqu	MAR	8	Ari	APR	14	Ari
APR	20	Tau	MAR	18	Pis	APR	1	Tau	MAY	23	Tau
MAY	21	Gem	APR	9	Ari	APR	26	Gem	JUL	3	Gem
JUN	21	Can	APR	25	Tau	MAY	21	Can	AUG	16	Can
JUL	23	Leo	MAY	9	Gem	JUN	15	Leo	OCT	4	Leo
AUG	23	Vir	MAY	28	Can	JUL	11	Vir	DEC	12	Vir
SEP	23	Lib	JUL	2	Gem	AUG	7	Lib			
OCT	23	Sco	JUL	10	Can	SEP	7	Sco			
NOV	22	Sag	AUG	3	Leo						
DEC	22	Cap	AUG	18	Vir						
			SEP	4	Lib						
			SEP	27	Sco						
			OCT	19	Lib						
			NOV	10	Sco						
			NOV	30	Sag						
			DEC	19	Cap						

1995

	SUN			MERCURY			VENUS			MARS	
mth	dy	sign	mth	dy	sign	mth	dy	sign	mth	dy	sign
JAN	1	Cap	JAN	1	Cap	JAN	1	Sco	JAN	1	Vir
JAN	20	Aqu	JAN	6	Aqu	JAN	7	Sag	JAN	22	Leo
FEB	19	Pis	MAR	14	Pis	FEB	4	Cap	MAY	25	Vir
MAR	21	Ari	APR	2	Ari	MAR	2	Aqu	JUL	21	Lib
APR	20	Tau	APR	17	Tau	MAR	28	Pis	SEP	7	Sco
MAY	21	Gem	MAY	2	Gem	APR	22	Ari	OCT	20	Sag
JUN	21	Can	JUL	10	Can	MAY	16	Tau	NOV	30	Cap
JUL	23	Leo	JUL	25	Leo	JUN	10	Gem			
AUG	23	Vir	AUG	10	Vir	JUL	5	Can			
SEP	23	Lib	AUG	29	Lib	JUL	29	Leo			
OCT	23	Sco	NOV	4	Sco	AUG	23	Vir			
NOV	22	Sag	NOV	22	Sag	SEP	16	Lib			
DEC	22	Cap	DEC	12	Cap	OCT	10	Sco			
						NOV	3	Sag			
						NOV	27	Cap			
						DEC`	21	Aqu			

1996

SUN			MERCURY			VENUS			MARS		
mth	dy	sign	mth	dy	sign	mth	dy	sign	mth	dy	sign
JAN	1	Cap	JAN	1	Cap	JAN	1	Aqu	JAN	1	Cap
JAN	20	Aqu	JAN	1	Aqu	JAN	15	Pis	JAN	8	Aqu
FEB	19	Pis	JAN	17	Cap	FEB	9	Ari	FEB	15	Pis
MAR	20	Ari	FEB	15	Aqu	MAR	6	Tau	MAR	24	Ari
APR	19	Tau	MAR	7	Pis	APR	3	Gem	MAY	2	Tau
MAY	20	Gem	MAR	24	Ari	AUG	7	Can	JUN	12	Gem
JUN	21	Can	APR	8	Tau	SEP	7	Leo	JUL	25	Can
JUL	22	Leo	JUN	13	Gem	OCT	4	Vir	SEP	9	Leo
AUG	22	Vir	JUL	2	Can	OCT	29	Lib	OCT	30	Vir
SEP	22	Lib	JUL	16	Leo	NOV	23	Sco			
OCT	23	Sco	AUG	1	Vir	DEC	17	Sag			
NOV	22	Sag	AUG	26	Lib						
DEC	21	Cap	SEP	12	Vir						
			OCT	9	Lib						
			OCT	27	Sco						
			NOV	14	Sag						
			DEC	4	Cap						

1997

SUN			MERCURY			VENUS			MARS		
mth	dy	sign	mth	dy	sign	mth	dy	sign	mth	dy	sign
JAN	1	Cap	JAN	1	Cap	JAN	1	Sag	JAN	1	Vir
JAN	20	Aqu	FEB	9	Aqu	JAN	10	Cap	JAN	3	Lib
FEB	18	Pis	FEB	28	Pis	FEB	3	Aqu	MAR	8	Vir
MAR	20	Ari	MAR	16	Ari	FEB	27	Pis	JUN	19	Lib
APR	20	Tau	APR	1	Tau	MAR	23	Ari	AUG	14	Sco
MAY	21	Gem	MAY	5	Ari	APR	16	Tau	SEP	28	Sag
JUN	21	Can	MAY	12	Tau	MAY	10	Gem	NOV	9	Cap
JUL	22	Leo	JUN	8	Gem	JUN	4	Can	DEC	18	Aqu
AUG	23	Vir	JUN	23	Can	JUN	28	Leo			
SEP	22	Lib	JUL	8	Leo	JUL	23	Vir			
OCT	23	Sco	JUL	27	Vir	AUG	17	Lib			
NOV	22	Sag	OCT	2	Lib	SEP	12	Sco			
DEC	21	Cap	OCT	19	Sco	OCT	8	Sag			
			NOV	7	Sag	NOV	5	Cap			
			NOV	30	Cap	DEC	12	Aqu			
			DEC	13	Sag						

1998

SUN			MERCURY			VENUS			MARS		
mth	dy	sign	mth	dy	sign	mth	dy	sign	mth	dy	sign
JAN	1	Cap	JAN	1	Sag	JAN	1	Aqu	JAN	1	Aqu
JAN	20	Aqu	JAN	12	Cap	JAN	9	Cap	JAN	25	Pis
FEB	18	Pis	FEB	2	Aqu	MAR	4	Aqu	MAR	4	Ari
MAR	20	Ari	FEB	20	Pis	APR	6	Pis	APR	13	Tau
APR	20	Tau	MAR	8	Ari	MAY	3	Ari	MAY	24	Gem
MAY	21	Gem	MAY	15	Tau	MAY	29	Tau	JUL	6	Can
JUN	21	Can	JUN	1	Gem	JUN	24	Gem	AUG	20	Leo
JUL	23	Leo	JUN	15	Can	JUL	19	Can	OCT	7	Vir
AUG	23	Vir	JUN	30	Leo	AUG	13	Leo	NOV	27	Lib
SEP	23	Lib	SEP	8	Vir	SEP	6	Vir			
OCT	23	Sco	SEP	24	Lib	SEP	30	Lib			
NOV	22	Sag	OCT	12	Sco	OCT	24	Sco			
DEC	22	Cap	NOV	1	Sag	NOV	17	Sag			
						DEC	11	Cap			

1999

SUN			MERCURY			VENUS			MARS		
mth	dy	sign	mth	dy	sign	mth	dy	sign	mth	dy	sign
JAN	1	Cap	JAN	1	Sag	JAN	1	Cap	JAN	1	Lib
JAN	20	Aqu	JAN	7	Cap	JAN	4	Aqu	JAN	26	Sco
FEB	19	Pis	JAN	26	Aqu	JAN	28	Pis	MAY	5	Lib
MAR	21	Ari	FEB	12	Pis	FEB	21	Ari	JUL	5	Sco
APR	20	Tau	MAR	2	Ari	MAR	18	Tau	SEP	2	Sag
MAY	21	Gem	MAR	18	Pis	APR	12	Gem	OCT	17	Cap
JUN	21	Can	APR	17	Ari	MAY	8	Can	NOV	26	Aqu
JUL	23	Leo	MAY	8	Tau	JUN	5	Leo			
AUG	23	Vir	MAY	23	Gem	JUL	12	Vir			
SEP	23	Lib	JUN	7	Can	AUG	15	Leo			
OCT	23	Sco	JUN	26	Leo	OCT	7	Vir			
NOV	22	Sag	JUL	31	Can	NOV	9	Lib			
DEC	22	Cap	AUG	11	Leo	DEC	5	Sco			
			AUG	31	Vir	DEC	31	Sag			
			SEP	16	Lib						
			OCT	5	Sco						
			OCT	30	Sag						
			NOV	9	Sco						
			DEC	11	Sag						
			DEC	31	Cap						

2000

SUN			MERCURY			VENUS			MARS		
mth	dy	sign	mth	dy	sign	mth	dy	sign	mth	dy	sign
JAN	1	Cap	JAN	1	Cap	JAN	1	Sag	JAN	1	Aqu
JAN	20	Aqu	JAN	18	Aqu	JAN	24	Cap	JAN	4	Pis
FEB	19	Pis	FEB	5	Pis	FEB	18	Aqu	FEB	12	Ari
MAR	20	Ari	APR	13	Ari	MAR	13	Pis	MAR	23	Tau
APR	19	Tau	APR	30	Tau	APR	6	Ari	MAY	3	Gem
MAY	20	Gem	MAY	14	Gem	MAY	1	Tau	JUN	16	Can
JUN	21	Can	MAY	30	Can	MAY	25	Gem	AUG	1	Leo
JUL	22	Leo	AUG	7	Leo	JUN	18	Can	SEP	17	Vir
AUG	22	Vir	AUG	22	Vir	JUL	13	Leo	NOV	4	Lib
SEP	22	Lib	SEP	7	Lib	AUG	6	Vir	DEC	23	Sco
OCT	23	Sco	SEP	28	Sco	AUG	31	Lib			
NOV	22	Sag	NOV	7	Lib	SEP	24	Sco			
DEC	21	Cap	NOV	8	Sco	OCT	19	Sag			
			DEC	3	Sag	NOV	13	Cap			
			DEC	23	Cap	DEC	8	Aqu			

2001

SUN			MERCURY			VENUS			MARS		
mth	dy	sign	mth	dy	sign	mth	dy	sign	mth	dy	sign
JAN	1	Cap	JAN	1	Cap	JAN	1	Aqu	JAN	1	Sco
JAN	20	Aqu	JAN	10	Aqu	JAN	3	Pis	FEB	14	Sag
FEB	18	Pis	FEB	1	Pis	FEB	2	Ari	SEP	8	Cap
MAR	20	Ari	FEB	6	Aqu	JUN	6	Tau	OCT	27	Aqu
APR	20	Tau	MAR	17	Pis	JUL	5	Gem	DEC	8	Pis
MAY	20	Gem	APR	6	Ari	AUG	1	Can			
JUN	21	Can	APR	21	Tau	AUG	27	Leo			
JUL	22	Leo	MAY	6	Gem	SEP	21	Vir			
AUG	23	Vir	JUL	12	Can	OCT	15	Lib			
SEP	22	Lib	JUL	30	Leo	NOV	8	Sco			
OCT	23	Sco	AUG	14	Vir	DEC	2	Sag			
NOV	22	Sag	SEP	1	Lib	DEC	26	Cap			
DEC	21	Cap	NOV	7	Sco						
			NOV	26	Sag						
			DEC	15	Cap						

2002

SUN			MERCURY			VENUS			MARS		
mth	dy	sign	mth	dy	sign	mth	dy	sign	mth	dy	sign
JAN	1	Cap	JAN	1	Cap	JAN	1	Cap	JAN	1	Pis
JAN	20	Aqu	JAN	3	Aqu	JAN	19	Aqu	JAN	18	Ari
FEB	18	Pis	FEB	4	Cap	FEB	12	Pis	MAR	1	Tau
MAR	20	Ari	FEB	13	Aqu	MAR	8	Ari	APR	13	Gem
APR	20	Tau	MAR	11	Pis	APR	1	Tau	MAY	28	Can
MAY	21	Gem	MAR	29	Ari	APR	25	Gem	JUL	13	Leo
JUN	21	Can	APR	13	Tau	MAY	20	Can	AUG	29	Vir
JUL	23	Leo	APR	30	Gem	JUN	14	Leo	OCT	15	Lib
AUG	23	Vir	JUL	7	Can	JUL	10	Vir	DEC	1	Sco
SEP	23	Lib	JUL	21	Leo	AUG	7	Lib			
OCT	23	Sco	AUG	6	Vir	SEP	8	Sco			
NOV	22	Sag	AUG	26	Lib						
DEC	22	Cap	OCT	2	Vir						
			OCT	11	Lib						
			OCT	31	Sco						
			NOV	20	Sag						
			DEC	9	Cap						

2003

SUN			MERCURY			VENUS			MARS		
mth	dy	sign	mth	dy	sign	mth	dy	sign	mth	dy	sign
JAN	1	Cap	JAN	1	Cap	JAN	1	Sco	JAN	1	Sco
JAN	20	Aqu	FEB	13	Aqu	JAN	7	Sag	JAN	17	Sag
FEB	19	Pis	MAR	5	Pis	FEB	4	Cap	MAR	4	Cap
MAR	21	Ari	MAR	21	Ari	MAR	2	Aqu	APR	21	Aqu
APR	20	Tau	APR	5	Tau	MAR	27	Pis	JUN	17	Pis
MAY	21	Gem	JUN	13	Gem	APR	21	Ari	DEC	16	Ari
JUN	21	Can	JUN	29	Can	MAY	16	Tau			
JUL	23	Leo	JUL	13	Leo	JUN	10	Gem			
AUG	23	Vir	JUL	30	Vir	JUL	4	Can			
SEP	23	Lib	OCT	7	Lib	JUL	29	Leo			
OCT	23	Sco	OCT	24	Sco	AUG	22	Vir			
NOV	22	Sag	NOV	12	Sag	SEP	15	Lib			
DEC	22	Cap	DEC	2	Cap	OCT	9	Sco			
			DEC	30	Sag	NOV	2	Sag			
						NOV	27	Cap			
						DEC	21	Aqu			

2004

SUN			MERCURY			VENUS			MARS		
mth	dy	sign	mth	dy	sign	mth	dy	sign	mth	dy	sign
JAN	1	Cap	JAN	1	Sag	JAN	1	Aqu	JAN	1	Ari
JAN	20	Aqu	JAN	14	Cap	JAN	14	Pis	FEB	3	Tau
FEB	19	Pis	FEB	7	Aqu	FEB	8	Ari	MAR	21	Gem
MAR	20	Ari	FEB	25	Pis	MAR	5	Tau	MAY	7	Can
APR	19	Tau	MAR	12	Ari	APR	3	Gem	JUN	23	Leo
MAY	20	Gem	APR	1	Tau	AUG	7	Can	AUG	10	Vir
JUN	21	Can	APR	13	Ari	SEP	6	Leo	SEP	26	Lib
JUL	22	Leo	MAY	16	Tau	OCT	3	Vir	NOV	11	Sco
AUG	22	Vir	JUN	5	Gem	OCT	29	Lib	DEC	25	Sag
SEP	22	Lib	JUN	19	Can	NOV	22	Sco			
OCT	23	Sco	JUL	4	Leo	DEC	16	Sag			
NOV	21	Sag	JUL	25	Vir						
DEC	21	Cap	AUG	25	Leo						
			SEP	10	Vir						
			SEP	28	Lib						
			OCT	15	Sco						
			NOV	4	Sag						

2005

SUN			MERCURY			VENUS			MARS		
mth	dy	sign	mth	dy	sign	mth	dy	sign	mth	dy	sign
JAN	1	Cap	JAN	1	Sag	JAN	1	Sag	JAN	1	Sag
JAN	19	Aqu	JAN	10	Cap	JAN	9	Cap	FEB	6	Cap
FEB	18	Pis	JAN	30	Aqu	FEB	2	Aqu	MAR	20	Aqu
MAR	20	Ari	FEB	16	Pis	FEB	26	Pis	MAY	1	Pis
APR	19	Tau	MAR	5	Ari	MAR	22	Ari	JUN	12	Ari
MAY	20	Gem	MAY	12	Tau	APR	15	Tau	JUL	28	Tau
JUN	21	Can	MAY	28	Gem	MAY	10	Gem			
JUL	22	Leo	JUN	11	Can	JUN	3	Can			
AUG	23	Vir	JUN	28	Leo	JUN	28	Leo			
SEP	22	Lib	SEP	4	Vir	JUL	23	Vir			
OCT	23	Sco	SEP	20	Lib	AUG	17	Lib			
NOV	22	Sag	OCT	8	Sco	SEP	11	Sco			
DEC	21	Cap	OCT	30	Sag	OCT	8	Sag			
			NOV	26	Sco	NOV	5	Cap			
			DEC	12	Sag	DEC	15	Aqu			

1. I seem to fit one sign perfectly, but none of my planets are there. Have I calculated it wrongly?

Go through the tables at the back of the book again to check you haven't missed anything. If you still can't find this sign represented by your Sun, Moon, Mercury, Venus, Mars or Rising sign, it's almost certainly **planetary interference** in your horoscope. This doesn't happen very often, but when it does, the planet in question will dominate your chart so much that the sign it rules seems to leap out of your personality, and your life!

If a particular sign seems to fit you — or someone you know — but no planets are placed there get your chart drawn up and check for the ruler of that sign in the list below. Chances are, it will be all over the place!

Aries — Mars	Libra — Venus
Taurus — Venus	Scorpio — Pluto
Gemini — Mercury	Sagittarius — Jupiter
Cancer — Moon	Capricorn — Saturn
Leo — Sun	Aquarius — Uranus
Virgo — Mercury	Pisces — Neptune

Jimi Hendrix was a good example of this planetary influence. He didn't have Taurus or Libra — the music signs — in his chart. Nevertheless, Venus, the ruler of Taurus and Libra, dominates his personal horoscope.

2. I was born on the cusp of two signs. Am I a bit of both?

No. You really will have that planet in either one sign or the other. The only way to calculate it properly is to make sure you have an accurate birthtime to give your astrologer, so that he or she can 'count in' the Sun to its correct sign. If you have always felt that you were influenced by both signs, you may well have been. But it's not the effect of the cusp — it's more likely that your Sun is in one sign, and one of the other planets — the Moon, Mercury, Venus or Mars — is in the other.

3. Are babies who are induced or born by Caesarian section still reflecting their birth horoscope?

Yes — sometimes uncannily so. Many premature babies have chart patterns involving the planet Pluto, which always describes a struggle for survival. In a perfect world, astrologers would prefer babies to be born naturally, just because horoscopes of these children tend to show a stronger link to the signs in their family tree. However, children who are induced still have an accurate chart.

4. What about twins?

Twins born minutes apart will live out the themes of their horoscopes in subtle and different ways, but also in literally identical fashion. In an obvious way, the broad similarities in the lives of twins may be the best argument in support of astrology. Changes are more obvious if the gap between each child's delivery is longer, which may give some twins different Planet signs or Rising signs and which will in turn result in different journeys in life, or different characteristics.

Just as interesting as real twins are time twins. These people are born on the same day, at the same time, in roughly the same place.

I did horoscopes for two time twins for the television programme, A *Current Affair*. Both women shared surnames, both had been given the same Christian names by their parents and both were gifted students.

Documentary evidence of time twins is fascinating. After Rudolph Valentino's death, when the search was on for his double, one of the shortlisted candidates turned out to have been born on Valentino's birthday, in the same area. If you've ever watched the BBC-TV series *To Play the King*, you may be interested to know that its scriptwriter is almost a time twin with Prince Charles. (They both married blonde women, too!)

5. If astrology works, how does it work?

Dr Percy Seymour, one of Britain's leading astronomers, has written a book called *Astrology: The Evidence of Science*, which explains things far better than I ever could. Geophysical cycles? Synchronicity? Magnetic fields? I can't decide either, but I do know this: nature organises us into cycles, patterns and groups in other ways — through the seasons, through the menstrual cycle and through genetic codes. Astrology may be just another part of this system.

6. How can an astrologer say that the future will be the same for every person born under one particular sign of the zodiac?

Sun sign predictions are the side of astrology most people know best. From the outside they can seem simplistic — how can everyone born under Aries be having a wonderful week at work, for example? It depends on the astrologer, of course (people like English astrologer Patric Walker were particularly accurate), but most of the time, the people who write syndicated astrological columns do get it right.

We astrologers talk about the future in a generalised way in these columns because the information we are dealing with is quite general and we're looking at just a few astrological factors, instead of a few dozen. We also have no idea about your age, sex, income, job or private life — and would you want us to? — so we are forced to paint the canvas with a pretty wide brush. For all that, it works.

In the same way that anybody could predict that 25th December is generally going to be a day of over-indulgence for the group of people known as Australians (a prediction based on previous evidence) so an astrologer can predict that any one day might be wonderful at work for the group of people known as Arians. We are also working with previous evidence — namely planetary patterns. In other words, we are taking a calculated guess.

7. Aren't the signs in different places now?

Yes. The twelve signs of the zodiac no longer match the constellations named after them, because the earth just keeps tilting, dammit. For example, between around 21st March and 21st April, the Sun, as it always has, enters an astrological slice of the sky which astrologers associate with Arian qualities and themes.

However, it now looks as though it's passing through Pisces. This is not a problem for astrologers, who have known about it since around 200 BC, because astrology is and always has been a symbolic system.

8. If astrology has always been accurate, how do you explain the fact that Uranus, Neptune and Pluto, which have such an important effect on our lives, were only discovered recently?

This is a bit like the argument that the medical discoveries and cures of the future will make meaningless virtually everything that works in hospitals today. The new planets are an amazing addition to the body of astrological knowledge that was in place before, but this does not mean that everything beforehand collapses. Even today, astrologers would be the first to admit there are plenty of grey areas and gaps in what they do. As we research and discover more, astrology will expand again.

9. I'd like to get my horoscope done. What's involved?

Some astrologers will see you face-to-face, others will send you a tape, but the majority will send you a written report or even a glossy booklet. If it matters to you that a report or booklet is personally written for you, rather than made up of pre-written paragraphs stored on a computer, then say so. However, you'll pay extra for the privilege, as it can take an astrologer days to piece it all together.

If you're clueless about who to hire, and where to start, I suggest going to astrology magazines, which often advertise very good written reports, tapes and consultations. In Australia, *The Astrological Monthly Review* is a good bet. If you can't find a copy in your newsagent ring 02 9713 7784 or e-mail the Editor, Ray Webb. He's at amr@one.net.au. Some of the biggest names on the Australian scene, including author Mary Coleman, advertise in *Astrological Monthly Review*.

In the USA and Canada, find a copy of *The Mountain Astrologer*, which is my favourite astrology magazine in the entire world. There are plenty of chart offers to choose from. You can also chase them on their website at www.MountainAstrologer.com or telephone (800) 287 4828 in the US and Canada, (44) 1202 424 695 in the UK and (617) 3216 6960 in Australia.

In England, get in touch with The Astrology Shop, 78 Neal Street, Covent Garden, London WC2H 9PA. Telephone (44) 171 497 1001 and fax (44) 171 497 0344. Robert Currey, who owns the shop, also puts out a great website at http://www.astrology.co.uk/index.htm where you can order charts on the spot. Not bad. If you'd rather get your chart in person, wander into the shop, which is five minutes from Covent Garden tube, and you can have your chart printed and bound on the spot — perfect for those of you with planets in Aries who can't wait for anything. Robert's chart service Equinox exists in Australia, too, in Manly, Sydney. Fax or phone (02) 9976 2015 for details.

Getting a big name astrologer to do your chart doesn't have to be expensive if you order a computer-compiled report. Robert Currey does one, so does the legendary English astrologer Liz Greene, and the grand-slam American writer Robert Hand. People often worry that these kinds of charts aren't personal — all I can say is, I've ordered my own computer charts from all three of these international stargazers, and the sophistication of the computer programmes they are using is so finely tuned that even I was staggered by the accuracy of the predictions and the spot-on character portraits. Expect to pay what you'd fork out for a good T-shirt — not bad at all! One idea you might like to consider is finding a magazine or newspaper astrologer who seems to be on track with you, then writing directly to them at the publication concerned. Many media astrologers are accomplished client-based astrologers as well — my friend Kim Farnell, who writes the horoscope column for *Company* magazine in England, is a good example. If a columnist has the time, he or she will be glad to hand-write and prepare a chart, or send you a tape — but do go via the publication concerned, and send an SAE.

In England, both The Astrology Shop and the Midheaven Bookshop (phone (44) 171 607 4133) sell these computer charts. If you've got a credit card handy, you can also organise everything over the phone. In Canada, try the wonderful Donna King, who can be found at The Astrology Shop in North Vancouver on 604 984 8782, or via e-mail as follows: celestia@conneti.com.

10. I'd like to take an astrology course. Where do I start?

Once again, magazines like *Astrological Monthly Review* in Australia, and *The Mountain Astrologer* in the USA and Canada are good starting points. The Astrology Shop and Midheaven Bookshop in London are also good sources for the many different kinds of courses on offer — someone behind the counter will point you in the right direction.

My personal recommendation is The Faculty of Astrological Studies in London. The Faculty offers correspondence courses around the world and in-the-flesh classes, too. You can do short courses or come out with an impressive qualification.

For more information contact The Registrar, FAS, BM7470, London, WC1N 3XX UK. You can phone them on (44) 7000 790 143 or fax on (44) 1689 603 537. The website is at http://www.astrology.org.uk and the e–mail address is info@astrology.org.uk .

If you're sure you're serious about investing your money and committing your time, you might want to drop in to one of the many special weekends or festivals now put on by astrological organisations — with luck there'll be some near where you live. Trade fairs at these events offer you a chance to meet the people who are putting on face-to-face and correspondence courses in your area. Once again, astrology magazines usually advertise these one-off events. In Australia, you might like to start with The Federation of Australian Astrologers, 24 Berryman Street, North Ryde NSW 2113. Their e-mail address is faa@peg.apc.org. Through them you can gain a Basic Certificate or (if you are a total girlie swot) the title of AAT — Accredited Astrology Teacher.

GETTING YOUR CHART DONE – FREE – ON THE INTERNET

If you're on the net and into astrology, you may already know about what's on offer. Basically, you can either get your own chart (signs, planets, house positions, aspects) calculated in the form of a wheel, which enables you to use books like this to help you sort out what it means — or you can get the whole enchilada, with written information on your personality and your future. Some astrologers on the net, like my friend Kelli Fox in San Fransisco, will give you a taster of a real chart interpetation by allowing you to download information on what it all means — as well as all the different signs in your astro-package.

If you're not on the net, or don't have a computer, or just find the whole thing baffling, I have just one word for you — internet cafe. For just a few dollars or pounds, you can try out the net while you have a coffee. Look in your local phone directory for the nearest location, or browse in any of the internet magazines on sale at your newsagent, as cafes are often mentioned or advertised there. The staff at these cyber-cafes are used to helping technobimbos like myself out, and I've always found them happy to assist. All you need to take in are the following addresses, written down on a piece of paper. (If you're online already, feel free to bookmark them.) By the way, if you want to make your life easier, write down your full date of birth, clock time of birth and place of birth (if you've got longitude and latitude from an atlas, even better) before you log on. Some sites will ask you for it, and if you haven't got it, you could be slapping yourself on the head à la Homer Simpson.

Here we go, then.

CHARTS THAT DON'T COST A CENT
The TwoStar Oracle

http://www.twostar.com/astrology/

Before you go here, make sure you have your full date of birth, the clock time of birth, the longitude and latitude of the place where you were born (or the nearest town) and make sure you know how many hours your birthplace was ahead or behind Greenwich Mean Time (GMT) in London. For example, if you were born in Sydney during daylight saving time, you are GMT + 11. If you were born in London when daylight saving time wasn't happening at all, you are GMT + 0. You'll notice several boxes to click on. Most of them are self-explanatory, but you may hit a couple which don't make sense. My advice is to click on the box which says Equal, the box which says All Charts, the box which says Display Interpretations and the box which says Display Transits. Then go! You'll get back a whole bundle of information and a chart reading. It's very handy if you need to double-check your Sun, Moon, Mercury, Venus, Mars and Rising signs in order to use the book you're holding now.

By the way, TwoStar Oracle uses the other term, 'Ascendant', instead of Rising sign. They're the same thing, though. Fear not!

This site also gives you information on curly astrological critters like Vesta and Chiron — it's quite an in-depth reading. I personally think there's more here than you need to know — especially if you happen to be a beginner — but it's a generous offer from TwoStar, and it's completely free. And one more thing, if you're in Australia a great place to order astrology books online is Earth Violets, which you'll find at http://www.earthviolets.com.au — this is the place to find the books which can help you make more of TwoStar and many other freebie chart sites.

Astrodienst

http://www.astro.ch/atlas/

If you don't know your longitude, latitude or time zone compared to GMT, use this. Astrodienst does it all for you, so all you need is your birthday, birthtime and birthplace. Begin by pressing Click Here To Find A City. Search the relevant part of the world — you can choose Whole World or, to make life easier, you can narrow it down to your own country. Type in your birthplace, or if it's too small and obscure, the nearest town to the place you were born. Click on Submit. A number of choices will come back — just click on the right birthplace. If you were born in Perth, Scotland for example you won't want to mix it up with Perth, Western Australia. After this you'll then be asked to put in your day, month, year, hour and minute of birth. Click on the box saying Update Time Zone then follow the signs to get your free chart.

Don't worry if it looks like a pizza drawn by Salvador Dali's cleaner. The stuff you want is in the box on the far right of the screen. Opposite 1st House you will see a number next to a sign. The sign is your Rising sign, or Ascendant as it's sometimes known. You'll then see a list of planets. For the purposes of this book, you're interested in Sun, Moon, Mercury, Venus and Mars — all of which will have a sign listed next to them — this is your personal astro-package. If you want to know what it all means, you can order a horoscope book from Liz Greene or Robert Hand from this site at the same time. Otherwise, jot down the main points in your diary, or print the whole thing out — and head for an astrology book. As well as the Earth Violets store online, there are many other good book sale sites on the internet. You can certainly use the chart you get from Astrodienst in conjunction with this very book — *The New Astrology for Women* — but if you want to go more deeply into your horoscope, do take a note of things like the houses because there are certainly books and websites out there which will give you all the required info on them.

Women Astrology Net

http://www.astrologynet.com/

Kelli Fox, an Australian astrologer in San Francisco, has created an amazing website with women in mind. It looks fabulous, and it's easy to use. The deal is this — you can try a free sample chart for yourself or a friend, then if you'd like more, you pay a very reasonable sum (around the cost of a pair of socks in New York) and back comes your chart, via the computer. The nice thing about the free chart that Kelli offers is that you don't need to know longitude or latitude for your birthplace, and if you don't know the time of birth, that's okay too. In other words, she's done all the hard work for you. Definitely worth checking out.

My Site!

http://www.jessicaadams.com.au

A lot of the people, ideas and services discussed in this book are directly linked from my site, so if you're into one-stop surfing, you might like to head here first. Part of my site is a special spin-off of the book you're holding now — *The New Astrology For Women*. Then there are the online sun-sign predictions I write, and sun-sign profiles, which you'll only ever find on the net. You can order more copies of *The New Astrology For Women* from this site, and maybe even grab a personally signed and dedicated book. This is one of those sites which you can come back to all the time and find something new. Check it out!

Astrolabe Free Charts

I was impressed with the speed at which my birth chart appeared on the screen after visiting this site. Once again, it's completely free, and you may even get a mini-reading at the same time. The address is http://www.alabe.com.

A word of caution:

The internet doesn't stand still. There's a chance that when you try out one of the addresses above, it may have moved somewhere else (don't worry, they'll usually tell you where to head next). At worst, it may have vanished altogether. If this is the case, head to a good search engine like hotbot, which you'll find at http://www.hotbot.com and type in a key word like horoscope or astrology. A whole lot of new addresses will come back, and among these there's bound to be a brand new free chart calculation service somewhere in the world. As time goes by, there should be even greater numbers of freebie charts on offer than there are at the moment. By the way, if you discover one, please e-mail me at jessica@zip.com.au and I'll mention it in future editions of this book.

A SIMPLE TEN DOLLAR CHART

Ray Webb, at Australia's *Astrological Monthly Review*, will do you a quick computer chart, called a Basic Horoscope for $10. It will show you your Rising sign and planet signs, and if you wish to go further into astrology, there will also be house positions, aspects and a few other crucial details. Write to Ray Webb, PO Box 122, Five Dock, NSW 2046 for more details. In other countries, check your local astrology magazines for a similar service. You shouldn't have to pay more than a few pounds or dollars. Better still, surf the net — these chart services are free.

WHERE ASTROLOGY IS GOING

It's easy to under-rate astrology. If you only know about the star-sign columns you read in magazines and newspapers, then you can be forgiven for letting your jaw hang open when you discover that modern astrologers do everything from statistics on insurance claims to full-blown psychotherapy. Astrology is every bit as big and complicated as modern medicine, with the same kind of weird and wonderful history. In the same way that first-aid kits don't really tell the whole story in medicine, star-sign columns (much as I love them) can only give a quick, superficial version of what it's all really about.

There are as many different kinds of astrologer as there are kinds of astrology. You can get women in purple cloaks with crystals hanging around their necks. You can get serious Wall Street guys in serious Wall Street suits. You can get academics — scarily brilliant, and often successful in 'straight' professions before making the switch to astrology. At the United Astrology Congress in 1998, there were two Ph.Ds speaking. Liz Greene, a pioneer in psychological astrology, also holds a Ph.D.

When you ask an astrologer what it's all for — and where it's all going — you'll get a different answer, depending on who you speak to. Spiritual astrologers will tell you that we're supposed to be using astrological knowledge and wisdom to help us become better human beings, so we can zoom up the ladder of spiritual evolution even faster. Astrologers who hang around race tracks with binoculars around their necks will explain that it's basically about getting the winner of the Melbourne Cup.

One of the trends that is worth watching is the new interest in hard research. ISAR, The International Society for Astrological

Research, keep figures on stock and commodity trading, and war and weather cycles. In France, Madame Suzel Fuzeau-Braesh, research director at France's National Centre for Scientific Research, has demonstrated that the majority of 238 pairs of twins with nearly identical horoscopes — except for their Rising signs — show personality differences which are exactly true of their different Rising signs.

Then there are the worst enemies of sceptics — the Gauquelin family, also from France. Their pioneering work in the 1950s showed something called the Mars Effect — proof that prominent athletes had Mars (traditionally the sporting planet, and ruler of Aries) prominently placed in their horoscopes. Scientists and researchers continue to argue over the Mars Effect today, but it just won't go away — as a new book, *The Tenacious Mars Effect*, points out.

Debbi Kempton-Smith, one of the world's favourite astrologers (and author of the brilliant purple tome, *Secrets From A Stargazer's Notebook*: Bantam) is taking stargazing even further. The last time I checked her website she was onto something called exoplanets — like 47 Ursa Majoris, and 51 Pegasi. One of the challenges for new astrologers after 2000 will be tracking the exoplanets in people's horoscopes to discover what they're all about, and what kind of effect they're having on us down here. Debbi also reckons that there's been enough of flat horoscopes (she calls them pizzas or pancakes) ... what this woman wants is a 3-D spherical chart which you can tilt and rotate.

While some astrologers continue to spend their careers putting together research (and arguing with sceptics) there are still thousands more who couldn't care less about proof on paper — the only proof they need is in their client work — or their successful predictions. To these astrologers there is a kind of mystery or poetry in their work, and to try and classify it and measure it would be like winding a tape measure around a crystal ball.

One of the interesting things about astrology is that it actually has an inbuilt stuff-up mechanism. And I mean that in the nicest possible way. Astrology's universe takes in the planet Uranus, which is eccentric, insane, chaotic and unpredictable and represents the x factor that always takes the world by surprise. By accepting Uranus into the astrological universe of meaning, stargazers also had to accept the reality of something which would always mess things up. Well — that's my excuse for bum predictions, anyway.

Prediction is still the part of astrology that people love and know best. After ten years in the business, I have no doubt that it works — at least, as well as weather forecasts, or economic forecasts, or any other of the straight, acceptable ways of peering into the future. It's not so mysterious, when you think about it. Astrology is about repeated cycles, and enough people have now been practising it for sufficiently long that it's possible to set up a hypothesis. If x happened when Jupiter was in Aries twelve years ago, then we can expect x to happen again ... Really, it's no more occult or bizarre than that.

The esteemed Australian astrologer Bernadette Brady specialises in using medieval war charts to help predict sports scores. And yes, she generally does do better than those TV experts in the matching sports jackets.

The only other question you have to ask about future prediction is probably a philosophical one. What's the point? What is it for? And if astrologers can predict the future, why aren't they all millionaires?

To answer the last question first, unfortunately a lot of them are seriously, revoltingly rich. You don't hear much about them (they're too smart to let their names or faces get in the paper, natch) but these canny stargazers not only have mile-long celebrity waiting lists, they also have an amazing way with Saturn cycles and the stockmarket.

Still, most astrologers will tell you it's not about that. And anyway, if you want to make money, you have to be born with a money-making chart, so it's a catch–22 situation. You could be the greatest astrologer in the world, with a terrifying ability to pick winning greyhounds, but if you were born with the worst Second and Eighth Houses in the history of horoscope-land, then you'll probably win the lot but be ripped off the next day by a garden gnome salesman.

I know that the inherent power and control in astrology — especially predictive astrology — worries a lot of people. All I can say in reply to that is that there are professional organisations designed to make sure astrologers behave fairly, ethically and nicely with you, the client. If we don't respect your privacy, if we don't handle you with sensitivity, if you have any complaints about us at all ... well. One report to our governing organisation and you can get us struck off the professional register. Now that's power, and it's all yours.

At heart, though, I don't think astrology is about power anyway. That's too Pluto, and astrology is essentially a Uranian/Aquarian thing — it's too chaotic and eccentric (try going to an astrology convention and you'll soon see what I mean) to turn into the sort of massive organisation where our representatives stand on street corners, harassing you with a biro and a clipboard.

Astrologers won't lock you in a room, refuse to let you use the loo during your 'lectures' or get you to force all your friends and family to join our lovely organisation. We won't give you motivation tapes to help you sell our products, or ask you for your bank account number, or insist that you marry one of our own kind.

On the contrary, the attitude of most astrologers I have ever met is this: 'If it works for you, great. If it doesn't work for you, great.' This is normally followed by a shrug, and then they just walk away. Astrologers can be like that.

Hitler tried to use astrology as a propaganda tool. It didn't work. And yes, I know the Pope keeps giving it the old papal thumbs-down, but it is not meant to replace religion either. It has nothing to do with people in black underwear drinking their own blood and dancing around skulls, and if anyone tries to convince you otherwise, run a mile. You have not been dealing with an astrologer.

Beware, too, the shonky breed of new astrologers who are appearing. If someone's making an awful lot of money from you, if they're not knowledgeably referring to planets in their predictions, if they seem to have tentacles on their heads ... well. Don't say the 99% of ethical astrologers out there didn't warn you. As the Age of Aquarius kicks in, astrology is taking off, and that means big money. By the way here's a list of things astrology isn't about:

Lucky leprechaun pendants
Spells to get your boyfriend back
Lotto numbers
Communicating with aliens

Okay, I'll go back on my medication now ...

Finally, a cautionary tale. A few years ago, *New Weekly* magazine asked me to predict the winners of the Melbourne Cup, in their correct order. The Sports Editor faxed me a list of the field, two weeks before the final draw.

All I know about horseracing is that whatever you do, some hopeless nag always wins. However, I had never done it before, so I looked up the planets on the day, thought long and hard about the horses' names and then faxed the whole thing off without trying to think about it.

I didn't have the birthdates of the horses, and I didn't have the birthdates of the jockeys or their owners. But astrology can sometimes be quite useful if you simply work off the symbolism of the horses' names in relation to the planets which are looking good on the day.

I chose (in order) The Phantom for first place, followed by Our Pompeii and Tennessee Jack. Then I totally forgot about it. On the day before the Melbourne Cup was due to run, I picked up a horse-racing newspaper. PHANTOM TO WIN the headline screamed, with a picture of the esteemed animal.

On the day of the race itself, to my absolute amazement, several of Australia's leading racing writers were picking The Phantom for first, Our Pompeii for second, and ... you guessed it, Tennessee Jack for third. In addition, a psychic who had also been quizzed by *New Weekly* also declared that The Phantom was it. I put down 30 dollars on the trifecta, told my boyfriend at the time (who told everyone at the TV station he worked for) and I even told the girls in the local printer's who were photocopying some astrology charts for me.

Eventually, it was time for the big race. Naturally, I had already worked out what a 30 dollar win on the trifecta would win me, and I was already planning my next trip to Paris. Naturally, dear reader, not one of the wilful beasts came home.

And the lesson is ... what? I can only think that astrology was having the last laugh on me. I don't have a gambler's chart, you see (the girls in the printer's still aren't talking to me). However, on reflection, something quite interesting was going on. Astrologically speaking, I was using the planets to predict the most likely outcome on the day.

It turned out to be so likely that half the country's best racing writers were picking one, two or all three of those same horses. It was so likely that The Phantom was a hot favourite at the TAB.

The whole experience was horrible, embarrassing and — I admit it — a complete waste of money. But the more I think about it, the more it makes sense. Astrology doesn't predict the outcome of future events, you see. All it can do is predict the likeliest scenario. And if the horse doesn't care about that, the horse doesn't care. The same applies to you and me. After reading this book, you may find out that you're in a Jupiter Cycle Seven next year, with Cupid poised for a direct hit. If you're not interested at the time, then nobody's forcing you to win the Melbourne Cup, if you know what I mean ... Ultimately, astrology is about freedom. And you have the freedom to tell it to get stuffed — just like The Phantom did, on the day I blew 30 bucks on the trifecta.

SOURCES

Arroyo, Stephen & Greene, Liz 1984, *New Insights in Modern Astrology*, CFCS, California.

Beal, G. 1992, *The Independent Book of Anniversaries*, Headline, London.

Birkbeck, L. 1996, *Do It Yourself Astrology*, Element, Dorset, Great Britain.

Bulfinch, Thomas 1979, *Myths of Greece and Rome*, Penguin, USA.

Contemporary Australians 1995/96, Reed Reference Publishing, Port Melbourne, Australia.

Harvey, Charles & Harvey, Suzi 1994, *Sun Sign Moon Sign*, Aquarian, London.

Hayward, A. 1994, *Who's Who on Television*, Boxtree, Great Britain.

Knowles, Elizabeth (ed) 1997, *The Oxford Dictionary of Phrase, Saying & Quotation*, Oxford University Press, New York.

Laufenberg, Frank 1992, *Rock and Pop Day by Day*, ed Hugh Gregory, Blandford, London.

Maltin, L. 1995, *Leonard Maltin's Movie Encylopaedia*, Penguin Reference, New York.

Monash Biographical Dictionary of 20th Century Australia 1994, Reed Reference Publishing, Port Melbourne, Australia.

Rodden, Lois M. 1990, *Astro Data IV*, AFA, Tempe, USA.

Rodden, Lois M. 1993, *Astro Data II*, AFA, Tempe, USA.

Seyffert, Oskar 1995, *The Dictionary of Classical Mythology, Religion, Literature and Art*, Gramercy, New Jersey.

SOFTWARE SUPPLIERS

AstroDatabank Company, Manchester MA, USA.

Electric Ephemeris, Islington, London, England.

Nova Software 1984, 1986, Astro-Graphic Services, Inc. USA.
Sherrill, Linda 1989, 1991, Celeste I Macintosh, Astrolabe, USA.
'Visions Program' 1990, Lifestyle Software Group, USA.

Many thanks to Mark McDonough, President of AstroDatabank Company, who ran many of the American and English celebrity birth charts through his computer. AstroDatabank is a fascinating resource for astrologers and students alike, if you haven't already discovered it. A lot of my English celebrity data also came from Data Plus UK, the only place with correct X-*Files* data — and more. Find them by fax or phone at (44) 181 381 4169. To contact Electric Ephemeris in London ring (44) 7000 171 666 or go to their website at http://www. electric-ephemeris.com.

Every effort has been made to verify the sources of birth data in this book. When the attempt has been unsuccessful, the author and publisher would be pleased to rectify any inaccuracies.

YEAR AND MONTH OF BIRTH

	JAN	FEB	MAR	APR	MAY	JUN	JUL	AUG	SEP	OCT	NOV	DEC
1930	Cap	Pis	Pis	Tau	Gem	Leo	Vir	Sco	Sag	Cap	Pis	Ari
1931	Tau	Can	Can	Vir	Lib	Sag	Cap	Pis	Ari	Tau	Can	Leo
1932	Lib	Sag	Sag	Aqu	Pis	Tau	Gem	Can	Vir	Lib	Sag	Cap
1933	Pis	Ari	Tau	Gem	Can	Vir	Lib	Sag	Cap	Pis	Ari	Tau
1934	Can	Leo	Vir	Lib	Sag	Cap	Pis	Ari	Gem	Can	Leo	Vir
1935	Sco	Cap	Cap	Pis	Ari	Gem	Can	Leo	Lib	Sco	Cap	Aqu
1936	Ari	Tau	Gem	Leo	Vir	Lib	Sco	Cap	Pis	Ari	Gem	Can
1937	Leo	Lib	Lib	Sag	Cap	Aqu	Ari	Tau	Can	Leo	Lib	Sco
1938	Cap	Aqu	Aqu	Ari	Tau	Can	Leo	Lib	Sco	Cap	Aqu	Pis
1939	Tau	Gem	Can	Leo	Lib	Sco	Cap	Aqu	Ari	Tau	Gem	Leo
1940	Vir	Sco	Sag	Cap	Aqu	Ari	Tau	Can	Leo	Lib	Sco	Cap
1941	Aqu	Ari	Ari	Tau	Gem	Leo	Vir	Sco	Cap	Aqu	Ari	Tau
1942	Gem	Leo	Leo	Lib	Sco	Cap	Aqu	Ari	Tau	Gem	Leo	Vir
1943	Lib	Sag	Sag	Aqu	Pis	Tau	Gem	Leo	Vir	Lib	Sag	Cap
1944	Pis	Tau	Tau	Can	Leo	Lib	Sco	Sag	Aqu	Pis	Tau	Gem
1945	Leo	Vir	Lib	Sco	Sag	Aqu	Pis	Tau	Can	Leo	Vir	Lib
1946	Sag	Cap	Aqu	Pis	Tau	Gem	Leo	Vir	Sco	Sag	Cap	Aqu
1947	Ari	Gem	Gem	Leo	Vir	Sco	Sag	Cap	Pis	Ari	Gem	Can
1948	Vir	Lib	Sco	Cap	Aqu	Pis	Ari	Gem	Leo	Vir	Sco	Sag
1949	Cap	Pis	Pis	Tau	Gem	Leo	Vir	Sco	Sag	Cap	Pis	Ari
1950	Gem	Can	Can	Vir	Lib	Sag	Cap	Pis	Ari	Gem	Can	Leo
1951	Lib	Sag	Sag	Aqu	Pis	Ari	Gem	Can	Vir	Lib	Sco	Cap
1952	Pis	Ari	Tau	Gem	Can	Vir	Lib	Sag	Cap	Pis	Ari	Gem
1953	Can	Vir	Vir	Lib	Sag	Cap	Pis	Ari	Gem	Can	Vir	Lib
1954	Sco	Cap	Cap	Pis	Ari	Gem	Can	Vir	Lib	Sco	Cap	Aqu
1955	Ari	Tau	Gem	Can	Vir	Lib	Sco	Cap	Aqu	Pis	Tau	Gem
1956	Leo	Lib	Sco	Sag	Cap	Pis	Ari	Tau	Can	Leo	Lib	Sco
1957	Cap	Aqu	Pis	Ari	Tau	Can	Leo	Lib	Sag	Cap	Aqu	Pis
1958	Tau	Gem	Can	Leo	Lib	Sag	Cap	Aqu	Ari	Tau	Gem	Leo
1959	Vir	Sco	Sco	Cap	Aqu	Ari	Tau	Gem	Leo	Vir	Sco	Sag
1960	Aqu	Ari	Ari	Gem	Can	Leo	Vir	Sco	Cap	Aqu	Ari	Tau
1961	Can	Leo	Leo	Lib	Sco	Cap	Aqu	Ari	Gem	Can	Leo	Vir
1962	Sco	Sag	Sag	Aqu	Pis	Tau	Gem	Leo	Vir	Sco	Sag	Cap
1963	Pis	Tau	Tau	Can	Leo	Lib	Sco	Sag	Aqu	Pis	Tau	Gem
1964	Leo	Vir	Lib	Sco	Sag	Aqu	Pis	Tau	Can	Leo	Lib	Sco
1965	Sag	Aqu	Aqu	Ari	Tau	Gem	Leo	Lib	Sco	Sag	Aqu	Pis
1966	Ari	Gem	Gem	Leo	Vir	Sco	Sag	Aqu	Pis	Ari	Gem	Can
1967	Vir	Sco	Sco	Cap	Aqu	Pis	Ari	Gem	Can	Vir	Lib	Sag
1968	Cap	Pis	Ari	Tau	Gem	Leo	Vir	Sco	Sag	Aqu	Pis	Ari
1969	Gem	Can	Leo	Vir	Lib	Sag	Cap	Pis	Tau	Gem	Can	Leo
1970	Lib	Sco	Sag	Aqu	Pis	Tau	Gem	Can	Vir	Lib	Sag	Cap
1971	Aqu	Ari	Tau	Gem	Can	Vir	Lib	Sco	Cap	Aqu	Ari	Tau
1972	Can	Vir	Vir	Sco	Sag	Cap	Pis	Ari	Gem	Can	Vir	Lib
1973	Sag	Cap	Cap	Pis	Ari	Gem	Can	Vir	Lib	Sag	Cap	Aqu
1974	Ari	Tau	Gem	Can	Vir	Lib	Sag	Cap	Pis	Ari	Tau	Gem

1975	Leo	Lib	Lib	Sag	Cap	Pis	Ari	Tau	Can	Leo	Lib	Sco
1976	Cap	Aqu	Pis	Ari	Tau	Can	Leo	Lib	Sag	Cap	Pis	Ari
1977	Tau	Can	Can	Vir	Lib	Sag	Cap	Pis	Ari	Tau	Can	Leo
1978	Vir	Sco	Sco	Cap	Aqu	Ari	Tau	Can	Leo	Vir	Sco	Sag
1979	Aqu	Ari	Ari	Pis	Can	Leo	Vir	Sco	Sag	Aqu	Pis	Tau
1980	Gem	Leo	Vir	Lib	Sco	Cap	Aqu	Ari	Gem	Can	Leo	Vir
1981	Sco	Sag	Cap	Aqu	Pis	Tau	Can	Leo	Lib	Sco	Sag	Cap
1982	Pis	Tau	Tau	Can	Leo	Lib	Sco	Sag	Aqu	Pis	Tau	Gem
1983	Leo	Vir	Lib	Sco	Sag	Aqu	Pis	Ari	Gem	Can	Vir	Lib
1984	Sag	Aqu	Aqu	Ari	Tau	Gem	Leo	Lib	Sco	Sag	Aqu	Pis
1985	Tau	Gem	Gem	Leo	Vir	Sco	Sag	Aqu	Pis	Tau	Gem	Can

DAY OF BIRTH

Day of birth	Count forward
1	0
2	1
3	1
4	1
5	2
6	2
7	3
8	3
9	4
10	4
11	5
12	5
13	5
14	6
15	6
16	7
17	7
18	8
19	8
20	9
21	9
22	10
23	10
24	10
25	11
26	11
27	12
28	12
29	1
30	1
31	2